ATTENTION, SEEKERS.

ALPHABETICAL MUSINGS ON
CHAKRAS, COLOUR, BORES, BULLIES,
HEALTH, LIFE, LOVE, POLITICS,
SPIRITUALITY, DOGS, CATS, CHICKENS
AND ANYTHING ELSE
THAT AMUSES, INFURIATES OR FASCINATES ME.

BY AMANDA MANSELL

Published by
Whippet Point Publications, PO Box 9988
Sudbury, Suffolk CO10 9WU

First Published 2007
© Amanda Mansell
The right of Amanda Mansell to be identified as the
author of this work has been asserted by her in accordance
with the Copyright, Designs and Patents Act 1988

A CIP catalogue record for this book is available from the
British Library

ISBN 978-0-9557421-0-1

Printed in Great Britain by The Lavenham Press, Suffolk.

ABOUT THIS BOOK

We have lost the old ways of Epsom Salts and bread poultices at a time when the National Health Service is floundering, superbugs abound and we are becoming an increasingly unhealthy nation. We are all being bullied. School ground bullying has taken on a new, more sinister mantle. Our politicians are deaf to the wishes of the voters and Europe has nothing less than federal intentions. We don't heal well, we are not being heard and are about to be taken over. We think we are impotent to the changes being imposed on us. We are not. We are far more powerful than we realise. Reclaiming our internal power base starts with each and every one of us paying attention to every small detail in our lives [hence the ant on the front cover], learning from our observations and then thinking differently.

This is a serious book written humorously. Throughout the contents, from defence of the realm, health, jewellery and intimate personal relationships, I have interwoven and interlinked the chakras so if you don't know anything about them you may need to read the 'C' section first. Alternatively, you can start on the first page and keep going.

For Larry

$\mathcal{A}$ Is for AUTOBIOGRAPHY

This is not the story of my life, heaven forbid, though you will get snippets. In between various humorous and silly bits, my bold intention is to enlighten you on certain things I have learned during my lifetime. The following musings, listed under the letters of the alphabet as the whimsy takes me, are on any number of subjects that fascinate, infuriate or amuse me. I am completely fascinated by psychology, health, healing, spirituality, colour and most people .... but please note *most* because you may or may not be in there. I am absolutely infuriated by politicians, any one will do, I'm not proud [not in that department anyway], and I am highly amused by me and my complete and utter ridiculousness, human nature and its related lunacy, my partner and my pooches.

In between such diverse subjects as Hattie the chicken and defence of the realm, I am going to illuminate you on the chakra system and when I am done you will know why you cover your forehead when you have lost your car keys and that your bank account is below your navel - there's novel for you - but don't go ferreting around in your knickers for your cheque book or people will get the wrong idea. I will cover colour in some depth so you will understand why you simply cannot wear the canary yellow jumper that cheery aunty gave you for Christmas and why you *need* to pay attention to black. I will give you my observations on clothing and why people wear what they wear and I will mention a bit about jewellery because the boys and girls who periodically battle with my greying hair are totally fascinated by my psychoanalysis of their rings and things. If you think you are a good listener please read on because I suspect you miss the important bits. If you are being bullied, either at school or by the senior flower arranger at church, there are some helpful tips on taking evasive action that do not require eye level hockey sticks or thistles at dawn. There's stacks about health because mine took a hike some time back. Though I am having a devil of a job persuading it to come back I have to admit I have learnt much in the process, so I am passing the information on. I suppose you could classify this as a self-help book but because helping myself is more than a full time job, let alone helping anyone else, I like to think of it more as a raising awareness/wake-up call book. I have read no end of self-help and 'pathway to enlightenment' books but few made me giggle, which is a pity because I am keen on giggling. I don't know about you, but I have a busy life and not much time for waffle, so I like to be given information the day before yesterday in sharp, snappy, bite size and easily digestible pieces and do please try to mildly amuse in the process. Maybe you are the same.

Is there a simple way to improve life? I reckon there is and it starts with paying attention and therefore raising awareness. Simple, really, but not *entirely* pain free so you may need an aspirin or a glass of Shiraz, but not both and certainly not together. Rather fortuitously, I thought, both attention and awareness start with the first letter of the alphabet so we shall get cracking in no time at all. Under 'A' there will not be a listing of 'answers' because I do not have many but what I do have are observations, with which you may or may not agree, and an infuriating habit of asking more questions. Now I come to think of it asking awkward questions seems to have been my sole raison d'etre [reason for living] - translated for you because I am absolutely infuriated by being given foreign language quotations that I do not have time to look up. Don't these people do housework? I am, after all, still 'cherchez-ing la femme'.... where the bloody hell is she?

AMANDA

I arrived in Surrey in 1954, polite and on time - me all over. Fairly soon I found that life was not making any sense at all. My father greatly added to my confusion by instructing me, from a very early age, to 'Question everything, ducky', an idea I embraced with enthusiasm. This did not make for an easy life. Even when I was quite small I was perplexed by relationships and completely baffled by religion. At the age of ten I was sent to prison [boarding school] and any hope of improving my brain vanished as I spent the next six years suffocated with ludicrous rules and Dickensian punishments for the mildest misdemeanours. As we were unpleasantly punished for talking in corridors, doing anything mildly naughty was not worth the risk. Extraordinarily, I was once on the breathless brink of being expelled for the heinous crime of taking a miniature pot of marmite back to school. I look back on my school days and absolutely marvel at the excessive amount of energy our various teachers spent on preventing us from becoming unique and creative individuals.

At school, aged eleven, I wrote my first book, a rather tame illustrated ghost story. It was found and confiscated by my form teacher, fingered with disgust by my headmistress before being thrown contemptuously on the fire in her study in front my disbelieving eyes. I am still in recovery; I am now fifty-three. This is my second book; I don't like to be rushed when I am being creative. I got parole at sixteen and my parents wondered what to do with my less than average brain. Mother thought a potential husband would appear shortly and what a huge relief that would be. My years of enthusiastic and rather good doodling of clothing designs had been diligently ignored by my teachers so it did not come as a complete shock that my suggestion of art school was instantly vetoed by my father who, cigarette and large gin in hand, announced, 'It was a *hotbed* of drug addicts'. So I learnt to type instead and blundered about for a while, doing this and that, before embarking on nurse training in 1975.

Six months into my training I had decided what was wrong with the National Health Service and what it would take to rectify the situation but unfortunately my views were not greeted with warmth and appreciation. The world [well, Hampshire anyway] was not ready for an opinionated young student nurse, which is a pity because I was alarmingly far-sighted and correct in my predictions for the future of health care. My 'question everything, ducky' policy had me standing on the long Nightingale wards in an agony of incomprehension. Why did some people heal and others not? Why did some diabetics lose limbs or go blind, but not all of them? Why did non-smokers get lung cancer? Why did some women die from breast cancer and others survive? Why right sided breast cancer or left sided breast cancer? I had no answers and it bothered me. I had even less answers but a thousand more questions as my life unfolded and things went from bad to worse. Then someone suggested I read a specific book which lead to another book which lead on eventually to chakras. Suddenly my life and everything in it started to make some sense, but because we only take on board what we are ready to learn [when the pupil is ready the teacher will come] it took me many more years of reading and observation before I could fully relate my chakras to me as well as see and feel the crucial difference, as I see it, between emotions and feelings. I learnt to pay attention and then I learnt to hear; more importantly I learnt to hear myself, which was an unpleasant and shocking experience because I found that though I tried to be honest with other people I could lie to myself until the cows come home.

From the chakras I began to see where my relationships, in all their forms, were coming from and leading to. I combined what I was learning with my enthusiasm for clothes and colour and began to realise that peoples' clothes, hair and jewellery 'talked'. More specifically they talked 'emotions'. Chakra related sickness and healing started to make sense and it even cast light on my own catastrophic illness [sudden, viral onset, severe Rheumatoid Arthritis] which arrived unannounced, without so much as a 'by your leave' and is behaving like the last drunk at a party .... refusing to leave. Ghastly though the illness has been I have to admit it has speeded up my spiritual learning process no end because without it I would have been in my usual state of busy, busy, doing, doing. I would have been having a nice time and as I have been saying for years 'you don't learn anything having a nice time'. When you switch from continuously 'doing' to regularly 'being' a whole new world opens up before your eyes and my illness forced me into a state of 'being' in double quick time. I know I was meant to get sick so I would study and learn rather than manically tidy my garden. I have found there is nothing quite like excruciating total body pain to render one still and concentrate the mind.

I am anything but an intellectual [six 'o' levels ... *by the skin of my teeth*] but I do have four things going for me - I am a people observer and a deep thinker. People fascinate me and I like excavating away at psychology. The other two things are drinking scotch and giggling, but I am not sure if they count. My life has been a series of seemingly inexplicable events a lot of which I have not enjoyed at all and because of this I needed answers so I have looked for them. It is amazing what you uncover if you persistently search. In between musings on any subject that takes my fancy I am going to distil down what I have learnt and offer it to you. You can take it on board or dismiss it entirely as you wish, I ask only this of you ... if you learn something from this book please use that knowledge with kindness. We are all here on planet Earth just trying to learn and get it right, even the morons among us. What I am offering is a smattering of the little knowledge I have picked up on my way but *all* knowledge is power, even the little bits, so please use that power quietly, with compassion and kindness, otherwise I may think you are a bully.

I offer you my discoveries and I hope you find it all fascinating and illuminating. If you don't you are probably very nice .... but not my type.

ADELLE

Adelle Davis. Now, she should have come under 'D' but I was in a tremendous hurry to get her in quickly because my reverence for this woman knows no bounds. Something of an institution across the pond, this great lady was writing about nutrition in the 1960's and despairing of her fellow American's diet even then. She is no longer with us, more is the pity, but if she were I should imagine she would be beyond tearing her hair out by now. I am certain she would be the first to say science and research has moved on but nevertheless her common-sense and down to earth approach to food and health rings just as true now as the day she penned her work and I just love her wonderfully humorous and compassionate view of human nature. I have all her books which are so well thumbed that they are falling apart. With her help I am hauling myself back to health, in fact if I had been braver, following her instructions to the letter, I may have got better a lot faster but being rather stubborn I could not believe I required such huge doses of certain vitamins on a daily basis. These days I have a better understanding of the state of my damaged gut, my exceedingly poor breakdown of food and my inconsistent take-up of nutrients [most of which relates to my third chakra]. Nowadays when my body talks I pay reverential attention because I have had a very serious body breakdown and I don't plan a repeat performance.

Though Adelle does not write about treating animals I have used her advice on treating infections in small children and applied it to treating really sick pets. From dogs to chickens the advice works. Try and get hold of 'Let's Get Well' or 'Let's Eat Right To Keep Fit' but look out for 'Let's Have Healthy Children' and I am talking about Adelle's *books,* NOT a website. Her advice is particularly pertinent now in these uncertain times of over-prescribed antibiotics [and the resultant resistant bacteria], unprecedented levels of chemicals and pesticides, a crumbling National Health Service, the threat to our health from a nuclear or biological attack and the suicidal tendencies of many, not least our youngsters, in relation to their recreational and nutritional habits.

Adelle's books are all out of print, so to get your sticky paws on one may take some tracking down. Once you get hold of one read it, re-read it, keep it safe and don't lend it to anyone because you know what anyone is like - unbloodyreliable. Before you pop a prescription pill, please, PLEASE read Adelle.

AWARENESS

I am putting this in before 'attention' because although I don't have much to say about 'being aware' it is, however, absolutely *crucial* in understanding and repairing or healing your life, health and relationships. We live our lives partially blindfolded, blundering into adulthood and then getting on the work, relationship, mortgage, family life hamster wheel, running and panting until the wheel drops off. There is a way to slow the wheel down to a manageable pace and make life easier but it requires some stillness and silence on your part. If you are in a perpetual hurry you are not paying attention to what is going on around you and if that is the case you most certainly are not paying attention to yourself. Big mistake.

ATTENTION

Please pay it. It is the first simple step toward self-discovery and I believe it is the most powerful tool of self-protection. Recently someone informed me, rather blithely, I noted, that we are living in interesting times; *I should cocoa.* We are heading smartly [if we have not already arrived] for extremely turbulent economic and political times and raising your levels of awareness will help you negotiate the choppy waters ahead. If you start by paying attention to the everyday and seemingly mundane, pretty soon it will become a habit. Suddenly you will find yourself paying attention to absolutely everything and that way you can sidestep trouble that is on its way towards you. The fastest and most interesting way to start paying attention [and therefore raising your awareness] is to observe and listen to others. When you have the others taped, as it were [and you have got over the shock of your observations], you can then start observing and listening to yourself. I guarantee you no end of entertainment as you listen to the complete and utter drivel you tell yourself and anyone else who will listen. I know all about this because I talked drivel for years.

We have all been floored by ghastly events in life and if you haven't yet, the chances are your turn is on the horizon. Hideous happenings teach you wisdom, usually in blasted hindsight. Unpleasant life-hurdles highlight what we are made of and make us strong or weak, less or more compassionate and give our lives definition and meaning, or not, as the case may be. I know if I had had an uneventful and smooth life I would have become tedious, unaware and unpleasantly pleased with myself. I am none of these things though my partner assures me I do have some highly irritating habits [I can't think what he means]. Unhappy events jar us out of complacency and set the scene for a life lesson from which we can learn if we wish. Some events cannot be predicted but most give warning signals for months or years. Unfortunately there are any number of ostriches amongst us who resolutely refuse to lift their heads from the sand to observe proceedings and take appropriate action. This is called self-sabotage. They will always have their reasons for preferring gritty, sand-filled eyes, but they usually blame their reasons on everyone else because it is easier than pointing the finger at themselves and accepting self-responsibility. You have to stand up straight to be able to shoulder the blame and ostriches [bless, I adore the real thing] are short on shoulders. For the rest of us miserable homo-sapiens, standing up and peering myopically at the debris of our lives, shattered by some ill wind, we can all have easier lives if we learn to pay attention .... sooner rather than later.

I am grateful for my upbringing. In a funny sort of way my parents taught me, at an early age, to pay attention even if they did not realise that was what they were doing. My mother taught me thrift, which meant paying attention to any form of wastage. This meant our Christmas wrapping paper was annually ironed and put back into circulation decades after its original purchase, compost-bin worms went hungry on the *tiny* slivers of vegetable peeling my mother offered and you could expect an inquisition if you used more than two sheets of loo paper [all of which was accompanied by good-natured humour - mostly]. My father enthused in me a love of art and you cannot love art without giving it your attention. On our occasional days of culture in London my father would urge me to drag my eyes from the pavement or shop windows and to, 'Look up, darling, or you will miss architectural treasures'. This was a 'pay attention' lesson and over the years I have gained much from it, including bruised knees, but probably the biggest 'pay attention' lesson he gave me as a child was when he pointed out that the body language between two people was at odds with what they were saying to each other. My mouth fell open, my eyes widened and suddenly there was an hint of an answer as to why I got these inexplicable feelings about people. Why I felt people, who seemed thoroughly nice, were thoroughly dishonest. My father was not an expert on body language and unfortunately I was a bit slow on the uptake, not realising books were being written on the subject, so it was to be a long time before I could see if someone was verbally telling me one thing but bodily telling me another. By the time I fully grasped this lesson, in middle-age, I had moved on to a point where it did not matter so much. By then I knew that everything boils down to love and fear and in that simplicity there is much more of a challenge for me, the challenge of minding my own business and finding my compassion. Minding my own business is not too difficult but as there is a mountain of fear to every molehill of love, there is much compassion to find and it's flaming difficult for me to locate at all when dealing with certain people.

Experience has taught me if you do not pay attention you walk through life getting only 20% of the story. By raising your awareness and paying attention to small details you have a much, much richer life, a safer one and you get the added bonus of becoming a more interesting person. Once you get the hang of paying attention to everyone else, and highly amusing yourself in the process, you can then start paying attention to yourself. This is not quite so funny and involves arm to arm combat with your ego. I would like to warn you your ego has been in very serious training for years so this may be a bruising time. My advice is to take it slowly and resort to a bottle of wine when it all gets too much.

We all say and do things we regret when we are nervous, it is human, but by training yourself to pay attention to every little detail in life you minimise the risk of putting your foot in your mouth, getting hitched up with the wrong person or getting shafted because you missed some tell-tale warning sign. This is really important if you are going to do business with someone and if you start training yourself now, with the every day minutiae of life, you will be fine tuned, hopefully, before you are sitting in a featureless office or busy restaurant about to do business with someone who is not who they appear to be. Learning to pay attention to tiny details and listen with extreme care is very difficult and can take years to perfect, mostly because we want to believe in other people. Believing in other people is a lovely thing to do but when you believe in someone, *but they don't believe in themselves*, then there is going to be a problem. People who don't believe in themselves fall into two categories - they either talk themselves up or talk themselves down. It is the former category that you need to watch.

I am going to cover chakras in detail later and also a bit about body language but I want to state now that there is a strong link to both. In order to get your attention early let me warn you about doing business with a person who keeps touching their nose because it can indicate deep grief or deep lying and you may well be dealing with someone with suppressed childhood rage, no matter how smooth talking and pleasant they appear. Watch for someone clamping their hands over their lower abdomen when they are talking about money [more under 'second chakra']. Observe shoes and feet movement because shoes speak volumes [more under 'clothes'] and foot movements often completely negate what is being verbally said. Is your business partner making eye contact? You will need plenty of practice at observing this because lack of eye contact can mean someone is unbearably shy, or secretly fancies you, or is about to take you to the cleaners … or worse. On the other hand I know someone who is as honest as the day is long but who does not make a lot of eye contact when talking to me, even though he likes me a lot [he is a man of *exquisite* taste and discernment]. What you will need to do is observe all the other body language going on while listening very, very carefully. This is not easy to do and requires much practice but it is well worth the effort. Read on for 'listening', it comes under L, believe it or not.

To embrace 'paying attention' you have to hug 'personal honesty' too. This is tough territory and it requires courage. It is all very well paying attention to another but you need to remember that you are interacting with them and because I have paid attention my personal belief now is every interaction means something and has a deeper significance no matter how small or mundane. I have been astounded by my observations and mighty humbled. To give you a tiny example - a quick conversation with someone in a bright red coat would seem unremarkable but I am going to tell you what red represents and a quick visual blast of the colour on your retina may have more effect on you in the hours after a conversation than you might think possible.

I don't want you to think I am preaching on the paying attention front because in the last few weeks I made a complete horlicks of a social encounter by overriding what I know about colour and miserably failing to keep my mouth shut. My partner has also had a nasty lesson on listening well but ignoring a gut feeling. I can think of two occasions in the last handful of years where I noticed a physical action/movement between two people which I should have taken as a warning to proceed with care [I did not] and another where I failed abysmally to heed my own advice about listening [a person made a derogatory remark about themselves - take it as read - and I refused to take it literally and as a warning because I was doggedly pursuing my own agenda - more later - of getting my needs met]. Both these instances led on to much grief and cost me money I would rather have spent on something pleasurable. Paying attention can be very cost effective and at the extreme end of the scale it just might save your life. It is also the start of the road to self-responsibility. There are certain events in life that we cannot predict at all, they just have to be dealt with as best as we can, but there are others that were preceded by flashing amber warning lights. There are some genuine cases of 'I didn't see it coming' but often, if we are honest, we chose to ignore the warning signals. I'm as guilty as the next person, so let's all try to pay attention together.

If you are not used to being observant then the first step to attention seeking is to try something easy. Go and visit someone you don't know that well, at their house. As you approach the building stop and ask yourself what the neighbourhood is like, then the street. Is it a pleasant environment? Does it feel safe? Is the street clean? Check out the cars parked nearby. What do they tell you about the folks hereabout? Look at your friend's house. Does it look and feel like a happy house? Take a minute to stand and stare at it and get a *feeling*. Some houses look happy, some look too happy, some are sorrowful or isolated or neglected or depressed. What colour is it and how does the paint look? Does it have a front garden and if so is it planted and well maintained, stuffed with flowers, a patch of unruly grass only or something else? What does all this information tell you about the person you are about to greet? Everything. It tells you everything, because people make choices that intimately reflect their inner selves so the choice and style of a front door will say much about how they view themselves physically and emotionally. Even the type of door knocker or bell will indicate whether you have someone who is forthright or elusive. The choice of plants in the garden, particularly the colour, will tell you even more. I always wondered why I was obsessed with old fashioned pink roses but roses represent heart and love, are often round shaped [heart shaped even], pink is the heart chakra colour but specifically, it is a heart healing colour and I had plenty of work to do on that front. I am not going to talk about plants but if you finish this book you may never look at a garden the same way again.

All houses talk and the colour of the paintwork says even more. A happy house usually has happy occupants. An immaculate house may or may not have happy occupants. A tired house may signify a tired occupant, depression, low funds, or that energy/funds are being directed elsewhere and that the house and its appearance may mean little to the owner. I take all this information in when visiting someone because it makes life easier and when I get into the house if I have noted a garden stuffed with plants it means I can bring up daffodils or dahlias if the conversation runs dry and I will know

I am on fairly safe ground, whereas tarmac and a multiplicity of motorcars means I am going to have to think of something to say about engines. Now, if you paid attention you might have deduced that I have limited interest in cars and probably enjoy gardening and you would be dead right.

Are you still awake? Right, let's pretend we are visiting an imaginary friend. Knock on the door. The door partially opens and a dog peeks round the corner at you. Quickly note the dog breed and behaviour because it often reflects the owner .... so while I am on this note I will whisk you off and tell you a story. Many years ago a colleague asked me what breed of dogs I owned. 'Whippets', I replied. When she had finished *howling* with laughter I enquired why she thought that this was so amusing. Apparently she thought something large and boisterous was more in keeping with my image; big, excitable and barky black Labradors or Rottweilers maybe, but definitely not whippets. I braked in the corridor as she progressed, her shoulders still shaking with laughter and the joke continued, told and retold for days to resultant gales of laughter. I was completely fascinated but the point of my fascination was not that I had amused her greatly and others besides, but that she was not fascinated by her inaccurate assumption. It would have stopped me dead in my tracks because I would have felt I had missed a vital piece of information, misread someone totally. This would have really bothered me and I would be right to be bothered because dog breeds and dog temperaments and behaviour do reflect their owners. People get dogs for many reasons [personal agendas included] but often their dogs are like them in personality or reflect the side of them they cannot project - like quiet mousy men who buy noisy 'in your face' dogs [or even attack dogs, and I do so hope their wives/girlfriends are paying attention] or razor tongued women who have soft white fluffy pooches. There are many more human-type and dog-type scenarios but I will leave you to work them out, 'go figure' as the Americans say [I love this expression, it amuses me greatly]. Meanwhile, back in the hospital corridor my colleague, missing the whippet point entirely, was getting the positive energy of multiple belly laughs while I was worrying, so I think she won on points. What is the whippet point? Well, my dogs are intensely home loving but adventurous at times. They can be neurotically nervy over trivial things but occasionally outstandingly courageous. They adore quiet cuddling up on the sofa and will take and give any amount of love. They are rescued, have had a rough time and therefore really appreciate kindness and gentleness. They laugh a lot [oh yes they do!] and are remarkably intuitive and empathic. Are they like me? Might be .... the difference being that my ribs have not been seen for *years*.

Let's get back to the front door. There stands the person you came to visit
…. let's make it a 'her' and call her Susan [apologies to all Susans]. Now,
how does she look? Obviously you see and hear the obvious, i.e., ethnic
origin, rough height and weight, voice/accent but what else do you notice?
Is this a happy lady or sad? Healthy? How many colours can you see in her
face? [I'll do this in more detail under 'health'.] How does her voice sound?
Is it high pitched, high pitched normal or high pitched anxious? Deep, deep
and confident, or fag smoking deep? What was the handshake like?
Confident, sweaty, fleeting? What do her clothes say about her and what
colours is she wearing? Does she spell rich, poor or managing the bills but
a Ferrari is out of the question? What style/colour are her shoes and what
state are they in? Shoes speak volumes about how people view themselves,
especially how they view their faces [spiv type shoes are not worn by
bankers who like opera - well not in my experience anyway]. Is she pleased
to see you? Does she want to talk? Presuming she does want a natter follow
her indoors while taking note of the hallway. Hopefully she will offer to
make you a cup of tea and before she hotfoots off to the kitchen she settles
you into the sofa. This gives you time to look around and reflect on what
information you have picked up already. What have you sensed? Smell?
There are the usual suspects of dogs, damp, cat pee, babies/milk,
cooking/food, technological equipment and so on. People talk of an air of
something and this does not necessarily encompass an odour but I can smell
despair and sadness just as I can smell optimism and hope. Is the latter
freshness? Lightness? Clarity? I am not sure but I can sure whiff it and it has
nothing to do with age. I can visit houses where the occupants are elderly
and the house smells optimistic. I can chatter away and let my conversation
be led by my host's body language, but if the house smells stale I will take
caution and tailor my conversation to suit, whatever age the occupant.
Sometimes I have to tailor my conversation into a straightjacket if I am
being led by body language that is warning me of multiple no go areas.

Now, settle back on the sofa and take a look around and ask yourself, 'How
does it feel?'. Check the colours of this room; how do they relate to the
chakra system [more later] and related colours? My rule of thumb is that the
more colours present the more topics of conversation you can broach,
whereas as a single colour scheme makes me much more careful and
attentive. Pictures, books and photographs give a mountain of information.
Most people have family photos on display but not everyone and if they
don't the reason might be very interesting indeed or it might simply be
because they can't stand their family. Obviously half a dozen pictures of

roaring lions, zebras and a giraffe or two might point to a much loved safari holiday or a spell in Africa, but what if there are half a dozen tribal masks, some witch doctor's paraphernalia or a row of stuffed animal heads on a mantelpiece? What would your thoughts wander to? Personally I would keep the conversation very light and listen very carefully because I would read masks and take scalps literally.

Having checked out the photographs and the bookcase [which will give you any amount of information] take a good look at the pictures. I make a habit of looking at people's paintings and pictures and note if they depict people or people interacting, landscapes, or still life as this will give me an idea of how outgoing and gregarious the house owner is. Sometimes pictures [or photos] are warm and vibrant but others can feel lonely, still, or possibly even a bit cold. From pictures and décor you can pick up if someone is stuck in a time warp, like the old saying 'you can tell when a woman stopped having fun by her makeup'. Watch for placement of pictures or ornaments and perhaps their grouping. In a kitchen I once saw a grouping of knives and hearts on a wall and knew to keep my mouth firmly shut about marriage or partnerships. Sure enough I learnt that the owner had felt stabbed in the heart by her ex-husband. I am certain she did not put the hearts and knives together consciously and would probably have been amazed if I had mentioned it but we do these things subconsciously and then display them for all to see, but for few to notice. Some years back I put an inscribed paperweight on the windowsill by my front door. To date no-one has noticed it and I will probably move it soon because nowadays visitors do not need to 'tread softly because you tread on my dreams'. My dreams are my reality now and they have well protected boundaries.

From my young student days I bought postcards from art galleries because it was all I could afford. I stuck them in groups on the wall in my bedroom but even then the pictures I chose said a great deal about me and my character. I have not, until the last few years, favoured paintings with people being drawn over and over again to landscapes and still life with the odd solitary portrait thrown in. This might lead you to deduce that I am not a people person and you would be partly right. I would describe myself as a gregarious loner. I love meeting people and chatting but only in short bursts and ideally on a one to one basis. I find it extremely difficult to concentrate on more than one person at a time because while listening I also get so much non-verbal information I simply cannot assimilate it. As I am a chatty person, people mistake me for a party animal but parties are a screaming nightmare for me because I'm on information overload and usually go home completely exhausted. After a party I used to spend days trying to decipher why so often people would be saying one thing to me while everything else about them was saying something different. I now understand these people are not listening to themselves as they talk, let alone as they think. I also used to wonder why, at parties, some people wore me out emotionally and others didn't. It took me ages to realise the people who did not wear me out had less agendas and were more authentically in touch with their feelings. The more authentic a person is the safer they make you feel because you can be honest with them and know your honesty is in safe hands.

For about nine years [interesting number - in the world I inhabit, nine hours, days, weeks or years is known as a significant birthing period] I had a large and beautiful but rather severe portrait of a nun in my house placed in such a position that it was the first thing you saw as you came through the front door. It took me some time to realise the connection between the picture, its placement, and the reframing of my internal landscape achieved during that intensely introspective and soul searching period. Then I went on a couple of trips to Asia, had a couple of interesting but slightly surreal spiritual experiences and on return bought a large, colourful and mainly pink landscape of India depicting a shrine. I put it on the wall where my nun used to be and moved her upstairs outside the bathroom. Not an unthinking placement because I am reverentially drawn to life giving water and feel blessed to be able to turn on a tap. Then I painted my bedroom an alarming shade of orange and a year later I met the man who is the love of my life. We now live together and share a more restful pale yellow bedroom with turquoise curtains, the colours chosen specifically because we are working on the related chakras. If you are unhappily single, before you rush out to buy orange paint for your bedroom in the hope that love will surely follow, please read all of the book first. Then ...... go paint.

Now, because I want you to pay attention because it makes life easier but I don't want to bore you to heaving sobs on the subject, I will paint a really silly scenario. Picture this.........

Imagine we are back on Susan's sofa and sitting there is a visitor, a full-blooded, lustful but lonely young man called John Fish and Susan is a head-spinningly curvaceous young woman. While Susan makes the tea, John, not paying enough attention, is filled with thoughts of conquest. In comes Susan from the kitchen teetering on two inch red silk mules decorated with those feathery things [can't remember - marabou? Caribou? Whatever!]. She is wearing a tight black leotard with a very fetching wide red belt and the entire outfit leaves very, very little to the imagination. She melts beside John handing him some tea which he endeavours to keep in the mug and not on his crotch, which is quite hot enough, thank you. Our Susan has designs upon John's person because she *has* been paying attention and has clocked the expensive shiny new car he parked outside her house [his Dad's] and the extremely expensive gold watch he is wearing [his Dad's, borrowed, well he is on holiday and it is a shame not to use it, besides it might impress someone and by gum it has]. Now Susan isn't stupid, she is wondering how a very junior dishwasher salesman could afford such a big brand new and shiny expensive car but she isn't planning on asking awkward questions because she is pursuing an urgent agenda. She is looking for a husband and babies and in John Fish she thinks she may have landed a sturgeon [they produce caviar for those not in the know] because she wants to land a sturgeon, whereas, in reality, it is not a caviar producing fish sitting on the sofa, it is a sea bass. Nothing wrong with sea bass of course, but their roe don't fetch much dosh. Susan now has a choice, she can either listen up, very, very carefully and get more information or relentlessly pursue her agenda and end up disappointed, or not, as the case may be. Meanwhile John Fish is jolted by Susan putting her hand lightly upon her knee and asking, huskily, if his tea is to his satisfaction. Now, in my experience the John Fishes of this world are neatly divided into two categories. The first category is the one where, at this juncture, he launches a full frontal assault and finds a tight leotard difficult, but not impossible, to remove. The other John Fish finds his Adam's apple playing nervous vertical ping-pong and grabs the first topic of conversation he can think of. Our little fishy is definitely in the ping-pong category. IF he had been paying attention he might have noticed the type of rings she was wearing and on which fingers [more under 'jewellery'] and noting the colours she was wearing would have given him more clues. Has he spotted the dozens of photos of baby nephews and nieces decorating the walls, or the limited contents of the bookshelf housing such classics as 'Plan Your Perfect Wedding', 'Teething, Toddlers, Tantrums', 'Learn To Knit In 304 Easy Lessons', 'The Art Of Seducing A Fish' and the enormous teddy bear slippers almost stuffed under the sofa? No, he has not. Hit by a sudden attack of nerves John violently hauls his brains from his privates and embarks on the one subject of conversation he feels safe with ..... rock climbing. This boy knows what women want! 'Ooooh', Susan says, leaning towards him but closing her left arm across her middle, briefly touching her nose, crossing her legs away from him and raising her toes [to be explained later in the book], 'I love rock climbing too'. John is thrilled. He can't believe his luck. A sexpot rock climber! Of course, she will have a devil of a job keeping up with him in those shoes but imagine the look on her face when he gives her a pair of proper walking boots. *Imagine indeed* ..... and like a lamb to the slaughter, because he is a lonely, sex starved, weekend rock climber and he hasn't paid attention, he pops the question. She says yes. Agenda sorted! Two weeks later they drive up to the registry office in Dad's car [he isn't back from holiday yet, thank goodness, thinks John] to get married. We would, of course, want them to live happily ever after but the problem is if you don't pay attention you might not get what you want.

So it came to pass, a few months on, that Susan, wearing a loose fitting pale grey track suit and huge pink fluffy slippers [colours to be explained] while bouncing a bonny baby on her knee, was very cross. 'He lied to me about the car', she thinks, 'and we can't afford the bills on a sea bass salary and here I am worrying and where is he? Half way up a bloody rock is where and I never liked rocks. He is just like my Dad, never around when you need him'. And there is John, all lonely on his rock, wondering where that sexpot rock climber went. Wondering where sexpot went, full stop. And the bills and three mouths to feed and she is only interested in the baby. He should never have borrowed his Dad's car .... if only he had paid attention.

*A*BSOLUTELY

Many years ago I had the pleasure of working with a most excellent woman. She was, I reckon, on the right side of sixty and everyone liked her and she got on with absolutely everyone. I was impressed and decided I was going to follow this woman around and learn her popularity trick. I was mighty vigilant, lurking furtively about in corridors and listening through keyholes but I could not work out her secret. Eventually I had had quite enough of furtive skulking so I pinned her into a corner, left hand on my hip, right index finger wagging under her nose and demanded to know her formula. 'Oh', she laughed, delightedly, 'it's simple really, I just agree with everyone about everything. Whatever anyone is moaning about I say, *absolutely*, whether I agree or not'. I stared at her with a mystified expression on my face, completely lost for words [this is unusual for me]. 'Could it be that easy?' After a lengthy pause I announced, 'I'm going to try that', and stomped off with a determined step.

It would be fair to say I didn't have quite the same success with 'absolutely' as she did though it was a helpful little tool in my kit box. I suspected people knew that when I said 'absolutely' I was being absolutely insincere. 'This is what you get for being an opinionated little prat, Amanda,' I comforted myself, unsuccessfully. Pretty soon I was back to lurking and skulking in corridors and doorways, listening to my friend and thinking, 'She is hiding something from me, she has another trick up her sleeve, I just know it'........ I never found it.

ALCOHOL

Love the stuff. I rarely meet a drink I don't like. Should you ask my first choice is definitely a neat scotch, preferably from some romantic sounding Scottish location where it tastes and smells like it has been slowly filtered through a smoking peat bog - oh, very heaven - but do let's get things in perspective. 'Hangover' sounds so reassuring, nothing serious, no harm done, bit of a giggle, right as rain in a day, but really a hangover is notification of liver damage. 'Little Ego' person may feel fine two days after the night before but 'Little Liver' person will be rectifying the damage for days, maybe weeks, maybe longer, depending what ingredients you chuck down your gullet that will, or will not, facilitate repair. Do engage brain, please do, you will be so very grateful in later life. If you don't know where your liver is, much less how it works and what it needs - LOOK IT UP.

ALCOHOLISM

Exquisitely unpleasant to deal with for the person in its midst and in my experience even harder to bear and watch if that person is someone you love. If the alcoholic wants help, you are blessed; if not, as is so often the case, you may have to encircle your heart with imaginary protective ironmongery and, while pouring out love and compassion, back right off. Addictions can tear the onlooker apart and wreak havoc on their liver too, make no mistake, suppressed anger can do as much damage to that organ as alcohol.

High alcohol consumption [and this includes routine social drinking in the evening] will GREATLY increase the need for the B vitamins, magnesium, vitamins A and C [for starters] so please put them back in. Eventually serious drinking will seriously skew your biochemistry if you drink enough, your diet is lousy and your feelings are unexpressed [and the same goes for recreational drug intake]. Life becomes a vicious circle which starts with 'feeling out of sorts' or 'feeling wound up' which calls for a soothing drink. Wonders! Let's try that again. Then the 'feeling out of sorts' or 'feeling wound up' comes not just because of unexpressed feelings but also because of mineral and vitamin deficiency which calls for a drink, or several, to feel better but which further depletes your mineral and vitamin supply, so another drink anaesthetises that problem and makes you feel better, temporarily, and so on and so forth.

My father died of alcoholic liver cirrhosis. I adored him. I understand why he drank and each passing year adds another level to the depth of my understanding. My father was not 'an alcoholic', it did not define him. He had a thousand plus points. He was an educated man, great company and an extraordinary father on so many levels. I miss him daily but I am sad that, in the end, I lost to a bottle because I would have loved the chance to have shared a few more years together. I think he would have been tickled pink at the woman I have matured into. I got the best of him but he did not get the best of me.

If you love someone with a drink problem you have my greatest sympathy because nine times out of ten things are only going to get worse. If you are young, fancy free and dating but hoping true love will be on the horizon in the future please read 'attention' if you haven't already and apply the lesson to looking for potential problems in potential partners. Alcoholics usually just start out liking booze; then liking booze a lot. Then it's needing booze; then needing booze a lot and when they get to that stage they can be mighty devious. When working abroad I once nursed an alcohol and drug abuser in her own home. She was a really nice woman and I liked her but I was naïve and slow on the uptake. She went for a Jimmy Riddle [piddle] and though only gone for a couple of minutes took a handful of pills and passed out sometime later. I couldn't believe I had been so careless and stupid to allow it to happen. Several hours later, when I had someone else in the house to watch over her, I got permission from her equally lovely husband to search the loo, the rest of the house and garden [but I speedily foreshortened my excavations when the gardener casually mentioned cobras]. Having searched, I couldn't *believe* the places she had hidden the caches of booze and pills - was she trained by MI5, I wondered?

Don't make excuses for a loved one if you see something in the early stages that you don't like the look of. Take courage, you are going to need it, and confront it early. In my experience and observation keep one thing firmly in your mind - instead of nagging about booze intake, hand out lashings of genuine compliments. Alcoholics, no matter how intelligent, and they often are, lack self esteem and a belief in themselves. Focus all your attention on their strengths and remind them of these qualities repeatedly. While you are doing that, improve their diet to the optimum level. To do this you may need to be as devious with ingredients as your loved one is devious in hiding the bottles. Get professional help from a nutritionist to learn your devious mineral and vitamin rich recipes, especially if your beloved is not picky with his/her alcohol but is picky with his/her food.

Alcoholism is slow suicide. If you are feeling really brave you could ask your alcoholic loved one why they have a death wish. You are unlikely to get a satisfactory answer but you may get them thinking, which is a start in the right direction. If you do get a satisfactory answer, as I did [and I knew there was nothing I could do] you must protect and be gentle with yourself. I am telling you this softly because I want you to take it on board before I get a bit brutal. You will hear and read all about help for the alcoholic, but you the carer, the coper, beloved one, need help too. You may also have an addiction - what is it? Are you a rescuer? Addicted to being needed? Addicted to being a doormat? Are you the financial provider and therefore the controller to a certain extent? Do you have unfinished business with the drinker? Can you realistically finish the business? Do you understand what love is? What are you most afraid of? Ask yourself some searching questions and while you are at it ask yourself, 'How do I see my life 10 years from now?'. Get some professional help and make DAMN sure whoever you turn to is kind to you. Turn instantly on your heels and walk away if they are not - your life is tough enough already.

ᴀRCHETYPES

You know when someone remarks 'He is such a clown' or 'She is a real femme fatale' they are talking about archetypes. Mentioned by Plato and explored by Jung, they are psychological patterns of behaviour derived from historical or mythical characters. There are dozens of archetypes, each one displaying light and shadow attributes and I think it is helpful to know about both these attributes, but particularly the shadow ones, because they may be at play in you, or me, or them. I will give you a few archetypal characters

... athlete, child of nature, victim, servant, gossip, seeker, engineer, artist, saboteur, hedonist, warrior, mother, teacher, rescuer, storyteller, Don Juan, martyr, thief, judge, monk or nun, prince, bully, queen, Samaritan, rebel, knight, addict, pioneer, visionary, angel. There are lots more. Recognise anyone you know?

Let's take one, say .... servant. This may be a 'literal' paid servant, but it may also be a person whose light [as opposed to dark] attributes are of taking pleasure in serving others. This may take many forms, it might be that one's work is service orientated or it might be preparing food, being on hand to do repair, maintenance, driving, fetching, carrying, nursing, babysitting work or something, but for no reward. This is all positive, in moderation, but there are shadow attributes of the servant [literal and archetypal] that need to be watched. It can be that someone slowly becomes completely dependent on a servant who then becomes controlling or manipulating, or it can be that the servant is using all the giving and care taking for free as an excuse not to get on with their own life, usually because they do not consider their own life worthy of that much attention. I have witnessed both of these types of servants over and over in many different types of relationships. I was certainly in danger of becoming a servant to my late mother, though how much this was related to a sacred contract [later], I am not 100% sure.

One of my archetypes is 'rescuer', animals being my speciality. They often appear well when I get them but develop chronic illnesses or unpredictable neuroses that require very gentle handling [could be talking about me, really ... probably am]. The light attribute of the rescuer is to play a role in providing support and comfort in times of crisis but the dark attribute hovers when it becomes time to release; the recognition that the work is done and the rescued are then free to find their own feet and pursue their destiny, for even in a shared home, destinies differ. This can be tricky with humans and possibly even trickier with animals who can form a great big needy attachment and personally I like being gazed at with adoration by my animals.

It can be tiring being a rescuer; I fancy a change of archetype and am looking at alternatives. Goddess struck me as a distinct possibility but its shadow attribute is exploitation of the female form and nature. 'Blimey', I thought, 'I may have to take my clothes off .... best not'.

I have tried to look studious and intelligent while reading Jung and Freud but I am an Aries and like my information in short staccato bursts the day before yesterday, so now, if I am puzzling a particularly knotty little problem and need to know what archetype(s) are in play in a particular person, I reach for the most excellent author Dr. Caroline Myss [there will be a tribute to her under 'M']. She has produced some archetype cards in a small red box that are just the thing for quick answers to knotty problems.

We are richly awash with archetypal well known figures at the moment. Some of these are having a tricky time because we are learning the 'second chakra lesson' that they have been teaching us [even if they did not realise that is what they were doing]. These larger than life people are reflectors, mirroring back to us our own dishonest, erratic, sometimes wild and inappropriate behaviour. We sneer and snigger at them, sometimes even boo and hiss while missing the point entirely. Their lifestyle and behaviour, writ large and displayed for all to see, may seem totally at odds with yours and my way of life but, within our smaller lives, we are all capable of boundless extravagance, inappropriate and sometimes dishonest behaviour and harbouring cruel thoughts.

In the comfort and safety of your living room you can watch your favourite soap characters and work out which archetypes are in play and what their shadow has to teach you but if soaps are not your thing, and they sure ain't mine, look at the major players in the newspapers and magazines and see if you can spot the dominant archetype. Rebels, addicts and hedonists abound, thieves and judges too. Though there are few in number of the real thing, archetypal kings and queens strut about, most of them not watching the pavement for banana skins and some, particularly the queens, are out and out republicans which amuses me no end. Try working out the famous before you turn your attention on your private inner circle of family and friends. You may see people in a very different light and the knowledge may startle or unsettle you, so I offer a word of warning ...... if you are examining close relationships up close, this is NOT now a game of spot the celeb archetype. Keep your mouth shut while you quietly digest any new information. Keep compassion and banana skins at the forefront of your mind. Knowledge is power, it changes you, so be aware that you are becoming aware and read on.

ATTITUDE

It took me far too many years to grasp how big a deal my attitude was to everything in my life. I understand now that if I am sad, I will see sadness and possibly even look for it. If I am angry I will see anger, invite anger and maybe even get anger chucked straight back at me, because we carry our anger within us and it acts like a magnet [the same goes for carrying fear]. I can see all this quite clearly running as a theme throughout my life. Nowadays, if I get up in the morning on the wrong side of the bed, thoroughly disgruntled about something [usually of little importance really] and having internally grumbled my way through breakfast, I then go out shopping, you can bet your bottom dollar I will encounter every other disgruntled person in the town. From the road hog blocking my impatient path, to the bad parker in the car park, to the unhelpful, or downright surly, shop assistant - do you know what all these little blighters have in common? Me! On the other hand, should I wake in the morning with a sunny smile and disposition and having kissed everyone I love in the house starting with my lovely man [he might get two], perkily eat my breakfast and then venture forth on my errands, I find I have a lovely day. If I am driving cheerily to shop for food, the road will be clear[ish], cars will allow me to pass and parking spaces that are just right appear. Adorable shop assistants will be helpful as can be and a giggle or two will be shared. The day will be gloriously mine no matter how tedious or mundane the errands.

How I wish I had grasped this concept when I was twenty one. For, verily I say unto you my precious ones .. ...'what you are is what you get'. Here endeth the lesson.

ALLOTMENTS

Use them or lose them. Forever. If you don't think an allotment sounds like fun, you would be very wrong, for they are hip and happening places. You meet all sorts, learn something of value every day, have a shed to play in [I love sheds] and get to take the fruit of your labour home to enjoy - but don't tell them at the Treasury, they will descend - you know how they hate us having good, clean, untaxable fun.

Wouldn't it be wonderful if some mega rich pop or sports star bought land

and donated it to local parish councils [with a 'no bloody building on it, ever', proviso] to be used as allotments for future generations to enjoy? What a gift to leave behind when your songs or sporting achievements are forgotten. What a fitting epitaph on a gravestone, 'Remembered in Cabbages' or 'Sadly Missed by Sprouts'.

AGE

You have chronological age and emotional age and the two are quite different. That is why you have seventy-five year olds who behave as if they were six, and eight year olds who make you think they are very old souls indeed. Many years back I was trying to decipher a middle-aged person's rather odd behaviour. We were chatting one day and I was musing on an upcoming birthday and commented that I did not mind being in my forties because I felt as if I had been born forty. I asked my chatty companion what age they thought they were and the answer came back, as quick as a flash, 'Sixteen'. They chatted merrily on while I gazed thoughtfully out of the window thinking, 'Yup, that'd be about right'. Suddenly everything about them and their behaviour made complete sense - in their emotional mind they had not yet left home. I do believe in young and old souls because I think we have multiple lives in order to learn and spiritually progress, but I also think you can emotionally shut down at a certain age because of a great shock or because you cannot cope with growing up, perhaps because there is not enough energy loaded into your first chakra [more later]. Anyway, try asking your friends and family what age they feel. Their answer may give you a shock or everything about them may suddenly seem perfectly clear.

AGENDAS

There are private agendas, hidden agendas, business agendas and any amount of political agendas. Virtually everyone has one or two and some people have multiple agendas all the time - must be exhausting! These people you want to avoid if you can but if you can't think carefully before answering a question or request from them as it may have long reaching implications.

Now, what's your agenda? You need to get to the bottom of it because agendas are tricky, they often take on a life of their own and have an unpleasant habit of backfiring on you. Agendas are always, always based from fear. We are all needy little bundles of self-protecting and fearful egocentricity so when one little bundle meets another little bundle both little bundles are doing their best to protect themselves. Lovely and fair is the day when you meet a bundle that is just plain nice and means no harm. You can have a little chat, feel warm and rosy and move on - but here comes that howling gale of a bloody-agenda-bundle. What to do? Well, personally, I leg it quick smart in the opposite direction, head home and bolt the door. Keeping my head below the parapet for a couple of days I assume [always dangerous] the coast is clear and answer the phone. Whooooosh, the hurricane is on the line. Just a gentle murmur of breeze to begin with, a few pleasantries, then the wind gets up a head of steam - an agenda is coming - take cover! I have been poor at fast verbal response all my life so I have been slow to think of an excuse for fending off an agenda-laden telephone caller. Nowadays I have improved tremendously and I just say, 'no'. I'm thrilled with myself if I can say no without offering an excuse, but that is warp speed and I am rarely able to go that fast.

Of course not all agendas come in at gale force. Some are silver-tongued, smooth as you like and a lot more difficult to spot. The dinner party invitation where you are there just to make up numbers or be the amusing performing seal, or the cup of coffee/drinks invitation where information will be extracted from you whether you like it or not, or the gift/favour that comes at a price, a price that will be exacted months or even years hence. Stop and think about it - how have you been used and how have you used? It is all about getting our needs met and to do that we use people [and sometimes animals] to some degree or another. We all do it and it will probably never stop because I have a suspicion that using people is the way most of us move forward and learn, but steady as you go, it can get nasty, take a deep breath - the agenda marriage that is maintained not out of love but because it supports a lifestyle, a hobby or something else. Please pay attention, even if you don't want to, because I see any amount of marriages that support a hobby rather than supporting a hubby [or a wifey]. This is dangerous territory and liable to go one of two ways, hitting the rocks or tailing off into mutual low grade hostility which hovers just below the radar screen. Then comes the ill health.

There is the agenda-laden parent that uses the child as a weapon, the child using the parent as an unlimited bank account. The controllers whose agenda is wanting to know every aspect of your life and then they tell you how to live it, usually because their own lives are out of control. The agenda friendships that are glamorous, just glamorous, or needy props, one way listening posts, or just useful. It comes down to self-questioning and honesty and integrity. This is painful territory so take it slowly and be gentle with yourself. To err is human, to forgive divine. Try some divinely inspired forgiveness of yourself and just seek to ask yourself on a regular basis, 'Is this making *me* happy?'. You might also try, 'Am I doing what I am doing for me or to make *someone else* happy?' Please be careful because any action that is laced with an agenda has a nasty tendency to head down a banana skin covered slope eventually and the 'eventually' may come at an age when picking yourself up, dusting yourself off and starting all over again is hard work and extremely daunting. Ask yourself on a reasonably regular basis, 'What am I doing, and am I doing it for the right reason?'. My days are filled with such deliberations and it can be exhausting, but I do find much reward in the questioning because life gets easier ..... honestly, it does.

Once you start to look for agendas and get good at recognising them you are going to be amazed, for truly, they seem to be the very life blood of homo sapiens. Even the most harmonious relationships have agendas being batted back and forth at some level or rather. You will never, I suspect, be able to live an agenda-free life in agenda-free territory, though you might manage it in a monastery, but you can make a start by asking yourself some honest questions, giving some honest answers and learning to be strong and stand alone, even if you are in a relationship.

I am fascinated by the political agendas. About twenty-five years ago I was perplexed when reading in the newspaper about a series of seemingly inexplicable events taking place, over some months, in a European country not given to high jinks. The events made no sense to me at all but some months later I was lucky enough to meet a journalist who had just returned from working in that country and he explained that the events were completely fictitious; conjured up to scare the public for the political motive of getting unpopular and expensive legislation through parliament and that the entire ruse had been successful. I was riveted - and I am sorry I am not being more specific, but this is a country I have yet to visit and I don't want to make myself unpopular before I get there. This insight made me look much deeper at current news, so now when I see something on the television or the newspapers that seems extraordinary and makes no sense, I look for the agenda. In this I am helped no end by Robert Redford in his role as the reporter Bob Woodward in the film 'All the President's Men'. I saw this film in New York in 1976. I was not much travelled at the time and walked around the city with my mouth permanently open in amazement. I went to see the film with two American twenty-somethings who I thought were incredibly hip. The cinema was crammed with more hips and the film started with a clip of the real President Nixon making a speech in response to which there was a barrage of noisy abuse from the cinemagoers. I got all hot and uncomfortable because we didn't *do things* like that at home but I wondered if it was a taste of things to come. Redford, as Woodward, had an unidentified informant called 'Deep Throat' and he met him in shady corners of underground car parks; I thought it was all exceedingly covert and glam, though rather dangerous. When Redford complained that he was out of leads and didn't know where to go next, Deep Throat told him to, 'Follow the money'. I took this very seriously indeed and since then I have, when confronted with complex political or business manoeuvring, tried to follow the money trail [and the power of course, because if it ain't one, tis the other, and often both] and everything becomes clear, if immensely dispiriting. I daresay politics has been chock full of agendas since politics began but I can only focus on today's shenanigans and I am hugely cynical about most political statements, especially if they are headline grabbing. I tut and then look for a deeper 'take' on the story. I have noticed 'power' often rests on knowing about skeletons hidden in closets [Hoover territory I call it - as in J. Edgar Hoover who allegedly kept files on everyones' shenanigans]. I snorted with derision recently as one senior politician was being excessively smarmy about another politician who did not deserve such pleasantries. 'Hello', I said, 'someone knows about some bones'.

I love 'spot the agenda' except when it is aimed at me. About twenty-five years ago, when I was working with a lot of young and lovely people and was rather young and lovely myself [if you will forgive my tootle on my trumpet], a young and lovely woman informed me I had been asked out to dinner by a young man. 'Well', I thought, 'things *are* looking up'. There was only one snag .... she had been invited too. 'I don't understand', I said, knee deep, possibly higher, in naïve thickness. 'Well', she explained slowly and with a hint of exasperation, 'He wants to takes us *b o t h* out at the same time'. The penny dropped with a sickening thud. An agenda! Outrage started its thunderous ascent from somewhere in my large bowel and was heaving its way to my head threatening red mayhem. I declined through gritted teeth and my fellow invitee left in complete incomprehension at my stupidity, but a red flag had been fluttered and I was, right on queue, snorting and pawing at the floor. I was far too proud to play double arm candy for an evening, but

... *if only*.... if only I had accepted the agenda graciously, smiled and smoothed my way into a restaurant seat and ordered the most expensive things on the menu, TWICE. *Noooooo* ..... not me. I was still puce in the face, snorting and pawing my way round London a week later.

ATTACHMENT

That most of life's grief and misery stems from attachment is a concept I understand completely. I would like to assure you, dear reader, that work is in progress. Meanwhile, with all due respect, I think you will find that is *my* glass of wine you are making off with and that is *definitely* my dog.

ASSUME

Don't do it. Some of my biggest mistakes in life have been because I made an assumption. Do not assume she has locked the door - check. Do not assume he has paid the bill - check. Do not assume there isn't a problem because your spouse or partner won't talk or look you in the eye when you ask them about the mortgage/bills/pension. In fact if you are getting this sort of non-verbal non-communication you need to keep calm and do some very serious checking indeed. Do not assume your hot date is hot in the right departments - check [but do it carefully]. Do not assume that that professional you just talked to knows exactly what they are talking about - check, especially if that professional is a white coated doctor and your gut instinct [third chakra - keep reading] knows they are missing something or misdiagnosing something. Don't be afraid. If you think it is serious, ask awkward questions and get second and third and fourth opinions, if necessary. If personal issues, health issues and monetary safety are at risk because you have made an assumption, you are skating on mighty thin ice.

My mother taught me a valuable lesson on 'assuming' as a child. We would occasionally go to London shopping and once she bought some shoes for me but before she left the shop she made me stop and check the box.'Don't assume the shop assistant has got it right, you don't want to get off the train and head home to find two left shoes or two right shoes in the box', she instructed me. I thought this was excellent advice and as usual have carried this to excess and now check all my shopping before I leave shop premises. It has saved me from hassle on more than one occasion as I have found exactly that - two left shoes in a box, or the right skirt but wrong blouse. I always finish off an 'away' shopping trip by getting into the car and checking my wallet to make sure I haven't left a credit card in a shop. So far this has not saved me hassle and merely made any companion shopper think I was completely paranoid. Sadly my mother's advice about assumption stopped shortly after shoe boxes, which is a pity because she 'assumed' at great cost in later life.

While travelling I do multiple daily passport, ticket and money checks because leaving or losing any of them while you are in transit is a bit of a nightmare [always leave photocopies of your passport, visa etc., at home with someone you can rely on, in case yours is stolen or lost]. It is helpful to get into the habit of a doing quick check of your belongings and crucial items before you get on and off trains, planes and things. Having checked into an hotel we always come out of our room and run our hands along the wall counting doors until we get to the fire exit. You can't see much in a fire with thick smoke, even in daylight.

Some years back, when I was a midwife, I was caring for a pleasant pregnant lady who made some comment about 'my type of life'. 'What type of life would that be?', I enquired. After a bit of umming and arrrring, she told me she assumed I was married to a professional man, lived in a smart country house with a couple of children, a couple of Labradors and drove a Landrover type of car. 'But I am not wearing a wedding ring', I answered. She had not noticed. I told her I lived in a tiny one bedroom terraced cottage, on my own, with a large mortgage an elderly VW Beetle and two whippets, who would now be snoring on my bed [given that it was about 2 o'clock in the morning]. She was amazed. Assumptions? You can be mighty off target.

ANGELS

I have never seen one, but by golly I'd like to. The full kit and caboodle. Wings, big ones, white of course, a long white frock .... and ....er .....tinsel? Well that's what they gave me when I was in a nativity play. I can remember it well, which is extraordinary, because there are vast expanses of my childhood for which I have absolutely no recall but I can remember being on stage dressed as an angel. I can even remember the smell of my angelic frock and feeling that this was all quite wrong but, strangely, quite right.

I have read a lot about angels. I read that they are beautiful but are neither male nor female.......bit worrying .... but interesting, because I got carried away recently and bought a largish Christmas decoration type angel in a closing down sale. When I got my angel home I was shocked at the size of her bosom - huge. Fortunately the bosom was foam and I set about radical surgical reduction. *'What are you doing?'*, my partner said when he got home. 'Angels don't have big bosoms, everyone knows that!', I retorted, then slumped in my chair and wondered where, exactly, I got that idea from.

I read that angels have wings but spirit guides do not. Well, now I am confused because I thought when I graduate, pop my clogs, I would immediately be awarded a pair of wings and as I only got one prize at school [no, I am not telling, I won't, I'm tired of being laughed at] I was really looking forward to approaching the dais with Kindly Great God Headmaster and being presented my wings, though I was a bit uneasy about how they would be attached - power drill? I decided not to dwell on that one because I was more bothered as to how I would get a decent night's kip. Would I have to stand on one leg and tuck my head under a wing? I read that angels don't sleep .... just another thing for me to worry about. When we die I think we should all get a pair of wings, it is only fair. When I get mine I am going to apply for a short commission and join the display team, 'The White Arrows'. Picture the scene .... great excitement while revving up on the runway with my team mates. I shall be tucking my white frock into my knickers and making spitfire noises, of course, then someone will shout 'Chocks away, Squadron Leader', and we will be off, performing great feats of derring-do!! Bit worried about my coloured exhaust though .... and people say there is no such thing as UFO's. Ludicrous!

Some people think there is no such thing as angels, but I think they are quite wrong. Why? Because when I get 'up myself' which I occasionally do, I can hear them. Behind me. Giggling, planning and eating bananas ....

When I was very little, my Mummy would often take me for a walk in the afternoon. This alone was intriguing as my mother could not see the point of walking anywhere unless it was to or from Peter Jones and we did not live in London [though I have to say, mention Bond Street to my mother and she could break into a gallop and *quite* see the point]. Most afternoons Mum would ask me where I wanted to go for a walk and the answer was apparently, day after day, always the same - I wanted to see the angel in the churchyard and very lovely she was too, only then, she was shining white marble, now she is green and sad. I predict she may well be restored to her former glory in the future when we are more appreciative of such things and find small metal hand-held objects don't feed the soul in the way restoration [in all it's forms] and staring at lovely sculptures do. There will be less of us then and we will be more sensible.

I am not psychic, I rather wish I was, but I did see the same woman on two separate occasions, a year apart, in a hospital corridor and I suspect she was a ghost, either that or she was the fastest moving geriatric in a blue dressing gown in history because I gave chase but could not catch her up. I have definitely heard heavy, loud male footsteps walking past an open door I was facing though I saw nothing and quaked for hours. I can sometimes sense the presence of ghosts which I take to be lost souls on another dimension. I once saw a colour photograph of a ghost showed to me by a women who was very, very mildly eccentric, but I *like* eccentric women - I am in training myself. She had taken a photo of the inside of an empty church and when it was developed there was a little old lady sitting in a pew. She told me she was astounded when she collected the photos from the developers because the church had, categorically, been empty at the time she took the picture. I had no reason to disbelieve her. Sadly she is dead now and I often wonder, when I drive past her house, what happened to her photo.

Some years back I heard Arthur C. Clarke was going to be interviewed on the radio. The dogs had to be walked at that time so I thought I would kill two birds with one stone and took off with hounds and trusty Roberts Radio perched upon my shoulder [I am not a technological beast, you understand]. So there I am marching along, radio to ear, and on comes Arthur. During the course of a very poorly led interview the subject of UFO's comes up and I pay serious attention because I have read much about them. Thousands of people have seen unexplained things and I am of the opinion that, for every thousand that gets in print, there is another thousand that on seeing something odd [or strange] whoosh past in the sky turn on their heel and return to the pub, musing on cocaine-stoked magpies pitching for MACH 2. I once charged down a road asking people if they had also spotted that round thing with a flaming [as in alight] tail that had shot over a neighbour's roof. Their reactions made me think questions like these are best asked *before* one is smelling of white wine. Going back to the radio, when the interviewer asked Mr. Clarke about UFO's, Mr. Clarke said he thought they were unlikely to be piloted by little green men [I was on full alert now] but he thought that extra terrestrials were likely to be light forms. The interviewer then smartly changed the subject, leaving me howling in a wood and shrieking at the radio, 'Ask him what he means, you thundering idiot'. The dogs [who don't like loud noises unless they are in the shape of a postman] were upset but I was absolutely beside myself with furious indignation and pouring forth a stream of sexist abuse at the male interviewer who had, by now, wound the interview up. I did eventually calm down .. years later … and then a funny thing happened ….

I moved house and quite soon I found myself seeing misty shaped things out of the corner of my eye and when I turned to look there was nothing there. Often there were things above my head. 'Bandits at twelve o'clock', I would think and look up - nothing. Once, though, I did see a black cigar shaped object traverse the ceiling at speed. I mentioned this to a friend with whom I could discuss such things and she advised me to get rid of it, but strangely I did not feel threatened at the time. Had I felt threatened I would have taken action immediately, clearing the supermarket shelves of garlic before fetching the vicar, and I'm only half in jest, but, a while later, a very strange thing happened. It was a summer evening and I was in the sitting room watching television. Something attracted my attention over my right shoulder and I looked up to see three gold orbs about the size of tennis balls move in slow stately procession, one behind the other, around the ceiling cornicing until they were in the far side of the room whereupon they faded away. Now before you call the men in white coats I can state that I was as astounded as you are sceptical. I was drinking *tea* and as I sat very still indeed, mug frozen in midair, watching said slow stately procession my mind shot through, and dismissed, the following options … alcohol induced hallucination - no, visual disturbance - definitely not, reflection of car headlights - no, strange holographic Wimbledon tennis match [don't be ridiculous], pawnbrokers [getting sillier], something I need to be concerned about ……… well, it was inexplicable. I was nonplussed. In those days I lived alone and had no-one, there and then, that I could have discussed it with. Nowadays I have a partner who, and I am so hugely grateful for this, is completely unfazed by extraordinary revelations. I can describe a sighting or happening that many would think bizarre and he will, in a phlegmatic, pragmatic, Virgoan analytical way, quietly discuss with me the possibilities ranging from the mundane to the extraordinary and mysterious.

I have never seen those gold orbs since, but a few weeks after their visit three bright flashes arrived. Take a deep breath and bear with me if you will, though if this is all just too much, please feel free to skip this bit. There are three flashes, different types and colours. I can't remember which one came first, but which ever it was, I would stop and stare and do much as I did with the golden orbs - a check list of possibilities. Well, I soon gave this up because there did not appear to be any rhyme, reason, or particular positioning for the displays, or so I thought then. The flashes are initially tiny, intensely bright, the size of a pinhead and sometimes they expand out to about half a centimetre. One is an intense white; one is a blue that is a cross between air force and royal blue and the other I cannot work out at all. It is basically another intense white flash with a dark edge, not black, more like charcoal grey, and it might be a in a figure of eight but I am not sure. Months later I started to realize that the flashes were in some way a highlighting device. No, that doesn't sound right - what am I trying to say? It seemed that the flash appeared when I was being instructed to pay attention. The first time I grasped that something extraordinary was going on, was when I had treated a client [I was practising as a reflexologist at home]. Many reflexology sessions became a chance for a client to discuss personal matters and I noticed that there was often a recurrent theme to the discussions. When this theme came up the flashes would often appear round the client's head area. One particular client had a lengthy reflexology session and a long chat with me afterwards. While we were talking the client seemed to have a moment of deep understanding about something that had been troubling her - like a major breakthrough moment and as it happened the three flashes burst forth like a repeating starburst around her head. I didn't say anything but, when she left, I was very quiet indeed. I began paying much more attention and I noticed that if I was reading a book quickly and I got a flash on the page, I would stop and re-read the sentence or paragraph carefully. To my astonishment, by doing so, I was getting answers to many of the knotty little problems I have in my life. Even more astonishing, as the months and years wore on, I found I could be deliberating a dilemma and, within a very short space of time, [hours], I would get a flash as if warning me to pay attention and the answer would come either by book, person, newspaper or radio. I try and pay attention most of the time now and I have noticed that, though the flashing persists, sometimes it is not as bright as it was and is more diffuse. Perhaps the batteries are low [joke] or maybe I have got the message.

What are these flashes? I have absolutely no idea, but I think they are *other* than me. I don't think I am nuts, far from it, I am an intensely practical, earthy, a let's have some common sense sort of person. Am I projecting them in some way? I don't think so. Are they within my aura? Possibly, but it would have to stretch out further than I thought. I do know, without doubt, that when I have made some kind of a mental or spiritual breakthrough, an 'aha' moment, I get a massive burst of flashing almost as if to say, 'Well done'. I call them my angel flashes because I don't know what else to call them. They are still about now, but in the last year or so I have been seeing other strange things - small shapes I cannot identify, whitish misty doors and something that looked like Chinese or Japanese writing [which I think is so beautiful] but was gone before I could get a good look. Often I see coloured lines that shoot out in front of me. Am I seeing ley lines? I have no answer for them. Why do I see these things? Don't know. Maybe it's because I want answers, I NEED answers and they are trying to give them to me. I am a slow learner and must drive them mad, poor things. I am intrigued by them but not frightened, not at all. Mankind scares the hell out of me - these do not.

AURAS

While we are in the general area I thought I would cover auras. In case you don't know what an aura is I looked it up in the esoteric dictionary I have and the description is … 'the psychic energy field that surrounds both animate and inanimate bodies'. I am not sure how far this energy field extends because I have read differing opinions but I take it to be a few feet and that it is roughly egg shaped. I cannot see full blown auras but I am working on it and as soon as this book is finished I plan to start working on my peripheral vision as apparently this is step one. However, I can often see the whitish energy field [just about two to three inches out] that surrounds everyone and everything and increasingly I can see patches of colour around people and this will give me an idea which chakra is being engaged or worked on at the time [see chakras] and the general state of someone's mental and physical health. If I couple this colour information with clothes and skin colouration [more later] I can get a fuller picture, as it were. I have noticed that people who are tuned in to their feelings choose colours that match [sometimes to the exact and specific shade] the colour, or colours, in their aura. As black and grey in an aura is rare and bad news it suggests to me, due to the swathes of black you see these days, that many people are not fully in touch with their inner selves.

Once, and once only, I was talking to a man who had a small patch of gold over his right shoulder I mentioned this to him……… because I could

.... and he said, 'Oh yes, watch this'. He stood still and centred himself then slowly raised his arm until it was out straight from his shoulder. The gold patch then shot out down his arm to his hand and slightly beyond. I was absolutely astounded. He talked to me afterwards but I was so stunned I can't remember a thing he said. What does this mean? Well, I took it to mean that I was in the presence of someone who was making really serious spiritual headway, we certainly had some fascinating conversations when we met. Years ago I went to a lecture given by two extraordinary people. I can't remember who was talking at the time this story was told and if they could both see auras but the tale was that one of them was walking through a shopping mall, in Australia, I think, and saw a gold aura emanating from someone up ahead. The storyteller gasped and rushed forward to find out who owned this truly unique energy field and found it belonged to a baby in a pram. A Down's Syndrome baby. And, as always, as I recount the tale, I am filling up with tears.

ARTHRITIS

I woke up one day with Rheumatoid Arthritis courtesy of a virus. I have a pretty high pain threshold but within weeks, just trying to get out of bed in the morning could reduce me to tears. Eight years on I am dramatically better, improving all the time and I profoundly thank God for my belligerence and refusal to continue taking the prescribed medication. In the last few years I have learnt much more than I bargained for. I could say I was a better person for the experience but 'truer' would be more accurate. I'm not launching into a 'them and us' against the medical profession. I have worked alongside doctors in Intensive Care Units, A&E and various hospital wards as a nurse and midwife. I have witnessed doctors tackle astonishing, exhausting workloads, maintaining courtesy and professionalism in the face of really shocking abuse. I have found much to admire. Should I ever be in a serious accident I shall be mighty glad and verbally thankful to see an anaesthetist and a surgeon. I am, however, absolutely appalled how little Western medicine has to offer when you reach a stage of chronic [more than six months] ill health. Here is my story, stick with it if you can because it may not be relevant to you now but none of us know what our health will be like next year or the year after. The information I give you just may help if you find yourself very ill, for any reason, and not improving.

In August 1999, aged forty five, I had left the NHS and was practising at home as a reflexologist, just about to embark on further training. I planned to do iridology [study of the iris], kinesiology [muscle testing] and either herbal medicine or nutrition, but I expect you have heard the one, 'Do you know how to make God laugh?....... Tell him your plans'. While I was busy making plans, I was not listening to my feelings because my feelings were demanding a life that I was not prepared to give them. My feelings wanted a recovery period from a really difficult decade [this is a mild understatement]. They wanted to sit by the sea for a year and do absolutely nothing. I thought they were being thoroughly unreasonable and offered holidays instead. Looking back now I can see my feelings had a chat with my body. 'Let's organise something to put the brakes on Amanda', my feelings suggested and my body said, 'Wilco' and lo, I woke up one morning with a really nasty headache and slightly swollen fingers. Over the next few days my fingers grew and grew. In a few days they were painful and solid thick sausages that I could not bend at all, my wrists had decided to join in and my elbows thought they might too. I took affirmative action and booked myself in with an acupuncturist. Sessions were had but meanwhile the inflammation had reached my neck and was thundering merrily down my spine. On my last appointment I noticed I could hardly get out of the car and I was reduced to a shuffling walk, for it was now making my knees into shapeless hot red blobs and eyeing up my toes. The lovely acupuncturist said it was time to see a doctor and I cried for the first time, finally confronting my denial that this was serious. My feelings and my body, looking a trifle smug, stood there with their arms folded, on strike. Arbitration was about to be on their terms only.

I shuffled to the GP where tests were done and viral onset Rheumatoid Arthritis diagnosed. Large doses of non-steroidal anti-inflammatory drugs were prescribed and I felt like a new woman. I did things, truly, unspeakably, enormously stupid things that you do during the normal course of a normal day but not when you are ill and your body is saying menacingly, 'Stop everything immediately! Disengage brain and listen'. A few weeks later the pain started to seep through the drugs and I had to engage brain because I was not better and I was amazed because I always got better. I came off the pills so I could see what was happening to my body, with interesting results. I found out I couldn't pick up my cat or negotiate stairs, up or down, unless I was on my bottom. I had about a nine inch stride and I could only brush my hair if I bent forward. Putting on a bra or jumper was extraordinarily difficult [though I did get enthusiastic offers of help with my bra from a male friend, who is adorable but not in the first flush of youth, though I daresay he would have made a sterling job of it]. I slept with four pillows behind me, another one under my knees and one on my tummy on which to rest my hands to which the slightest knock from a concerned pet would make me scream. Getting on and off the loo was so painful it reduced me to tears. When I could detach myself and look on my condition with dispassion I was completely fascinated at my body's control over me and that I had absolutely no idea I could withstand such levels of pain. I began to realise there were two of us in this predicament, egotistical me and my body. I had yet to realise there were, in fact, three. My feelings were lying low and waiting.

I had to admit this was going to be more than a walk in the park and told my clients I was completely shutting down my reflexology practice because I could not heal myself - mildly embarrassing to say the least. My next hurdle was a friend's wedding, planned and mostly paid for before I got sick. Problem was it was in New Zealand and I was going, come hell or high water, because she was a good friend and getting married for the first time at the age of fifty. She was, therefore, a petrol-soaked flaming beacon of hope for single old me. Little did I know my beloved, the light of my life, the man I now adore, was only two months away - bloody late arriving but well worth the wait. I went back on the drugs to get me to New Zealand and back. Got there and back and came off the pills and found I was much worse, with no-one to blame but myself.

I could not wear clothes with button or zips, or ordinary shoes, or get into a pair of Wellington boots because they were all too painful to negotiate. I lost a lot of bladder control and getting caught short on a dog walk was a damp and challenging affair with binocular-armed bird watchers being a particular menace. Sometimes I lost my sense of humour - so it was pretty serious. On the plus side my bottom got smaller because I spent so much time shuffling about on it. I could not hold a telephone handset for longer than three minutes, so lengthy calls were taken with the handset on the arm of my sofa and me leaning into it. I didn't tell people I was doing this and now I wonder what on earth I thought I was trying to prove. I was being ridiculous.

I shuffled into my hospital appointment with a Rheumatologist in April 2000 and he manoeuvred my limbs, with limited results and then showed me my joint-damaged x-rays. I stared at them in horrified silence. 'Oh shit', I thought, *'I'm in trouble now'*. I asked him for a blunt opinion without sugar coating. He told me it was very serious and I could expect a lifetime of drugs, physiotherapy and occupational therapy to minimise further damage. 'But I want to get well', I said. 'You are not going to', he replied. Well he was, bless him, wrong. Though not fully better, I am hugely improved. This improvement, which is still on going, has not been resolved spontaneously but rather from scraping away layers of physical and emotional accumulated rubbish. I found out all about me and my body while at the same time my spiritual fumblings became highlighted. I started to allow my feelings equal say in my every day life [my feelings have just snorted with derision - ok - I allowed my feelings much more of a say in my every day life].

After that hospital appointment I hobbled home and had a serious think. 'He can stuff that diagnosis up his hair shirt', I thought belligerently, 'and I won't take any more drugs - I just won't'. I trawled through my medical history from when I was a child trying to build up a comprehensive picture. It looked like my immune system had never been prize winning, my digestive system was suspect, my endocrine system functioning below par and my adrenals might be tired, verging on exhausted. There had been clear warning signals for some years and though I definitely had not been oblivious [as I had been seeing various therapists and been taking vitamin and mineral supplements] but I most definitely had not taken the fast drastic action I now realise I needed to take. Two years earlier, I had seen my doctor with a persistently reddened eye [sclera - white of the eye] and had been seen, at my insistence, by a hospital specialist who tested me for absolutely everything, but came back with no answer. I wondered if this had been another warning sign [now, as a practising iridologist I can say yes, it categorically was a clear warning sign of an internal - gut/digestion orientated - inflammatory process]. At that time I had also gone vegetarian and had stupidly not seen a nutritionist and discussed changing my diet. A year into my veggie period I found my previously strong body struggling to lift objects that I would have normally have managed with ease. Following a chance encounter with a therapist who remarked that I looked severely protein deficient and I needed to take my vegetarian diet much more seriously, I decided to go back to eating meat. I wondered if that protein deficiency had anything to do with my problems now.

'Changes must be made!', I announced to myself. I hoiked out of my shelves all my books on healing and diet including 'Your Body's Many Cries for Water' by Dr. F. Batmanghelidj [definitely worth a read] and I started on three litres of water a day. My day went like this ... bed, loo, kitchen, loo, dog walk, tree loo, kitchen, loo, sofa, loo and so on. I started to feel fractionally better. I excluded all the main suspects from my diet beginning with alcohol, red meat and then dairy produce. As my evening alcohol was my only pain relief this was not easy. Later I excluded wheat, by which time there was so little that I could eat and drink that I was beyond caring. I read 'Curing Arthritis the Drug Free Way' by Margaret Hills S.R.N., and followed her recommendations on removing acid from my diet. I stopped drinking tea and drank other fruit or herbal things that were perfectly ghastly. I felt a little better but nothing too dramatic.

My postman delivered a steady stream of books on every aspect of healing, ordered from a couple of bookshops that did mail order. My trusty Adelle Davis 'Let's Get Well' was being picked up daily and cross referenced with other nutritional books, but any other lead I heard, read or picked up from friends or acquaintances was followed up. I started experimenting with different courses of minerals and vitamins. I hit the sack at 9pm every night and often much earlier. Adelle [and many others] reminded me that anger was frequently at the core of arthritis and that arthritics are often rather good at not blowing their top but rather smiling politely and gritting their teeth. *'Mmnn',* I thought, 'rings a bell', so I wrote furious letters to everyone and anyone who had pissed me off during my entire lifetime. These letters were all ritually burnt in the fireplace. Did this help? I have no idea. Adelle said kick pillows and swear like a trooper - so I did. Did this help? Well, I have a sneaky suspicion it may have done, a little. It certainly alarmed the dogs and astonished the cats.

In May 2000, on recommendation from a friend, a Shiatsu practitioner walked up my drive with a futon mattress over his shoulder. Shiatsu is Japanese acupressure [like acupuncture but without the needles]. I deafened the poor chap by screaming throughout the treatment because my joints, in particular my wrists, felt like they had broken glass in them. I apologised profusely and he said he was used to big reactions as he also treated horses and they had a tendency to bite. I promised him I would keep my teeth to myself. The screaming continued for several sessions but, bit by bit, I got a little better.

'Emotions!', I thought 'I must deal with them. I shall plumb my evasive depths ... hypnosis, that is what I need. This is it! This will cure me'. Off I shuffled to a very nice lady hypnotherapist and sessions were had. Two extraordinary things came out of them. Under hypnosis I was asked to recall a sad event and how it made me feel. At the end of the session the hypnotist told me that I had given her a factual account of the event in great detail but, despite repeated promptings, I had failed to say how the event had made me feel. The hypnotist wondered if perhaps I was living in my head and could this be because living in my head and my body simultaneously meant dealing with a flood of emotions I couldn't cope with. Shocked silence. Hadn't occurred to me and it should have done because we discussed fifth chakra blocks, mine in particular because I knew I had one [more under 'chakras'] and suddenly vast expanses of my life that made no sense at all were suddenly not looking so complicated. I could swear I heard angelic popping of celestial champagne corks - not least because right at this moment my fifth chakra block [neck/speech] was being strenuously challenged by my ascending feelings. I was falling in the most serious love with a man that I could not countenance not being with. What better way to challenge a fifth chakra problem than have an explosive blast of feelings charge through the road block in my neck, wave cheerily at my tonsils and approach my brain [that was bristling with practical defence]. Next session - another bombshell. I was asked if there was anything I particularly wanted to explore. There was. I wanted to find out if there were any other reasons, other than the ones I had thought of, that I might have arthritis and not .. say, cancer. Down I went into such a deep hypnotic state that when the session was over I asked if I had been asleep. No, I had not, but on being asked about the type of illness I had and the best way of healing it, I had not volunteered anything other than an enigmatic, 'I am not ready to get well yet'. I took this statement home and stopped the hypnotherapy sessions. Stranger still, I accepted, unquestioningly, the validity of this statement. Deep within me a little voice was saying, 'Yup, that'd be about right'. I then left the statement alone. Now this is very unusual behaviour for me, normally I would have been like an energetic Jack Russell puppy at your favourite slipper, all sharp teeth, pulling, mauling and ggggrrrrrrrrrring until I collapsed in a heap of shredded leather, the insides revealed to my satisfaction. Much later, feeling braver, I would ask myself, 'Why am I not ready to get well yet? Did I engineer sudden viral onset Rheumatoid Arthritis? Is this a purely physical problem or a magnificent co-ordination of mind, body and spirit? Is this a contract, a sacred contract even, and if so when did I make it? Was I [ego] involved at all? Is there something I am supposed to be learning from being ill?'.

Have I learnt something from being ill? Yup. I have learnt that an incapacitated body requires a very strong mind, wobbly brain bits have to get their act together quick smart and thought debris must be removed. My ego [and there is plenty of it] has been humbled by my physical body and sternly lectured to by my feelings. I have learnt to shut up and listen when my body is talking and, in the process, I have gained much in terms of respect for my physical form and in attaining a level of personal power. Then there was the spiritual breakthrough. I knew I was not going to find the cause of my problem by medicating it, though I did resort to buying anti-inflammatory medication from my chemist occasionally for the odd social occasion, important appointments and not least taking my animals to the vet when I didn't want to look disabled. These pills would give me 24 to 48 hours of normality but I always felt much worse after taking them and the pain level would sky rocket, so for that reason I would take nothing for weeks on end and suffer the consequences - but something interesting was happening - I found I was not alone. Yes, the lights were flashing [from 'angels'], but that was not all. It was as if I was being watched and helped. Every day small tasks were seemingly impossible - packets, food wrapping and tins were often unopenable to my swollen and painful hands and household objects were too heavy to lift. Each and every time I was confronted with the impossible I silently asked for help and it came within minutes or hours *every single time.* It was too often to be coincidence, far, far too often. It was all the more extraordinary because I do not have many visitors, as I like quite a solitary life. I would be fighting tearfully with a tin that I could not open, put it down and say, 'I need help', and within a short space of time there would be a delivery man, delivering or lost, at the door, or a friend or neighbour calling in unannounced. I would ask them to help and they were all, not least the delivery men, so kind. This was a lesson for me as I am not good at asking for help like this. My mother asked for help all the time, even before she became ill and actually needed it. I disliked this trait in her and vowed not to follow her example. She is now tittering at me from her cloud but I ignore her and ask, 'Am I being taught to have faith? Is this what it is all about, this exquisitely painful incapacitation, a journey of faith? Faith in myself and/or faith in my God'. I am reminded of the saying 'you cannot describe faith, only experience it'. I don't know who penned these words but they are having resonance with me. I spent years living life at breakneck speed; if I was not at work I was furiously tending my garden or allotment, or sewing and making things. I thought a day without some evidence of achievement was a day wasted. Incapacitation has forced me into silent contemplation and the road to wellness has vastly increased my level of gratitude for life, but probably the most important lesson for me has been that I am no less of a person and no less valid here on earth for spending days at a time [sometimes even weeks] sitting and staring out of a window, while my body, at snail's pace, heals and I clear my mind. I was often told I was lazy as a child and I think I have spent my adult life trying to prove that I was not. How ridiculous was that? Wearing myself out because of a few ill-judged comments made over forty years ago, by people who were probably admonishing themselves for laziness, but doing it the easy way by pointing the finger at me.

I am now into 2001and making good progress and about to make more, I got food poisoning. I spent a week sitting on or looking at the loo, but as I got weaker my joints got better. 'Golly', I thought from the throne, 'I have the answer - don't eat!' This 'eureka' moment had limited appeal but pointed the way very clearly to the fact that my problems were food and gut related. More radical exclusive diets were embarked upon each one seemed to help a bit but nothing produced a complete cure. I tried different minerals and vitamins in varying doses. While out shopping I narrowly missed being run over by a speeding car because I could not accelerate my legs across the road and the experience taught me how old age feels. An extraordinary lesson to learn at the same time as learning that I was deeply loved by a man despite my slow and crunchy joints. My poor deafened therapist, the love of my life, became my partner and with infinite patience he gave me shiatsu treatments, moxa therapy [heated cigar shaped herbal preparation used on acupuncture points], prepared ginger poultices for my aching kidneys and nagged me relentlessly when I was being stupid and doing things my joints hated. He helped me into cars and hauled me physically out again, pushed me upstairs and stood in front of me on the way down so I could lean on his shoulders. He ploughed through endless books, researching every possible lead and spent hours and hours in the kitchen at the weekend, preparing food and liquids that helped reduce inflammation. He observed recently that he didn't know how bad I was until I got better and he could see what I was capable of doing. I would sit and stare at him thinking, 'How amazing that he can love me when I am like this'. This was a major life lesson for me.

During 2001 and 2002 I tried Homeopathy and Bach Flower Remedies. I did not get dramatic results but improved bit by bit. An iridologist told me bowel cleansing was a priority and I embarked on colonic irrigation. My unchewed food sailed down a well-lit glass pipe. I came home and told my partner who rolled his eyes to heaven in an exaggerated manner, *toooo* exaggerated for my liking. He is always telling me to eat slowly and I hate being confronted by my shortcomings. I started taking digestive enzymes with my food, plus acidophilus [to put good bacteria back into my gut] and chlorella [powdered green algae that helps detoxification]. I was troubled by slight abdominal distension and that prodding my tummy produced pain. I asked a doctor but was assured it was due to the arthritis. I thought otherwise. I thought the abdominal pain was producing the arthritis in some way. A friend told me about a visiting healer [Ray Brown] and as she spoke I had a spectacular bout of light flashing, so I paid attention and made an appointment to see this man. Apparently he becomes St. Paul of Damascus when he is healing - frankly I didn't care if he turned into Mickey Mouse, I just wanted someone, anyone, to take the pain away permanently. Ray, or whomsoever, sat quietly and listened to me, then he told me what my bowel movements were like, i.e., days of diarrhoea or very watery poop and then suddenly a perfectly normal shaped stool. I was amazed. He then prodded my abdomen and told me my colon was in spasm at the hepatic [liver] and splenic [spleen] flexure [bend in the colon] and gently probed my tummy to release the spasm. I felt two jets of heat, like really hot water, shoot down either side of my abdomen. I was stunned and asked what it was. Ray said it was just the blood supply getting through. I thought about my anatomy and physiology and was more than doubtful, but I was still incredulous at the experience. My partner drove me home and out came every single book we had on bowel, bowel conditions, spasm and anything else we could think of. Taking emotional tension aside, there were several vitamins and minerals, or lack of, that kept coming up, potassium and pantothenic acid being two, but the one that got all the razzle dazzle was magnesium. Back to the doctor and a request for my blood magnesium to be checked. The results were 'within normal limits'. I pondered on this. What if my body is taking from my superstructure what it needs to maintain my blood chemistry and therefore my life? What if it is so desperate for magnesium it is taking it from my joints? Why not access it in the middle of my bone? Is it taking it via my joints because that will immobilise me but not seriously endanger my life? Do I need much more magnesium than someone else? Is this a genetic problem? Despite my dietary changes, is my body *still* too acidic and is the acidity eating away at my joints? What exactly is going on with my so called auto-immune disease? Why would a body attack itself? [this has never made any sense to me especially having witnessed, while working in various Intensive Care Units, just how hard an unconscious and sometimes desperately ill body will fight to live.] Are some of my cells damaged in some way and therefore seen by other cells as alien? Are these cells poisoned? Am I poisoning them with my diet? My thought patterns? Am I poisoning them because I am not chewing my food or do I have a major digestive abnormality? How much is this related to fear? Or anger? I was not exactly knocking myself over with answers to all these questions, but at least I was asking them.

I saw Ray Brown again a few times but I did not feel I was moving much further on, but looking back the information he gave me was of enormous help and significance. I started taking a combination of magnesium and vitamin B complex three times a day. Barely three weeks later, I am, on personal recommendation, being treated in a pleasant but clinical room by a seriously highly qualified person who specialises in functional biochemistry and uses muscle testing. My muscles test strong one minute and then won't work at all the next, and I mean *really* won't work - it was unnerving. I am told I am desperately, but not catastrophically, low in magnesium and vitamin B6 at a cellular level [but my earlier blood results were normal]. My thyroid is not too sharp either. I am given pure bio available supplements that can be easily used in the body because mine was not accessing the type of magnesium I was taking. Fascinating information was racing past me at a rate I could hardly compute. This was followed by raging discussion with my partner in the car on the long drive home, covering food, farming [low magnesium in the soil], digestion, elimination, nervous tension and low B vitamins [a definite link], constipation, a lot of poop, more poop and inherited factors and, in particular, is it possible I incurred damage from my mother while I was in utero from her catastrophic constipation? Could the faeces hanging around in her colon for days and days and days have leached out into her body poisoning her, and therefore me, while she was pregnant? Was my nervy mother putting enough minerals and vitamins in for both of us when she was pregnant with me? On the next session my partner also gets treated and a zinc deficiency is found, which we sort of suspected, but was nevertheless surprising in the face of our varied diet [which seemed so nutritious,] the fact that he always took a multivitamin and I would frequently buy seafood, particularly whelks and crab, to eat at weekends. Could his ancestry have something to do with his low zinc in spite of a good diet? Did his Gibraltarean and Spanish forbears eat far more seafood? Was the seafood less polluted and did it have a higher zinc content? We looked up zinc and although we were already incorporating them into our diet we nevertheless bought industrial quantities of wheat bran, wheat germ and nuts. Suddenly oysters [extremely high in zinc,] which my partner adores, were looking more of a necessity than a treat for him.

Around about this time I was getting grumpy at home. I was better [not fully better] but I definitely need to stretch my brain, such as it is, flexible but not bursting at the seams. I decided I was well enough to pick up my 1999 plans to do extra training. My hands were not strong enough to restart reflexology but I thought I could manage iridology [study of iris]. So I did. I love to learn, and boy, did I learn. A few weeks in, I bought a small, round, self-examining magnifying mirror and took a really good look at my eyes. My now slightly trained eye noted multiple contraction furrows in both irides (the plural of iris is irides) which confirmed I used up minerals and vitamins faster than most. I had a weak lymphatic system [no wonder my ankles got so swollen on long flights] and the area denoting my large and small intestine was not a pretty sight, in fact it looked positively alarming. I booked in with a different colonic irrigationist. 'You are not chewing your food properly. You are malnourished because you are not breaking down the food particles enough and your body is having to work too hard .... your stomach doesn't have teeth you know!', she admonished me. *No way* was I telling my partner about this session, though he looked highly suspicious every time he finished his food and I was still half-way through mine. 'I will wear my teeth out at this rate', I thought.

I was getting heaps better but my stride was good some days and poor others. Walking after driving was unbelievably difficult and I viewed large car parks with a sigh as I knew it would take me ages to cross them. I was weary but not pole-axed with tiredness, so that was a great improvement. I am put in touch with a lovely lady whose husband got arthritis suddenly and went from very sporty to crawling across the floor, like me. He had taken liquid minerals and got better. I was so touched by this lady and her kindness, meeting me on Christmas Eve to give me her supply of the minerals so I would not have to wait until after Christmas. I took them - no major result, but it is great to know someone has got better.

I did a test and found I was low on stomach acid [see 'bicarbonate'] and now take supplements with some meals [the heavier ones] but not all. Also the magnesium has helped me enormously but failed to stop the gut spasm completely. I found taking potassium helps, but DON'T try this at home! Potassium can be dangerous, ask your doctor. Olive oil is good and I aim to slap it on something I eat nearly every day. I take flax seed oil, a good handful of vitamins and minerals daily, plus chlorella [a green cleansing algae]. I drink meadowsweet tea [I don't like it much], to keep an alkaline balance and try to cut back on ordinary tea, which I love, but I have to be careful not to overdo the meadowsweet as I find if I get too alkaline I get urinary tract infections. By 2005 I am sometimes able to descend stairs normally, instead of my usual sideways, one step at a time, crablike shuffle. In June 2005 I met up with a friend for lunch in London and managed over 200 stairs in various places, descending normally. I was neither fast nor elegant, but so thrilled with myself and so wreathed in beaming smiles at the bottom step that I startled onlookers. I can't make a fist and I still cannot squat but I can, at last, get down on the floor and up again unaided, though I doubt my performance would impress the English National Ballet.

Early 2006 was grim but I was not disciplined with my food. I tried the Gasteiner Heilstollen clinic in Austria, near Salzburg. Its natural low level radon caves, at different levels of humidity, have arthritics from all over Europe and beyond, attending year after year getting months and months of drug-free pain relief. I heard many people, with a multitude of problems, including severe fibromyalgia, praising the treatment. If you are shy, do not be put off by the brochure full of naked Nordic beauties of both sexes. In reality, the men and women are strictly segregated in the caves, the average age is probably 60 plus [though small children are treated] and the average size is lumpy. The nearby thermal spa at the small town of Bad Hofgastein has every 'wellness' facility imaginable and each hotel has its own basement spa but there is a large central spa in the town [where you can get a massage from someone who has had two years full-time training and really understands muscles and bones]. You can rent a small apartment easily if you are looking for a cheaper option. The treatments certainly helped me.

It is now early 2007 and my progress is speeding up but still on-going. I am presently on another course of herbal remedies for bowel cleansing and to clear parasites [I am hearing over and over from different sources that a huge percentage of people are carrying parasites, pet owners especially]. My skin looks better for it and my tongue is becoming clean and pink. Early in the year we spent three weeks in Southern India, eating meals for twenty pence in local restaurants that have no cutlery - fabulous food and we had absolutely no health problems. I returned with no stiffness at all but it has crept back a bit. I have been seen by a TFT [Thought Field Therapist] and am doing tapping exercises on acupuncture points to release emotions. He tells me white sugar is a major problem for me and so is my toothpaste. The sugar is not much of a surprise, I eat very little of it but sugar is in tinned food and I do love the odd biccy. I am astounded at the toothpaste because I buy it from a health food store, but he is right, I sleep with that toothpaste in my mouth and absorb it all night long. My first night after the treatment I got a vivid parachuting down and safe landing dream, whereas I normally fly night after night, year on year. The therapist has given me a simple test to check my body's reaction to toothpaste and I am amazed to find most brands have my body saying, 'No thank you'. Shortly after my appointment I developed a nasty eliminatory rash that had a smell like stale urine. It was gone in four days but at the same time I was poorly, headachey and vomiting. I see both these as positive signs and I continue tap, tap, tapping. I am currently under the care of a teacher of nutrition. Although I am waiting for her to analyse all the tests I have had done [mostly urinary], she has, nevertheless, come up with a probable diagnosis to my current problems that is so astounding in its simplicity that it makes complete sense to my nurse trained ears. I am enormously hopeful that, under her guidance, I will get well. I feel it is time now and I am put in mind of the ancient Greek temple at Delphi which has 'Know Thyself' carved above a lintel. I am, however, utterly dispirited that, though I live less than an hour by car from Cambridge, I had to send my urine samples for comphrehensive testing to America. I would rather my taxation went to fund a urine testing laboratory here than to Domes and Olympics.

I shall sum up. How is your health? Are you sick? Research. Please don't just sit there. Research and learn. Question professionals, check and double check, get second and even third opinions, if necessary. Give your body a break by having just juiced fruit and veg for a couple of days and see if you feel a bit better - if you do, even if it is fractional, then you know you have work to do on your diet. If you have a list, large or small, of piddling little minor health complaints that do not keep you from working but worry you at night, start some serious research. A bunch of small niggles is your body asking for help, be aware that all those little niggles may be the road map to a major problem so pay attention before your body starts screaming for help. I paid attention to my endless small bodily complaints but abjectly failed to get in touch with my feelings. Never forget you are unique, no-one has had your life and your experiences, so what helps one person may, or may not, help you. Read the 'health' section in this book. Think gut, whatever your illness is, even if it is something completely unrelated to digestion. This is your body, you own it, you manage it, you must take responsibility for it. Try everything; even if you find all wanting, you have been courageous and that alone may heal you. Talk to yourself and far, far more importantly, listen to what you have to say. You have one language, your body has another. Learn it's language and remember when it talks 'pain' you have missed *all* the preceding conversation. It was talking, you just were not listening. Pay attention, please do. I'm not preaching, I'm just learning and it has been a long and exquisitely painful lesson for me.

ARGUE

I learnt how to argue when I met my partner. I was useless at it all my life. I would silently rage but be unable to find the words because I was clouded with seething emotion. When my beloved came into my life we had some corkers of rows. Those major blow ups were important for both of us because love allowed jets of pent-up stored rage to spew forth safely. We learnt to stick to the point - absolutely crucial for a constructive row. 'And another thing', was not permitted. Gradually the heat was expelled and rows became arguments, arguments became debates, debates became squabbles and squabbles dissipated into giggling. We are still learning and barristers we will never be, but I am grateful for this lesson [actually we both are] because having learnt how to argue we have both become more powerful and united. I repeat, because I think it is important, having learnt how to argue constructively, without malice, sticking to the point, we have become more powerful and united.

I view with suspicion those who say, 'We never row'. There may well be a few exceptions to the rule but there are, in my view, many 'who never row' where one person is relentlessly backing off and the other is getting their own way. Energetically [and you will need to read 'chakras' if you think I am talking about your electric light bulbs] this is lethal territory, it almost certainly will damage your health in the long run.

I have witnessed many rows and been told many stories of couples who row continuously. It is interesting how instigators of rows often need attention and by creating a scene that is exactly what they get - full eye contact, full on attention and I wonder if their bottom line is an abject fear of abandonment. Rowing couples are together for a reason - to release emotion. This is healing, but if the rows persist then there is not much forward movement nor a degree of resolution and peace; there is only fear. Next time you see two people screaming at each other, know you are seeing raging fear on both sides.

May I make a plea? Do not row in front of children or animals. You may be doing actual physical damage, grievous bodily harm. Watching loved ones in an uncontrolled screaming match rips open some children's and some animal's bellies energetically as surely as a surgeon's knife. I have comforted a cringing and whining dog while its two adult owners screamed at each other; the screamers displaying their fear for all to see and terrifying the dog in the process. A kinesiologist [muscle tester] can give you a demonstration of how damaging unkind words are to muscles, it will surprise you, vicious words can do untold energetic damage and even a cutting look can make your muscles go weak. You can test this yourself by standing up and extending an arm sideways. Get a friend to place their hand on your forearm and try to push your arm downwards while you think firstly about nice things and secondly about nasty things. Your muscles will go weak with the latter, even if it is only fractionally. A good row may be therapeutic to some, even sport, but may be absolute hell for onlookers, so take your rage outdoors, comfort spectators afterwards, seek professional help if it is getting out of hand and, above all, ask yourself what you are *really* afraid of.

ANGER

There is so much of it about these days, have you noticed? It seems twenty-four hour shopping, travel and luxuries beyond the reach of our fathers and mothers have made us rather tetchy. It is sad, I think. We do need to look at our individual anger because it is a dangerous tenant. Appropriately used anger is a useful tool and can energise you to action, but anger swallowed and unexpressed can lead to halitosis [bad breath], a jammed jaw, neck and spinal problems, headaches and do untold damage to your abdominal area, not least your liver and gall-bladder. It will spread across to your pancreas and spleen and not for nothing do we have the expression 'vent one's spleen' in relation to anger, or that something is 'galling'. I have a problem with my gall-bladder meridian [which runs near my shoulder into my neck towards my ear and continues further down from my hip, down the outside of the middle of my thigh towards my knee]. When my joints are playing up one or other, or both, of these meridian lines is painful to the touch. Try running your thumb midline down the outside of your thigh. Does it make you wince? It shouldn't. Now, I daresay it is 'ouchy' because you are not eating the food your liver likes, but if your liver is tetchy and your gall-bladder is also in a mood, adding the wrong grub can only make matters worse. It is difficult being good all the time, I know, I can be good for days at a time but then I spot the goat's milk cheese and think, 'Oh yum .... just an incy wincy bit won't hurt'. My gall-bladder, still in a huff about something I conveniently cannot recall, now has to deal with cheese so it gets even more cross. 'I'll show her', it seethes, sending an armoured division up my gall-bladder meridian, into my neck and giving me achey pains. Who do I blame? My neck of course. Poor innocent piggy in the middle of my egotistical desire for my favourite cheese and my disgruntled gall-bladder storing an old emotional file marked, 'Dr So and So, arrogant pig, humiliated me on a ward round, circa 1976'. I can't really remember the ward round that well, but my gall-bladder can. This, I believe, is how anger is stored away and pops up later as an '...itis' or an achey something.

Anger is often buried under niceness - so are you nice? A nice person? Excessively nice? A people pleaser? Is this because you are just nice or do you have low self-esteem? You don't like yourself much so you need to be liked by one and all? It is nice to be liked, to be popular, don't get me wrong, I like being liked but I have to accept there are people out there who do not like me one little bit. Of course these people are raving lunatics and I forgive them. Please be steady on the need to be liked though, we have a regular presenter on our local television who practically turns herself inside out trying to be nice and I worry about her.

Please do try to explore your hidden depths and seek out and release buried anger. While excavating, remember it is very, very important to do lots of deep breathing and drink lots of water. If nothing else, this will make you feel giddy and pee a lot, so there will be less time to be grumpy. My partner [still clearing his emotional filing cabinet - more later] is exquisitely calm until someone cuts him up on the road and he turns into a mad rabid dog, while I infuriate him further by advising, 'Enlightenment, darling, enlightenment' ... which reminds me of a story. There was a guru, or some such, who sat in the lotus position in a cave up a mountain in India. He was visited by many, many people because he was extremely famous for being enlightened and calm and serene and spiritual. One day he came down from his mountain, stubbed his toe on a supermarket trolley and lost his temper.

The release of anger will do your health no end of good. Buy a punch bag, put a picture of your boss on it, or anyone else who annoys you, and box its ears. Wallop the living daylights out of a very large cushion. Kick a pillow round the room. Try writing letters, any amount of disgusting language will be permitted, but do not, repeat do not, send the letters. Burn them, or rip them to tiny pieces and chuck. I did once send a furious letter to some poor unsuspecting person who had not been fully attentive to the fact that I had been, for some time, a pressure cooker about to explode. I did apologise with a letter and a gift later. So do as I say and do not do as I do. Learn to argue your point, quietly and politely from an early age, it will save you considerable grief in later life. If you are someone who 'is not heard' or is constantly interrupted you will pick up some helpful hints under 'clothes' and 'colour' and possibly 'boundaries', but if these do not help feel free to buy a large mallet and learn to shout.

If you are thinking the above may be relevant to you and you are going to do something about it, please understand this: you are instigating healing and even taking a small step in that direction will bring changes. You know about this, oh yes you do. Down, down, in the deep, dark cavern where you keep ancient knowledge of all things, you will know that a small step towards self healing = movement, and movement [don't panic] = c h a n g e. Most people do not like change [I hate it] and that is why healing, in any form, even releasing some old anger or rift is frightening territory for most. It changes you and it changes your vibrational rate [more later]. People, family, friends, loved ones will sense the change in you and either draw close or pull away. It is the latter which frightens us.

*A*LONE

Who doesn't like being alone? Hands up. I don't mean half an hour or a weekend when the spouse has taken the tribe on a sixty mile hike up some mountain, a long way from you and the sofa upon which you blissfully relax. No, I mean completely alone. Living alone. How is it for you? The world is split neatly, in my opinion, between those who like their own company and those who do not, but allows for a few oddballs who don't like their own company or anyone else's for that matter. There are a number of people who think and say they want a companion but actually prefer living alone but will not admit this preferment to anyone, much less to themselves, and I am beginning to suspect this is now an increasingly large proportion of women and, to a much lesser extent, men.

When things start to go wrong in your life in relation to relationships of any type, you need to stop still and ask yourself one single question, 'How can I change?'. You see, you can't change other people, you just can't. You are wasting your time and breath trying to do so. It may be that you enjoy wasting your time and breath trying to change someone because by doing so you don't have to move on and you can just stay where you exhaustingly are, preserving the ghastly status quo [existing state of affairs]. If that is the case, that is your business and good luck to you. You should get bored eventually

.... hopefully. If you want to do something constructive about improving a relationship you have to instigate some sort of self-healing, some emotional repair work, so when you have finished blathering and complaining about 'them' to everyone who will listen, and tired yourself out in the process, you are then going to need some 'alone' time. Take the phone off the hook, quiet down and look within to find the answers. It is only with this alone time that you can start to change your outlook on life and start accepting responsibility for your actions and your words. It takes two to tango and ghastly as it may be, we all need to see where we stepped on other's toes, no matter that those toes were kicking you in the shins at the time.

When you have finished looking at your relationships through thoughtful eyes, you may need to make a choice to stay where you are and erect better emotional boundaries or leave. Sometimes it is not just one person that has to be left, but whole families, sometimes whole tribes, if we are to heal or, at the very least, not sustain further damage. Many people cannot make this choice. It is understandable, as the thought of walking away from the familiar, coping with what people might say and living alone can be daunting. It takes tremendous courage and a leap of faith [I am not talking about religion, but you might be] that someone else, a special person, or a replacement family, or a more appropriate tribe [or better still, no tribe at all] will turn up at some future date. It is often easier to retreat to the familiar and stagnate than face the fear of aloneness. Better the devil you know than the angel you want, but cannot see. Better the mild or even outright hostility, the multiple agendas, the rows, the sniping, the carping, the ignoring, the silences and the lack of being heard .... than being alone.

For me, aloneness has always been the better option and I am a better, wiser, stronger and more empathic person for having spent many years living on my own. Learning to enjoy your own company is *crucial* for healing past relationships and creating healthy future ones. For you, if you are in such a dilemma, I can assure you sunnier pastures and nicer people await, you just need courage. Don't be afraid of living alone, it can be wonderful, it just depends how much effort you make to enjoy it.

𝔸LEXANDER TECHNIQUE

One day when big, interfering, silly and expensive government has gone away this will be taught in every school to every child in the land.

I once went to a woman, who was made of India rubber, for Alexander Technique lessons. She wafted around me as graceful as a ballerina. Standing beside me she took my upper arm in one hand and my wrist in the other and sweetly requested, 'Relax, let go and give me your arm, Amanda'. So I did. Smiling, she said, 'No, give me your arm'. My eyes shot east to west rapidly and back again, my brain whirred and then I gave her my arm. 'I want you to try and give me your arm', she said, but I detected a hint, just a hint of a sigh. I flattened my lips while thinking, 'What does she want me to do, get a bloody Black and Decker and remove the screws?'. I relaxed utterly [after all this was costing me money and I like to get my money's worth]. I gave her my arm. She put my arm down and smiled politely. 'Ooooooops,' I thought, 'I have seen that sort of polite smile before'. 'Shall we reverse roles? I'll be you and you be me', she suggested, helpfully. Well, I think anyone who suggests being me, even for a very short period, is a jolly good sport and I am prepared to go along with such an heroic gesture. She took up the 'me' position and I endeavoured to graceful ballerina over to her position. I took her arm and smiled encouragingly. 'Give me your arm', I commanded. She did. I swear to God I nearly removed it from its socket. Not that I was pulling, you understand, she just gave it to me. I stood in stunned silence, the full horror sinking in. Her body was indeed made of India rubber, mine was made of solid 100% concrete.

Concrete bodies are made up of emotional body armouring. Mine was such that I had not only armoured but built a veritable Sherman tank around my neck, shoulders and anywhere else I could think of. She taught me that I was such an habitual muscle tightener that I was perpetually carrying my shoulders about half an inch higher than they should be, maybe more. I was pulling my shoulders in and up and locking. Now, let's check you out. Where are your shoulders? If you relax do your shoulders drop down from their current position? If they do, get some professional help because you may need to be taught how to unwind your body. If you have nice solid concrete shoulders and neck you are exhausting yourself. Muscles are being permanently tightened using up lots of minerals and vitamins you probably are not replacing fast enough or in sufficient quantities, so the rest of your body is paying the price because it needs them too. You are compressing your neck, possibly damaging bones and probably getting more headaches than India rubber people, so do something about it. Several times a day try to massage your ears with your shoulders but not when you are driving or in the cinema, especially if I am sitting behind you. Get a massage from someone who knows a lot about muscles so you can ask questions, find out just how bad the situation is and start to rectify it. Simple really.

Now here are three major lessons I learned from my most excellent India rubber Alexander Technique teacher. First, stand in front of a full length mirror and look at yourself. Starkers is best, if you can bear it. I want you to check your thumbs. Where are they? Don't be silly, of course they are on your hands. Your thumbs should be facing the mirror, not your knuckles. If you are presenting your knuckles to the mirror you are doing the Neanderthal look - most unattractive. Get help from someone who knows about bones and muscles because you are rotating your arms forward and this will have a knock on effect on the whole of your upper torso, and neck and head. I suppose it might affect your lungs too. Probably does, come to think of it.

Next, get a friend, a sober one is best. Then get a large book and put both hands underneath it and put it under your chin to obscure your downward vision. DO NOT look down - no cheating. Place your FEET PARALLEL to what you think is the width of your hips, or to put it another way, a hip's width apart. Do your feet feel parallel? Don't look! Now relax. Keep very still but give the book to your friend. Look down. Are your feet perfectly side by side, a hip's width apart and are your toes pointing to twelve o'clock? Get your friend to hunker down and look at your heels. Are they straight and parallel? Usually they are not. Ask your friend to shift them into the correct position - you will now almost certainly feel like a duck. Relax your knees, stare at your feet reflectively and vow to do better - better still, go see an Alexander Technique specialist. If you are strapped for cash this does not have to be expensive, just tell them you can only afford one or two [try and make it three] appointments. Most therapists understand limited finances and, if they do not, find another one who does, quick smart [I am less than keen on therapists, of any description, who rely on your *repeated* attendance to pay their mortgage]. You can always get an Alexander Technique book out of the library if pennies are really tight but just one Alexander lesson from an experienced teacher will be hugely beneficial and may change your life by teaching you to rebalance. A straight and well-balanced body aids a well-balanced mind.

Meanwhile, back at the Ponderosa, you can amuse yourself looking through the local newspapers at photographs of important men in groups [or men who think they are important] because they are usually the worst offenders. Their feet will give you no end of entertainment. Are their toes pointing to twelve o'clock? I doubt it. Five to twelve, ten past twelve, eleven fifteen, quarter to three, you will spot them all, and come fifty, or earlier, they will be wondering why their knees and hips hurt, and possibly their ankles too.

Now, stand sideways on to your pal and ask them to look at you, while imagining a ruler or plumb line running from the top of the middle of your head and going right through the centre of your body. This ruler or plumb line SHOULD drop down the side of your body and on that line SHOULD be - your ear, the middle of your shoulder, your elbow, your middle finger, the middle of the side of your knee and your ankle bone, which your middle finger should be pointing towards down the centre of your thigh. Clear as mud? Now ... how many ears are in front of shoulders? Elbows behind hips? In front of hips? Hands in front of thighs? Thumbs hidden because backs of hands are Neanderthal pointing to twelve o'clock? If your ear is ahead of your shoulder, your neck is out of alignment and that has a knock on effect on your whole spine, plus you look like a tortoise. Get professional help because it may well prevent years of pain in later life. Look after yourself, take care of your body, because no-one else can do it for you. You will be so proud of yourself in years to come because you will know, right down to your bones, that you can be reliable, sensible and forward thinking.

Last little exercise - lie on the floor and relax. Can you slide your hands under your lower back and meet hands or worse, hold hands? Your lower spine is out. Get help now.

My wonderful India rubber teacher gave me a 'lying out exercise' to take home with me. This is far more 'lying out' than 'exercise' and took minimal effort, so it is *just* the sort of exercise I like. I cannot begin to tell you the fantastic difference it made to my back that had been giving me problems for years and I got a double whammy from my Alexander lessons - my twenty-three years of severe period pains stopped completely. When I decided to have my Alexander Technique lessons, years ago, I asked a friend, who recommended me to my wonderful India rubber teacher. My friend strictly warned me not to do anything after my treatment, especially as I had a very long drive home. 'Come straight back, Amanda, you will be exhausted'. I then saw another friend, an actor, who also said I would be tired and that Alexander lessons had been taken by a friend of his and it had changed his life. 'Well', I thought, 'I'm up for that'. I had my first lesson and I hardly knew what my teacher was doing half the time. It was such small, gentle movements and afterwards I felt the same as I did before the lesson so I ignored all advice. Being in a town I don't often visit, I thought I would have a little furkle around the shops. Then I drove home and feeling chipper, walked the dogs. I had an early supper, switched on the box and quite suddenly I felt like I had been hit by a BUS. I crawled to bed, I am not exaggerating, and slept like a log for twelve hours, so please take the advice I ignored.

Alexander Technique needs to be a statutory form of health prevention taught to every child [before they hit their teens] in this country. God alone knows how much money it would save the taxpayers.

𝒜NIMALS

Ever since I was a small child, my mother would tell everyone and anyone who would listen, 'Amanda loves animals', with a tiny amount of pride and a huge amount of incomprehension in her voice. I would stand there politely, elongating my mouth and exposing teeth in what I hope passed for a genuine smile while thinking, *'Noooo, that's not it'*. Problem was, I didn't know what was it. As a child I relentlessly begged my parents for a dog but it was not forthcoming on the grounds that we were an Air Force family and a posting abroad was a distinct possibility at any time. I finally got a cat when I was ten years old, just as I was sent to boarding school. I suspect the two events correlated. I worshipped that cat but it was still to be many years before I fully realised what I had been too embarrassed to face - the fact that *I needed* animals, but specifically, I needed the company of a dog. I have cats and chickens and some fish in the pond and I love them all dearly, I especially love my cats, but I *need* a dog. I find a calmness in the presence of dogs. I have heard all the arguments about them giving unconditional love and how they fail to comment on the extra half stone that indecently bulges behind your zip. These observations are true, but it goes deeper than that for me. It is not just the wonderful unconditional love - it is something else, something indefinable.

Do I love animals? Well, I certainly find them absolutely fascinating and I could, if I had the time, lie on my stomach for hours in the garden on a summer's day, watching ants going about their extraordinary lives, but I don't need an ant. I find snakes fairly compelling and I could probably watch a cobra for hours, as long as there was a large sheet of bullet proof glass between me and it …….. which puts me in mind of a fabulous trip to Namibia where our enchanting and most excellent guide Dwayne noticed a cobra trail in the sand heading to a tree. 'Let's see if we can find the cobra!', he suggested in a jolly tone. 'Good idea', thinks uncompetitive me, 'and I plan to spot it first'. 'What do we do if it comes out of the tree?', asks my sensible partner. 'Run!', says Dwayne. The three of us circled the tree until I found my nose perilously close to the outer branches and I backed off to a sensible distance. We did not spot the cobra. Shame. No, I definitely do not need snakes but they are fascinating.

I don't know what it is exactly that I love about animals, dogs especially, but I do think the longing to be in the company of animals is a longing that *should not be ignored*. We understand little about the 'energy' we possess and pass to others and I rather suppose it is the same with animal energy. Perhaps I specifically need the 'energy' that a dog emits. Perhaps I was a dog in a previous life. Perhaps there is a dog in me still….. woof woof.

ADVICE

I watched a tragedy unfurl through my parent's inability or downright refusal to ask advice. It made me acutely aware of how important advice is and who to ask for it. Nowadays we are bombarded with advice. These days magazines, newspapers and television programmes will tell you how to live, to die, remove your cuticles, get a divorce, get a cat, buy a house anywhere you can think of, change your job, or finance your finances. This sort of advice was not available to my parents at the time they needed it. In those days magazines told men about manly things, like shooting small birds, and advised women how to make that rabbit pie go a little bit further with a bit of racy information on what shade of pink nail polish was going to be fashionable for the next two years.

My advice, for what it is worth, is this - if you are faced with a mountainous dilemma, write down what you really, really want and what you really, really don't want, so you are clear in your mind about both. If your 'want' is proving elusive and so is the exit to your dilemma, find someone [preferably two or three people] for whom you have respect and who will keep your secrets and tell them this … 'I have a problem I would like to tell you about and though I am not asking for your advice I would value your opinion on the matter so that I can make my own judgment later'. Then listen carefully, no matter what they have to say, because whatever their answer is it will inevitably be coloured by their life experience, so therefore it may or may not be relevant to you. By asking them to listen and give an opinion, but not asking specifically for their advice, you are free to follow up on their idea or ignore it. Remember to thank whoever you asked for their opinion, because manners matter.

ART

I adore visiting art galleries. I definitely lean towards preferring traditional, representational works of art. A portrait by a Dutch master would send me into raptures but I covet [though I am unlikely to get] a Mark Rothko painting. A few years ago, my partner and me walked through the Tate Modern. We were relatively unmoved by the experience, yet, a year later we were thrilled at the sight of such fantastic creativity in the Museum of Modern Art in Havana, Cuba [restriction can have such interesting results]. Still, I did not understand why some modern pieces of …. erm, art [?] really annoyed me. I could not just dismiss something as ludicrous in my mind, without having a reasoned argument for my dismissal. Then a friend informed me when it comes to a work of art, 'You have to be able to work like a master before you can break the rules'. There is *plenty* of scope for argument in that statement, but still, for me, my friend's information made me think, 'Phew!'. I found my annoyance abated and I could drift serenely around a museum or art gallery. What a relief. I do like having a little box for my botherations.

$\mathcal{B}$ Is for Bragg

As in Melvyn. I always think he is *such* a good idea. I scan the Radio Times and alight upon one of his philosophical discussions. 'Mmmmmmmn', I think, 'I'll have me some of that - get meself ed-oo-cated'. I put big highlighter pen marks around the programme and come the big day I rush around doing all my jobs in record time and walk the dogs even faster. Then I sit down with quiet jobs, some sewing maybe, turn the tranny on and listen, head cocked in a hopeful posture looking much like one of our chickens at feeding time. On comes Melv. Golly he's smooth, isn't he? We are off. Streams of intelligent intelligence in very long sentences. I begin to stumble and the first hurdle isn't even in sight. I'm not looking so perky now and I begin to slouch a bit. My eyebrows are drawn together in fierce concentration and I am muttering, 'I'm not thick, just a bit slow on the uptake, that's all'. I'm grappling with a sentence and suddenly we are three sentences on and I have lost the plot completely. In my imagination, Spike Milligan and Peter Sellars are before me, pointing at the radio and then pointing at me and laughing. 'Bugger off', I tell them, 'I'm trying to better myself. Make yourself useful and put the kettle on'. It's no good. I adopt a familiar posture I perfected at school - staring out of the window. I sigh. Sentences are still coming out thick and fast and I am none the wiser. I could swear someone used the word perspecivity, sounding like persperkivity - what the bloody hell does that mean? I rush to the diccy - can't find it. We are half way through the programme and I am lost. I hurl myself back on the sofa, palm to my forehead in a theatrical manner reminiscent of Hedda Gabler, crying, 'I'm thick! I was thick, am thick and will always be thick'. Spike and Peter are causing mayhem in the kitchen of my mind. I think I will join them. We start making rude comments about Melv's hair. Much tittering.

A few months later, because I never learn, I put a ring around Mr. Bragg's programme.

$\mathcal{B}$RIGHT

I am not particularly bright and I am a bit bored trying to convince people of this unavoidable fact. I suppose I measure myself against the guests on

Melvyn Bragg's programmes and find myself miserably wanting. There are vast expanses of things I know absolutely nothing about, however, in between those vast expanses there are the odd crevices where I can spout forth with a modicum of certainty. I am trying to think of one or two of my knowledgeable crevices but I'm not having much success just now - well I am making myself giggle [whippet behaviour, charity shop shopping and the art of giving an enema circa 1975] and as I enjoy giggling that is always a winner. Of course there are a few people on this planet who think I am very bright indeed, a font of all wisdom no less. These people I like a lot.

I don't happen to think being bright is the be all and end all - well, I would say that wouldn't I? I would rate an enquiring mind as high as being bright. I have an enquiring mind as long as it is not confronted with anything that looks like an engine. When I was a youngster my father would periodically lift the bonnet on the car and diligently explain the workings therein. He noted with amusement that I was most definitely his daughter most of the time but, when confronted with an engine, I immediately became my mother's daughter and adopted her polite but glazed expression. I would look down on a sea of pipes, more pipes and messy oily things, examine my fingers nails and think, 'Not blooming likely'. I am glad to report I haven't changed a bit.

BOSOMS

They are everywhere these days, have you noticed? I don't know where to look. Now, heaving mounds and silicone gun turrets are all right, if you must, in low light or high fashion but I don't particularly want them in my line of sight while I am buying Brussel sprouts or paying for petrol. I think it is getting ridiculous. Nancy in 'Oliver' looked adorable with bosoms, but that was then and this is now and anyway, Nancy had the sense to call it at day at mammary glands, whereas nowadays we practically get an anatomy lesson. Naked bosoms on the beach are quite the thing, whatever shape or age they are in. Men's eyes will, quite naturally, be drawn to such edifices, much like a spaniel to a steak, but I don't think it is fair because I very rarely find staring at a man's chest enthralling and men in tight swimming trunks make me giggle.

I am not a complete puritan, bosoms are lovely, but I do think they have been so very cheapened and even my partner, who thinks bosoms are a very fine thing indeed, has recently remarked they are too much and too everywhere. Bosoms at nine o'clock in the morning are inappropriate outside of a bordello and I am not sure why women expect anyone, let alone men, to take them seriously when they are exposing their bosom in the office. Would you take a man seriously if he turned up at the office at nine o'clock in the morning wearing a cod-piece? I suspect not. I certainly wouldn't, but I might buy him a drink at lunchtime for being a helluva good sport, assuming the cod-piece was not a daily occurrence.

I think over exposure of lumpy bits is a bit like swearing all the time. A well-timed expletive [and I make good use of them myself] can make people pay attention, but continual expletives lose their emphasis and eventually become really tedious. I liken continual swearing to continually shouting at a wilful dog. Eventually the bored dog switches off and uses its owner's verbal barrage as a sort of pinpoint echo-location finder so it knows where to return to, should it feel like it, while it continues on its silent, sniffing and merry tail wagging way, watering every blade of grass in a three mile radius.

BABIES

I wrote a whole section on childbirth and then chickened out. I decided being a midwife with views that were not mainstream had been tough enough. I do want to say this though, please take your diet ultra seriously when you are planning to start a family and, obviously, when you are pregnant. The more research I do into my own ill health, the more I think I probably arrived, at birth, with a problem and I wonder if my grandmother's eating habits and her wish to be severely slim, had an effect on my mother before she was born too. A pregnant women needs to be in the best health she can possibly be to give her baby the best start in life. As a midwife I used to tell the mums to listen attentively to their food cravings as long as they were reasonably healthy things to eat. Each baby is growing continuously day and night but often in spurts. Each bit of the growing baby needs different minerals and vitamins to grow and may need extra during one of those growth spurts. You may hate vegetables or fruit but your baby will need it and it will need regular intakes of protein [please read 'backache']. Don't glug sugar, it is not good for you or your bump. Think of your growing baby with every mouthful of food you put in your gob because the NHS is not too perky, there is a desperate shortage of midwives [who have been treated abysmally] and you need to give you and your baby the best possible chance of a safe delivery, as well as a healthy future life.

One more point. If you are pregnant or a mother, please always remember that you are the expert on your baby or your child. Doctors are experts on what can go wrong with a child, but they are not the expert on your child because only you are with them all the time, observing. Be guided by that knowledge and listen to your intuition. When your child is sick see a doctor quickly but always look at the food you are feeding your son or daughter. Think diet, stomach and intestines. If your child is always getting infections, its immune system is not strong. You *feed* an immune system to make it healthy. What are you giving your child's immune system for breakfast, lunch and dinner?

B VITAMINS

I am going to give you what little I know about vitamins and minerals under 'vitamins' but I want to just get in early with the B's. They are essential, not stored [give or take an inch or two] so you need them daily and, due to paying attention and my personal experience, I have a mounting concern that both the B vitamins and magnesium are so undersupplied in our diets today that it is becoming a really serious matter. Frazzled nerves need B's and magnesium to soothe, but most of us reach for an alcoholic drink when we are frazzled and that depletes these essential vitamins and minerals even further. If you are tired all the time, try increasing your B's [there are lots of them] in your diet. Change your diet before you start taking supplements and take the supplements only if your improved diet is not helping. Beware of taking one B vitamin in isolation, it's much more effective to take a multi B compound [B complex] and don't panic if your pee turns bright yellow, it's ok, it's just your body throwing off unwanted extras [I think it is the B2 that turns the pee yellow]. All pee is a wonderful compostable thing but bright yellow pee doesn't half put the wind up foxes, which is probably not interesting if you live in the middle of a city, but heavingly relevant to those living in deep paraffin country with chooks clucking about.

I have always been fascinated at tales of harvesting in ye olden days. How did folk manage to perform long hours of such strenuous manual labour in the fields when their lunch consisted only of a hunk of bread [no butter, so I am told] and some cheese? Could it be the bread was different [as in higher B vitamin content] to the bread we eat these days? Was the cheese different?

I remember cheese went rock hard in a couple of days when I was a child, but not now. Perhaps the farm workers were permanently hungry. Perhaps they drank ale and that lubricated their limbs sufficiently, but then ale has B vitamins too. I seem to have a very high daily requirement for B vitamins [perhaps it is the whippet in me]. I am a big fan of Brewer's Yeast which is a very rich source of all the B's and some minerals. If you think you have intestinal candida don't take Brewer's because it is, obviously, a yeast.

Brewer's Yeast is one of the cheapest supplements and has been an age old remedy for maintaining health. You can get it in pill or powder form [check labels for maximum contents - I recommend Solgar's Brewer's] and I add the latter to soups and gravy. I also sprinkle it on my dogs' food daily, I find that it calms them. One of my rescued dogs was frightened of loud noises but since giving her Brewer's she is much less bothered. We now give her extra to get her through the ever lengthening firework period in November, with good results. There is a link in humans between magnesium depletion and reacting to loud noises [they made my mother *jump out of her skin* and I now realise, in sad and belated hindsight that she was almost certainly grossly magnesium, B vitamin and zinc deficient at a *cellular* level]. I have read that you need to be adequately furnished with B Vitamins, especially B6, in order to absorb magnesium. I don't know if this is true but it makes sense to me. I am of the opinion that B vitamin and magnesium depletion has already reached epidemic proportions in this country and probably all over the Western World. I have no proof but in my bones I think this is part of the reason why we are seeing so many allergies, reactions to drugs and vaccinations, gut problems and ground down tiredness. I also suspect that the gut problem comes first and that affects absorption and manufacture of these vitamins. I daresay our hectic lifestyles do not help one iota.

BREAKFAST

Did you have breakfast this morning? I take no credit for what I am about to write, it is my partner's observation. Aside from late night mountainous meals or raging hangovers he suspects that most people who skip breakfast are nervous of the day; frightened of work or school [but possibly good at hiding their emotions] with their stomachs in early morning knots they cannot face the thought of food, but later, having broken into work/school, nerves have settled, they then feel peckish and guess what? There is only unhealthy snacks available, so that is what they have. Adelle Davis was bemoaning the lack of protein eaten in the 1960's, heaven only knows how little we are getting now and we wonder why we get sick and can't repair. If you eat at 6pm, skip breakfast the next day and grab a sandwich at 2pm you have just gone 20 hours without protein, unless you count the milk in your coffee as you skate out the door for work. We all need protein daily, children and adults alike, for daily repair. If you are ill you may need even more protein to help make and replace the cells that are dying off even quicker than usual. Think about the dust in your bedroom, it is mostly dead skin and this is the dead skin you can see, but lots more has gone in the wash, down the plughole or up the vacuum cleaner and this is just the skin cells we lose on the outside of our bodies. We lose MILLIONS of cells, inside and out, every day. To make new ones we need nutritious food and especially protein. Engage brain, please do, put the necessary food in your mouth three times a day if you want to heal that cut on your finger quickly, generally stay well and not age too fast. In these days of manic face-lifting we need to remember that we will stay youthful looking longer if we drink water and put balanced meals in three times a day, than we ever will dieting or nibbling on lettuce leaves, besides, you need protein and any amount of minerals and vitamins to recover from a face-lift. It is surgery, which is trauma and all trauma needs building blocks to do the repair work.

Stating the obvious, children grow. Growth requires protein and plenty of it. If your kiddywink refuses brekkie at least furnish him/her with a protein snack and also some healthy carbohydrates [to give slow release energy] to take to school and eat when nerves have settled. Try and ensure protein goes in at lunch and/or dinner, preferably both [but don't forget the fruit and veg]. It doesn't have to be difficult, you can make a smoothie - liquidise tofu [high in protein], add yoghurt and flavour. Eat nuts if you can [most nuts are high in protein and lots of other good things], either whole or ground in a coffee grinder and then sprinkled onto cereal. Powdered skimmed milk is also a good source of protein, you can put it dry onto porridge, cereal or muesli, or add water and have as ordinary milk. Try something different for breakfast every day - eggs on toast, tinned fish on toast, cheese on toast, marmite on toast, peanut butter on toast, kangaroos on toast [just testing to see if you are still paying attention]. Be inventive and make that toast from the most nutritious bread you can buy [and brown bread does not necessarily mean it is better for you, read the labels very carefully]. Wholemeal bread with lumpy crunchy bits is usually better but make your own if you can. We are highly blessed with a fabulous local bakery and both their produce and our home-made bread is the bread I remember from my childhood, absolutely delicious, but it goes mouldy within a few days as it always used to. I bought some sliced brown bread in the supermarket some months back because it was on its 'sell by date', well reduced in price and I love a bargain. That night I made it into a bread and butter pudding that was beyond divine, but the bread left over was still soft and fresh looking days later. I wondered how much of a bargain I had actually got.

BACKACHE

Do you have it? What did you have for breakfast? Not relevant you think? Think again. Backache usually means injury, injury = repair, repair means new cell growth and new cell growth requires food, healthy food. My partner had a classic middle-aged male client recently. The poor man arrived for his emergency appointment listing at 45 degrees, in agony with his back. Following a successful shiatsu treatment the now upright gentleman was quizzed on his diet and it transpired he survived on a certain sugary breakfast cereal, often eaten for breakfast and evening meal. Lunch was frequently skipped. Occasionally in the evening the boat was pushed out with spaghetti bolognese. Vegetables and fruit were virtually non-existent in his life. His only fluid intake was coffee and snacks were usually of the chocolate variety when his blood sugar dropped. He wondered why his body was not repairing. Frankly, we both thought it was nothing short of a bloody miracle he was still standing. My beloved told him he was being a bit of a mug [or words to that effect] and the gentleman not only agreed but came out with the now familiar response … 'I needed someone to tell me straight'. It was interesting that this man had watched several of the healthy eating programmes on the television but had not applied the lessons to his own life and I suspect he is far from being alone.

To come from an entirely physical angle I will ask again, 'Do you have backache?' If so, drink a litre of water per day because your body is largely made up of water and the squishy pads between the vertebrae [bones] of your spine are not an exception. I'm prepared to bet those squishy pads, given a choice, would prefer water to coffee or tea. As my partner says, 'Would you wash your hair in coffee or shower in tea with milk and two sugars?'. Bodies need washing inside and out with nice clean water. Don't drink a lot of water with your meals because you dilute the acid [and probably interfere with the enzymes] in your stomach that you need to digest your food - wine does not count, of course, says me, removing my tongue from my cheek. Review your diet diligently. See an Alexander Technique practitioner or an osteopath. Ask either of them about getting a 'Hang-Up' [we have nicknamed ours the batmobile - or batmobeel as we pronounce it]. You sort of climb on, shove your feet in a thing, clamp them in, then put your arms over your head and whoooosh, you are hanging upside down. It stretches the spine nicely. We use ours daily and it has been of great benefit but check with your doctor first because they are contra-indicated in some medical cases and especially if you have high blood pressure. I was told it was highly unlikely I had adhesions under my appendectomy scar but the first time I hung upside down I had tremendous pain and pulling beneath my scar site, so if you get one and you have had surgery, check with your doctor.

Now ..... wacky stuff, I just love it. Do you have backache? Upper, middle or lower? Emotions play a *huge* part in back problems. Let's split it into three sections but first I need to explain that in the complementary medicine world it is generally recognised that the body is *energetically* split and the right side of the body is male and the left side is female.

Lower back corresponds with second chakra, or possibly, first chakra ['chakras' are coming up shortly] and, when it goes haywire you can be pretty sure money, or power, or both, is the issue. The man [and it usually is - though it is changing now] who says, 'I was absolutely fine, then I bent down to pick up a book and, bang, my lower back suddenly went', needs to relive the events of the last couple weeks. Usually there has been a worry over money and then the energy seeps from the lower back but look at partnerships, work or living arrangements, anything that is troubling you or possibly making you feel unsupported and therefore weakening and creating energy loss. This includes unpleasant phone calls or letters, either from family or work/business related. Check whether the pain is right sided [a male problem, so therefore a woman irritated with her husband or boss may experience pain on her right side] or a left sided problem [which will have a female bias]. Are you with me? Maybe this sounds too 'away with the fairies' for you but note it, because it is, by and large, more likely to be men who have problems with their backs and they are, bless their cotton socks, notoriously bad at saying, 'I'm really worried about money, or work, or whatever'. Please read the section on 'colour', it is relevant especially if blacks or greys are being worn a great deal, but read about stripes and checks under 'clothes' too. Try and do something constructive towards fixing the emotionally troubling situation as well as improving your hydration and diet. You may well have a boundary issue, you may have a problem saying 'no', or you may have an emotional trigger point that one look, comment, criticism, letter, or bill sets off and your back 'goes'. Just being *aware* that the issues you are facing can have an impact on certain areas of your body helps toward healing.

Middle back is more likely to be relationship issues. Maybe you have been metaphorically stabbed in the back by colleagues, friends or family. Are you needing to watch your back? In which case you may find the 'fat' section interesting. Do you feel *overloaded with responsibility*? How is the front of your back - do you have a happy heart? What colours are you wearing? Don't be afraid to look at the problems and ask for help, this alone can trigger change. Do something constructive, please do, because this area incorporates not just the heart, but also the liver and the pancreas and if they start yelling for help things can get serious. More and more, these days, we look at problem areas in isolation but the whole body is connected. An unwelcome and unpleasant letter from the bank manager can lay into your lower back because there is an energetic connection, just as stage fright does not only affect the brain that registers the fear, it gives you butterflies in your tummy too. Pure terror can knock your knees and even evacuate your bowels: my grandfather told my mother that, in the First World War, the soldiers frequently emptied the contents of their lower colon into their trousers in sheer terror as they were ordered 'over the top' of the trenches - poor things.

Upper back is literally upper back and shoulders but also includes the neck, jaw, mouth and teeth. Problems in these areas, in my opinion [and I speak from experience], is energetically related to repressed anger, fear and emotional guarding. There may be a control issue going on, one of feeling controlled or being controlling, possibly a problem with not being heard or understood and/or an inability to see things from a different or wider perspective or from another person's viewpoint. Not for nothing do we have the expression 'bull-headed'. You don't have to be male with a large neck to go into that category because women can be intransigent too, at times [*though, of course, it is extremely rare*]. It may be accompanied by shallow breathing, recurrent headaches and muscular tension, jaw, mouth [speech], teeth and ear problems and anything going wrong around the neck and shoulders. Anything sound familiar? Have a gentle prod of your neck and shoulders, if anything feels like concrete or makes you go 'ouch', you have a problem. Shoulders should be loose and swing free but often they carry heavy burdens and/or the high expectations of others. I have a hunch [and the shoulders are a good area to get one] that tension in this area *can* deplete your zinc supply. If it does, it will have a knock on effect on your *stomach digestion*, immune system and your ability to repair [I often wonder about rugby players and their enormous neck and shoulder muscles]. I have no proof that my hunch is right and I daresay I would be poo-pooed by academics and doctors but if you have read the bit about my arthritis and my magnesium levels versus blood results, you might wonder too. Bear in mind that the state and health of your gastro-intestinal tract has a huge bearing on your bones and muscles including the whole of your back. Get your neck looked at by someone who understands muscles, bones and connective tissue tension but bear in mind that in Oriental medicine there are two meridians connected to the neck. The gall-bladder meridian runs across the back of the shoulder and up the side of the neck and the bladder meridian runs up the back and neck, over the crown to the forehead. You cannot, therefore, completely disassociate your bladder and your gall-bladder from your neck problem [my partner can often release my stiff neck by pressing a bladder meridian point in my leg]. If you are ready to tackle the emotional block causing the problem try the very subtle therapy of cranio-sacral therapy or somatoemotional release. You could also look for someone who does fascial/connective tissue release [there is an osteopath practising this in East Anglia who is wonderful] but never forget, only you know and hold the emotion that needs to be released. You are the expert on that and the time for release of the emotion is in your hands only.

BOND

I have never been a fan of the James Bond films but I am completely fascinated that the new Bond is Daniel Craig. Previously we have had several actors portray Bond ending with Mr. Brosnan who is a good -looking man, beautifully handsome, you might say, but he doesn't look lethal to me, whereas Daniel Craig does look lethal and he may be a powder puff in real life but if I met him in a dark tunnel on a dark night I would leg it smartly in the opposite direction. Allowing for the fact that films often point the way to future trends and because, in my view, Western democracy is already on very shaky ground, I am wondering if we are going to visually look for 'lethal' in our heroes, or possibly our leaders, in the future. By 'lethal' I do not mean loud mouth bullies. Plenty of those about.

In my mind I am surveying the current crop of political leaders, or potential

ones, and looking for 'lethal'.............. bit thin on the ground, with one
notable exception. Perhaps I am looking at the wrong sex.

*B*ULLIES

Bullies arrive when you have flat boundaries, the two go hand in hand.
When you have flat boundaries you have low input into second chakra and
your third chakra [self-esteem] needs repointing [like brick work]. I am
doing 'bullies' now and 'boundaries' next, but both crop up again later - when
we get to 'chakras' this will start to make more sense.

There are two types - aggressive bullies and passive aggressive bullies.
Aggressive bullies are loud and shout a lot and generally wear everyone
down so that it is easier to give in and join their gang, or tiptoe out of the
room. One aggressive bully can infect the atmosphere in a very large
building full of people but it goes belly-up eventually because all aggressive
bullies *need* people to victimise and there comes a time when retirement or
old-age means there are less people about, then the bully is liable to
implode. If the bullying has been on a one to one basis and the victim
decides they have had enough and pull away [or even die] then the bully is
left without a power source and is in deep trouble. Passive aggressive bullies
are *much* quieter but *equally* controlling. They manipulate by non co-
operation. They are not confrontational and rarely raise their voices. Often
they will not engage or discuss problems, or they engage and agree to do
something but then do nothing or the opposite. By perfecting this evasive
technique they relentlessly get their own way.

Bullies home in on their victims like heat-seeking missiles. On an energetic
basis a bully will register a victim the *very moment* they set eyes on them.
A male bully will home in fast on a women he instinctively knows he can
manipulate, bypassing any amount of available but trickier females, no
matter how gorgeous they may look. The same goes for bullying women,
though women often favour the passive aggressive bullying procedure and
will actively look for a compliant partner. Both bully and victim have a
major self-esteem problem [third chakra] and both are acting out their drama
in second chakra where one has found temporary refuge in the external
power of energetically bludgeoning a victim [this can be just verbal
bludgeoning] and the victim is unable to find a refuge at all. BOTH are here
to learn MAJOR spiritual lessons in the reality of internal [as opposed to

external] power. I was expertly and aggressively bullied at boarding school where there was little refuge and complaint would have made matters ten times worse. Many, many years later I was astounded to see my tormentor, looking much the same, sitting in a pub and while I felt the familiar fear and tightening in my gut I watched her reaching for a drink - there were multiple healed slash marks on her wrist. I forgave her. Bullies are here to *teach* us boundaries. Bullies, who are the most fearful among us, are here to *learn* forgiveness, self-forgiveness, love and self-love.

Serious school ground bullying may need serious measures such as the removal of the child from a school, but bullying goes on all through life and seems to be more prevalent today than ever, in our relatively wealthy but fearful society. You will never stop bullying but you can learn some techniques to deal with it. Learning about maintaining boundaries [coming up in the next section] is crucial in repelling bullies but I will also cover eighth chakra conversations later under 'chakras'. I have advised many a friend and client who is dealing with major work bullying to wear navy blue and put a mirror down their bra, this is because I mainly deal with women who mainly wear bras. Now, please do NOT remove the mirror from above the fireplace and shove it up your jumper on your way to work because you will look ridiculous and you may fall and do yourself a nasty. A small mirror is sufficient [facing outwards] down your bra [for the boys, a shirt pocket will do the trick]. The mirror is a *tool*, nothing more - it is you taking pro-active physical action while mentally saying, 'I am not taking this nastiness, I am *reflecting* it back to you because it is your problem not mine'. If the bully is in full throttle, try standing in your navy blue clothing and facing them but focusing on their mouth [no eye contact, it encourages them] while folding your hands across your third chakra, which is just across your tummy above your tummy button. Do not fold your arms, this is an aggressive posture. In case they have got hold of this book too and are checking your chest for mirrors [hopefully not manually] you can implement the mirror and hand clasp just as effectively with mental imagery, but you will need a bit of practice. Imagine you are holding a large mirror up in front of you or imagine yourself in a mirrored cape and holding a shield over your tummy. These techniques work but you have to work at them. Repeat, these techniques work but you *have to work at them*.

BOUNDARIES

This subject is of particular fascination to me because it is only recently that I have started to get my personal boundaries in place and in good order. You may think that I am off in the land of the fairies again but I will tell you straight, if your boundaries are not in place then others will impinge on you emotionally and physically because *that is what they are here to do*. Their job is to show you that your boundaries are down. If your boundaries are flat on the ground then expect a battering emotionally and possibly physically. Don't shoot the messenger! I am not preaching because I am still fingering my imaginary shotgun over a recent boundary infringement which infuriated me but taught me a profound lesson. My problem is that I am chatty and gregarious when out and about and, when being so, I let my boundaries down. Before I can say, 'Back off please', someone is through my lowered barrier taking advantage or bossing me about *and I don't like it*. It would, I suppose, be much easier to be cool and aloof but I can't see much chance of changing my character now. I am slowly trying to learn to strike a balance between being warm and being a refrigerator, between approachability and keeping my distance. I understand now that this is a profound spiritual lesson. I used to think lessons like this were just about personal relationships and how to handle them, but really the lesson is in handling yourself and your level of personal power.

In my view there are over-enthusiastic defenders of boundaries [who ask all about you but won't give anything away about themselves] and over-enthusiastic attackers - both need help. Occasionally you get someone who is both [I call these people 'screaming nightmares']. In my experience many people do not recognise when someone is stepping on their toes, so to speak, especially if that person is family or a close friend. It helps to be on the look out for small early signs of boundary infringement so you can nip things in the bud before it escalates. By doing this you are strengthening your third chakra [more later] and building your self-esteem. Signs to watch out for are repeated, uncalled for and unamusing personal comments about your hair, name, looks, clothes and personal belongings. Laugh them off, if you must, but be warned that you have a problem and don't get in a muddle about teasing - we all tease the ones we love but teasing is NOT teasing when it starts to hurt and I have been in the company of friends and families where the teasing was way out of hand. Regular derogatory remarks made about you are designed to disempower and keep you occupied by feeling resentful, that way you skulk about and fail to establish a healthy sense of self-esteem. A friend of mine was kept constantly skulking about by a domineering mother who always managed to find fault with her clothing. 'You look nice dear, but what a pity you chose those shoes', was a favourite, always hit the target and would be followed by weeks and weeks of my friend wailing, 'Why can't my mother *just* say something *nice* to me?'. Total preoccupation until the next visit when the scarf was criticised, or the handbag and this went on for years because my friend failed to learn the lesson and take her internal power back. This was a control battle and the mother was calling the shots.

The next step up of boundary infringement is someone going through your handbag, briefcase, diary, mooching round private rooms in your house when your back is turned and maybe even opening a drawer or two. This is NOT acceptable behaviour. This is theft of your privacy. It is, in fact, the rape of your privacy. Harsh words but true. It is hateful to be on the receiving end of an invasion and a perpetrator would not like the experience either … and they know it. I have experience of invasion and it took me a while to understand that the infringers had no respect for me. It took me even longer to work out that this was my problem. I am still working out how to unpick years of intense childhood training to be nice so that I can stop boundary infringers invading in the future.

Poor boundaries denote a lack of self-esteem and an inability to voice feelings. Though not everyone has problems 'voicing' virtually every single person on the planet has a lack of self-esteem to some level or other, so you will never be lonely. However, low self-esteem will make you needy and in relationships [of any kind] this will either attract a bully or another needy type whereupon a 'control battle' will ensue, though it might take time for that to be evident. There can be any amount of ways of controlling and I am endlessly fascinated at the controlling that goes on within partnerships or marriages.

How do you get respect without frightening people? It is a tough one and I am still working on it. It definitely helps if you keep conversations light and give little away about yourself. Revealing your thoughts and emotions is read as being weak but much worse, sadly, being kind is often viewed the same way. I think this is a huge mistake on both counts. Lending is a boundary minefield. No matter what the loan is [books often, but money too] if the return is proving a hassle you can rest assured the borrower thinks you are a bit of a wimpy walk-over. Shakespeare cautioned, 'Neither borrower nor lender be' [Hamlet], but this is difficult to adhere to throughout a lifetime. I have noticed that for most of the population respect and fear go hand-in-hand, which is a pity. Be aware that an unreturned, lost or broken object [whatever it is] that is not replaced is a clear signal that the borrower is not remotely afraid of you because if they were the borrowed, lost or broken object would be replaced in a jiff. If your boundaries are down it is time to get them up and looking purposeful [the 'chakra' section will help in this].

I like to think of my personal boundary as being an imaginary white picket fence. I always fancied a garden full of roses, not a weed in sight, surrounded by a white picket fence like you used to see in the old Hollywood movies. I suppose that makes me an old fashioned romantic, which reminds me of another story. I once had someone to help me design a garden. 'What sort of garden are you looking for?', the designer enquired. 'Romantic', I enthused. 'Romantic, highly scented, sweet smelling roses, clouds of white, pink, yellow and blue, honeysuckle, jasmine, old roses, more roses and even more roses', I sighed in ecstasy. He came back with a drawing. I immediately pointed to an ominous mound near the front door 'What's that?', I said. 'Red Hot Poker', he replied. Someone had not been paying attention and I had completely failed to set my boundaries.

At home or in your work place are you put upon, unheard, overworked, undervalued, bullied? Let's look at your personal boundary, however you imagine it to be [you can copy my white picket fence if you like]. Is it all perkily upright? Neatly in rows, nicely spaced, well painted and just high enough to repel intruders? No? Oooops. What, you mean it is broken, damaged, not well maintained, or even non-existent? Oooops indeed. Perhaps it is fifteen feet high, metal, with sharp as you like tips? Golly, no snuggling up with you then. What we want to aim for is an attractive protective barrier that gives onlookers the impression that you are having a nice life, everything is in reasonable order, you do know how to say 'no' without swearing and you are capable of taking care of yourself thank you very much. We want people to look at you and think, 'That person has self-respect', that way they will pause at your picket fence admire your smart garden and then approach your front door respectfully. They will not barge through your front door and make rude comments about your hair, curtains and furnishings, or worse, ask how much you paid for them. Many years ago, when my boundaries were in poor shape, I had a visitor who asked me the price of pretty much everything in my house and tutted if anything was over £2.50. I wore myself ragged fending her off. It was not my visitors fault, she was just a bully, it was my fault entirely for having boundaries as flat as pancakes. Imagine having a cup of tea with Her Majesty the Queen and telling her you *really* don't like her sofa and how much is it worth anyway? I think not.

Whatever age you are, if you are being controlled, teased, targeted with nasty comments, or someone has been borrowing and burrowing through your belongings [making allowances for a genuinely concerned parent checking on their children for evidence of dangerous activity], your next step is to set about doing something constructive so that boundary infringers leave you alone.

Step one. Learn to say 'no'. Practice, practice, practice, but not on the people who genuinely love you. Next. Stop the self-criticism by patrolling your thoughts from the moment you get up. Don't 'should' on yourself [as the most excellent author Iyanla Vanzant says] and when you have dropped the habit of self-nitpicking with, 'I should have done this', or, 'I should have done that', get into the habit of not 'should-ing' on other people. Boundaries invaders are people who like telling other people they 'should do this' and they 'should do that'. Tell them to bog off.

Now, get out a pen and pencil and list all the things you are good at and I mean everything. I absolutely insist you list ten things to start with, I could even say you *should* list ten things, but I shall resist, *resist*. You can't think of anything? Can you boil an egg? Bake a cake? Clean out the gerbil cage beautifully? Park a car reasonably well? Remember special dates and birthdays? Know the makes of modern cars? Tie your shoelaces? Know a barn owl from a tawny owl? Do maths? Build anything? Knit? These are skills so please list them. Give yourself a rest and a pat on the back. Do the list next week and list twenty things you are good at and thirty things the following week. Focus on your strong points and NEVER on your weaknesses. We *all* have weaknesses, we are *meant* to have weaknesses, we are human for God's sake.

If your boundaries are being flattened by nasty comments from bullies, keep in the forefront of your brain that all bullies are desperately unhappy people and, in my observation, often end up with sad and lonely lives. Seek out people who make you feel good about yourself. Spend time with them and be generous with your compliments to them. Genuine ones only please, don't get smarmy. Read 'attitude', memorise and frequently repeat 'what you are is what you get'. Pay attention in 'colour' because I have yet to meet someone who truly understands what colour means and how blindingly important it is. Always remember that if you are an internally strong but kind person, people will seek you out like a heat-seeking missile because you will be good to be around.

Having spent several weeks writing out all your positive traits you may be running out of paper or ideas. You will, by now, be liking yourself a lot more so it is time to take the next step - cultivating self-sufficiency. This is a tough one. Try and be your own best friend. Take liking yourself to loving yourself and encompass looking after yourself. This means tending your thoughts [nice thoughts only, or no thinking at all please] and tending your body, so read 'health' and take it seriously. A healthy face and body oozes confidence. Posture says everything about you and you get taken more seriously if you stand up straight. Aim for silent strength because people are intimidated by not knowing what you are thinking [I am useless at this, so don't use me as a role model]. Watch the Queen, she knows a thing or two about maintaining personal boundaries though she does cover her third chakra with her handbag, but then I would if I were her. The Queen dresses well, whether you like her style or not, she is always immaculately groomed and this makes people alert in her presence because immaculate grooming enhances personal boundaries. Combat fatigues aside, that is why the forces put considerable effort into looking immaculate on parade. It makes them look serious.

We can't all be the Queen but we can all copy those attributes of people who know how to maintain their boundaries. Think of someone you would not dare to ask a favour from - what is it about them that puts you off? Note how many favours have been asked of you lately. There are millions of people out there who cannot say 'no' [especially to their children]. How are you doing? Start practising, but inevitably you will start practising on easy targets, those who love you, so do try not to piss off too many kindly folk in your search for a new picket fence. As someone I am fond of [who was useless in the 'no' department] said to me the other day, 'You have helped me so much', to which I replied, 'I'm delighted, but don't you start flexing your new found 'no' muscles at *me*'.

Getting your personal boundaries in good shape may be an uphill struggle at first, especially in this day and age where respect for others and other people's property has not been drummed in from birth. Take courage and keep going, but know the challenges will get harder. Reward yourself hugely for saying 'no' while stating your reasons with clarity and without malice. If you can pull this off, it seriously calls for a cream bun, but just one. Mine is a doughnut, but don't tell my partner. Some time back I managed such a corker of a 'no' that I decided to buy two doughnuts [nearly choked on the price, so you can see I don't do this often]. I triumphantly drove them home purring with contentment as I imagined the cup of fresh coffee I would have as a perfect accompaniment. I emergency braked in the drive when I saw my partner's car. A client of his had cancelled their appointment so my beloved was at home and would, no doubt, be patrolling the kitchen. Hell's teeth!! My partner is into green tea, healthy living and supervises my diet because he loves me, hates to see me in pain and knows sugar and arthritis don't mix. My doughnuts stayed in my car, hidden under my seat and *tortured* me for the rest of the day …. and night.

BURGLARY

Here we have a boundary issue and a half. Another form of bullying. When I am not furious, I am curious as to why we have declared war on international terrorism yet have permitted years of escalating home grown terrorism. Massive boundary infringement and terrorisation is perpetrated against honest citizens on a daily basis all over the country. It is a cancer eating away at the bedrock of our society [and we wonder why cancer, particularly second chakra area bowel cancer, is on the increase]. We are not protected from it and the loss invariably has to be accepted with a shrug of the shoulders. We have to be stoic because the police can't cope, the courts can't cope and the prisons can't cope and worse, burglars have 'rights' within our homes when their intention is purely to cause harm.

It is quite extraordinary. Some prime minister, or other, stands up and makes yet another utterly meaningless speech about being tough on crime and gets a *round of applause*. For just words. Why? Silence would be so much more appropriate and powerful.

BROGAN

Brogan was a much loved whippet who was two years old when I got him and he was looking for love. The man I collected him from said, 'He lifts his leg occasionally in the house'. I think this goes down as an historic understatement. He also failed to mention that Brogan was rather neurotic and screamed a lot. I soon found my darling dog hated me talking to anyone and for the first six months he would interrupt all conversations with screams. It was no good, screaming aside, piddle or not [and there were puddles of it], he was mine and I loved him from the moment I set eyes on his blonde good looks and ludicrous Cleopatra styled kohl eyeliner. In fact I worried about Brogan in that department because he always preferred girly things and 'nice' smells, seemingly oblivious to the smells he deposited here and there and everywhere. I needn't have worried because I later adopted another lady whippet who instantly came into heat and though Brogan's equipment had been removed in the hope it would stop him marking round the house [it made not a jot of difference], the arrival of Elladora and her hormones set Brogan into a frenzy of manic lust filled behaviour. I didn't know whether to move out and let them get on with it or ignore and hope her heat would quickly wane, but I have to say the sight of Brogan panting round the house and garden with his eyes on *stalks* looking for the object of his desire was hilariously opposed to his usual posture of artfully composed relaxation on the sofa, for twenty two hours a day, while occasionally inspecting his nails.

My most precious Brogan became very sick. I will not go into a long and detailed history, but suffice to say he started snorting one day, possibly due to an inhaled grass seed. He then began producing mucous until it was coming out in industrial quantities of staggering proportions. Without exaggeration he could sneeze out thick ropey strands that would touch the ground. I would clean it up and twenty minutes later the next lot would come out. At night his laboured breathing, obvious pain and enormous mucous production meant little sleep for either of us. Huge sums of money were spent at the vet and at Cambridge veterinary medicine school. Every possibly piece of advice or 'alternative' lead was followed up and we spent hours in the car together while driving to see someone or other, hoping for a cure. I tried raw food, cooked food and endless different types of nourishment. Looking back I should have given him a lot more B vitamins but I did not know that then. I found that massage helped him tremendously though I had no idea why. I massaged him daily until I got sick with arthritis and my hands were so painful I couldn't do it. Then a miracle appeared in the shape of my future partner and shiatsu treatments. In the space of six weeks with weekly treatments Brogan was transformed. Yes, he still got a bit of a dribble, but not much and his quality of life was really good after three years of absolute misery, poor wee lamb. My partner said it was definitely stemming from his stomach and gut, with the spleen and an adrenal output connection [we couldn't pinpoint the problem]. The massage I gave him suddenly made sense because I was probably, unknowingly, hitting one or two acupuncture points in my 'blundering about' effort. I think shiatsu is marvellous for animals because needles are not involved and they respond so quickly. My partner has treated many different four legged animals. Though he specialises in horses, with great and immensely rewarding success, he is not brilliant with sick chickens, it has to be said. Chook-chook acupuncture points are hard to find.

Brogan was a complex dog but I loved him dearly [though I have to say the day he ate one of my most magnificent charity shop trophies took some getting over]. He is in heaven now but I offer up his story in the hope that some poorly woolly woofer and his/her distraught owner might glean something helpful from the tale. Look out for Juliette de Bairacli Levy's books [details at rear] giving natural remedies for dogs and cats, you might find something helpful if you are desperate.

BACH FLOWER REMEDIES

Apparently pronounced batch and who am I to argue? How do they work? Beats me, I just recommend them because I have heard amazing stories from acquaintances and clients [you can put a few *rescue remedy* drops on a problem elbow, knee, tummy - or even mozzy bites - as well as on the tongue, or in water]. If you are in an emotional jam and cannot see a way out, try them. They are relatively cheap and you may be amazed.

BICARBONATE (of soda)

If you are having any problems in the bloating department and your poop is not prize winning try this - first thing in the morning, on an empty tummy, put one teaspoon of soda bic [you can buy it at a supermarket in the cake making section] into a small glass of lukewarm water and drink this most unpleasant drink. Don't be a wimp. Wait a moment for the soda bic to mix with your stomach juices and produce gas and … wait for it ….. burp. Possibly several. The more the merrier. If you do not burp at all you may have little hydrochloric acid with which to digest your food which means you have a problem and it could get serious because undigested food is sailing through your body providing little nourishment, possibly doing nasty things and probably producing unpleasant odours. You may know about these. Your loved ones might do too. Do something about this immediately and I mean immediately. If your diet is calamitous see an experienced nutritionist because you will need advice on hydrochloric acid, diet and/or food absorption [you may be putting good food in but your body can't break it down and access the nutrients] and specific vitamin supplementation. Do not ignore.

Right, that is the purely physical side of things. Now comes the tricky bit. We have an increasing problem with malfunctioning stomach and intestines [that includes the bowel] in this country. My belief is that all illness starts with an emotion. Diet is crucial, but you eat badly when you don't care about yourself - that is an emotion. Low or high stomach acid is the body trying to deal with an emotion and basically not coping very well. What, *exactly*, is going on emotionally that is so affecting your gastro-intestinal system, particularly your stomach, that you are failing to produce the acid in the first place? [You may, by the way, be producing too much acid and you will know if you are always buying antacids - think low magnesium - from the chemist, either that or an iridologist will tell you, and the following equally applies.] Is your stomach in knots about something? Is it a boundary issue? Are you afraid? Are you exhausted and/or feeling overloaded with responsibility? This can affect the pancreas, which produces digestive enzymes. Is it someone or something specifically that is upsetting you? Is it at home or at work? The emotion will always boil down to fear eventually but you may have to go through other layers first, so …. are you angry? Sad? Ask yourself if you are more given to barking at an inconsiderate driver or crying over a sad film - there is the clue.

Now, go and find someone really kind, preferably a friend who knows you well. Take them a bottle of wine [because they will need it] and a huge box of tissues for you to blub into. Tell your friend what you think the problem is, then ask them to gently cross-question you about it while watching your body language like a hawk, particularly hand placement [see 'chakras' and 'jewellery']. Ask them just to listen carefully to what you have to say, not to try to fix the problem or offer solutions. As you talk, pay attention to any sensations you have of heat, cold, flushing, itching, sweating, choking, swallowing, big or small physical pain. Any one of these is your body trying to talk to you in the ONLY language it has. Be alert to anything like throat clearing or coughing because that is truth being blocked - so for instance if you say you love your work and then clear your throat, or cough, you are probably telling yourself an enormous porkie. This is more serious than telling someone else a porkie because your porkie may not damage them, but your porkie to yourself is definitely damaging you emotionally and probably at a cellular level too. Having done all that you should have a clear[ish] idea of where the problem lies so you can set about fixing it.

Do not expect your friend to be a free counselling service. Get professional help if you think the problem is too big to handle yourself. It is now up to you to fix your problem. There will be lots more helpful hints at helping yourself in the rest of this book but, meanwhile, take affirmative action. Try Bach Flower Remedies, reduce your workload, or whatever, if you can. Say 'Thank you' for the lessons a relationship or a job [no matter how ghastly either of them have been] have given you and silently affirm the time has come for you to move on to something or someone better. Keep silently repeating this until events change. This takes discipline. Sometimes things get slightly worse before they get better; have faith - in yourself if you don't have faith in anything else.

BEING

There is an anonymous quotation which goes 'being is more compelling than doing'. I love it. I spent years doing but I now find being so much more restful and constructive. We all seem to be caught on this relentless hamster wheel of doing, doing, doing. As most of us are continually doing work or chores that we do not much love we need to remember to insert some 'being' time to allow the body to drift, repair, dream and explore possibilities. This is when feelings come bubbling to the surface and we need to let those bubbles rise, because when we do not we allow trouble to brew.

Should we all go off on retreats every year? Probably, but far more challenging is to go on retreat at home. To tell your loved ones that you are having a day or a week of being. Essential tasks only will be carried out first thing in the morning, everything else can pile up or the family can get stuck in because you are going on a solitary retreat into your head. If necessary you will stare at a wall all day or take yourself on ultra long walks where you will put your mind chatter on hold, just silently 'be' and you *categorically will not* make Christmas shopping lists in your head, fornicate with Mr. Darcy or play rugby for England. I bet you can't do it. It is not easy but do, please, try and do this every now and again. You are permitted, it is ok. I mention this because I have observed that at some stage of the proceedings a time of 'just being' will normally come into play. In most people's life there will come a calamitous event that will catapult one into a state of being because doing suddenly becomes irrelevant or not possible. I have had experience of this when a big happening in my life seemed to make me a silent non-participatory watcher. It put me on 'still', as if I had switched a 'hold' button, while all around life and people went by me in an out of focus display of doing - doing that seemed to lead to nowhere. Just round and round. Most of us will experience this momentous stilling in some shape or form and it is a spiritual time of reconnecting with the very essence of you. For many it will come at extreme old-age with enforced 'just being' because of infirmity and may or may not go hand in hand with regret. In my nursing years I listened with great sadness to elderly patients expressing regret at opportunities lost. It was a powerful lesson for me. You don't want old age regrets if you can avoid them. By allowing yourself some hours or days of just 'being' on a regular basis, while being attentive to what pops into your head you will get in touch with your feelings. This will give you a chance to look at your life and explore your options. By just 'being' you may be able to see your 'doing' is not bringing you happiness. You can then look at other ways of 'doing' that will change your way of life, hopefully alleviating acres of regretful 'being' in old-age.

There is a saying that 'life is not a dress rehearsal', so try and ensure you are living your life in the right play with kindly fellow actors, whose company you enjoy. Take courage, change the play or change the cast if necessary and if you are a reading this and you are in your teens or twenties please know this - life speeds up dramatically as you get older. With each passing decade the years go faster and faster. I am not sure why this is, perhaps as we get older we just get slower at doing and everything takes longer, or maybe older life is way too full of tedious things that have to be done.

I am consciously making more time for being these days and I am surprised at the results - it is redefining me. I decided some time ago that I did not want to arrive at the Pearly Gates, at the end of my life, and have someone important in full feathers ask me, 'Who are you, Amanda Mansell?', or worse, 'What are you?'. I didn't want to conjure up an image of me holding an animated yellow duster while holding a bottle of washing-up liquid. 'Fat chance', my partner would say to this idea, not unkindly, but with an emphasis that has me rushing to fetch the duster and polish because I see dust as my failure, which is ludicrous because he doesn't see dust as his failure, in fact, he rarely sees dust at all. I do not want to be standing at the celestial reception desk trying to define myself in relation to how busy I have been or who/what I am in relation to others [daughter, partner, friend, whippet snogger, nurse/midwife, gardener, iridologist]. I want to be able to define what is the essence of me because I have a sneaky feeling if I can do that well I might get a better room with a nicer view [this is a joke]. I want to be able to say, 'I am fearless', and, 'I have attained detachment', but I can't, so at present I am looking at the prospect of being booked into a small broom cupboard in the basement of the heavenly hotel.

When you have cracked 'being is more compelling than doing' and really understand it you will have made a huge leap of consciousness. 'Being' is more compelling because then the 'doing' becomes so easy. Once you are fully 'being' you are in the here and now and you are 'being' yourself, not someone you want to be or someone you think you should be. At this point you gain a level of detachment and realise that everyone else is heading towards their state of 'being' too, but at varying speeds. It is a snail's pace for most and that is fine. Just leave them alone to go at their chosen pace while you trot ahead on your own and very individual path, giving them a kind word, a smile and a cheery wave.

$\mathcal{B}$IG

In response to my plaintive wailing of an unfair life and some monster behaving monstrously toward me, my father's advice was … 'Rise above it, ducky'. It never failed to deflate me utterly. I simply could not imagine myself rising upwards graciously and forgiving when I wanted to pick up a cricket bat and do something very, very nasty indeed. Because it had this effect on me I do not use this expression, though I appreciate its sentiments. Instead I remind myself to be big. When someone behaves outrageously toward me I immediately reach for my imaginary pistol and before I pump them full of bullets I remind myself I have to be bigger than they are. This is not easy and, if I carry on at the rate I am carrying on, I shall be very big indeed.

BURNS

The best burn cream is Vitamin E. Keep some capsules in your kitchen and when you get a singed hand from cooking, bite the top off the capsule and pour the liquid onto the burn. It will take the pain away in about ten to twenty minutes. Repeat the application in about four to six hours. It should heal quickly, if it doesn't your digestion may be poor [read 'health']. I am, obviously, talking about small burns though if I was in hospital with major burns I would ask my partner to bring me bottles and bottles of vitamin E. We always take it on trips abroad to use if we have sunburn and here comes the wacky bit [sorry, I cannot resist].... if you do get a burn while cooking, stop and ask yourself what were you thinking just before it happened. You may surprise yourself because burns are linked with anger. Best to start paying attention to matchstick and cooking burns before the fires get out of control.

BREATHING

I am a shockingly shallow breather. If you have never given your breathing a second thought, just try to be aware now and for the rest of the day how you breathe. If you are not sure how you should do it, find someone who has a nice relaxed baby lying flat on its back and watch its little tummy going up and down as it breathes. This is what your little tummy should be doing. How is it going? My littleish tummy only goes up and down when I concentrate on my breathing because I have completely lost the knack of doing it naturally. I suppose I should do Tai Chi or something but then I *should* do a lot of things, and that is before the things I shouldn't do. Gosh, it's a very full life of being, doing, not doing and worrying.

Take a breather. Breathe away. I will put the kettle on and then we can all have a little worry and hyperventilate together.

BODY LANGUAGE

I love the language of the body. Took me years to decipher what I know now and I am still only a beginner. We chatter away, trundling stuff and nonsense out of our mouths, meanwhile our body is moving this way and that saying,

'Rubbish', and, 'I don't mean that at all'. It is hilarious when you get the hang of it. I have been pretty good at reading other people for a long time, but poor at reading my subtle body signals because, you may be surprised to read, I do not spend much time talking to myself in front of a long mirror. It was, therefore, a revelation some years back to be sitting in front of a kinesiologist on a hot summer's day, with me wearing a scoop neck top, hair up in a pony tail and long dangly earrings. Toward the end of a 'talking' session she asked me if I wanted to get married. 'Yes, absolutely', I replied. 'Then why are your earrings swinging slightly from side to side?', she enquired. Total verbal denial on my part. Insistence on hers. Silence. Big, and I mean BIG penny dropping that had such an effect on me that, on my way home, I went round a roundabout three times, dazed and confused and unable to find the appropriate exit on a road and route I knew like the back of my hand. This event still makes me marvel. I still wonder at the extent to which I would not face my truth and lie to myself, but when I met my partner and experienced the 'as never before' effect he had on me, I wondered if in fact I had had a deeply hidden unconscious agenda - in that I was waiting for him. This would be the realm of a sacred contract which I will cover later. On the other hand, we have been together for seven years and we have still not married, though every six months, or so, we idly discuss tying the knot [such an interesting expression] and possible locations. That's about as far as we get.

In our technological age we are becoming worryingly distanced from human contact and having less chance to watch bodies as they talk and do business. These days, teenagers, with their mobile phones surgically attached to their lugholes, get less and less chance to watch bodies talking. If you cannot actually see someone's face as you communicate with them you don't have much idea if they are being honest, if your chitter-chatter is causing them emotional pain or if you are boring the pants off them. As a quick exercise I jotted down how many signals I might get from someone who was silently requesting that I shut-up. I came up with 34 in under two minutes, 21of them were linked to the head. How many can you come up with? I can be in mid-flow of chat with someone when I spot them clasp the little finger of either hand and I know to instantly veer off, taking my conversation in another direction, like a car avoiding an oncoming vehicle. Would you know to do the same? I will cover the meaning of little fingers under jewellery but suffice to say if you see this gesture you can take it as read that the person doing it is feeling threatened to some degree. Same as hands clasped over the pubic bone, but more later under 'chakras'.

My partner and I were flying abroad recently and we spent most of the flight transfixed by a nearby young couple. He manically foot tapped during the entire flight. She was very loving but, bless her, she seemed completely oblivious to the almost continuous small signals from him of his dislike for her, many of the signals appearing to be playful but all with decidedly unloving intentions. I did not see any wedding rings and sincerely hope they are not married now. Not much attention paid there, sadly. Try and watch people as you talk to them, because what comes out of their mouths may not be reflected in their posture. Often the signs are quite subtle but I do remember one incident that was about as subtle as a Sherman tank. In the middle of a hospital night shift, I watched, open mouthed with incredulity, as a senior member of staff lectured an exhausted medical student on the finer points of some procedure or other. I could scarcely believe my eyes. She droned on and on, and on … and on, as the medical student's eyes closed and his head literally bounced off his chest in an effort to stay awake. On she droned, completely oblivious. Least I hope she was.

BOWELS

I cannot even begin to tell you how important this subject is. I really do believe this is the starting point of a huge amount of illnesses all over the body. Think of your lower bowel as a dustbin that needs not just regular emptying, but keeping clean. Imagine if your dustbin got saggy and baggy, it would collect smelly rotten deposits that would stink to high heaven. Bowels can get saggy and baggy too and they get old and tired as we age and droop. Use your imagination and treat it with some respect. You would help a little old lady struggling across a busy road, try being as considerate to your bowel.

I am going to cover health in enthusiastic detail later but I should point out that I will use the word gut and bowel or colon interchangeably which is naughty of me because it is not correct. In case you don't know, your gut is your alimentary tract and encompasses everything from your mouth to out, including your bowels. Your small intestine starts from the exit point of your stomach and incorporates your duodenum, jejunum and ileum. The small intestine wiggles along until it gets to the bottom right hand corner of your lower abdomen whereupon it becomes the large bowel. It goes uppity-up [ascending colon] towards your liver, then turns sharp right across the middle of your tummy to the left side under your ribs [the transverse colon] near the spleen, then turns sharp right again and it skips down [descending colon] towards the final exit via the rectum.

Your entire gut is important in food digestion and absorption because things start happening in the mouth with your saliva [that is why it is so important to chew your food well] and things continue to happen right through your small and large intestine until the time you head off for a roost in the smallest room with a heap of magazines or silly books [you might even be taking me with you - now there's a thought to conjure with]. I talk to lots and lots of people and I get the impression that they think they have bowels ... *and* an immune system. That they are separate. Like a refuse collection and a flying squad, both being run by completely different departments. If you think like this you would be wrong, wrong, wrong. You might sit there thinking, 'Well what, exactly, has tonsillitis got to do with my bowels?'. The answer would be EVERYTHING, because flying squads need refuse collection and they wouldn't be able to move fast if rubbish was piling up in their panda cars. If you can imagine getting on a really overcrowded bus or underground train, people jam-packed together, that is how your abdomen is. Its full of organs and bowels and bits and bobs all hugger mugger together. If your bowels are not functioning and getting mucky or constipated, your liver can't just up and move house. It has to sit there, day and night, up extremely close and personal to an unpleasant neighbour, but your liver is crucial to a healthy immune system. Are you with me? Please just stop for a minute and think about this because we spend acres of our day worrying about school work, jobs, rows and relationships; all these things are usually temporary but your bowels will be with you, working away, until the moment you take your dying breath. I BEG [Bowels, Emotions, Gut] you to spare a thought to your hard working body [I will do emotions later, but you have to get through chakras first]. How do you know if your bowels are functioning properly? I will tell you under 'health'. Really it is just a matter of paying attention to what your body is telling you and then doing something about it, but please read on to 'iridology' because you can see your bowel in your eyeball. Dead clever the body is, you know.

For now, let us keep our bowels open once a day, at the very least, though preferably more, and ideally after every main meal. Let us eat lots of fresh vegetables and fruit. You have heard it all before. Five fruit and veg a day but my partner assures me his clients j u s t can't seem to grasp this one, so let's try it again. One, two, three, four, five, that's 5 different types of fruit and vegetables a day. Easy peasy. A banana for breakfast, apple for elevenses and then you choose which three veg for dinner. Spuds don't count and neither does a sliver of iceberg lettuce in that sandwich you bought, bolted and called lunch. Next day, have a pear with your cereal at breakfast, an orange for elevenses and three different from yesterday veg. Next day, change again. Drink one litre of water a day between [not with] your well chewed meals and don't forget roughage - think fresh chopped cabbage, lightly steamed, or elephant sized muesli.

Remember at all times to 'keep your bowels open and your mouth shut'. This will make your life much easier.

BORES

I have met a few. Sadly, bores have not heard from their feelings for a very long time. This calls for yellow, pink and pale green clothing, but also for an urgent need to study body language.

C Is for CONNECTION

This whole book [even some of the silly bits] *is connected*, just as our whole physical body is connected and that in turn is connected to our emotional body. *Clothing* and your choice of *colour* reveals your *emotional* state. *Alexander Technique* is as important in learning to deal with *bullies* as is understanding our *emotions* versus our *feelings*. Knowing what *chakra* lessons you are currently being faced with will help in erecting *boundaries*, repelling *bullies* and regaining or maintaining your *health*. A crucial element to all types of *relationships* is to get the hang of *listening* and that includes your *relationship* to *money* which is another *chakra* lesson. I have covered all these highlighted subjects and there are some more to come - so read on for more connections. The next bit is my favourite. I love chakras.

CHAKRAS

I have been talking about chakras for years and I find people respond by either adopting a worried expression or they take the piss. I am bothered by both responses but I am improving my levels of botheration due, somewhat, to advancing age, wisdom and general tiredness. Occasionally I come across someone who is curious and this often results in the statement, 'You should write a book, you should' …. and here we have it.

Chakras is a Hindu word referring to the seven major energy centres of the body. They are also known as the seven emotional centres. As I am emotional *and* untidy finding out about chakras was a huge relief to me because I finally had somewhere appropriate to put all my hysterias and I could have a *jolly good tidy up.* Imagine, if you will, that each chakra is a specialised computer that loads in specific information. These computers are much like most computers, bless them, they need to be plugged into an energy source, will resolutely refuse to deliver if you do not programme them correctly and they are deaf to expletives delivered in any language or volume. Each chakra computer is like a control centre where we store life lessons and having fully learnt the lesson we move on to the next challenge and that is often, but not always, the next chakra. I call this spiritual progression. You can call it anything you like. Health is also chakra territory and the link is very interesting, so join me later when I shall invite you to stick your tongue out. By then you may feel like doing just that.

The chakras are contained within our auras. I can't see them but my partner can sometimes feel the chakras spinning which is apt, because apparently they look like small wheels. I am going to go into each chakra in depth but I want to just start by skimming through what each one represents and where it is positioned. Interestingly, if you observe body language you will see that when someone feels threatened by a specific emotion they will often protect the related chakra, such as placing a hand over their throat, hand to heart or clasping their hands over their pubic bone. If you pursue this subject you will see pictures of chakras on the spine but for the sake of simplicity I will line them up the front of the body - so if you imagine someone standing towards you the first chakra is in the pubic region and represents the tribe. The second chakra is across the hips up to the belly button and is split into four sections - money, sex, external power and one-to-one relationships [as opposed to tribal or family relationships]. Third chakra is at the solar plexus and represents internal or authentic power and self-esteem. Fourth chakra is at chest level and relates to heart, love and true forgiveness. Fifth is at the throat and is about speaking one's truth as well as speaking up for oneself. Sixth is between [but just above] the eyebrows and represents our ability to see the bigger picture and the seventh chakra is at the crown of the head connecting us to our perception of the divine. I am covering the meaning of colour shortly but each chakra has a related colour - please note it because I have observed that *politically* red is making a comeback in Russia and orange is cropping up across Europe.

You can block or load chakra information as you wish. For example, if you meet a clean, smart and thoroughly presentable person for the first time but smartypants has you thinking, 'I don't know what it is about you but I just don't trust you', you are loading information from them [and about them] at your third chakra [solar plexus - gut level]. If you think you can handle yourself and them, you will just take on the intuitive feeling and carry on talking to them while being cautiously wary. If you feel threatened by them you are likely to take a defensive position. This may involve putting your hands together or bringing one arm across your body, or both your arms together in a low fold. If you are carrying something [or holding a drink] you may pull it across your tummy as a sort of barrier. If smartypants is making you feel very uncomfortable you may turn your body away, possibly crossing your legs as you do so and if you feel restrained in your conversation you may well cover your throat [fifth chakra] with your hand. As most people are in a low level state of fear, whether they recognise it or not, there will be about a dozen deflective gestures towards smartypants rather than an open body posture. It takes significant third chakra input to hold an open body posture, keep still, face smartypants and hold eye contact while thinking, 'I receive you, but I don't I trust you'.

Chakras one, two and three are the most crucial. These first three are going to give you a sound rooted sense of yourself and where you came from, a level of personal power and a belief in yourself so that you know you can cope whatever life throws at you. Insufficient loading into these three computer stations, your foundation blocks of life, will mean a life of almighty struggle and tricky, if not disastrous, personal relationships. Everyone has problems at one or several chakras so it is no good feeling smug because I am bound to hit a raw nerve somewhere - giant egos beware. Chakra blockages occur either with ill health, lack of self-belief, feeling overwhelmed, bullied, put upon, lacking an identity, lacking a purpose in life and all of them always boil down to one basic ingredient - love. Usually the lack of it. There are tools you can use for clearing your clogged up bits, colour is one and I will explain this in the colour section but love gets a section all to its self under, yes you guessed it, 'L'. Read on, read on, I am bound to bore you to sobs eventually.

Apparently, there are one hundred and fifty or more chakras spinning on the body [especially on joints]. I have no idea if this is correct, probably is, but I am just concentrating on the major seven and I think it would be safe to say the whole world, with a handful of exceptions, is basically operating out of first and/or second chakra, but simultaneously engaging the other chakras to some degree or rather. Our aim, well my aim anyway, is to head smartly towards third chakra [while fully engaging the other chakras] and, having secured borders, live there. Sadly this is not a walk in the park.

Once chakra lessons are fully learnt you cannot go backwards. There will be new and challenging tests but you cannot slip back into old thoughts and beliefs because they will not sustain and empower you and you will see them for what they are - limiting and false. Also, like a flock of birds that moves as one [because, *I think*, while they are amassed in flight they form a single consciousness], once a critical mass of people have learnt a chakra lesson their combined new thought form pulls a big chunk of the population forward toward self-empowerment, while leaving a few stragglers behind [the gaining of women's suffrage would be a classic example]. Right now the whole world is going through seismic change which is linked to the chakras. The first chakra tribal societies are being shaken to their roots and family tribes are being disrupted with divorces and breakdowns. Much of the Western world is crashing unpleasantly through second chakra lessons and that is why we are being bombarded with images of pornography, super-wealth and materialism. The general awakening and shifting of consciousness in second and third chakra is causing belief and trust in politicians and large organisations to crumble away as a critical mass of people are seeing through all the meaningless speeches, the bullying and controlling. Increasingly, voters are thinking independently and are putting out collective challenging thought forms and there is an growing number of people who believe not a single word politicians say. This loss of trust is thoroughly unpleasant but crucial and necessary because from it we are learning to put our trust in ourselves [individually] and we are starting to engage with our third chakras. This is growth, it is spiritual revolution before evolution. Not nice, rather unsettling, but ultimately good news because things have to get bad, really bad, before individuals wake up, stand up, stand firm and start insisting on having more control over their daily life.

If you look at chakra growth from this angle, what is going on now is tremendously positive and it is why we are experiencing turbulent times. However, it would be nice to think that a significant number of boys and girls at Westminster were reasonably au fait [well acquainted] with 18th century French history and are paying attention, but I do wonder sometimes. No, I am not suggesting we are heading for some kind of storming of the Bastille in this country but personally I am extremely worried and paying so much attention that I am standing on tippy-toe and scanning the future horizon very, very carefully

FIRST CHAKRA
At the pubic area - colour RED.
The tribe.

It is about survival because as a baby and small child you are unable to survive without help from your family [tribe]. You grow up surrounded by the tribal rules and values you were born into and it does not matter if you were born in Essex or Estonia, Mongolia or Missouri, Australia or

Greenland you will come from a tribe. Firstly it will be your family tribe, which may or may not incorporate a tribal religious belief. Next, a county or local area tribe and then your nation tribe. Information loaded into first chakra will be about how families function, the roles of men and women according to your tribe, how you behave in your society and your degree of tribal loyalty [which may or may not be mightily tested if you want to leave or marry outside the tribe, or the tribal religion]. Children are taught their tribe's political and religious views and how the tribe views government, policing, the law and its enforcement. A form of tribal clothing is usually adopted and it is not just small societies in lesser known areas of the world that have a distinctive and recognisable dress code. Tribal clothing can be seen on any street in Britain, from chavs to sloanes, eco-warriors to city gents, they all have their distinctive way of dressing so that one tribal member can instantly recognise another.

The most important feature of the first chakra is *safety*, that you grow up in a safe environment feeling safe as a baby so that you develop groundedness, can put down roots, develop a sense of belonging [to a family, tribe or nation] and a connection and reverence to earth and nature. A lack of input into first chakra can result in cruelty to animals and children and it includes littering too, on a small or large scale, because the tribe teaches their young their beliefs on reverence [dropping litter indicates a lack of reverence for the earth; we must be the first generation not to venerate what keeps us alive]. Full first chakra input is crucial because without it you may get an adult who simply cannot cope with adult life and this can come about within what appears to be a 'normal' family, if the baby or small child feels insecure because of tension in the home [and I do believe that a baby *can* arrive frightened if it has had 9 months in the womb feeling its mother's insecurity or great unhappiness - this may have an impact on its health]. At the extreme end of little, or no first chakra input you may get a feckless adult dropping partners, children and pets as if they were litter because they simply do not have that first chakra energy to hold a family life together. It is hard to reproduce something if you have never witnessed it. The feckless adult then expects the state, seen as the parent, to pick up the responsibility and the tab. Lack of first chakra input can also produce an adult that views the world as a hostile place or a child that lives in a fantasy world because that is a nice safe place to live and that is how their life can proceed, as fantasy, not being able to face reality or to ground themselves into the daily routine of school or a job. This calls for the colour brown, but more of that later.

You cannot tackle second chakra life lessons without at least a partially loaded first chakra, you just cannot do it. You have to go back and repair the damage before you move on. You can look at it like this: no good repeatedly filling the cracks in the walls of the house if the whole foundation of the building is built with poor quality cement because you will always get more cracks. I think the whole country needs a network of mentors and not just in urban areas because youngsters needing some input into a partially empty first chakra do not necessarily need a lot of time, they can make huge leaps forward with a little concentrated listening, a few words of wisdom, encouragement and love.

The questioning of tribal values and beliefs will not start in earnest until children become teenagers when they decide they have dinosaurs for parents. They start to challenge the tribal mindset and this disruption goes on until they decide if their tribal beliefs are relevant to their adult life. In some cultures the beliefs will not be questioned at all and this is often because the tribal religion will not tolerate individual thinking. Tribes have to have beliefs and rules that its members abide by, that is what binds them, but we can see these tribal rules are being challenged and broken everywhere with same sex marriages, couples from different religions and ethnic origins uniting and, of course, there are more and more people living alone which is distinctly untribal behaviour. There is nothing wrong with tribes, they have successfully sustained life for millions of years but the problem we have now is that more and more tribes [nations] have nuclear weapons. If one tribe does not like the look of another tribe we could all go … boom! Therefore, our shifting out of tribal consciousness and our challenging of the leaders of the tribes is becoming increasingly urgent. The notion 'we are all one' is NOT a first chakra understanding, it is a sixth chakra perception, grounded in third chakra and overseen by the fourth heart chakra. Mass travel and migration is the fastest way to the realisation that 'we are one' but the problem now is the phenomenal speed of human movement in the last few years is making for a bumpy flight and uncertain landing.

There has been much disruption within the tribal family too. Unsurprisingly, as a result of family fragmentation there has been an escalation in gangs where youngsters seek out a clan or tribe to provide some sort of surrogate family and then comply with all the fascinating tribal rules, clothes, language and the inevitable tribal leader. These gatherings, having tested loyalty [sometimes brutally] give a feeling of belonging and security initially but, unfortunately, they rarely encourage study and growth because it is difficult to hold a tribal gang together if people learn, question and leave. If members get too bright they might make the gang leader look stupid - disaster! Such gang or tribal behaviour is not restricted to urban street gangs, it can be seen within terrorist organisations across the globe and within families right across the social spectrum. I have witnessed bright, questioning children being ridiculed by a dogmatic, frightened parent and watched the facial shutdown of the child as it learns to be silent rather than push tribal boundaries. The child has to be silent, it cannot yet survive on its own. Stamping down on the learning that questions tribal loyalty can take place in sink [such an interesting expression] estates and very grand country houses where, sometimes, learning is encouraged but tribal loyalty is non-negotiable. A classic example of this is can be seen in a very big house indeed, Westminster, where political party tribal members are encouraged to think as one, or else.

Later on in life different types of gangs can take the form of a tight knit circle of friends, again across the social spectrum, where often one person takes on the unofficial role of leader and to whom the rest defer, though the deference may be subtle. Although this has changed a great deal since the 1960's there is often a dress code for the tribe which can be observed at any formal or informal gathering. It can be seen in any number of clothing styles from country shooting outfits to black clothed and white faced goths, Ascot racing ensembles [quite a challenge to the tribe going on there at the moment, I notice], top-to-toe and instantly recognisable designer clothing or hairy biker's studded leather gear. Nowadays one large hairy biker sipping champagne at a designer clad polo match might be tolerated with amusement [and you can switch the scenario] because the biker is unlikely to be seen as a threat to the polo playing tribe, whereas the arrival of 200 bikers [a tribe of bikers as it were] would be seen as threatening, maybe even physically threatening and would change the atmosphere somewhat. I am not sure how a tribal invasion of 200 polo fans would affect a biker's convention but I can imagine amused unease. I daresay there would be copying and teasing of accents, which is low grade sign of inter-tribal tension. The sudden arrival of Bill Gates, of Microsoft fame, on or off a bike [but probably off, because I can't quite picture him in leather and tattoos] at either a polo game or biker's convention would also cause a stir, but it would be a ripple of deferential attention. Bill is in a tribe all of his own, bless him [hope he isn't lonely, he can always invite me, but he would *have* to send a private jet]. Money always talks, but 'mine is bigger than yours' starts talking in first chakra, is shouting loudly in second but fortunately it is learning to shut up by third chakra. I reckon Bill Gates is on good terms with third chakra, he is certainly a magnificent reflector of what we are all capable of doing and then being. Interestingly, snobbery is tribal, the inference being that 'my tribe is better than your tribe'. It actually stems from third chakra fear and is played out in second chakra.

Chakra learning is not exactly chronological from one to seven like a stepladder, you will take whatever you have loaded in first chakra into second chakra and third and so on. However, lessons start early and can be seen with one outraged toddler biffing another toddler on the head for swiping a favourite toy [second chakra - what is mine, is mine], tilting their head back and screaming blue murder when he/she does not get what he/she wants [fifth chakra - expression], accepting praise [third chakra] for kissing and making up and then happily snuggling up to a parent [fourth chakra - heart/love]. I think very small children have fully activated seventh chakras [divine or spiritual link] but these are usually closed down by tribal customs. Similarly, I have met children who drop simplistic pearls of wisdom from their sixth chakra [the wider perspective] until this too is discouraged. I daresay littlies can see auras as well, this may be why they paint Mummy with green legs, orange arms and purple hair - why else would they choose these colours? We could be learning from these small humans and instead of correcting, 'But your Mummy has brown hair', we could be coming out with a much more appropriate, 'What else can you see?'. Is it beyond the realm of wild possibility that a tiny child could see a specific colour over a specific organ and therefore diagnose illness? Just a thought.

Somewhere, in the last fifty years, we failed, as a nation, to fully load our collective first chakra. We had a fourth chakra heart-led response to poverty without comprehending that poverty does not deliver unloved, uncared for and rootless children [I have seen plenty of children living in expensive houses where love, care and grounding were absent]. Our 'collective' first chakra loves, guides and disciplines our children. It raises them within family tribal units and a nation tribe that offers protection but also an understanding of adult responsibility and self-sufficiency. Basically this means reaching adulthood with the *absolute* understanding of working for a living, being socially responsible and providing for a family [the young *and* the old], come good times, come hardship. I worry a great deal how we repair this damage, collectively, when we are a nation obsessed with living in the limelight and we have a culture of permitting and, worse, applauding footloose behaviour. That first chakra wheel has to be spinning clearly, cleanly and efficiently for second chakra lessons [and the other chakra lessons] to be fully tackled, otherwise the second chakra wheel rests on a void. I suspect the repair will be some sort of return to tribal life. I am not hugely looking forward to it, but I am tentatively hopeful.

First chakra physical protection is crossing legs, when either sitting or standing. Body fat distribution in this area is another sign and you may have a devil of a job shifting the fat, you will need to shift the emotion first. First chakra illnesses [please read Myss under 'M'] usually relate to the whole body and involves 'structure' such as bones and muscles, but it also encompasses the immune system and health problems involving the area you sit on. Think rectal area, roundabout, and all things related. For most, fear, to some degree or other, is loaded into first chakra during childhood and its level or intensity [according to the individual, remembering what is stress to one person is challenge to another] is often the guiding principle in the development of disease. Why might someone develop rectal problems at fifty-five when they were terrified at three years of age? Good question. I think we 'file' fear, stash it, hide it until some event or thought pattern opens the file. Very often emotions resurface years on [Saturn returns, for those of you astrologically minded] and the problems of later life, with a less robust physical body, can produce feelings of fear linked to security and safety [first chakra], fears that a more vigorous, youthful mind and body would shake off easily but fears that one might feel as a small and not very strong child. Please note that having money does not necessarily make someone feel safe and secure.

SECOND CHAKRA
At or around the belly button - colour ORANGE.
Money
Relationships [one-to-one]
Power [external]
Sex

The full scale pull out of first chakra started with the First World War when returning soldiers took a dim view of the perceived tribal hierarchy of the country and caused a political shift, on going through and beyond the Second World War. The second chakra lessons over money, relationships, sex and external power were all put on fast forward and given maximum exposure. There was an escalation in home ownership [second chakra] and a rise in the divorce rate [second chakra] because tribal rules [first chakra] about divorce were relaxed in the face of the monumental and bloody upheaval of war. Post 1945 women joined the workforce in increasing numbers out of choice, not wartime necessity. In doing so, they faced criticism because the tribal belief was that their role was child care at home, in the cave, not out hunting with the boys. The sixties brought even more challenges to tribal rules and all sorts of roles and institutions [that kept people rigidly 'in their place'] came tumbling down. There was a huge amount of colour introduced into our lives and dress codes changed or were abandoned. Homosexuality stepped out of the closet into the path of the religious teaching of my childhood; 'we are all God's children' took on more meaning than many could digest and religion was questioned as never before. There was a lot of visible skin, a lot of visible sex and a lot of people making a lot of money very quickly. People started living together rather than marrying - another kick in the teeth to first chakra beliefs as we talked about our 'partner' instead of 'wife/husband' so that relationships could start to be *heard* as equal. There was an explosion of spiritual shortcuts in the form of drug-taking and we sang along to songs that seemed to speak of promised lands and love, love, love. The problem is you cannot shortcut a spiritual path, sooner or later second chakra lessons come and bite you on the bottom. You have to do the spiritual graft and take the spiritual examinations, no matter how challenging and difficult they are.

This extraordinary time [less than a hundred years, just a blip on the time scale of mankind on Earth] has seen more challenges and change than ever in our known history. Today we are bombarded continuously with information, imagery and noise while being exposed to extremes of human behaviour, much of it pretty ugly. It's money, more money and what money can buy; twenty four hour sex, bullying, hating and killing, some of it real and some so-called entertainment. We are informed, through the newspapers, of underhand financial dealings going on at the highest levels to the highest bidders while we are being watched, monitored, manipulated and controlled to an unprecedented level. I do believe all this is happening for a reason, we are being bombarded and compressed in order to grow. The compression at the moment is extraordinary but then as far as I know we have never been faced with the potential destruction of the planet at man's hand. Nuclear weapons aside, we are polluting and using up the earth's resources at an unsustainable rate so we need to wake up and grow up fast …….. or else. I think this bombardment is beginning to have the effect of a general switch off. People are starting to retreat inside of themselves and, as far as possible, shut the world out. There is a realignment beginning, a return to earth. In this quiet retreat, almost a meditation, people will come to their own individual conclusions about how life is, how life should be and what is and what is not important. They will make their own rules. This will be the move into third chakra, the changing of individual minds and the moving into a new way of thinking. We are about to birth a new consciousness, a new baby; we need to be vigilant and prepared for the delivery. Perhaps you can see why second chakra orange has been the colour of choice for the quiet velvet revolutions going on at present in former eastern bloc countries.

I am now going to cover the four elements of second chakra but it is difficult to separate them because they are all interlinked. Money comes or goes with relationships. Money buys sex, sex makes money. Relationships begin and sometimes end with sex and relationships often go hand-in-hand with external power games.

Money. Your attitude and beliefs about money will mean you attract or repel it, hold it or lose it [I am going to do a section on money later]. I have mentioned it already under 'backache' but second chakra is in the lower abdomen and that is where your energetic bank account is so money issues will hit this area, usually in the lower back.

From the cradle we will all have heard money being talked about positively or negatively and hear Mum tutting over the price of rusks and little shoes. From the first battles over pocket money onwards, the issues about money are ongoing all through life. The lessons to be learned are if you are controlled by the lack of money or controlling in the getting of it. For most people it is the former though the latter is becoming increasingly common. Second chakra lessons are also in the losing of money and having the power base to rebuild what you have lost, but here there is a very strong link to third chakra [because you need grit and discipline to rebuild]. I suppose it is also about the amassing of large amounts of money too, or the point at which you can say, 'I have enough, what I have makes me feel safe' [emphasis on safe]. Really vast wealth removes the super-rich from the rest of humanity but ultimately it can isolate the holder to the degree that he/she loses a sense of perspective and reality. Sometimes they can lose their marbles too and even here there are second chakra lessons to be learned. There is an interesting energetic shift going on at the time of writing [July 2006] in the way the super-rich are perceived by the masses, especially if they are high profile. I am noticing a flavour of cynicism which I expect to accelerate so I daresay there will be yet another flurry of high profile, highly visible charitable donation, but there is a problem here in that we have reached a stage where there is a broader understanding of second chakra external power viewed from the wider perspective of sixth chakra. I wonder if anyone in the super-rich echelons, apart from a handful of notable exceptions, is paying attention to the cynicism. I rather doubt it. I feel we are approaching a time when amassing vast amounts of money will be viewed with distaste, in the West anyway. It is as if national socialism will be replaced by a global call for socialism. I am fascinated by this.

Comparative monetary wealth has brought an indifference to the family and the tribe [also to neighbour, village, town and nation], but each chakra has its sacred lessons and you cannot by-pass any of them. We are seeing a return to the first chakra tribal mindset and an economic downturn will fast forward this. Now many adult children are returning, or failing to leave, the tribal family nest because they cannot financially manage on the outside in an intensely second chakra world. Introduced to second chakra materialism at too early an age they have missed the grounding survival lessons of first chakra [new bikes - instead of learning how to repair the old one, knowing how to cook and eat on a minimal budget, that sort of thing].

Money and the acquisition of excess material goods is a profound second chakra lesson. We are all dragged into this testing ground, whatever our position and income. We are presently besieged with images of high profile people living lives that few can dream of; all of these people are teaching us. I followed with interest the recent court case involving Conrad Black. The participants of this courtroom drama are some of the greatest teachers we have today. They are reflectors, mirroring back to all of us our own rather strange sense of priorities. We all lust for external power to some degree or other. We have all been wildly extravagant in the acquisition of material goods, even if that extravagance was spending £2.50 more than we could afford in a charity shop on some item we did not actually need. Wanting to be famous is wanting a second chakra power kick. Buying a huge television, that is not essential, is another second chakra external power display. All of this acquisition is indicative of only one thing - an empty third chakra. Look up [sixth chakra] and around at the celebrities and pop singers we once admired and now sneer at and deride. They are reflectors. Mirrors. They are our teachers.

Relationships. These are not the tribal or family relationships of first chakra, they are the one-on-one relationships of best friends, lovers and spouses, though they do, to some extent, incorporate your interactions as an adult with individual members of your family. The soaring divorce rate in the last forty to fifty years has partly been the result of unions made that were 'out' of tribal control - before this marriages were hatched within communities [sometimes very small communities] between people with common tribal beliefs. The attitude to a bad marriage was 'put up and shut up' but after the Second World War, when people travelled more and met 'foreigners' [literally or from another part of the country], they began to look for love, and at love, in a much broader way. Greater freedom of movement, job opportunities and slowly increasing spending money meant it was not crucial to live within a tribe for survival and tribal religion started to lose its hold. Now people started facing all the second chakra lessons about relationships that were made 'on their terms' and with it came the power struggles, money lessons and then sex came out from under the blankets.

The initial exploration of second chakra relationships begins with a baby assessing how much control it has over its parents [if you are childless - or childfree - and are wondering how soon most babies start assessing control issues, think 'day one'. I could tell you a tale about big baby George - enormous feet - who was barely out of the birth canal before he got the better of his tiny frazzled mother, but I must stick to chakras]. Further exploration continues when the child and their 'best friend' spend a lot of time together to the exclusion of other children. This continues right through adulthood with friends, partnerships and spouses and the inevitable power battles within close relationships. We are meant to learn to stand our ground and voice [fifth chakra] our personal authority in our most intimate relationships at home but few of us learn the lesson. Everywhere you see controlling spouses, of either sex, who have no power *outside* their home and controlling workmates or bosses who have no power *in* their home. Now we have the new and absolutely extraordinary epidemic of parents who are frightened of, and controlled by, their children. I can see that this is a necessary exploration of second chakra for both parent and child now that first chakra tribal rules have been slackened [and in some cases rewritten] but it bodes ill for the long term economy. I shall be watching with fascination how this generation of children handles future parenthood. There will be much for me to learn and I am wondering if one of the lessons will be how to dodge a severe pendulum swing.

Second chakra relationships are about finding trust with another who is not of your family or perhaps your tribe. It is about holding your own within that relationship and is the realm of the bully and the victim about which I have already written. This is backache territory again, the back 'giving' because of a perceived lack of support. The bully/victim drama starts in the home and from there it is taken to the classroom. Through life and work the bullying continues and now [it really worries me] we are being intensely bullied by government. We are continuously told 'now' the government is listening while it does absolutely nothing of the sort. Worse, we have the opposition playing the same game. This is resulting in the breakdown in our *relationship* with government and this comes at a crucial time because we are no longer the worker ants who know our tribal place, we have been growing through second chakra lessons and are taking peaks at third chakra [authentic power, self-esteem]. We have also been spoiled with material goodies and if the going gets economically rough, which I think it will, we won't take kindly to having our toys taken away. To me this spells trouble. All for the good eventually, of course, but trouble is usually unpleasant to live through.

Power. This is not internal or authentic power, which is third chakra territory, it is external power only. It is the world of materialism and how the getting, having [or not having] material goods and money affects you as a person. Think control, because controlling people are operating out of second chakra. Here agendas and game playing abound and this is one of the reasons why we have had an explosion of soaps and reality television. These programmes are in abundance in order for us to watch and learn how agendas and games are played out. Most people pay far more attention to the television than to their own lives and many cannot or do not want to see the agendas and games played out in their own kitchens and living rooms because it is too painful to face. To deal with second chakra agendas, which invariably includes a degree of bullying, you need to establish boundaries, both of which I have already covered [though establishing boundaries is a third chakra issue]. To deal with emotional [agenda loaded] game playing you need to stop your own personal dishonesty. Game players need other players to play with - full stop. Both agendas and games need an attentive ear and I am going to cover 'listening' later.

We tend to think of the powerful as being monetarily rich. I don't. I think some people have the ability to amass a lot of money; I am not deriding it because accumulating money is a necessary second chakra lesson and it takes tremendous drive, focus and, sometimes, skill to amass vast wealth, but it can then hinder growth as the money stacks up like a fortified castle around its amasser, distancing him or her from reality and a sense of perspective. My perception of power is someone who can heal themselves from major life threatening diseases and huge emotional wounds. It is also someone who can manifest what they *need* by no more than a thought [taken to its *most* powerful limit, I would think about loaves and fishes]. The arrival of such a state would nullify the need for acquiring or amassing of anything and would present as humility in the face of the absolute knowing of a greater guiding power. This is not second chakra territory, not alone anyway. I suspect it is a state reached by having six fully loaded chakras and an open seventh.

If your sense of power and self-esteem rests on your work status, your position in society, the content of your bank account, your house, your wardrobe, your vehicle or the person you step out with you have some serious work to do on yourself and no time to waste. If you are very sick [no matter what or where your illness is] please read that last sentence again and think about it, because to heal well you need a mighty amount of internal power and if you are leaking energy over externals you are in trouble. Just how important to you is your house, your rank, or the look of your lover?

If you are young, I want to point out something to you [apologies if you have already grasped this]. At some point in your life when the shit hits the fan, as it inevitably does, you will need a friend to offer support and it will not matter to you a single solitary jot what your friend does or does not have, or wear, or own. This is because it is their second chakra strength, not their weakness, that will give you comfort and you may well be stunned at just who is a brick in your time of need. I certainly was. The least likely person I could possibly imagine rose so majestically to my sad, sudden and overwhelming occasion that it still astounds me today. When this happens please understand you are being taught a powerful spiritual lesson, so pay attention. At present we seem to be hell bent on achieving our self-esteem through our clothing and possessions - tragic - but a necessary transition through second chakra. This morning alone I read an intelligent young woman writing that you could not cut it these days without spending a jaw dropping amount of money on your hair, nails and fashionable clothing. I thought 'cut it' was such an apt expression, as perceiving life in this way is almost an act of physical vengeance against yourself and vengeance is second chakra territory. The present media obsession with launching an assault on anyone with fat, wrinkles or unfashionable clothing is frustrating for many, I am continually tut-tutting and sighing but really it is a necessary tool for change. We are approaching visual saturation point of unrealistic and minimally clad bodies and a really worrying overload of body shape obsession, surgery, silicon, botox and muscle enhancing drugs. Our bodies, already on overload with chemicals, preservatives and status anxiety, were not meant to be so invaded by aliens [why buy organic food and then have botox?]. This epidemic of body enhancing, fuelled by fear, is stemming from an insufficiently loaded third chakra. Long term, although it has arrived already, this is the area [second/third chakra, mid body] where many of the physical problems will emerge and I suspect the end result will be hampered immune systems with the inevitable knock-on effects. When we see too much sickness, rampant allergies, sweeping infertility and inability to repair health in enough numbers then, and only then, will we see some common sense [third chakra], a desire for substance over fearful vanity, restful friendship over relentless competition, wisdom over perfect skin and a respect for the years of experience gathered by the older among us.

Managing your power base so that external threats do not overwhelm you and you can take some level of control over your life so that you are not excessively manipulated, is a tough call for most. When bullied, whether by family, friends, bosses or complete outsiders we tend to react with anger and want to lash out physically, even if this is only in thought [the urge to bite someone is, interestingly, strongly linked to babyhood fears and therefore first chakra insecurity]. Traditionally we carry our weaponry at second chakra level and I frequently want to pull out my imaginary pistol from its *hip* level holster and do away with bullying and controlling politicians who are intent on the theft of my second chakra power base. This is intensely childish of me and I must grow up because my sixth chakra knows full well they are performing a sacred service, even if they have absolutely no idea of it themselves. We have to be curtailed and hemmed in to grow well - like pruning a rose bush [but unfortunately the politicians are not experienced gardeners and some have yet to grasp that too savage pruning can cause disease and can even kill].

Second chakra external power-plays include cruel displays of highbrow intellectualism, designed to humiliate the less intelligent [you can see this in the media and at your work-place]. The refusal to share information or knowledge [displaying a fear of being overtaken] which could be expressed by someone unwilling give you a cooking recipe or the address of a favourite shop and continues through to a co-worker withholding vital work-place information or a teacher deliberately failing to fully explain a subject. Power-plays go on to encompass the ubiquitous displays of materialism [mine is bigger than yours]. From large conkers in the playground to instantly recognisable designer clothes and handbags [tribal uniform in some cases] and onwards and upwards to designer yachts and private planes that show the onlooker that the owner of the plane or yacht is different, elevated and superior to the masses. I am not knocking it, it is the realm of the second chakra writ large, painted on a huge canvas for all to see. These displays teach us all to aspire and that is growth and a wonderful thing but today there is so much to aspire to and there are millions who see the goodies but do not have the power base to acquire them. For some this will prove the trigger to absorb the image of what they want and move forward purposefully toward acquiring it. For many more, though, staring into the shop window and not having the power base to 'acquire', there will be a growing feeling of discontent. Most will grumble [some will get sick] but others will not stick to just muttering discontent and this is where the violence starts. A thought form initially, then a mugging here and a burglary there and onwards and upwards. This problem has to be dealt with within a first chakra framework because the rising tide of illegal activity threatens the *safety* and *security* of the tribe [nation]. The bulk of the tribe, handcuffed by governmental legislation, failed to get a grip on this early on and the problem is now, inevitably, escalating. Condemnation and retribution has to come from the tribe, I don't see our *present* law courts as being tribal enough, but I suppose that is inevitable with large populations. I have long been in favour of extremely localised trial and retribution and have been howled at for my views. Staring, recently, at a picture of an American woman caught shoplifting [standing outside the shop she had targeted, she had been forced to wear a placard announcing her theft] I wonder if America will lead the way and we will follow - but it will not happen here until the downward turn in the economy starts to really bite. Then there will first chakra cries for swingeing punishment.

Sex. It is linked with the lesson of external power in that you have enough power in your sexual relationships for you to learn to have a fulfilling adult relationship with a significant other, but not get bullied into sexual practices that you do not want or feel ready for. There is, therefore, a powerful link here with third chakra and self-esteem. So very much has been written, filmed and generally exposed in relation to sex in the last twenty odd years that it leaves me with little to say. It seems, to me, that sex has lost much of its connection with care and tenderness. We do not, yet, understand our auras - how very close physical contact means two auras almost combining and what effect that can have, short and long term, on two people. I am saddened by the serried ranks of sex-based magazines in newsagents, promoting second chakra sex. The message is, 'pleasure me now'; the heart chakra an irrelevance, yet we all long to be truly loved. There is a place for this literature but not in the sightline of small children [can we not give them a chance at childhood?]. It speaks of more and more people unable to make human-to-human contact and within that contact create a place of safety where sex can be explored in a loving framework. Collectively, women have yet to comprehend how much power they hold when it comes to sex. I do not see a realisation of this arriving sometime soon. For many women today it is all about being used when it comes to sex, or using sex to gain external power and/or making money. This will be corrected, as everything that is out of kilter is, eventually, put back into balance. Growing infertility will bring the sacred back to sex.

Sexual abusers have no self-esteem or second chakra power base and therefore seek to bully the most vulnerable [I don't understand why it is called sexual 'abuse' - 'torture' would be more accurate]. Sexual abuse, especially of children, will be registered in this chakra and can cause emotional and physical havoc then or later in life. These wounds are devastating and hard to heal. I suspect sexual abuse has been rampant, but hidden, in families forever, but even so, it says so much about the state of our nation that so many individuals are lacking second and third chakra power that they seek out targets, related or otherwise, to sexually abuse and even murder. No doubt most sexual offenders have also suffered as children, but as adults you make a *choice* - continue the violence or stop the cycle. It is appalling in this time of so-called sexual liberation, when adults are free to fornicate at will, that so many children are at risk of abuse. I think it is outrageous that children are not protected by swingeing laws and punishment for offenders. You can throw in any amount of fourth chakra compassion and counselling once offenders are locked up and out of the sight and grasp of younsters. We are slammed fast enough for tax evasion, our lawmakers making the silent statement that money comes before protecting our children. This is the very worst of second chakra politics, the compassionate heart chakra nowhere to be seen. Our government is still [but only just] seen as a parental figure, guiding and leading our nation, and it is failing to adequately protect the most weak and vulnerable in our society. Intuitively children and teenagers understand this. They know they are not protected, they hear that money is more important and we wonder why so many youngsters are going off the rails. Intention, intention.

Second chakra is also about betrayal. This is usually linked with what was, or is, a sexual relationship and I don't need to go into graphic detail about being 'dumped'. I am sure everyone has had that experience at some time or another, but betrayal also comes in non-sexual *relationships* and business *partnerships* and this is what I mean by all the elements of second chakra being closely interlinked. I can remember a particular instance of betrayal [non-sexual] in my life and I walked away from my betrayer and felt as if my guts were spilling on the pavement. Not for nothing do we say, 'I felt gutted', for this emotion is entirely second chakra territory, as opposed to 'I felt choked' which is fifth chakra [voice] blocking a fourth chakra heart feeling. 'Feeling gutted' is a sensation of being energetically disembowelled in the lower abdomen. Please note that unkind words can disembowel you as fast as unkind actions and witnessing screaming rows can do the same, as I mentioned in 'argue'. If you have been on the receiving end of an 'I felt gutted' you need some serious quiet reflective time. A person disembowels another out of fear, though it may not seem or feel like it at the time. This is a major spiritual lesson and it may be that you have failed to read the warning signals of an imminent disembowelling. Back track. Think things through. Have you moved on or moved forward in some small way? Have you empowered your third chakra enough to frighten someone who is still rooted in second chakra, or even first chakra? Have you unknowingly threatened someone's second chakra external power base? Try not to shoot the messenger, no matter how badly you feel let down. Be honest with yourself but also remember this: after an emotional 'disembowelling' you will have a damaged aura and be emotionally and physically vulnerable, so be proactive in your approach to repair. You might get an instant tummy upset or cold, or you may put a lid on things and press an 'on hold' button, but be aware that emotional wounds like these can fester and erupt years later as a second chakra illness. Personally, I would wear navy for a few days to give protection and stability, eat healing foods, avoid cold situations [I'm talking weather and people] and generally give yourself time to heal and reflect. This will be one of your important life lessons - an examination. Forget 'A' levels, they are piddling by comparison to this spiritual hurdle - and hurdle it is. Only you can chose to fly over it or dig your heels in. Only you will know where the fear came from and then have the strength to find the compassion. You may think I am away with the fairies but I do believe our angels and guides are very close to us at this time. You may be weeping from your disembowelling but they are there silently, just behind and around you, offering unseen support and healing. Just ask for their help, though sometimes you don't even have to do that - on a couple of 'in crisis' moments I have felt their unseen healing hands.

While I am here I want to talk about compensation, because I couldn't think of anywhere else to put it. This is not a diatribe [such an interesting word] against compensation in general, though the subject does worry me. I want to talk about the very second chakra habit, for that is what is has become, of seeking retribution in the law courts for rude or sexist remarks made in the workplace. Lay down your second chakra pistols please, if you are bristling, because I take your point, I most certainly do, BUT please know this: you are taking your grievance to someone else to decide if it is right or wrong. It is a bit like asking your Daddy to punch the school bully on the nose for you. You might get temporary satisfaction but you have grown not an inch, you have not learnt the lesson and lessons ALWAYS come back, but often dressed differently. In court you may be awarded financial compensation which enriches you but very rarely does it empower you. A fat compensatory cheque may give you a more comfortable materialistic life but it will not prevent the lesson from recurring later, sometimes years down the line. The money may bring you a house with better burglar proof security but it will not stop someone, at some time, from infringing on your boundaries, either literally or emotionally. This is the lesson that has to be learned; how to become empowered to the point that someone does not make a sexist remark in the first place. It is a tough lesson and it is especially hard for women [I have found it enormously difficult], but learn we must. Boundaries, boundaries, boundaries.

Second chakra protection is hands clasped or gripped together over the pubic bone, or just above it. The whiter the knuckles the more you need to pay attention. You will see this position adopted when people stand near royalty, this is because they think they are in the presence of power, but you can spot it in all sorts of photographic line-ups or anything that confronts second chakra issues - like interviews. You may also see this posture adopted by someone being cross-questioned about money if they have big issues on the subject, usually because of the lack of it. If you are doing the questioning and the object of your interrogation is clamping down over their pubic bone it might help to change your approach because if you do not you may just get someone defensively shutting down and going completely *deaf*. This is as applicable to the infuriated father to the spendthrift son as it is to the bank or building society 'driven by targets' manager to the overdrawn customer or mortgagee. Try to get underneath them and be supportive, otherwise you are probably wasting your breath by either terrifying or infuriating the clamper and any advice or instruction given may not be heard at all. Offer really basic and easy to comprehend strategies to escape from monetary muddle. Keep it simple.

Please also be aware of protective second chakra belts [read 'jewellery']. The recent fashion trend of exposing the flesh of second chakra is fascinating me. I can talk to a youngster wearing a breathtakingly low slung skirt or trousers exposing their lower abdomen and only just covering over their pubic hair but if I cross question them on second chakra issues they will invariably do a protective hand clasp over the area. Bless. Such mixed messages. Such muddle.

Second chakra illnesses are situated in the lower abdomen, right across the hips, and include anything to do with the reproductive organs for men and women [ovaries especially, ladies, please read about red and black in 'colour']. For men it extends to prostate problems even though that would appear to be in the first chakra region. It would include all the organs around and below the navel especially bowel, bladder, appendix [have you had yours out? If so, what was going on emotionally at the time? It is right sided, so what did your father - or some significant male later on in life - say, or do, or not do?]. Our diets are pitiful these days but not for nothing are we seeing a rise in bowel cancer in these second chakra times and - while I think of it - there is growing evidence that cancer often appears two years after an emotional upheaval.

I have a happy mental image of most of the population, including me, getting into a lift in a department store and disembarking en masse at the second floor [second chakra] marked 'purses/wallets [money], counselling services [relationships], lingerie [sex] and weapons [external power]'. There we lurk and skulk about, muttering, complaining, partaking and learning painfully. Occasionally we see the lift door open from whence a yellow glow emanates and a sunny voice announces, 'Going up, third floor [third chakra], sunshine and more lessons'. '*That sounds nice*', we all say ..... but no-one gets in.

THIRD CHAKRA.
At the solar plexus, just below the breast bone.
Colour - YELLOW.
Personal [authentic and internal] power and self-esteem

This one is about authentic personal power. It is not the same as second chakra power, which is needed to deal with our outside and extremely material world. Authentic power is about self-control, doing the right thing [no matter how uncomfortable], self-discipline, self-esteem, the pride you take in yourself and in your life and your personal honour code. It is your level of integrity.

What is your work ethic and are you punctual? Can you keep secrets and keep your word - keep them for others and yourself? How reliable are you? Can others rely on you and can you rely on yourself? Do you constantly let yourself down? Do you start a diet on Monday and jack it in by Wednesday? You could remove the word 'diet' and put in its place smoking, drug-taking, criticising or over-spending. How much does it bother you if you are not liked? Do you over self-analyse or over self-criticise? Are you an approval seeker? Do you name drop? Are you a people pleaser or a rescuer? Do you rescue animals [I could win gold prizes at this] or people? Do you do everything for your family and nothing for yourself? Do you feel overwhelmed by responsibility? Are you a carer? Are you trying to save the planet, politically or environmentally? If so [to all of these mentioned], you are losing energy at the level of third chakra. I am not suggesting that you do not rescue animals or save the planet, but I am saying do not do it at the expense of personal energy loss and subsequent ill health. An overloaded sense of responsibility, for whatever reason, can energetically overload the pancreas and too much thinking exhausts the spleen. Both are smack in the middle of third chakra territory.

Before I go any further I want you to conjure up an image and take it away with you. It's important, so please pay attention. I want you to imagine that your upper tummy, solar plexus, has an electrical socket right in the middle of it. Do you know those outdoor sockets that have a snappy lid on them to keep the rain out? Some people have these, but far more have open sockets and they leave their front door, metaphorically, open. In walks the low battery. Low batteries come in all shapes, sizes and ages, male and female, nice and not so nice but they all have the same thing in common, the swines, they plug their recharger into your solar plexus socket and drain your central supply. Read on for third chakra protecting mechanisms and then check out 'blue' in the 'colour' section. I am serious about this, because if you are being repeatedly drained you are going to get very ill sooner or later and you may not be able to heal yourself. Get yourself a snappy socket lid. Avoid two-legged low batteries at all costs. Think about self-protection and start learning to say, 'No!'.

Ok. Let's get back to people pleasing, rescuing and approval seeking [name dropping included] because they are major contributors to third chakra energy loss. I have realised, late in life, that it is absolutely essential to approve of yourself because it is damn dangerous trying to get someone else to do it for you. If you are not good at this and seek approval from others for your hair, your clothes, your boy/girlfriend, your house, your job, your decisions and your life in general then you need to take urgent action because you have an addiction. I didn't realise I was an addict until someone disapproved of one of my shopping purchases and I lost it - went ape. My filing cabinet [more under 'emotions'] was already full to bursting with disapproving comments. When I calmed down I realised I was addicted to getting approval from other people, particularly women, about my purchases. My need for the approval had stemmed from an early childhood incident where I had taken my birthday money and purchased something I desperately wanted but about which my mother had severely disapproved. That one seemingly trifling incident [it was over some small, plastic farm animals, believe it or not] set up a chain reaction that initially encompassed anything to do with animals. If I was given china animals or pictures of animals I was in heaven but if I wanted to buy them for myself I sought approval, which invariably I did not get. What started with animals went on to encompass other items including clothes because my neediness had no brakes. My long dead mother would have been absolutely aghast and extremely sorry that such a piddling incident could have caused such a long term drama. I am also absolutely aghast that a seemingly piddling incident could have caused such a long term drama, but there were two problems here: one was that my mother was also seeking approval so she could not empower me on that score and for me the initial purchase was not the *plastic* animals, it was *the* animals. These ornaments were the substitute for the real thing that I absolutely craved but our lifestyle would not permit. My mother's disapproval was of something I needed [and still do] and the recognition of this, plus the fact that she most certainly would not have disapproved had she understood the enormity of the need, heals a hole in my pockmarked third chakra. Eventually, when I fill in enough pockmarks [there are quite a few holes in my second chakra too] I will be fully well again. I know this. I feel this.

Third chakra is also about having personal boundaries - another major problem area for me that is why I wrote at length about recognising early boundary infringement and boundary maintenance. Third chakra is also about trust, trust in yourself and in your ability to heed your intuition. I expect you have heard the one 'intuition is God's only way of talking to you'. I have thought about this one a lot. If God does indeed talk to you via your intuition and if your intuition is indeed your gut feelings then your third chakra and solar plexus needs a great deal of serious attention. It is interesting that this area is beginning to be talked about as the area of the second brain. Learning to pay heed to one's intuition is essential for a calm life. Both my partner and me have had a couple of recent and painful lessons when our ego over-ruled what our intuition was telling us. We failed to pay attention because we did not like the message and we paid the price. The lesson is now fully learned [we sincerely hope].

I have a belief that everyone gets confronted with issues of third chakra trust at some stage of their life. It may come as a dark night of the soul for those of intense religious belief but for everyone a leap of faith is required at some stage of the proceedings. The leap for the non or mildly religious may come at marriage, parenthood, divorce, bereavement, change or loss of work, bankruptcy, major illness, or just making a pivotal decision in life [maybe you can think of another] and the challenges faced require a great belief in oneself and one's ability to pull through, whatever life brings. If the foundation blocks of chakra one and two are insufficiently loaded this is going to be difficult. I always think of one of the Indiana Jones films when Indy is being chased, as usual, and comes out of a tunnel to face a huge chasm. He realises a leap of faith is required and steps out into the abyss to find a rope bridge [or was it a stone path?] forms magically under his feet. I think this is how it goes, anyway it had a big impression on me and it got me thinking about the difference between 'risk' takers and 'leap of faith' takers. I think risk taking comes under the remit of second chakra and can indeed be risky. There is generally more movement [both literal and fidgety] and the outcome, if successful, is material. The leap of faith [a gut feeling of success] is much more still and calm and the successful outcome is often not material, though it may appear to be in some instances. I have watched many falter and refuse when a giant leap of faith in themselves was required but I have also watched in open mouthed amazement as some have taken the leap with grace and humour. I visited a leaper recently who had faced an appalling tragedy but had decided on life affirming action and had carried it through with dignity and courage. It was just so lovely to see her serene and content and I was full of admiration for her. She uplifted me [for it has a ripple effect], though she will laugh her wonderful raucous laugh when I show her this book and point and say, 'That's you'.

A really genuine compliment can empower two people at the level of third chakra. Please don't think I am talking chat-up lines [which is second chakra manipulation], I don't, I mean a gut recognised [third chakra] but heartfelt [fourth chakra] compliment that recognises another's strengths and flair. A sincere compliment giving such recognition is a beautiful thing because it gives grace to the giver and empowers the receiver. These days we are fast to condemn and complain but slower to genuinely praise what is genuinely worth praising and it is doing more damage than we can possibly comprehend. It seems to me our entertainers are overly praised to the detriment of everyone else, yet a good bricklayer's work will stand as testament to his endeavour long after the celebrity is dead, gone and forgotten.

In your solar plexus you hold your level of reliability because third chakra is about saying you will do something and then doing it [this also encompasses fifth chakra]. It is having the discipline to do the right thing, even if it means putting yourself out or pushing yourself a bit further than is comfortable. It is obeying the rules but it is also about breaking the rules if you know it is the right course of action, no matter that the consequences may be personally dire. You damage your third chakra by letting anyone down, not least yourself. Keep promises, it is essential. Stick at things through rough patches and give up only when you have fully discussed with yourself and then acknowledged that this is the wrong pathway for you.

I see the word 'integrity' as being integral to third chakra and I love the word. I once stood in an art gallery in front of an enormous and completely incomprehensible painting that was described as having 'great integrity'. I stared and stared but for the life of me I couldn't see the integrity, though I wanted to. I thought it was all a bit frenetic and tiring, though I liked the colours. Eventually I started to giggle, so that was good, as I can often find integrity in laughter. Fortunately I have no problems recognising integrity in a person. My dictionary definition is 'honesty, incorruptibility, wholeness, soundness'. How beautiful. I reckon a fully loaded third chakra [not too many about] is as the dictionary describes.

One last point on third chakra. I have talked to many people who were kind, reliable, honourable and true [third chakra attributes] but had one disaster after another in their lives. For years I did not understand it until I came to the conclusion that we can [possibly/probably] arrive here with a partially loaded third chakra, or we can acquire it during childhood. However, some people with partially loaded third chakras and a reasonably healthy level of self-esteem have no second chakra power. They can't hold onto money, relationships are a minefield, sex gets in a muddle and there is bullying here and there. Without a reasonable loading into second chakra, the partially loaded third chakra has no firm foundation to sit on, as it were. It's hovering over a void. Your solar plexus third chakra wheel will keep dipping down into the quagmire that is your empty and malfunctioning second chakra. Is this making any sense to you? If it is resonating with you, try and understand you *have* to start shoring up your second chakra. See every ghastly incident you have faced in the sex, money, one on one relationships and external power department as lessons brought to you to learn from. Stand back and look at the lessons in dispassionate perspective. It does not matter if you think you failed. We all fail repeatedly at different things and I have been a serial failure. Get a handle on being able to say, 'no'. Learn to listen [more later]. Sort your boundaries out. Use the colours navy, orange, turquoise and possibly red [more coming up]. Give relationships a miss for a while, get your finances sorted, keep reading for more helpful hints and, above all, be kind to yourself [especially if everyone else is not].

Third chakra protection is hand [or hands] over the solar plexus, a single or folded arms, or the more dramatic warding off gesture of a palm first outstretched hand, either fully outstretched and imploring or the less obvious 'waving' about. Back off when you see it and if you are paying attention you may see the 'waving about' in the most unlikely situations coming from the most unlikely people [as I did recently from a professional .... erm, let's say helper, who was supposed to be helping me - I gathered they were out of their depth]. If there is a low battery heading your way and you need to implement third chakra protection [snappy socket lid] either bring one arm, preferably the right, across your upper abdomen or interlace your fingers and bring your hands to rest on your solar plexus. This is subtle protective body language, whereas double crossing your arms is like swearing. If you are carrying something you could bring that up as a barrier - whatever, it really does not matter, the whole point is you are paying attention to your weakness and making an effort to strengthen yourself.

Please also read the section on 'fat' and its distribution. Illnesses relate to the area and all organs situated in and around the solar plexus, below the ribs down to the level of the umbilicus [tummy button]. This includes the liver [the seat of anger, repressed or otherwise] all organs in the middle section of the body [gall-bladder, stomach, kidneys, adrenal glands - they are major players in 'burn out' - pancreas, spleen, upper gut, etc.] and it also encompasses illnesses of the so called 'auto-immune' type and arthritis. TAT [tired all the time] is frequently a third chakra energy loss often related to boundaries, though there may be a link to a blocked fifth chakra [unable to speak out] and subsequent thyroid dysfunction or possibly a blocking of seventh chakra [spiritual link]. Because of my own experiences of ill health and healing I am beginning to think third chakra plays a much more important role in healing any illness or injury.

FOURTH CHAKRA
At the level of the heart. Colour - GREEN AND/OR PINK
Love, compassion and true forgiveness.

Fourth chakra compassion is a wonderful thing but a bit of an empty vessel without third chakra discipline and second chakra power in the external world. It is the third and second chakra that charges up behind the compassion, moves and shakes, starts up charities and/or changes social conditions. We are on the turn now, but for too long there has been an over-emphasis on compassionate fourth chakra understanding and caring without the back up of the other chakras - it has not had a healthy outcome.

One of the major lessons of this chakra is about forgiving and the damage done when we cannot forgive and 'carry around' a wounded heart. I think it is the hardest lesson of humankind to tackle, to truly forgive those who have hurt, abandoned or betrayed you or your trust. It is imperative to forgive if you want to heal physically. If this seems like a monumental task start with just accepting that you cannot change the past but you can have a mighty impact on the future. Unkindness or cruelty done to you in the past cannot be undone but its impact can be lessened if you refuse to be unkind or cruel to yourself, or to anyone else, and that includes animals. Over twenty years ago, I sat ashen faced [I wasn't well at the time, but still] as a lovely plumber fixed my kitchen sink while telling me appalling tales of his impoverished childhood and of being beaten black and blue by his father. He said he had made a promise to himself to never, ever raise a hand in anger to his children. His happy children were now grown and he had kept his word [third chakra] and in doing so he in some way made an act of forgiveness toward his father [fourth chakra] for you cannot undo the past, only make a commitment to change the present. This man was so lovely to me, kind to my poorly state, fixing my sink for little money because I had little, while giving me a major spiritual life lesson. Sometimes towering figures come to you quietly holding tool bags. We need to pay attention or we might think they are just plumbers or electricians or some other repair worker. Repeat 'repair' workers.

Obviously this chakra is also about everything to do with love, unconditional or not. Love and respect for our fellow man and our fellow animals, for it is their home too, though we seem to forget this most of the time. I always think it is about kindness, just kindness. I never cease to be astounded at how kind this country can be. I am sure other countries are too, we just don't hear about it, but it seems that the Brits do seem to be extraordinarily kind in their response to international disasters. If they are suffering from compassion fatigue I can hardly blame them, they have given magnificently over many, many years. My worry is that addressing a disaster or poverty, either nationally or internationally, through the fourth heart chakra has its dangers. The giving nationally [I am particularly thinking about welfare in this country because I think it was originally a fourth chakra response to desperate poverty but now it has become a really shocking second chakra manipulation] and the giving internationally in aid must take into account that you cannot lift someone out of poverty, you have to enable them out. This allows them to learn the necessary lessons of second and third chakra so they can build their personal power. Second chakra lessons cannot be bypassed through gifts of money or material goods unless they are very small donations. You cannot hand someone third chakra self-esteem but you can recognise, nurture and compliment real commitment and effort. You cannot give personal power, you have to learn it and earn it. Without enablement the receiver will be lifted to a place where the giver may feel comfortable but the receiver is not. The receiver will then, inevitably, slip backwards or self-sabotage. This is why some people lose large sums of money they have suddenly acquired, their second chakra energy and third chakra self-esteem [or lack of it] cannot hold on to it. They will blow [note the word] the money until they get back to a financial situation that they understand and feel comfortable with and then they will blame everyone and anyone else, except themselves, for having lost it - self-sabotage is fascinating and can be seen in any number of different situations. A giver or donator needs to understand that the receiver has to be ready to receive. I will give you a different scenario that has the same lesson ....
imagine going to stay at your brother's disgustingly filthy bachelor flat and

spending all weekend cleaning it. Three months later you pitch up again to find it is in its original filthy state. *You tried to lift* [notice the emphasised words] your brother to somewhere you felt comfortable but he did not. He was not ready for the lift [or had different priorities] and you were actually subtly bullying and controlling on a second chakra level, so therefore you were bound to have the lesson rebound and hit you in the face. It might have been a better, more *heart-led* approach to take your brother out for a cheap meal and listen to him, that way you might have found out why he was living in a pigsty. Less physical effort than cleaning, far more productive, educational [for you] and healing for both of you, but more emotionally difficult because you would have had to tame and silence your ego. Pigsties, by the way, are home to pigs; highly intelligent, fun loving, truffle hunters, much maligned ..... and while I am snuffling about, please buy your bacon from farmers who grant, allow, permit their pigs to lie down comfortably. Such a very small third chakra allowance for a farmer to make to ward off large karmic debt or a small and patient angel with a huge spanner.

Nationally we have had a fourth heart chakra response to immigration with a muddled sense of guilt [poorly loaded third chakra] when we actually needed to work solely on strengthening our national second chakra and third chakra, that way we could have dealt comfortably with floods of immigrants who are still firmly rooted in first chakra. With the kindest of intentions it is a balls-up and I don't like the look of the outcome, though I understand the spiritual necessity of it all.

To me fourth chakra is all about giving from the heart in whatever context that is - giving love, kindness, forgiveness, care, time, attention, money, food. Wondrous and fabulous all that giving is but I think we need to be aware that giving needs brakes, moral brakes even [third chakra], because there are plenty of people out there, starting with family and friends and moving out nationally and internationally, who will take and take and take - not much spiritual growth there folks and that is morally wrong because it is disempowering people. This happens within families. My own mother took time and energy from me until I was exhausted. It was my fault entirely because I had insufficient boundaries [third chakra] where she was concerned. When I finally put my foot firmly down and laid down the ground rules, she knew I was serious. She was dead in a fortnight. I really believe in that moment of my putting my foot down [I actually made a slicing movement in front of me with my hand, as if drawing a line in the sand] and telling her I would not be on call 24 hours a day [I was getting calls, sometimes abusive, day and night] and set out the exact time each week in which I would be there for her, other than for emergencies, I empowered my third chakra to such an extent that she knew I had moved forward. I saw fear in her eyes as she lost control over me. In my experience the 'takers' of this world [you name the different type of taking, for there are many] end up very depressed and angry because they are taking but not growing.... and they know it. Growing emotionally is painful and you absolutely have to do it yourself because no-one can hand you the growth.

I should say something about receiving at this heart chakra level. It is as vital as giving. You might ask yourself how good you are at receiving love. If you cannot accept a compliment without shrugging it off or being dismissive, you have a problem. In a perfect world, if we were all giving out kindness everyone would be receiving heart energy. This is sadly not the case. There are many sad and lonely hearts about, and some are in long term relationships. We all need to learn to be kind to our bodies but we especially need to be kind to our tickers. If your ticker wants to go walkies, it is best to put your coat and hat on and go along for the ride to wherever or whomsoever that may take you ...... or your unheard ticker might walk you to somewhere where, traditionally, the yew tree grows [graveyard]. Deep and unreleased grief [mostly stemming initially from childhood] will rear up later in life and can play havoc with the heart. It can also affect the lungs, especially if the childhood grief was linked to fear.

I am pondering on hiatus hernias [such an apt name]. My mother had one, amongst other things. Could it be a third chakra hiatus rising up into fourth chakra and knocking on the ticker's front door, asking for attention? Hmmmm.

Taking aside the reaction to a sudden death, or behaviour at funerals, when this sort of gesture is entirely normal, fourth chakra protection is hand over the heart or, more unusually, a cupping gesture under the heart [please step and speak with care when you see it]. It might be a single hand and arm, usually right, diagonally across the chest, a high criss-crossing folded arms gesture or anything that has been held [handbag/book] but is brought up to cover the chest area. Please read the 'nose' section under health [not for nothing do our noses go red when we genuinely cry *heartfelt* tears] and also read 'fat'. Deep grief is often expressed by a single pat or repeated patting, or even a blow over the heart area by an open palm. This specific gesture is doubly fascinating as many in the new-agey world I live in will recognise the 'thymus tap' and its related 'giving of courage'. The thymus is situated sub-sternally, mid chest and a thymus tap is given singly or repetitively with the flat of the hand. Grief can also be shown by hitting the chest with a closed fist [often thumb foremost, the thumb the first part of the hand to make contact with the chest - this is interesting in relation to what the fingers represent - see under jewellery]. If the chest was being tapped or thumped in grief and the thumb was foremost to the chest I would be alert to someone almost trying to subdue or subjugate their grief. If I was a family doctor witnessing this gesture I would be doubly alert. However, the thumb foremost gesture is used a lot in conjunction with a cough. Most people ignore the body language of a cough or coughing when it comes in the middle of a conversation. A cough [excluding head colds and chest infections, of course, but even here there is a link] indicates fear and that some emotion or truth is being held back, so pay attention to the words and think back - what was the conversation about? [Interestingly, if you tell someone the awkward truth and the truth has annoyed them, they often need to urinate shortly afterwards. If you tell someone the awkward truth and the truth has frightened them, they often need to have their bowels open shortly afterwards. If you talk to someone who starts coughing, they are either holding something back themselves or requesting that you do so.]

Clothes and colours worn are also an indication of a heart that has been broken [as in protective armoury or a heart on the mend], I will cover this later on. Illnesses relate to the chest area, the heart, lungs [can involve the thymus, though I think the thymus - such interesting central body positioning - may be in a class all of its own and may be linked to grief and/or recognition of the self] and breasts - ladies, are you loving and nurturing yourself, or everyone else but you? I read any amount of material on the latest empirical studies on breast cancer, the latest scientific breakthroughs, but we define our roles and we learn what to think from our parents. I do believe we all start reacting to our mother's thinking when we are in the womb, well before we watch our mothers, listen to them and define our role [as a woman] using them as a role model or a model to kick against. Learning to nurture ourselves healthily [not doughnuts] is something taught to us as children by our parents or something we have to learn later in life, often as a result of an angelic spanner.

Please read the colour section, particularly black, grey and green and the clothing section under stripes and checks.

The heart needs a voice too, so …………………………..

FIFTH CHAKRA
At the level of the throat. Colour - TURQUOISE.
Speaking or voicing your truth
Willpower

You know when you say 'I was choked' or when you get an emotional lump in your throat, this is the heart energy of fourth chakra trying to force its way up to your head past a block in your neck - fifth chakra. The heart is in charge so you can only try and block this lump in your throat for so long before the heart launches a full scale invasion and possibly becomes a sick heart in the process. I am sure you can think of the odd occasion when you came under a verbal mauling and later you thought of the perfect 'put down'. It is absolutely infuriating when you cannot pull a verbal 'rabbit from the hat' when you need to because, at the time, you were clouded with emotional fury or resentment. Learning cool detachment, so you are able to find the appropriate words, can be a lifelong lesson. It is one I have really struggled with for many years and I am nowhere near done yet, but I have found that looking at unpleasant events in my life and seeing what chakra lesson they brought has given me a sense of perspective and I have become a lot less emotional. In the last ten to fifteen years, or so, I have noted, with interest, that the over emphasis on 'niceness' of my childhood, which severely frowned on tantrums, particularly from girls, has been over compensated for by a huge pendulum swing in favour of endless negotiating with angry small children who are roaring from their fifth chakra. A bit of balance is required here, I think.

A partially closed fifth chakra can open up when a separation occurs between two lovers, or during a bereavement. The intensity of the emotion roars up from the heart and blasts through any blockage in the throat. The voice then voices and the anger or tears are spilled. I believe that everything that happens in life happens for a reason and sometimes when we lose something it can actually heal us or even save our life. Many times I have seen small accidents, which required some surgical or nursing repair, but during the patching up process a much bigger and more dangerous physical problem was revealed. In a similar way, we see a furious row or lover's split as a sorry sight but I tend to see it as life affirming because often it is the only release valve people have. If you stifle and shove your emotions back down, over and over again, they become like a pressure cooker. A sudden row releases pent up anger, which can cleanse the liver. A lover's separation can clear years of previously unshed tears, thereby healing the heart. The same is true, but bigger and deeper, in a death. I think it can be that a much loved person or pet can give you as much in their departure as in their life. Their painful leaving allows you to freely express years of unreleased grief or anger; their death the trigger to allow wailing and tears, bringing release and a level of healing. Are we in the realm of sacred contracts? Is it possible that someone you love [or a pet animal] comes to you and agrees to leave early so that you can cry and heal your long broken heart? I do think that this can be the case, but I hope you do not think I am being insensitive and way too wacky. Further in the book I will discuss my views on reincarnation; I am beginning to suspect we can bring unresolved grief with us at birth. We see death as calamitous because we see it as final but I don't think it is remotely final at all. I do believe in multiple lives and that on the 'other side', for want of a better expression, time has no meaning. I have stood over babies in cots on postnatal wards, with my hands on my hips and my mouth open, while I marvelled at SO much character in tiny little humans that were only hours old. 'Well, you've lived a bit already, haven't you?', I would say to a particularly tiny but seemingly old soul.

Fifth chakra has a strong link with second and third chakra because we all need to learn to speak up for ourselves, but we have to have enough input in the other two chakras to be taken seriously. Nowadays we seem to be inundated with mouthy youngsters who have much to say, loudly and sometimes rudely, but they lack punch in the third chakra department [unless you classify 'punch' as being the physical second chakra variety outside a pub on a Saturday night]. I hear a lot of calls for 'respect' from youngsters who completely fail to comprehend that they will not get it until they have a level of self-respect and this requires intense self discipline - not much of that around these days. A person with true third chakra power has a strong base of disciplined will power and is often quiet and doesn't say much. They don't need to because their power is fully loaded and things happen without a lot of talking, or yelling, or gesticulating, or punching.

Fifth attributes are about speaking your truth, being honest and speaking kindly but also verbally holding your ground and therefore expressing your willpower. As a child, my expressed feelings often frightened and occasionally angered [linked to fear] my mother, especially when they generated opinions that went against our tribal beliefs, so I had to learn to keep my mouth shut on certain subjects. Apart from every day chit-chat [where I was capable of talking the hind leg off a donkey - still am], for years I was rubbish at verbal expression of feelings, because I got too clouded with emotion. I am improving now, but overcoming that childhood 'shutdown' has taken some doing. Speaking up clearly and with power is a major challenge for many and possibly, even these days, a tad more difficult for woman than for men. Even now, rather a lot of very little boys are listened to and taken more seriously than very little girls, especially in certain countries. For the young today, standing their verbal ground and saying 'no' is a daily multiple challenge, though I daresay if you are a parent you are rolling your eyes to heaven and thinking, 'My children do not find saying 'no', especially to me, any sort of challenge at all'. I am, of course, talking about youngsters interacting with their peer group. In my youth it was a continual challenge of keeping unwanted roving male hands away from my underwear but alcohol, drugs, gangs and violence were not a problem as they are today. Alcohol would have been a nice problem but we couldn't afford it. Half a lager [and a shared packet of crisps] in the pub had to go a long way.

For most of us, standing our ground verbally can be a lesson that lasts a lifetime and we tend to be challenged within our intimate relationships the most. It is hard to say to our parent, sibling, partner, spouse, or anyone else you can think of that this behaviour, or that event, or maybe the whole relationship doesn't make us happy. We put up and shut up, tell ourselves lies and lie to everyone else. 'How's everything?', we are asked. 'FINE!', we reply, in a voice pitched to shatter glass, and we wonder why our thyroids go haywire, we get sore throats, teeth and jaw problems or worse, get cancer [there is an energetic link between long-held, deep-seated resentment and cancer].

Speaking up for yourself starts in childhood and is going to be a problem if controlling Mummy answers every question that has been directed at the child. This may be compounded by an authoritarian Daddy issuing a stream of directives about 'in house' and 'out house' behaviour to which the child shuffles about, plucking knicker elastic, but fails to verbalize any disagreement. The parents might get peace now but can probably expect trouble later, possibly in the form of wildly inappropriate behaviour or loud love interests [the now older child choosing a boyfriend/girlfriend who can do the 'voicing' for them]. More worrying is a serious medical problem in the throat/lower facial area which may have started as something minor in childhood before the fifth chakra blocking goes beyond infections [inflammations and anything ending with 'itis' usually has a link with unvoiced anger] and appears as something more permanently medically defined and problematical. Please read the 'colour' section under turquoise and reading the 'emotion' section may be of help, but not if you are five years old and your anger is coming out as yet another dose of tetchy tonsillitis because your feelings are unheard. Early warning signs are sore throats, teeth problems, glue ear, or tightness in the neck, jaw [especially] and lower head area. Health concerns in this area have a strong link to unexpressed anger and usually stem from not being permitted to express feelings as a child, or, from not having feelings *validated* [might help to read 'listening'].

I have a suspicion that singing out loud helps to clear fifth chakra blocks and it would probably be helpful if all children sang together on a regular basis, as they always used to and still do in many other countries. I quite enjoy my singing, but no-one else does, so I choose to do so in front of the dogs. They usually leave the room. Occasionally I will let rip in front of my astonished partner and I can be quite tuneful for a couple of seconds before losing the plot, tune, tone and everything else. I probably should have singing lessons, but then I probably should do a lot of things and this is tricky when I am trying not to 'should' on myself at all. I once met a wise, gentle and kind man who pointed out to me that my red flushing neck [which infuriated me with its impromptu displays, especially at dreaded parties] was a classic sign of a fifth chakra block - my body talking when I would not. 'Hardly surprising, my dear, judging from my discussions with you', he added. 'If you said what you really think at parties everyone would leave the room'. My past years of recurrent sore throats started to make sense.

Please take this chakra seriously because, having had so many problems in this department myself, I am now able to recognise it in others and am surprised by how many 'others' there are. Despite all this fifth chakra blocking you may wonder at the relative, or friend, or colleague who has no concept of a block [but you sincerely wish they had] as you come in for yet another vicious verbal mauling from them and your polite fist is behind your back, not smashing them in the gob where you would like it to be. The verbal mauler who is savaging you is releasing pent up anger from their second chakra, usually, [bypassing fourth, because their heart has been emotionally damaged too] and the anger is roaring out through their throat. It may not seem like it, as they use disembowelling words that slice through your second chakra, but their outburst is absolutely rooted in fear. I dreaded some ward rounds as a nurse, knowing a few consultants who relished roaring at and humiliating medical students. They would finish off the nurses too, given half a chance [with the poor patient lying there, sheet up to their nose, looking terrified]. As a youngster you need a lot of constructive input into first, second and third chakra, not to behave like that. I did not know it then but that shouting and roaring consultant felt very unloved and insecure. Perhaps I should have interrupted the ward round and offered him a cuddle. That would have been interesting.

Fifth chakra blocks are strongly linked to the heart and several medical problems, so you may be interested to read the 'health' section later. It is a sweeping generalization but generally I find nice people are blocking their fifth, it is probably why they are so nice to be around. Fifth chakra protection is hand over throat, but read jewellery, clothing and fat. Health problems and illnesses encompass everything from the lower neck up to about the level of the nose [but I will talk more about facial features under 'health'].

SIXTH CHAKRA
At the level of the third eye, between eyebrows or just above.
Colour - INDIGO
Vision, being visionary and the ability to 'see' the bigger picture. Wisdom.

I think of this as non-sight vision and the gaining of a wider perspective [or viewpoint] and from that point comes wisdom. The gaining of wisdom takes time, years and years mostly and that is why it is sad that the old are so dismissed these days. Perhaps, ultimately, sixth chakra is a global viewpoint and the understanding that we are all one. I think this chakra can be a bit of a collision point between what you are taught versus what you see, perhaps that is why we get so many headaches here. I wonder about depression and sixth chakra, I believe I see a strong link.

Sixth chakra is up close and personal to seventh chakra. It is next-door neighbouring your energy supply from the divine. Divine wisdom does not always seem to make sense, so you might be thinking, 'I want my freedom', then you have a nasty accident, but upon reflection you find that through your physical healing journey you have gained your freedom or maybe the accident has given you time off from a busy life, the chance to reflect and to plan changes. This is sixth chakra vision, viewing the accident as a blessing in disguise, seeing the silver lining in a cloud.

If you are shut down at this third eye level you are unlikely to see much significance in 'coincidences'. You will not be paying attention to the small signposts in your everyday life. You may listen but fail to hear, especially to the mighty piece of information that could change your life that was dropped at you over the counter at the supermarket or on the golf course, for this is how angels talk to us, through ordinary folk. You may not like taking risks or following your hunches. You may not read all of this book ...... but you could surprise me. If you are closed off to small nudges from the universe that are trying to get you to question and possibly change a way of thinking or doing, you are, as they say, cruising for a bruising. You know the one: 'God talks in whispers'; let me take it further. Having whispered quietly, God then shouts. If you are still deaf and blind to celestial instruction, God will instruct an angel to hurl a spanner at the windscreen of your car as you are driving' .... and you, you little sweetheart, with your closed down sixth chakra shutters, what do you say? 'I was ONLY doing thirty five miles an hour and then a bloody spanner came out of *nowhere* ... it's not MY fault'. I am not talking a 'literal' spanner, just in case you are confused. Angelic spanners are usually in the shape of another car whose driver has also failed to hear God bellowing.

Personal physical accidents are read in the same way as car accidents. Both are seen as having something to do with the future or past issues depending on whether you get hit in the face or head-on [future], or hit on the back [past]. Sideways? I'd look at close relationships [male - right side, female - left side]. Therefore, stubbing your big toe [big toe - same as thumb - represents the head area; what were you thinking before you went, 'Ouch!'?] would be a present or future issue, whereas damaging your Achilles tendon would be a past issue. Is this too wacky? I am terribly sensible, you know. You would think I was quite normal if you met me.

Virtually all of us have problems seeing the broader picture in some way or another, for some it will be, 'All foreigners start at Calais and I don't trust any of them', or ,'We are all one, but football is full of foreigners these days'. It depends on your level of sixth chakra shut-down-ness, if there is such a word. A closed down third eye may have you thinking that synchronicity is a bunch of fetching maidens swimming in a circle. It isn't. Synchronicity is when the help arrives and you thought it was just luck. Pay attention - be attentive - open up your sixth chakra and you will find your synchronicity speeds up and you are likely to be chuffed to bits because answers, help and things you need move much more quickly towards you. The answers, help and things are always there, we don't move towards them [though we think we do] they move towards us but only when we are ready to receive. The answers, help and things are waiting for you to press your 'activate' button. Interestingly, in order to have the ability to find and press your personal 'activate' button you have to begin by de-activating. Being not doing. Become a human being, as the saying goes, not a human doing. Doesn't take much, you can start with being aware of your breathing. Is your tummy going up and down? Practice, practice. Oxygenate, oxygenate.

Wisdom is acquired through life during the gradual ascent and detailed exploration of all the chakras but, possibly, the blossoming occurs when the acquired wisdom meets the questioning of one's life purpose and meaning. I reckon this is sixth territory. I think this sort of questioning requires quiet introspection and, for the life of me, I cannot comprehend how so many adults manage to activate sixth chakra, hold down a job, pay a mortgage and raise a family. Where do they find the time and the silence? My admiration knows no bounds. I am, between spurts of gregariousness, deeply introspective, but then I have had plenty of time to plumb my depths, my purpose, my meaning. Without that time I think I would have gone quietly mad. Too much introspection is probably as damaging as too little so if the thoughts go too deep for too long a bit of earthing may be required. A spot of bashing around in the garden soothes my furrowed brow [note the sixth chakra positioning] very quickly, but if dahlias don't do it for you, try making something. Anything creatively formed from your hands will have the effect of earthing you, though I am not sure if brewing home-made beer counts … probably does. Definitely does if you are sharing it with me.

My acceptance of 'what is and was' in my life started to come through gaining what I call a bird's-eye view of life in general; getting a wider picture and a wider perspective where I could see where I was coming from, in the lead up to some of my major life events, my part in their going wrong and why I repeated the same scenario a few years later because I had not learned the lesson first time round. Things suddenly looked clearer to me as I stood back and viewed the larger picture. I found much comfort in being able to rise above my problems, view them from a wider perspective and I began to realise that the purpose of my life was not about work, a job, having or not having a family, it was about being me to the very best of my ability. This book is about me being me to the very best of my ability and I will whisper you a secret. Come closer. Not long after I was born, my late Godmother went to see a numerologist [they can tell things from numbers -

amazing - I look at numbers and see nothing but blind panic because I am useless at maths] and this numerologist told my Godmother that I was going to write a book. My parents waited with baited breath for my pen to hit paper, excitedly anticipating literary fame and maybe some riches .... and then they waited some more. Though they often enjoyed long entertaining letters from me they realised the letters were unlikely to keep them in the style to which they could rapidly become accustomed. I had absolutely no sympathy, they sent me to a book-burning boarding school, what did they expect? Meanwhile, I resolutely told myself [and anyone else who would listen] that there was not a shred of a book in me ..... nope, not a chance ..... until last November when my partner asked me what I was thinking about and I said I was going to start writing a book as soon as the Christmas deck was clear.'Yes dear', he replied. You know the tone of 'Yes dear' don't you? Hideous. Well, was he in for a surprise. I look back now and realise that this book could not possibly have been written a day earlier, because it was fifty-three years in the thought collection and event gathering process. This is a sixth chakra realisation.

To help activate your sixth chakra, try looking at your childhood passions. Be whimsical. Raid your memory bank and remember things you adored doing as a child. Look for little events during your formative years that you can recall with utmost clarity, no matter how tiny or fleeting. They may involve a person, thing, colour, shape, or perhaps a song, an animal, a smell, but you will have remembered that something, however little a something it is, for a reason. Now look at it from a wider sixth chakra perspective and ask yourself, 'Has something been speaking to me over the years? Have I held a memory for years and years only for it to become meaningful much later in life? Is this memory trying to tell or teach me something?'. Ask yourself how did you know to hold onto this image, out of all the images we are bombarded with on a daily basis since we could focus our baby eyes? How indeed? Are we on a specific flight path? Are our lives one glorious predetermined path of experience and growth? I reckon so .... though I have something of a bone to pick with my angels about their air traffic controlling of *my* flight path. Spanners at dawn.

Sixth chakra illnesses are, obviously, located in the head [and face] area and can range from eye/nose/ear problems, sinusitis [there is an emotional link with unshed tears], headaches, tumours and even psychiatric conditions. Migraines have a strong link to the liver/gall-bladder and often are sparked when you cannot 'see' why life is going wrong, despite your best efforts, or when someone is treating you badly for no apparent reason. This is also the realm of the pituitary gland that covers all things hormonal and that is why, when we get to colour, you will see why I keep mentioning old indigo [dark blue/*purple*] medicine bottles if there is a problem with hormones or infertility. We instinctively close down sixth chakra when we have lost something and are trying to remember where we put it; hand across forehead blocks out the wider perspective to narrow our focus down so we can find the flaming car keys that we know we put on the kitchen table but are now nowhere to be found. Don't know about you but this gesture is a regular in our household. Hand across forehead can also be used when someone is confused by another's behaviour and can't see where they are coming from. I have seen no end of this gesture in offices by rattled office managers, but do not muddle it with the two handed cupping of the forehead [which may also cover the eyes] which is a sign of grief linked to disbelief. Also watch out for furrowed brows, hair across the forehead [from a forelock to a full fringe] and headgear, bandannas or indeed any fabric [watch for the colour] covering the forehead for whatever reason. Stop and think about this, it is interesting.

I am pondering the deeper meaning of the sixth chakra covering ubiquitous baseball cap and its rapid take-up all around the world - it is bothering me. I also wonder if William Hague's [the politician] choice of this headwear [at that specific time], and its positioning, was an unconscious symbolic gesture of reassurance to the public, whereas you may think it was just a baseball cap and be calling me Tinkerbell. That's ok, I am usually proved right even when I would much rather be wrong.

SEVENTH CHAKRA
At the crown of the head. Colour - PURPLE or VIOLET
Our connection with the divine

Don't get confused with pictures of religious deities who have gold coming out of their crown, because that's them. The rest of us hoi polloi have purple [on a good day]. I find this one really hard to describe. To me, it is a lot like sixth chakra but more exaggerated. It is our direct link to the divine but I am not sure we can fully activate it until we have a well-stocked third chakra and our other chakras are humming along nicely, but I am not sure, to be honest, because me and seventh don't know each other very well. I do know that our energy, ki, chi or prana is supposed to come in from the God force [or the universe] constantly through the seventh chakra [the crown of our heads] and speed down through the body to the feet and back up again. If you take 'energy' literally, when we see no purpose to our lives we become depressed and we lose our vitality and energy. I think maybe the idea of prana flowing down your body is a bit wild for many but most of us, at some time or rather have asked with a sigh of exhaustion, 'What is the point of my life?'. This is partially a seventh chakra question that needs an answer with a lot of sixth chakra help. Later in the book I will talk about how I define 'the point' of my life and you can decide if it resonates with you at all.

I like to use the word spiritual but it may make you feel uncomfortable, so feel free to insert something else that makes you feel at home. Try 'strength'. We all want to be strong and able to take life's bitter pills when they are dished out and to be able to come out the other side of disaster, or sadness, intact. Seventh chakra does not have to link you to a God of a religion but I think it links you, in some way, to the rest of humanity and a belief that your life is meaningful and so is everyone else's. Most people need to see a purpose to their life. I certainly do. Once I started to widen my sixth chakra perspective the purpose of my life became further clarified and I think, but I am not sure, that this was a seventh chakra awakening, to some small degree. When I linked my 'disasters', as I perceived them, to the lessons of the chakras I realised each 'disaster' had a specific lesson and though the lesson was horrid, I became stronger for it. Life, for me, was no longer a morass of incomprehensible events, it was a clear cut path. My problem is that I am impatient and I have no sense of direction. I kept taking detours and getting hopelessly lost. Had I always stayed on my designated path, quietly paying attention, I may well not have needed such large and unpleasant lessons to make me stop and think. When I slowed my life right down, shut-up and paid attention, I slowly understood that I was learning and getting answers - that I was growing. Within this growth came a level of internal power retrieval and I began to realise exactly what Dr. Caroline Myss means when she teaches that life is all about 'taking your power back'. I also learnt that 'niceness' and 'taking your power back' often did not go hand-in-hand, which meant a major reconfiguration of my thinking. In the last few years this growth has become hugely important to me but my conscious awareness of its importance came about from a remark made when I had had a tad too much vino over dinner with a much loved friend. The next bleary morning I remembered [but could scarce believe] that I had said, 'My spiritual growth is the most important thing in my life'. My friend did not comment on it, much to my relief.

Does hope come down through seventh chakra? Don't know, but I rather like to think so. What does it mean when you get that funny, slightly itchy, hair lifting sensation on the top of your head? Could it be a angel with a spanner and some lubricating oil, desperately trying to shift the rust on the hinge? Maybe.

Depression has a link, I believe, with seventh chakra. I think the old adage 'depression is anger turned in on itself' has a ring of truth but is just too simplistic. It provides no tools for digging yourself out of a big black hole. I like and need tools for tackling life, that is why I have written this book. My mother was labelled a manic depressive and treated with the inevitable drugs, drugs and more drugs. Her life ended with several bottles of pills. She never challenged her religious beliefs and in the end they brought her no solace. In the last couple of years of her life we talked a great deal about spirituality but I am not sure if this helped or confused her. I would talk about my 'new agey' beliefs and she would listen to me with open mouthed amazement until, putting her hand across her forehead in a sixth chakra closure sign, I knew to shut-up. Sadly I did not, at that time, have enough knowledge about nutrition to tackle her problems on a physical basis and I sometimes wonder if I had given her big doses of minerals and vitamins and sorted her bowels out, whether she would have had a longer life. Would the physical easing of her symptoms have enabled her to have the strength to tackle the spiritual? I don't really have an answer but I know when my illness gets the better of me, all spiritual matters take a back seat, unless you call sleeping a spiritual practice .... perhaps it is. I think most of us are asleep most of the time, sleepwalking through the illusion that we call life. I know that making a major spiritual breakthrough can erase illness at a stroke but this is a tall order of Himalayan proportions. I am having a hell of a climb [and I don't like heights].

Your seventh chakra connection is intensely personal and needs some reflective time. I think spirituality and/or religion needs to be fairly quiet. I am immensely bothered when it is too noisy because, as I have already said, I believe God talks in whispers. If there is too much activity and noise you cannot hear any message being sent. Even if you 'get' the message, you will need some silence to relate its content to your life and where you are going. An activated seventh chakra is having a connection to a spiritual pathway that is one's own. It matters not whether it be within one of the major religions. It could be having a lust for life, or sun worship, or animal worship, or something else entirely. Whatever it is it must bring a degree of serenity and reverence. I am a bit of a sun worshiper myself and incy-wincy ants, capable of such extraordinary feats, have my utmost respect.

What I love about my spiritual path and my connection to what I perceive as the divine is the excitement and the one-to-one privacy. When I stopped piddling about and being silly, got on my path, shut-up, paid attention and concentrated, I started a two-way conversation which was rarely verbal [makes sense because I am highly visual - read on for 'eye-positioning']. I now get lots of messages of all descriptions. Burning bushes don't feature much [this is a joke] but animals do. I don't want to reveal too much because this is between my angel/guides and me but I will tell you about one instance. Magpies have always featured heavily in my life; one for sorrow, two for joy etc. The only time [to date] I have been done for speeding was when I was making a journey of about fifteen miles. I was in a *needless* hurry to get somewhere. During the course of that journey, on three separate occasions, three single magpies flew so close and so low across my path that I had to brake to miss them. The message was clear - slow down. I ignored it and got a fine and three penalties. I am much, much more attentive now. In consequence, the messages are subtler requiring more concentration. My level of commitment is being tested. That is what I love about it - the path is individually tailored to fit each and every one of us [it is often animals for me, but it might be cars, clouds or conversations for you]. The journey is exquisitely personal, highly addictive and quiet. You have to pay attention. It is up to me how far forward I want to go, or if I want to stay where I am and continue drinking scotch and being rude about politicians. It's a tough call. I *like* being rude about politicians and I especially like scotch, but often what I like is not actually very good for me.

I understand reverence. Even in my darkest hours [and I have had a few] I have been uplifted by the sight of a cloud, tree, flower or wagging dog tail. All four spelt God to me. It is only in the last few years that I have begun to understand the deeper significance of the natural world around us. Our land, our seas and our animal life are SACRED. This is a seventh chakra understanding.

Seventh chakra protection is hands on the crown of the head, a gesture sometimes seen at times of total disbelief [interesting word]. Often seen on the football pitch when the opposition [dare I say opposition tribe?] has just scored a vital goal. Not to be confused with cupping the back of the head which is reproducing the maternal cupping of the baby's head and is therefore a comforting gesture. I am often puzzled by the wearing of hats and the fact that they are rarely worn these days. It is interesting to note that many religious orders have some form of headwear [often vertical, which amuses me no end], that monks used to shave the tops of their heads and that so many men are losing their hair these days.

Seventh chakra illnesses can affect the whole body, the nervous system, the body's structure [bones] and its ability to move.

EIGHTH, NINTH AND TENTH CHAKRA, AND SO ON

Apparently there are another seven chakras over and above the crown. I don't know anything about them but, interestingly, I was chatting to a most excellent repair man the other day who was standing against a whitish wall and for a fraction of a second I saw something that looked egg shaped, vaguely silvery and shimmery above his head. I pondered on this sighting afterwards and I wondered if, having fully activated your seven body chakras, you then pootle off somewhere else to fully activate the next seven. Where would you go and what would you look like? Would you be a silver and shimmery martian? Haven't a clue.

I will talk briefly about the eighth chakra because it is helpful if you are having a really difficult problem with one person in particular because you can have an eighth chakra conversation with them. Yup, away with the fairies again ...... let me explain. What you do is this - think about the problem and formulate a short succinct conversation [no swearing or shouting please] with the person who is driving you to distraction in the forefront of your mind. Having done that, go somewhere private and quiet and project your short succinct conversation upwards into your eighth chakra which sits, egg shaped, a couple or so inches above your head, then silently project that conversation from your eighth egg shaped chakra to the other person's eighth egg shaped chakra. The object of your disdain can be as far away as Australia [you probably wish they were] for this to work, they do not have to be in the vicinity, but equally they can be in the same room. This is quite difficult to perfect because we tend to think of thinking as being behind the forehead but it is no good projecting from your forehead to their forehead, if you get my drift, no, you must project up to your eighth egg and over to their eighth egg.

I have been telling people about eighth chakra conversations for quite some time and I have had some very positive feed back. It even works if you need to talk to your animals but for them the conversation is best done in images, not words. This works, oh yes it does, but ... only when done for the highest possible spiritual good. Intention, intention, intention. Do not try Mafia tactics here, dear reader. Think BIG angels chucking down very BIG banana skins .... best not.

COLOUR

If I gave you a bright canary yellow jumper could you wear it? Why not? What about tomato red? Purple? To my gentlemen readers, what about a baby pink jumper? Noooo? It is just a colour, is it not? Well, I will tell you why your toes may or may not curl at the thought of wearing a bright cerise pink polo-neck. It's wacky stuff, so fetch a stiff drink and brace yourself ...... it's because the colour does not resonate with your current spiritual vibratory rate. Retrieve rolling eyes from the ceiling please, shucks ..... anybody would think you can't take me seriously.

Before we get cracking on colour - fabulous subject - I want to explain, briefly, 'vibration' and 'vibratory rate' because it crops up here and there in the book and you may be wondering what I am on about. All living things vibrate, cells vibrate, colour vibrates. I believe we vibrate at a specific level. When we meet someone and we instinctively don't like them I think we are unconsciously picking up their vibratory rate [possibly emanating through their aura]. When we make a spiritual shift forward, no matter how tiny, we make a small upward adjustment to our vibratory rate. A medium to big spiritual shift will go hand-in-hand, for most, with a change of clothing colour and often, at this time, relationships get rocky because one person may be vibrating at a different level to another. I'll talk about this more later in the book.

I have had a love affair with colour for as long as I can remember but for years it was, for me, 'look and admire but don't touch'. I thought it was just as basic as liking or not liking a colour or thinking the shade did not suit me. When I had learned about the chakras and their related colours, pennies dropped, but the chakras are only seven [eight if you count the heart chakra as two - green and pink] basic colours and do not cover colours like black, brown, beige and a whole host of shades of colours. I wanted to know what all the different colours meant. The only way for me to learn was to watch people in earnest and learn to listen with precision to all conversations, no matter how fleeting or light hearted. Gradually I started to build up a picture and I was completely fascinated with the results. I am still learning, but it is easier now because as a therapist I can ask people *extremely* personal questions - I could not ask strangers these sort of questions without them feeling the need to urgently summon the police. My observations have revealed to me that our choice of colour represents our emotional state and that we are walking around parading our innermost depths for all to see.

I have found that the *repetitive* wearing of one particular colour, any colour, represents an emotional holding pattern and sometimes a specific combination of colours mean specific health problems could be looming. Colour sends out distinct messages whether we receive them consciously or unconsciously; if you think this is a load of old baloney then just watch the politicians who are using colour all the time now - watch the ties. I believe that colour worn is a direct link with chakra blocks or possibly chakra [sticking my neck out now] maturity and there is, of course, a whole world of difference between wearing a colour because it resonates with your internal landscape and using colour for the gain of external power; bit dangerous that is, angels and banana skins and all that. You can use colour to heal and to protect and give strength but for a politician to slap on a pink tie, making out he is cute and coming from fourth chakra whereas, in reality, he is barely out of first and flexing unpleasantly in second, is downright naughtiness in my book. Their names have been noted. I am watching them and waiting, not to mention hoping.

You see we arrive on planet earth and are immediately put into a uniform, the uniform of the tribe you were born into. Now I am going to talk about my tribe because it is the only tribe I can talk about with knowledge of insider dealings. First a white nappy was slapped on me, a cute but ludicrous idea, especially as my mother did not have a washing machine. Then a variety of cream, white, washed out pinks and yellows arrived. Pink for a girl because girls, according to our tribal rules, need to have their heart chakra opened up and fully activated so they can love and nurture; light blue for boys so they can open up their throat chakra and have a bash at that inordinately difficult boy task of 'saying how they feel' [and, even worse, being honest about it]. Now these washed out colours are cultural and although cultural rules really started being shaken up in the late 1950's onward they still apply to most areas of this country. I went to Kenya in

1981 and was amazed at very small babies in searing fuschia pink, lime green and royal blue. They looked wonderful and had me wondering why we didn't do the same thing back home. Some ten or more years later I saw an advertisement for baby rompers in outrageous colours - aubergine, purple, indigo.'Fabulous!', I whooped, nearly spilling my tea. 'That'll liven things up', but it didn't seem to catch on outside of Chelsea and other trendy areas. This is because it is outside tribal rules and Mum has to feel very confident indeed before she can slap a brown nappy on baby bunnikins and top it off with a burgundy romper suit and a purple and tangerine bobble hat because this combination is unlikely to be received with universal nods and smiles of approval. It is more likely to be met with polite smiles but also furrowed brows [sixth chakra] because tribal rules are being broken and baby bunnikins isn't supposed have high blood pressure or to be tackling second and seventh chakra yet and this will make onlookers nervous. What am I blathering on about? Keep reading, it gets clearer.

Later as kiddywinkles grows up more daring colours will be offered and then come the clashes of clothing being refused by an outraged toddler or beyond, probably because the child instinctively knows what colours it needs for growth or possibly for protection. Mummy may think yellow with white daisies is cute and quite the thing but her foot stomping and red-faced two year old damn well knows *it needs to be blue with orange bunnies*! I recently tried my best to enjoy an outdoor restaurant meal while a small and desperate toddler at an adjacent table ran amok, struggling, thumping and screaming its head off. We finally got some peace when he was given a small plastic bike, whereupon the toddler set off with a beaming smile, pedalling at speed. It may have been a one-off tantrum event but he looked like a seasoned hand to me. He was wearing a black and white thick striped top with matching socks and black trousers. This is not a style or colour combination I would have put on a little boy given to tantrums and who so obviously relished his speedy freedom. I will cover black and white in a minute and stripes in 'clothing'.

During the teenage years, but maybe sooner, the desire for growth activated by colour is rejected or embraced. Nowadays I look despairingly at all the youngsters in black, it is a worry and it needs to be addressed. In 1968 as a fourteen year old I asked my fairly conservative parents for a bright purple and tangerine orange bedroom. My parents thought this was hilarious and did their best to comply but we were all oblivious to the real meaning of the request. I can see now I needed the purple to deal with religious questioning that I was struggling with at the time. The orange was to help me deal with the complexities of second chakra which were even more of a headache to me. Next time your child asks you for some particular colour, please pay attention, it probably will have more significance than you think. Watch out particularly for the request for brown as it is an instinctive recognition of a need for grounding.

I have noticed something interesting about groups of people meeting up on a regular basis [please note regular]. A newly formed group will grab a seat and position themselves according to how vulnerable they feel, the most vulnerable invariably choosing to sit as far to the back of a room as possible, or near the exit door. As the group starts to feel comfortable the seating pattern will alter. People will tend to gravitate toward others wearing the same sort of colours [orange to orange, or bright orange next to peach, or brown next to peach, or pink next to brown - blue to another type of blue, or blue to lilac]. When seat positioning suddenly changes it means people want to sit next to others who are working through similar chakra related issues [don't be fooled if they 'appear' as different as chalk and cheese - chakra lessons come to us all]. It is extremely unlikely that someone wearing predominantly beige would choose to sit next to someone in bright orange or bright red, but they might gravitate to someone in pale peach, white, brown or possibly dark blue. Similarly someone in bright red might not choose to sit next to someone covered in dark navy [because the two different colours convey different and somewhat opposite messages]. If you are teaching a group, or trying to get a point across, allow people to sit where they want or you might find two people in opposing colours are so uncomfortable [but don't know why] that they cannot concentrate on the meeting or lesson. The same would go for dinner parties.

Before I ramble on any further I will list the various colours and their meaning, in my opinion. I have covered the basic colours but not all. If I have left a colour out and you are wondering what it represents, just look at the colours that make up that colour. You have only got to try and choose a colour to paint your house to see the dizzying array of different colours, not to mention shades of colours. If I am staring at one particular shade and cannot make it out I will separate the component colours and work out the emotions from each of them. If I am doing this while talking to someone I can get more information from body language, clothing, jewellery and from listening carefully. All colours have their place but like everything else in life we need balance. An excess of one colour over another usually means things are emotionally out of kilter. I am particularly fascinated with someone making a personal statement that said one thing and wearing colours that said quite the opposite [as I saw in a female politician in the photographic leader of the Sunday newspaper today, in response to which I did a lot of cynical tut tutting]. As I have already mentioned, I can see colours around people sometimes, though I cannot see full blown auras. In my experience people who are in touch with their feelings are usually wearing, either roughly or exactly, the colours that predominate in their aura at that particular time [colours in an aura change]. Therefore, people who are not fully in touch with their feelings will not wear the colours that feature in their aura. If this lack of contact has resulted in ill health PLEASE change your clothing colours quickly. To find which colour or colours you need to wear, just look around at anything colourful you have bought [or decorated] recently. If you like the colour but could not wear it that is generally the colour you need to put on. Also [but be careful and go slowly on this one] any colour you absolutely hate is generally indicating a major chakra block. If it is not one of the specific chakra colours, break it down to its component parts and see which chakra it relates to most. Tackle the colour slowly and you will start to make an energetic breakthrough.

One more point and this is IMPORTANT. There is absolutely NOTHING WRONG WITH ANY COLOUR, or colour combination, as long as you are physically well and emotionally happy. However, if things in your life are not sunny all round a quick peek in your wardrobe will reveal much and the information I give you on colour will give you an easy tool for changing things ... hopefully. Anyway, read on and feel free to take it on board or dismiss utterly, as you wish.

BLACK

Or, B lack, to get you to look at it another way. I am covering this colour first because it is the one that worries me the most. Black is an enormously protective colour and not for nothing does this country have a tradition of wearing black for mourning and funerals. The wishes of the dead at their funerals should be respected but there has been a call lately for bright colours to be worn. I think this is a lovely idea of celebrating a life lived, but I would like to point out that many people will instinctively reach for black because it is protective and therefore gives comfort in a grief stricken time. I find many funerals intensely moving and the thought of having to attend a funeral of someone I held dear, wearing bright colours, would fill me with absolute dread, because I am comforted by black at sad times. I cannot see chakras, I would dearly like to, I can only surmise that they either close down during times of intense grief or open up excessively and bleed energy. The crown chakra is particularly vulnerable in times of grief, therefore wearing a black hat at a funeral would give much protection to that area. There was a long period between my mother's death and the funeral, as the cause of death was being determined. I reached for black clothes instinctively the day after her death, up to and beyond the funeral, not for some want of observing some Victorian styled mourning but simply because I could not cope with wearing any other colour. I was physically repelled by bright colours, though my wardrobe was full of them. For the last ten to twelve years I have found it extremely difficult to wear black at all, though last year I did find an absolute corker of a black cashmere coat in a charity shop and I must say I look *pretty smooth* in it. I have a feeling it is going to be just what I need for a while.

As a therapist I always ask what colours people prefer to wear. If black is the predominant colour I am going to be highly attentive because to me it says I am in the presence of someone who has a major issue of buried grief and has yet to identify or deal with it, so I am going to be very careful what I say. When I ask why black is a favourite I usually get the response that it is a slimming colour, but excess weight can be put on [extra protection] to cope with grief, or just to cope with life, full stop, and black is slimming but so is navy and you can look pretty slender in chocolate brown or very dark green.

Now, I want to talk about grief so please pay special attention to the next few sentences because we are on VERY delicate territory. Grief comes in many forms and is extremely personal. It does not have to be forever linked with a human death, it could be a much loved pet animal, but it could be the absence of someone, or something. It could even come about with being unable to fully connect with someone who was actually physically present, maybe in the shape of a preoccupied father or distracted mother and a child unable to get any, or enough [for them] completely undivided attention. It may be a mother wanting but failing to connect to a child and grieving for the lack of that connection. It might be a husband grieving because he is failing to be heard by a wife. It might run from sibling to sibling or friend to friend. It might be a feeling of loss from love unfulfilled from childhood, or a need [maybe a dream] unfulfilled for any number of reasons, something to do with work but also, possibly, a creative need.

I don't want to sound as if I am making a big issue over black. Though I despair at the vast amount of teenagers I see who are smothered in either black or dark grey, I am fully aware that this can represent a protective blanket while they are going through the usual adolescent growing pains whilst facing the very unusual future of our modern times. For it to be seen in such large numbers, like a cloud, I do think it represents a mass thought form but I cut a lot of slack seeing as we are going through such a massive chakra and spiritual shift. Recently I chatted to a shy teenager who was drenched from head to foot in a curtain of black, nose visible but not much else. After gentle questioning, I gathered that he was not quite sure why he was dressed thus. I knew it was only a phase for him because I could see right through his protective curtain. Behind the screen was an adorable sweetypie whom I rather suspected was going to be a giant hit with the girls. For phases, then, black is your man, but if black or dark grey is being worn continuously and the wearer's face looks pale, unwell, or sad, I am going to be concerned. You absolutely can wear black as an emotional barrier to the outside world while simultaneously having a happy internal life, but I see this rarely. You will need to read the section on 'health' where I have written about what colours to look for in a face, but usually I see pale faces if black is worn a lot and this makes sense if there is an element of grief. Think of the grief link to the heart [and therefore circulation/oxygen] and the absence of pink in the face. If there is a darkish hue around the eyes and repetitive wearing of black I would be more worried. My partner always looks for specific colours in faces and notes an overall [we still argue about under the eyes - more later] blackish or blue/black hue will mean the energy of the spleen and stomach meridians are out of kilter, the voice may be groany and there is often a craving for salt [which may mean tired adrenals]. I find the stomach connection interesting because I think that great 'attached' love is sort of gustatory and linked with the stomach. We say in spirited moments of passion, 'I love you so much I could eat you', and the heart is also very close to the stomach, sitting just above it.

I worry about black because we energetically feed off one another and I am not sure black is helpful. We are surrounded by an aura which is hopefully colour filled and bright and we exchange energy at this level when we interact with other people. I have watched a positive exchange only once but was open mouthed to see two people talk face-to-face and an misty energy exchange take place at the level of their lower chest and abdomen. I could see that this was a mutually beneficial exchange from the happy expressions of the two participants but most of us will have the experience of seeing someone we know approaching and inwardly groaning because we know when the conversation is over we will feel drained [snappy socket lid required]. If you wear black all the time you may be unable to enter into fruitful exchange on an energetic level. This may isolate you and can lead to depression and physical illness. I am not saying it always does. If you take a look at people who wear black a lot, they don't just lose colour in their face. Black drains you in two ways. At a very basic level the tone pulls colour from your face [my mother always used to say to me, 'You can wear black, darling, but you must wear colourful make-up with it'], but it also drains you energetically and this can have a knock on effect on your health. It is interesting to note how many women who wear black favour bright red lipstick. I have more to say on red and black later.

Please be careful when dealing with someone wearing black all the time. I have learnt from experience to walk on eggshells because a suggestion to wear a different colour has been met, more than once, with anger. It is a hugely protective colour so its wearer will only remove it when they are good and ready. If you are the wearer and feel it is time to move forward try easing yourself gently into other colours. Move into grey first, if the thought of any other colour makes you shrink. Then try moving from grey to dark navy blue [also protective but navy is much more open than black] and slowly incorporate other colours. I would recommend pastel shades at first. Try a pale pink, apricot, or very pale green shirt or t-shirt under the black first perhaps, before you venture into the blue shades, this will help the heart chakra mend. When you are ready put gentle colour around the rooms you use a lot by changing the colour of your towels, curtains and bed covers. Try putting some flowers on a table you regularly sit at, fresh flowers if you can afford it. A large picture on the wall opposite your bed will be the first thing you focus on in the morning, but look for one with a quiet, restful theme and gentle colours. Try putting a blue [the colour of the old medicine bottles] glass object in a window that is in your direct line of vision on a regular basis, this will help you to activate sixth chakra vision. Not for nothing do people wear coloured glasses but they do worry me a bit because I would not recommend a continual visual saturation of one particular colour. If you are having specific medical or emotional problems I would suggest you re-think the coloured specs. I am not talking dark glasses, by the way, but coloured prescription glasses, though dark glasses speak a language all of their own. Ponder on it for a bit, if you will, for very dark glasses are a barrier to the world from inside out and from outside in.

If you are a distraught parent with an unhappy black-clad teenager and talking is getting you nowhere, you can try subtly introducing colour into the house, presuming, of course, the teenager has not got hold of this book before you have and knows exactly what you are about. Read the section on orange, look carefully at the colours you, as parents, are wearing or using. Watch out for a tendency to buy objects of one colour while not using that specific colour for clothing as this can represent an emotion you want to deal with but are not quite ready to fully tackle as yet. Be particularly attentive if you wear a lot of stripes or checks [more later].

Don't get me wrong, there is nothing wrong with the colour black. It has its place and looks wonderful at times. I am interested in the concept of the 'little black dress'. I have one myself, except it is a 'little large black dress'. Black is associated with sexy and that is exactly right. I can say, 'Black suspenders', and my partner can immediately disassociate his brain from the football match he is consumed by and turn in my direction. I don't try this often because it annoys him, unless of course I am wearing black suspenders and little else. At my age I need more than a dash of alcohol to pull this off convincingly, in fact I damn near need an anaesthetic. A little black dress fascinates me because black is protective and yet the dress is often scanty these days so a mixed message is being sent out, one of 'come on, but back off'. Interesting. Pay attention boys and read the signals.

As a therapist the continuous use of black would alert me to the heart, the blood and circulation, the adrenals, thyroid and the brain. The brain would encompass the physiological brain but also the thought processes. Depending on what information I was getting I might also focus attention on the intestines, particularly the transverse colon [there is a link with depression and I think 'transverse' is so interesting, linking the right side to the left side of the body]. For a woman I might recommend regular breast check ups. For either sex, drenched in black, I would proceed with extreme caution, listen intently and be mighty attentive to body language. I would be alert to any kind of depressive tendencies, would wonder about a lack of nurturing and try to assess 'emotional' age which I have covered already. If there was a serious health problem and the sufferer could not ditch the black in favour of other colours, I would think along the lines of someone unable, or even refusing, to look at issues of grief in their life [especially if their 'smile was too bright']. I am going to take a deep breath and say....... in my experience, only the very spiritually mature can wear black continuously. Having said that, it would be nice to see vicars and priests given a choice of cassock colour. I don't think wearing black all the time is helpful for them and then, of course, there is that white dog collar. So interesting.

GREY

Black but less so. It is not as protective as black or as blocking but I would still be concerned at the level of resistance it affords. It might be a bit clichéd to say grey indicates a lack of colour in one's life but that is what it would say to me and it would also say there may be a lack of 'involvement', possibly a degree of aloofness. There is still an element of bereavement and so it would give me the same concerns, only not so accented as black. I would concentrate on the same physical aspects as I would with black but I would also wonder about the heart and lungs, prostate gland in men and ovaries and uterus in a woman. I would not be worried if there was a lot of pure white worn with the grey and the grey was a pale silvery colour. This would indicate to me spiritual thought processes were in place, in fact I would find this distinctly cheering as long as there was not too much of it being worn and a person did not appear to be too 'head in the clouds' with an obvious need for grounding. Anyone living in grey would do well to make a slight shift into a light blue/grey colour and then start introducing pale pastel versions of the lower chakra colours slowly into their life.

WHITE

Apparently white contains all the colours. I have had a jolly good look and I can't see them. I love white and find it an interesting colour to wear because of the way people interact with me [depending on how I present the white]. My personal experience has been that it has authority and also in some way defines boundaries, therefore giving a degree of protection. I wondered if this is why it was the colour chosen for doctor's coats, because it is a perfectly daft colour to choose otherwise. The protection aspect is particularly fascinating to me as I watch the current crop of 'how to' television programmes. In the 'how to raise your children' genre I watch a mother trying to control her unruly children and wonder why she would chose to wear white - possibly as a barrier to the screaming kids. I am usually bellowing at the television, 'Put some navy blue on, woman'. She can't hear me, poor thing.

I pay attention to people wearing white only, all the time [though I do not count someone in white as a uniform or someone dealing continuously with the public]. White alone is a colour representing purity of thought but wearing a lot of it might be expressing a need to create a barrier, or to stand back and reassess life. It might be someone going through a period of celibacy or requiring privacy in their lives, or both. While making allowances for hot sunny days, when white looks quite the thing, I would like to point out that when white is worn a great deal to my way of thinking it can indicate that some spiritual work is being done, no matter how small. Therapists and gurus who waft about in all white garments put me on high alert and I listen very attentively to make sure they are what they are saying they are. I am usually disappointed, but not always.

I am still struggling with white when worn with black [all the time]. The black will still represent an element of grief and if worn on the lower half of the body I would align it with the lower chakras, upper body with the upper chakras. I am not talking about uniforms here, but black and white worn as casual 'off duty colours'. Usually I see a choice of white top and black trousers and, to be honest, I am still trying to work this one out. I think there is a spiritual link to the upper white and a grief link to the black but I am a bit stymied by the polarity of it. Maybe it is just that - polarity. I suspect it is a very strong 'holding pattern' colour combination. I've a mind to think along the lines of needing to be contained or restrained. Of course, traditionally, waiters wear black and white. Repeat … waiters.

I am amused by the celebrity ladies who choose white outfits, with the serried ranks of cameras in mind, immediately after their celebrity husband/partner/boyfriend has wandered. It would not be my choice of colour. It is an interesting statement, but do I detect a little hint of an agenda?

RED

First chakra, in case you had forgotten. Pillar box or tomato red is a great enervator but it also infuriates, red rag to a bull and all that. It represents sex and sexuality and probably does not have the 'little black dress' message of 'come on, but back off'. No mixed messages here, just 'come on'. A love of the colour red does not necessarily mean it has only a sexual basis, it can represent an appetite for life.

A fear or dislike of a particular colour is saying a lot about your emotional state and this will affect your physical state somewhere down the line. It is healthy to be able to incorporate every colour into your wardrobe and this includes red. To have an intense dislike of red or to be unable to wear it at all might point to a first chakra block, a sexual block, or possibly a fear of connecting fully to womanhood or manhood. I think it can indicate a failure to connect to our warrior spirit [whether male or female] and often a leaning towards being or trying to be 'a nice reasonable person'. If this applies to you please try and tackle your dislike of red because I have observed that the universe will bring a lesson that will be linked with a specific colour and these lessons are invariably unpleasant, so you want to try and pre-empt them by changing your vibration yourself. The section on turquoise may also be helpful. If you cannot bear the idea of wearing red buy a small red hand towel or cushion first, then progress to something like slippers, a beanie hat, a scarf or gloves. You can do it in stages by going for a soft red, or terracotta colour first and move towards a clean pillar box red, but at a pace you can manage. Avoid darker reds while you are going through this phase [read burgundy].

An overload of red clothing would concern me because any excessive colour choice indicates a lack of balance and balance is required in order to cope reasonably well with life's major ups and downs. Because it is the colour of first chakra, if red is used to excess it might indicate some hidden anger at the 'tribe' or, more interestingly, unconscious anger at the opposite sex. I would offer that if red is in excess in your wardrobe it may need to be tempered with blue, some dark navy, some royal blue and/or indigo and a good sprinkling of turquoise. Remember the saying 'I saw red' which indicates the head area. Please take this on board because you DO NOT want to mess with or overload your head area, so give it a break and calm it down with some blue.

Don't put overactive or argumentative children in red or around red, it is asking for more trouble and if they are having problems at bedtime make sure they have soothing colours in the bedroom. Fire engines and sporty car motif duvet covers for little boys are fun but not restful on the eye or hyperactive mind.

The use of the colour red also includes the dyeing of hair, from pillar box red to plum. The very bright red may be saying something about the owner's libido and this is fine but as I have said - watch the head area. The plum colours are tinged with purple but also black [see 'red and black'], with all the connotations of that colour and as this colour is usually seen on women I would wonder about an unresolved problem with authority or possibly an authoritarian father. I have noticed a fashionable swing towards men putting red stripes in their hair, which is usually dark. I would take careful note of this combination.

Major life events often provoke a change of colour in clothes, cars and houses. Red is often used in response to being angry, so watch out for a new red front door. It is not so much the red car that is in more accidents than any other colour but rather the state of mind of the owner of the red car. Red nail polish can look stunning but I am wary if it is worn a lot [same goes for red toenails] and even more alert if the nails are long. Be careful what you say to someone wearing red shoes, they may look like pussycats and be smiling politely but be privately [so privately that they don't even recognise it] longing to kick someone in the proverbials and the same goes for red socks if they are worn a lot. Don't confuse the odd day or a phase of wearing red shoes or socks which means someone is using the colour with intent to assist growth, either consciously or unconsciously. Put red in the bedroom and your sex life may well soar but you may also have less than restful sleep. Watch out for a lot of red in people's houses, I would keep my mouth fairly tightly shut and listen carefully [this goes for red and black also].

If you are having problems conceiving I would definitely recommend wearing red especially over the lower abdomen. A pair of large red knickers will stimulate the reproductive centre [it's probably best to put something on over the knicks, but each to his own]. Add a turquoise scarf because there is a strong link between ovaries and throat [fifth] chakra. On a daily basis get a dose of rich blue [back to the old medicine bottle on a windowsill] because this is the sixth chakra colour. Doing this will widen your perspective and may bring a helpful insight but sixth chakra is also the domain of the master endocrine gland, the pituitary, which governs all things hormonal.

RED AND BLACK

This is a combination that worries me because it speaks of unresolved grief and anger. I do not see red on its own as angry, necessarily, but I definitely do when it is worn with black. I have looked at this colour combination from every angle and talked to a lot of women who favour it. My observations are, time and time again, that this is worn in conjunction with anger and grief and these emotions are strongly linked to the father, or father figure, and may also encompass grief led anger towards male authority and/or a male dominated religion. Over the years I have had far more opportunity to talk to women than men and I have found that this combination is most often directed at an absent, authoritative or bullying father. If this is an unresolved issue they may well have attracted a mate who displays the same characteristics. Now, if this is being read by a father whose daughter is wearing black and red, please lay down your arms, I point no fingers. A daughter may perceive authority or inattentiveness where there has been discipline and a heavy workload. My major concern would be for her health. I link red and black to ovaries, in particular, but also the area across the lower abdomen. Because that area can silently brew major health problems please be attentive when you see red and black worn or used a great deal. If there was a history of infertility my advice would be to get out of these colours quickly because I think they act in accordance with unconscious emotions as an ovary function suppressant [an interesting response ... suppressing the egg, the line]. I would look at the lower bowel, uterus, bladder, lower abdomen generally [particularly the right side], liver, breasts, the neck and throat area. If this is ringing a bell with you please look at the further reading section at the back of the book, particularly the most excellent Dr. Caroline Myss.

I am highly alert to this colour combination but I am definitely not pointing a finger at it. It looks stunning and can pack a punch. I have a beautiful evening outfit in red and black that I bought in Vietnam and I love it. Wear these two colours, by all means, but try and become aware of the level of emotional influence our choice of colour says about us.

BURGUNDY

A colour favoured by men, but we are still in red and black territory here, only the colours are combined and tinged with maybe a smidgen of blue. You don't often, these days [different political landscape], see men in separate red and black, but sometimes black or charcoal grey suits are chosen with red or burgundy [or oxblood] ties. Out of work, a burgundy jumper or sweatshirt might be worn. If this is a favourite colour I would be mindful of an anger issue, possibly stemming from a parental [or any first chakra] issue, but now directed at a social condition, at a religion or a fury [silent or otherwise] at authority. It might say to me that this person was angry but unable to pull away from his/her tribe or tribal [first chakra] thinking in whatever context that may be, or it might indicate that the wearer was angry with themselves, maybe for mistakes made or opportunities lost. I would look at the same physical aspects as I would for the colour black but I would focus also on the prostate gland, liver and bowel. I would then take a good look at the facial colouring and be alert to heart problems, circulation, raised blood pressure and generally anything to do with the blood [such an interesting connection if you think of the colour of blood and the way we associate being of our parent's or tribe's blood]. If this is rings a bell with you please avoid this colour and go for light to mid-blue, but not navy. If you are feeling brave you could wear a turquoise scarf to open up your fifth chakra [throat]. This would be most beneficial for you but maybe not those closest to you. Try it and see what happens. If you start barking and swearing at your nearest and dearest, wear the turquoise in the garden or sulking shed only, but don't frighten the dog and steer clear of saws and sharp implements. Have stock of band-aid handy and some chamomile tea, it's calming, but I can see your point …. the watering-can is an ace place to hide the scotch.

There is a story about me wearing a turquoise scarf later.

BLACK AND PINK

It comes from the same place as red and black but the whole emotional impact is watered down and lessened, but still, please pay attention to the combination. Pale pink is from the heart chakra, it is kindly, warm and affectionate and healing. Bright pink [fuschia or cerise] is fun loving and outgoing and therefore is also healing. There is still the element of grief with the black and I would look on it as either that there was not so much anger in the first place or some emotional heart work has been done and the result has been the softening from red to pink indicating some level of acceptance had been found. I would still be careful about my approach to someone in this colour combination and wary of the black.

PINK AND GREY

Same combination but watered down even further. I think it needs the same attention as pink and black but with much less urgency. I would ask if red and black were a favoured combination before pink and grey were worn as this would indicate a degree of resolution was being reached. Were you paying attention in 'attention' to Susan's clothes? Of course you were …. sorry.

ORANGE

Second chakra, in case you had forgotten. Orange is a warm, gregarious and a 'talk to me' colour. In the sixties and seventies orange was invariably chosen as the colour of chairs in conference centres, doctor's surgeries or meeting halls. We have come over all designer since then and a year or so back I was sitting in the waiting area of a large well known financial establishment where I noted, with a frown, that my chair was a combination of dark purple and royal blue. I wondered if this choice was intended to make me feel secure. I thought it was an interesting combination but absolutely not one I would have chosen for anything to do with money, especially in this day and age. As I scanned round the premises my frowning continued because within a sea of vertiginous high-heeled shoes I could not find a single face over thirty years of age with whom I could discuss my finances. I found this sight a great deal less than reassuring and I do wish these financial institutions would grow up. It is high time, particularly as the financial future looks so rocky.

I am sorry to be a bore but, because we are ALL tackling second chakra lessons, I am going to go over them AGAIN, because it is seriously important. The four components of second chakra are money, one-on-one relationships, external power and sex. If you have a problem with any of these and you cannot bear the sight of orange, let alone the thought of wearing it, please look at tackling the colour before the universe presents one of its oh so perfect, but oh so unpleasant second chakra block challenges. Most of us have financial concerns. If you are not facing them or dealing with them in a sensible pro-active manner the universe will bring you an unpleasant slap in the face in some form or other. Perhaps in the form of a huge unexpected bill that you cannot, or will struggle to pay or some other ghastly financial happenstance that assures you of endless sleepless nights. This is how the universe works. I blame the angels myself, they should have to take out a mortgage on their cloud and get a loan for the harp, then we might get some empathy from them [this is a joke - I can hear a sharpening sound behind me, always a worry when my angels lose their sense of humour]. These days second chakra lessons are being speeded up and come in double or triple whammies, like a divorce [relationship] that is stripping you of your external power base and emptying your bank account of money. I am sure you can come up with more horror stories. If you are not being HONEST with YOURSELF and standing up for what you are, in all your fabulous glory, you can expect a lesson to turn up to make life unpleasantly topsy-turvy. If it is a sex issue you may get an unfaithful partner, a newly appointed work colleague that shivers your married timbers, or something else that is sexually related. If it is a platonic relationship/friendship that is not going well and not being dealt with you can expect a happening to bring things to a head. If it is power and you are a bully you may find the tables are turned suddenly on you. If you are a doormat you may change jobs and find that nice fluffy person who interviewed you turns into a raging fire-breathing dragon once you have settled into your desk. Is the dragon reflecting your inner dragon - or do you need to swiftly remove your inner doormat when the dragon is wiping his/her feet? These are the major 'rug pulled under your feet' lessons, but there are plenty more lower down the scale. I am sure you can think of one, I certainly can, I had one a few days ago …. nasty. Try not to blame the messenger, look within. I am sure I have said it already but it is an immensely tedious fact of life that we learn nothing having a nice time. It essential to recognise who is our chakra teacher even if it is in the form of a dog [oh yes - woof woof!], the man you cannot take your eyes off at the office or the shortly to be ex-wife with the fabulously expensive divorce lawyer. What I am hoping, rather arrogantly I suppose, is by the time you have finished this book you may be able to spot trouble way before things get nasty and by doing this you will be changing your vibration and moving more into third chakra. Utopia looks good to me.

Back to the colour. You want to aim for the ability to wear a really bright tangerine orange - emphasis on 'ability to wear' rather than 'the wearing of'. You don't need to wear it, but you need to be able to wear it, if that makes any sense. Do this in small incremental stages if the colour makes your skin crawl and I have met many who simply could not wear the colour at all to begin with. If you are suffering at the hands of bullies please start wearing orange out of school or work as it will help to strengthen your external power base. If it is a colour you loathe, try brown or rust first then move to peach and strengthen the orange colour slowly. Bit by bit your confidence will grow. I could not handle the colour for years, then I bought a bright orange top [a sudden 'had to have' choice] and lived in it for about eighteen months [two sets of nine - if you 'new agey' think that way]. It was some time before I realised that my attitude to the way I lived my life was profoundly changing and I was becoming slightly less rattled by the second chakra problems that life inevitably throws up. I was starting to centre and stabilise myself. I am still strengthening my second chakra, I have nothing like passed the four exams with flying colours but I have rubbed the sharp edges off the worst of the lessons and, having done so, I do not need to wear the colour orange so much. I have a much loved tangerine dress that I wear when I am feeling punchy and a vivid orange scarf that I haul out when I need a bit of a lower back boost [it is a really helpful colour for those of you with recurrent lower back pain]. Neither of these bits of clothing get an airing when I am in a reclusive mood. While I am in this territory I have noted with interest that aloof individuals will invariably shy away from orange. You can shy away from the colour but the lesson will be on the horizon so please try and tackle the colour before something happens in your life that enforces people on you in a way you might not have envisaged or wanted.

On a recent trip to Austria my partner was astounded to see so many people, from the old to the very young, wearing bright orange. I had never been to this country before and while attending a special parade I was transfixed by the range and amount of tribal costumes, which I thought were fabulous. I think the amount of orange being worn represents an awakening of second chakra, but I hope the baby is not thrown out with the bathwater and the glorious national outfits will be retained by the next generation because they are so stunningly beautiful. In this day and age of 'anything goes' [as far as clothes are concerned] stunningly beautiful is such a rarity that it always stops me in my tracks when I happen to spot it. Orange is not an easy colour to wear unless you have some second chakra power and, at the risk of repeating myself again, one of the components of second chakra is power in the material world, so not for nothing has orange been chosen as the colour representing change in the countries where the political landscape is being challenged by the people in the so called 'velvet revolutions'. There is plenty more of this on the horizon as the voting public in large numbers are finally recognising the level of manipulation and bullying going on by those *they pay* to govern them. People are taking their second chakra power back. Perhaps it's time to hit the tangerine button in the UK and give Westminster the jitters.

If your life just seems a bit stuck for some reason, either emotionally or financially and you want to move things along, change direction, job, relationships or make new friends, try wearing orange. This is particularly relevant if you are starting a new business venture and you need to kick start the money section of your second chakra. If money is an issue get stuck into orange, big time. Start with pale apricot if tangerine is too ... too. If you are a big butch boy with zero conversational skills but longing for a girlfriend, orange is your man, so to speak. If apricot is a tad too effeminate try a tangerine t-shirt under a mid or light blue sweatshirt, with maybe just a tiny bit of the orange showing at the neck to add a bit of dash. It does work, honest, it doesn't matter if your conversational skills verge on Neanderthal grunting, wear these colours, listen well [especially to women] and smile a lot - your popularity rating will go right up.

As I pointed out in 'red' the dyeing of hair to orange is making a second chakra statement as much as an item of orange clothing. In fact I think it emphasises the statement but [and this is a big but] I am alert if the hair has been dyed bright orange but the clothing is black, grey, or generally dull coloured. I would be ready for someone who could talk well but maybe not receive so fluidly. I would also be attentive if the hair has gone from dyed red to dyed orange. I would suspect a certain level of transition from first to second chakra has been made, or some degree of resolution had been reached over a first chakra problem. It would make me think intimate relationships were being examined in a new light [watch out for the wearing of some indigo blue - but not too much - because to see something in a different light means there has been some sixth chakra opening].

BROWN

The colour of the earth, with a strong link to orange and therefore second chakra. Dark chocolate to mid-brown [I will do beige separately] are colours I loved and lived in, but have not worn for several years. Years ago I was told brown was the colour of the monk and I thought a lot about that because I suspected I had monkish tendencies, but then I also had a couple of friends who wore a lot of brown and they were much more outgoing and party loving than me. In my view the wearing of a lot of brown not only represents an emotional holding pattern colour but also that extreme inner work is being carried out. I am therefore going to be alert to the possibility of someone undergoing some level of inner hibernation and of a link to relationships. I think this colour is transitional to orange [there can be a little or a lot of orange in brown] to some degree or other. I think it denotes someone who is, or can be, outgoing at times but also needs time alone. It may mean someone is going through a period of reflection, maybe a breather between relationships or reassessing existing relationships. You can start to deal with second chakra issues in this colour but because brown is the colour of the earth it is a colour choice of someone who is, or has been, full of thoughts and needs a bit of grounding or stilling. This certainly applied to me and even now, on quiet cosy evenings when we are snuggled on the sofa, my partner can ask me to 'turn my brain off' because he says he can hear it whirring. I note he is not the first person to comment on this and I have pondered on the possibility that my chakra wheels [or singular wheel - maybe sixth?] actually speeds up when I am over-thinking so that it can almost be heard - perhaps on an energetic level. For many years I favoured brown flat shoes and I am sure they were an unconscious grounding, earthing choice to combat my excessive and fast thinking. I do not wear them much these days but my thinking is much more linear, targeted and restful whereas I just used to go round and round in circles thinking, 'Why?'. I am going to stick my neck out now [because I am speaking about my personal experience] and say I think brown may have a link with unexpressed anger. I suspect brown may be one step away, or up from red and black. Brown has a link with excessive thinking, which in turn has a link with the spleen. You 'vent your spleen'. The spleen is third chakra territory, yellow, and there are some shades of brown that look as if they contain a dab of yellow. Therefore, if I saw this being worn my mind would wander to a level of retreat, aloneness, grounding and third chakra repair. I am wondering if the wearing of brown continuously earths you so much that you cannot lift your thoughts upward and outward, to explore, to heal and then to face the inevitable change. Wearing brown to retreat is great if the retreat is constructive but not so great if it is a muddy stagnation. I just don't have all the answers to colour, I wish I did. I am still learning and every few days I am taught something new by a chance encounter.

Earth colour brown is great as an antidote to a stressful job where you have to engage brain all day long. It is also a useful colour if you find people are commenting that, 'You are not being realistic', as long as they are accurate in their assumption and not talking about themselves. If I had an excessively day dreamy child I might think about a putting a brown rug, throw or carpet in their bedroom or offering brown socks or shoes. Failing that an introduction to gardening might bring an excessively wandering brain and imagination down to earth, or a 'hands on' creative outlet like splashing paint about or prodding and moulding clay. Thinking about it, the clay would be better. Someone in head-to-toe brown continuously might think to introduce some light blue, maybe with a touch of violet to combat the excess of grounding and allow thought processes to flow and also to introduce some autumnal shades in to ease the transition to orange.

Brown shades in the skin of the face say 'gut problems' to me. Read on to the 'health' section.

BEIGE

The 'I don't want to be noticed colour'. It is a fade into the background colour but also a mix of the earthing brown and spiritual white. I love it because I find it restful and I suspect that is why it is becoming increasingly common in houses everywhere as it is a fulfilling a need for peace and tranquillity from an increasingly demanding and hectic world. Beige is not demanding, it asks nothing of you. Beige and light grey used to be the colours of the elderly. In years gone by I was always amused by the sight of a coach disgorging its contents of elderly tourists, because you could bet your bottom dollar it would be a sea of beige, but not now. I was out walking the dogs a couple of years back and stopped to chat to a large group of absolutely delightful grey haired ramblers from another part of the country. I was so busy chatting that I failed to pay attention to their clothing as a group, but a little while later I saw them all progressing along a top field at a distance and was struck by how wonderfully colourful their clothes were. Not a hint of beige or grey but a fabulous caravanserai of rainbow colours.

Beige has its place and I wear it when I want a rest and when I want to be peaceful but I would not dream of wearing it for an interview or to give a talk because I would be sending out a mixed message of 'listen to me' but also 'I don't want to be noticed', thereby confusing the audience. The wearing of light brown continuously drains the colour from your face but not as dramatically as black. With a colourless face and colourless clothes you will blend into any situation unnoticed and that is just fine as long as that is what you want. It is not a helpful colour if you want to be noticed, remembered or are struggling to maintain personal boundaries, particularly when dealing with unruly children, unruly relatives or unruly work colleagues, because it is not an authoritative colour. I would just add a word of caution about the excessive use of this colour in clothes or in houses [and cars] because choosing a sea of beige can denote an inability to cope with the intense emotion that the introduction of colour may provoke. I think it can represent a 'lid' on emotions - this can be dangerous territory. Just be aware you may be on course for an unannounced angelic 'lid-lift'. Not nice; best be pro-active and get in touch with your feelings. Have a chat with your third chakra and ask yourself what you really want in life, then ask yourself about 'safety' and what the word means to you.

YELLOW

The colour of third chakra self-esteem and the solar plexus. There needs to be an element of self-esteem to tackle this colour but I am inclined to be wary of someone in a repetitive overload of any yellow, particularly bright yellow. Any overload of any colour represents imbalance. Too much yellow would alert me to keep my mouth shut, listen very carefully and be highly alert to body language, particularly if hands were coming up over the solar plexus or to cover or support the lower face. I would wonder about unacknowledged emotional damage and I would also wonder about a link between ego and very deep, possibly well hidden, fear.

It is essential that we can manage to wear this colour even if it is only something in the very palest wild primrose as we are all dealing with an element of self-dislike, even the most pompous among us [pomposity being a cover for lack of true third chakra contact]. If you really hate this colour, try and ask yourself why. Do you trust yourself and your hunches? Do you let yourself down? Do you let others down? Repeatedly letting others down damages your own third chakra. Do you keep your word? Is your self-esteem jammed and wedged in second chakra materialism? Are you self-critical and, if so, where did you learn that? Who started the criticism? Was it justified or were they actually criticising themselves, but doing it the easy way by criticising you. Tackle the issues and the colour when you are ready by putting some pale yellow into your life. Towels, curtains or cushions are a good first step. A canary yellow coat might be a bit overwhelming initially, but give it a whirl if you have the energy.

If you suffer from depression try putting yellow into your house and clothes, especially if you are heavily attracted to the colour navy blue. Personally, I am wary of the combination of black and yellow [think wasps]. I would approach with caution, while wondering about a severely damaged sense of self-esteem in childhood, possibly by a domineering parent, linked with grief, but I would like to repeat that I would be thinking it but not saying it. Remember we are aiming for kindness and compassion at all times. We do not know what other people have been through in life and sometimes their stories can astound, amaze and humble us.

I try and incorporate yellow into my wardrobe on a regular basis because the solar plexus area is the bane of my life and I can and do haemorrhage energy here. I am a recovering rescuer and have been slow to get myself a snappy socket lid. As if that is not bad enough, my excessive thinking wears my third chakra energy out which has a direct knock on effect on my digestion. I know that if I could switch my brain off, cruise more, my digestion would improve no end. My problem is I like things that are bad for me and thinking is one of my most favourite things because it amuses me no end. I can be all alone staring out of the window, just thinking, and then get a massive attack of the heaving giggles. This causes passenger consternation on trains. My giggling is fine, it's all the thinking and worrying between the giggling that does the damage. As my most favourite type of thinking is with a neat scotch in hand or an enormous mug of 'thick as mud' tea, neither of which is greeted with enthusiasm by my stomach or my joints, I have to admit to being weak and pathetic at times and, as my green tea drinking and health conscious partner says, 'A right royal pain in the bottom at other times'. Let's do green.

GREEN

Heart chakra! I love green and it is a healing colour, I suppose because healing always encompasses the heart. Interesting to think of operating theatre 'greens' and certainly they were just that when I was a student but interestingly they started to change from theatre 'greens' to blue, while still being referred to as 'greens'. At the time, though I was curious, I did not understand the point of this, but now I can see that blue was needed to activate fifth and sixth chakra in readiness for the change in healing that is very slowly but inevitably coming. Green is a healthy colour to wear, off and on, but there is a specific shade of green and yellow that nature can probably get away with but to me spells deceit. It makes me wary. Interestingly, I rarely see it worn but sometimes people will paint their houses in these two shades. I am not saying the occupants are deceitful but I am alert to all possibilities when I see it.

Pale green will activate and soothe the heart energy and for someone with heart or lung problems I would advocate a mix of light green [definitely not dark green] and pale pink [come on guys, don't be shy, my very masculine partner looks great in a shell pink shirt and blue jeans]. A lot of green clothes and house furnishings might [probably would] say to me someone who prefers the status quo and will not rock the boat. If the green was excessive I would proceed with caution because the green may be chosen in excess to unconsciously mend or stabilise a heart that cannot take further rocking. If there was a lot of dark green involved I would be mighty careful and would think along the lines of chest 'armoury'. Please remember that what rocks or hurts one heart may be of no moment to another, so tread with care and remember the darker the green the more black there is. Read the 'health' section paying attention to the bit about cheeks and noses. I have noted that mid-green is often a shade chosen by ex-army personal. Army life may well rattle your fourth chakra anyway but also the status you hold in the army may disappear when in civvy street. I wonder if that is why the colour is worn.

All colours have various shades and green is no exception. There is a lovely dark bluey-green which always makes me think of the Atlantic ocean and I once painted my front door this colour. I see it as a mix between heart and sixth chakra and therefore a heart responding to a widening perspective. Lime green is obviously green and yellow with varying degrees of white and is a border [boundary] colour between the third and fourth chakra. I would suggest it is a colour representing love and boundary issues and also a heart healer for a damaged self-esteem. In that respect it is a very important colour because we all have damaged self-esteem to some degree or other and most have had our hearts broken at some time [a major spiritual lesson] and not necessarily by another person. Any shade of lime green is, therefore, a major 'repair' colour.

I would pay serious attention to the mixture of green and black in a clothing combination. I have already covered bottle green, which is favoured more by older men. Nowadays the green and black would more likely be presented as separate items of clothing worn together and would alert me to unresolved, possibly well buried, issues of heart-led grief. Be careful when you see mid to dark green clothing [upper body] with black stripes or checking - the thicker the black stripes the more alert I would be, because to me it spells 'heart' and 'trouble', the element of black bringing the message of grief and restriction [or constriction]. I am not talking camouflage [or combat] fabric, which I mention briefly later.

My mother suffered from manic depression for many years and was addicted to wearing navy blue. She thoroughly disliked green and I cannot recall her wearing it at all when I was young, but about two years before she died she bought a mid-green tweed suit, a couple of light to mid-green jumpers and wore them a lot, interspersed with a red jumper or a pale blue jumper. I was not so attuned with colour and its meaning when she bought that suit, but I do remember being in the shop with her at the time and being puzzled that she was repeatedly asking me if I thought the colour was a good idea. I encouraged her while thinking the choice of colour was highly unusual but it was much later that I realised the full significance. I also realised, much later, that I wasn't supposed to understand it at the time. Although my mother ended her life with a bottle of pills she was, in some ways, quite 'heart' led in her last couple of years and I look back at conversations we had and realise she was challenging her 'red' first chakra values with her 'green' heart chakra, albeit like a boxer ricocheting against the ropes. It was an exhausting match to referee.

PINK

Also the heart chakra, pink is soothing too but it is more lively than green. Pink is intensely feminine but it is creeping in for men and becoming more acceptable as they get in touch with their feminine side. I hope this does not mean men in pink sarongs, filing their nails. Long live the rugby playing male, I say, but that rugby player can cook a meal and change a nappy without losing his masculinity just as I can, joints permitting, change a tyre and clean out our really disgusting back drain if necessary, without losing my femininity. I may lose my rag, my fingernails, my hairstyle, my lipstick and probably my decorum but never my femininity. I have to say it, I can't stop myself, the positioning of that open drain [designed for maximum all year dirt collection] was most definitely not planned by a pink wearing architect and don't get me started on the staircase positioning in our house, I'll have a burgundy explosion.

Whereas red is all about first chakra survival and warrior spirit, pink is about compassion, love and feeling good about yourself; essential and life affirming self-love. Pale pink is soothing, soft and loving. Bright pink is cheery, non-threatening and resonates 'I want to have fun'. I love them both. I have a big bright pink fleece jumper with a very wide high neck that almost comes up to my nose and it gets hauled out nearly every homey evening in the winter because it cheers me up no end. I have a pale pink cotton raincoat, bought years ago, much loved and would be much more worn if only I could stop all the dogs I meet from hurling themselves at it with muddy paws - perhaps they are responding to the colour. There is a thought that too much pink indicates a failure to grow up. I am not sure if I agree with this. Any colour to excess indicates an imbalance but then who is genuinely balanced? I am all for balance but if we were all completely balanced I think life would be deadly dull. A lot of pink says to me a lot of heart kindness and that repair work is being done. There are days when I could wear pink from head to toe. We are not to know what has gone on in other people's lives and what they may be unconsciously trying to heal, so if you see someone in a sea of pink think twice before you make any remarks that are less than kind and remember, always, that people heal emotionally at their own speed and sometimes that is years and years of snail's pace ……. and that is just fine. How is your healing going? I can [and have] read clothing outfits and their colour with accuracy that has astounded friends and clients. It is humbling for me. The more I observe and learn the more I realise how this needs to be treated with great tenderness, it is NOT a party trick. I watched with dismay one of those clothing programmes on the television a while back, where some woman was being reprimanded for wearing pale pink because it did not suit her. 'They are completely missing the point', I said, sadly.

My rule for the colour is - pale pink for gentle healing and bright pink for fun, fun, fun. I find it difficult to find pink clothes that I like. I love pale pink [shell pink] thick sweatshirts but can rarely find one without some flaming slogan on it [you can read what I have to say about written messages on clothes later, under 'clothes']. I would recommend pink [not too bright] for a woman if you are looking for love as it is hard not to be tender when wearing it. Go for the brighter pink when love has arrived and settled down with you. I have already mentioned bright red underpants to woman with infertility [worn with turquoise on the upper half of the body] and I might also combine the colours with a pink top to support the heart chakra. For a man looking for Miss Right, but not having much luck so far, I would recommend a pale pink shirt or t-shirt worn on a daily basis until an energetic shift has been made. You will know when that day has arrived, because you will be thinking differently ...... and you never know, Miss Right might be smiling back at you over the breakfast table. I love happy endings!

I suspect pink will become much more in evidence in the future, at least I sincerely hope so. If not pink at the very least let us hope for a coast to coast carpeting of bright orange, because I do so worry about a national outbreak of green, brown and beige in the shape of combat camouflage fabric. I usually worry well ahead of everyone else, unfortunately, it is exhausting. Still, by the time the others have caught up I am usually feeling quite perky and upbeat.

TURQUOISE

The colour of the fifth [throat] chakra. My partner and I argue endlessly about this colour. He thinks turquoise is pale blue, I think he is colour blind. Turquoise blue is the colour of the sea in the shallows before it goes indigo in all the glossy magazines showing some divine little beach in the Mediterranean sea from the high vantage point of some equally divine old Italian house. My partner calls this pale blue. He is, of course, completely wrong *and* colour blind. We are talking kingfishers here. That is turquoise as far as I am concerned, but the important thing is, when you need to activate fifth chakra, that you wear whatever you call turquoise.

In my view this colour needs to be practically compulsory and, if it was, you would have far happier relationships and probably less marriage break-ups, because if everyone wore turquoise on a regular basis, and said what they really think, you would get less romantic hook ups that are no hopers……. I love dreaming of cloud cuckoo land where everything is pink and rosy. As I mentioned in 'fifth chakra' some years back I met an interesting male therapist and healer and we talked about me [always a fascinating subject] and he enlightened me about my chakra block and resultant flushing red neck that infuriated me. I still have the odd flush when I talk, but not often, but much more irritatingly I can flush when I am thinking. Yes, I flush when I am lying to myself. Big sigh. I so thoroughly dislike being admonished by someone as close to me as my own skin. I now make a point of wearing a turquoise scarf on a regular basis and my neck still glows but not nearly as often.

This is the colour for 'speaking one's truth'. It is called for when you are having problems verbally standing up for yourself. For all those of you who seethe after the event, thinking of some perfect one-liner put down that would have squashed that impertinent little toad into his/her grovelling place, turquoise is the answer [with navy - but let us not get ahead of ourselves]. This is a great colour for releasing emotion. I think the wearing of this colour has allowed me to be outspoken and honest about my personal [very personal] feelings, with interesting and helpful results. It is fascinating to ponder on the Mediterranean hot-blooded personalities because the people in those countries, and probably hot countries in general, see far more turquoise than we English. We live for most of the year in a landscape of grey skies and green and brown landscapes. I wonder if these colours account for our historically buttoned-up personas. Why do we all feel better when the sky is blue and the sun comes out? Well, yellow and blue colours are bright and cheery and the heat makes us feel better and probably the knock on effect is of muscles relaxing, but I wonder if it isn't more than just the cheery colours and the heat. In the hotter countries exotic colours are around in the vegetation and wildlife for more months of the year. With the heat come vibrant colours of clothing and then there is that fabulous turquoise sea, not to mention the blue, blue sky. Perhaps the fact that we are spending more time abroad on holidays and drinking in the blue is making us more volatile. There certainly seems to be plenty of shouting on the British television soaps and a rather tedious amount of blubbing on talent competition shows. I went to Venice for a week in 1980 and I couldn't afford to eat in restaurants so I lived on slices of pizzas bought from delicatessens, eaten while sitting on pavements. This gave me a terrific vantage point to look up and listen to the Italian women leaning out of their windows talking to each other in the way only Italian women do; gesticulating wildly and using a language I understood not one jot of, but seemed to say they were going to have their husband's guts for garters when they finally got home. I knew nothing of colour therapy then I just loved all that passion, flashing eyes, heaving bosoms and gesticulation. I tried copying one of the women but my pizza topping flew off. Disaster!

Fairly recently someone pressed my buttons and made me cross. I realised it was a buried issue that needed dealing with and I needed to be livid to clear the block, so I thought wearing red would do the trick, because I didn't think it was a fifth chakra issue. Red was worn and absolutely nothing happened. I tried my bright turquoise scarf, but also nothing. About three weeks later I popped into a large supermarket I do not usually visit and noticed they had some clothing for sale. I nearly bought a cotton jumper for my partner in what I would describe as a divine sea glass green. I was in love with the colour but the price helped too [slashed to seven quid - I do so love a bargain]. I tried it on, as you do when you are buying something for someone else of the opposite sex, but it didn't look good on me so I didn't buy it for him. 'He wouldn't have like it', I consoled myself as I drove home, while feeling strangely bereft. The very next day a small parcel came through the post and in it was a thank you present from a friend. It was a scarf exactly the sea glass green of the top I had not bought the previous day. I was thrilled and wore it straight away with a fetching white top. Then I barked at my partner. The next day, in the same outfit, I was snitty, spoiling for a fight and the day after, in my scarf but with a different top, I drove into our local town and I was so angry I was positively vibrating with temper, so much so that I was shaking the steering wheel of the car. What was I so cross about? I wondered. Then I remembered that I had forgotten the original issue of some weeks back. Aha! Did it clear the issue? I am not sure, I will have to wait until I get my buttons pressed again and see what my reaction is, but meanwhile my partner has requested I only wear the scarf when he is away from home - spoilsport. This got me wondering if you need a specific shade of a colour to release a block and I thought about this sea glass green and decided it was made up of blue, white, green [turquoise] and a hint of yellow and that maybe the issue I was trying to clear was related to speaking up for myself but that I had been repressed by heart [fourth chakra/green] and self-esteem [third chakra/yellow] and possibly spiritually [white]. Are you following me? Don't worry if you are not, it was heavily relevant and clear to me and that is all that matters.

I can see the opposite colour of clothing or an object. I have to be relaxed and breathing as I should be and then it suddenly appears as a sort of piping or edge around someone's clothing, or round a book, or vase, or something. Interestingly, I have bought a jumper in bright tomato red in the last six months and this sea glass green is the exact opposite colour. Perhaps I need to wear the two colours together to get a balance. I will try that.

I would chose to wear turquoise for interviews and examinations [no matter that they are written exams and not oral]. I think turquoise is a great colour for a school uniform, certainly pale blue and navy would be a good mix. One of our local schools has a red and black uniform, not a good choice, especially for children. Turquoise would be a great colour for counselling rooms and boardrooms and frankly, seeing as we pay for it, it should be the colour for every single room in 10 Downing Street. Imagine! *No more porkies.*

BLUE

Indigo blue is the colour of the third eye and sixth chakra. There is a hint of spiritual purple in deep indigo and I just love the colour as for me it is stabilising, peaceful and safe. There is a thought in the wacky world that although most jeans are not indigo, their blueness and their rapid spread throughout all corners of the earth opened up sixth chakra globally. I rather like this idea. Dark blue is a great transition colour from black, because it gives a lot of protection but allows energy exchange and a degree of opening up the third eye thereby promoting clear thinking.

Not for nothing is navy blue the colour most often chosen for uniforms where it denotes authority and stability and I think that is exactly right; the idea of a couple of pilots in lilac suits with yellow piping in charge of a Boeing 747 would not make me a relaxed passenger. Navy and pure white really stamps its mark, no messing with these colours and is just great as a uniform [as long as that is what it is]. If it becomes a personal uniform, worn daily, it can isolate and cool you, almost bringing aloofness. If this is exactly what you need then it is a great choice but I have seen more than one case of navy being worn to excess and it leading to an emotional break-down. It needs to be balanced with 'talk to me' orange and 'self esteem' yellow, and I would suggest introducing pastel shades of these colours in, bit by bit. I have talked to sane and sensible people who hate a colour so much they cannot even wear the pastel shade, so I then suggest a tiny piece of fabric of the problem colour tucked into underwear. Who would think colour could be such an issue?

I have given the advice to many people, who are struggling with bullying at work, that navy is the best colour to wear to give strength and protection. The choice of navy indicates wishing to have a level of control, so the constant use of the colour in clothes might indicate a control issue, but not always. Too much of the colour can inhibit freedom and can close down the sixth chakra, restricting a wider view, perhaps the ability to see things from all angles. I always note if navy is worn on the lower half of the body because I link it with the lowest two chakras, and if navy is worn on the upper half of the body I link it with the heart chakra. Either would make me pay attention and listen carefully. I would like to stress, again, if you are favouring navy most of the time it is absolutely fine if you are healthy and happy. You stick to your blue and stick two fingers up at me. If you are not healthy and happy, try introducing other colours in gently. If I was acting as a therapist and the predominant colour was navy and it was being worn to excess, I would say little, but make a mental note to watch, look and listen for anything to do with the brain and muscles, lungs and surrounding area, nerves and the digestive tract - but then virtually excessive colour makes me look at the digestive tract.

Light blue is associated with thinking. It's a good colour for students of any subject to wear, but not if you are an excessive worrier. I love it and find it incredibly restful but for someone smothered in light blue all the time a little bit of brown, for grounding, is a good idea.

VIOLET/LILAC/PURPLE

Not for nothing do little old ladies start wearing these colours in old-age [though little old men tend not to sport much lilac - perhaps they get enough of the colour from staring at their little old wife]. These colours have always been linked to spirituality and such questioning is inevitably going to come to the forefront when one's funeral is on the horizon. Purple is the crown chakra colour and violet and lilac are purple and white. I suppose you could shove mauve into this category, but as it has a hint of pink so I would think it would be heart-led questions of spirituality.

I think vicars would look great in lilac or violet, but they would have to have the option to wear black if they needed to. Purple is worn by the ecclesiastical hierarchy, presumably because they are closer to God than your common or garden vicar [must be the tall headgear that has a direct phone line]. Then of course there is royal purple about which I am mystified, although I do know the origins of it. There is a belief in the new agey world that too much purple indicates immaturity or a refusal to grow up. I don't fully agree with this, but I think there can be an inability to pull the spiritual overview of one's life purpose down through the chakras, so that the events in one's life make some sort of sense. It is just a question of balance with all the colours, too much of one particular colour usually negates the positive effect that colour brings. Too much purple could be balanced by a bit of bright red.

I would not think that a teenager favouring a purple pullover was about to do God's work but I would be alert to the fact that spiritual questioning was taking place at some level. This is as delicate a questioning as sex, so please TREAD WITH CARE if you see this colour worn on anyone, but especially the young. I think there is more depression stemming from spiritual crises these days than sexual, monetary or power crises. Many youngsters are experimenting with drugs which take them on a shortcut into realms only the spiritually advanced can handle. These spiritual insights and experiences can destabilise a youngster who is not ready for, or does not understand them, and worse, there are not enough people out there to help.

I would offer a word of warning about old ladies in lilac. Many years ago I was nursing a ward of elderly ladies and my colleague and myself collected around an elderly lady's bedside to settle her down for the night. She was such a pretty old dear, with a beautiful complexion, cornflower blue eyes, pink little cheeks and a halo of pure white curly hair. Tiny she was, a little powder puff dressed in a pink nightie and a pale lilac mohair bed jacket. I can't remember her name but I will call her Mrs. Dulcie Diddlydoo. We popped her on a commode and put her back to bed, gave her her pills [because that is what you did] and water and sorted out her teeth. My colleague who was just a tad on the efficient side and spent more time than I did in church, finished tucking her up and then leaned in dangerously close to the powder puff's nose and shouted, 'Goodnight then Dulcie, sleep tight and don't let the bedbugs bite'. 'Oh f**k off', came the clear and certain reply. My colleague shot out of the cubicle with flaming cheeks, leaving me, silently heaving and listing like a ship, behind her.

Never underestimate elderly powder puffs in lilac.

GOLD/SILVER

I don't know anything about the upper chakras [over the seventh] other than that they are a profound spiritual link. I believe they are made up of gold and silver type colours. I suspect our human range and perception of colours may be limited. I have already mentioned that I have seen something shimmering above someone's head. I don't think this means that something profoundly spiritual had taken place in its owner, but I might be wrong [he is not inordinately chatty, so I don't know him that well], but maybe I was meant to see it, or on that day I was open to seeing it. We all have these upper chakras, dormant for most it seems.

If I see people dressed in silver or gold I am probably going to read it in a very basic way. Gold would say a toned down yellow to me, but it would also say gold, literally, as in precious metal and silver would say toned down grey, as well as precious metal. I might think 'materialistic' but with extraordinary 'potential'. I would definitely suggest some indigo blue to open sixth chakra and pink to generate compassion. I don't see people dressed in silver foil or sheets of beaten gold too often, so I don't have much experience of the subject. Sorry to be so unhelpful.

CLOTHES

A fascination to me because an outfit tells me a whole story about the wearer. I have often done an analysis on a friend's or client's clothing [including accessories and jewellery] and they are always amazed at how their choice of clothing and colour represents whatever emotional state they are going through at that time. I am going to give you a rough guide on how to read clothes in a minute, but it is only a sketchy outline because it is easier for me to read clothing if I have someone standing in front of me. First, though, I want to talk about clothing in general because I have a lot to say, it's my book and I'll whinge if I want to.

Women's clothing, since the Second World War, has gone from the tailored, fitted and somewhat constricted look through to the sumptuous fifties, short sixties, messy seventies and power shouldered eighties. I am not sure what happened in the nineties, perhaps I was not paying attention, but now we have the 'anything goes' look. Invite 'anything goes' and you get a rather a mess, in my opinion, but this is obviously a necessary transition, an exploration of one's internal wardrobe, as it were. All this experimentation and 'internal wardrobing' has been a very necessary exercise, it is part of our shift of awareness from second to third chakra; challenging the expected, the norm and doing your own thing. This used to be the domain of the rebellious teenager but now we are all spiritual teenagers challenging the rules. All this exploration has been greatly assisted by silliness in the money and external power department of second chakra, the 'mine is bigger than yours and mine has better labels too' school of charm.

I have always loved the idea of smart tailored clothing but I have only been able to pull it off on special occasions. My life seems averse to high heels and crisp shirts. I remember returning from abroad to my parent's house, dressed in dust covered trousers and boots, a bulging rucksack and with camera equipment bursting out of every pocket of a voluminous and rather tired jacket. My father commented that I was dressed like a refugee and my despairing twin-set and pearled mother blamed my clothes, my boots, my dust, my rucksack, my travels, my life, my everything on my father because it was always his fault for putting ideas into my head. 'Why can't she marry a banker, live in Hampshire, wear a skirt and *stop all this nonsense?*', she wailed, to which I launched into a mild attack on how life had moved on since the film 'Brief Encounter', where one could totter decorously down a train platform on immaculately polished heels in a fitted tweed suit, with gloves and hat and have some porter huffing and puffing behind carrying your suitcases. My mother snorted with derision and added tartly, 'I could always find a porter'. And she could too, dammit! I never could perfect the helpless look that she so specialised in. Later, scrubbed and dust free I pondered on apparel and wondered if my clothes had resulted in a 'porter' [husband] free life and if a daily diet of high heels and pencil skirts would nab me a nice spouse. How I wish I knew then what I know now. The answer is, of course, categorically no.

I like plain clothes and I can scrub up quite well for occasions but mostly I aim for clothes that support my lifestyle, which always seems to involve mud, either wet or dry. My daily routine of cheap trousers, long in the winter and short in the summer, and some sort of top, both of which are usually decorated with something from the countryside by the time I have fed the hens, spilt my breakfast and muddy dog walked. I love the idea of dog walking in a fetching hat and tailored tweed suit but my outward bound stomach always threatens to ruin the line. I hate tights and stockings with an absolute passion and bramble infested styles are damn difficult to negotiate in pencil skirts. Still, I take comfort from dancing. Before the war people held on to each other and moved smoothly about but a few years later they danced alone, hurling limbs about in a strange and hectic fashion. Now we have come full circle again and dancers are holding on to one another again and moving smoothly about, even if they are doing it in clothes that would make a field of sheep flinch. I daresay the same thing will happen with clothing. The 'grab-and-slap-together-whatever-looks-truly-bizarre-but-original' look has, hopefully, nearly had its day. Acres of flesh has been done to death and, with luck, soon a smart cover-up will be deemed quite the thing. What a relief.

These days I can skim through a large glossy magazine and see not one item of clothing I would want to buy, but perhaps this always comes with age and more lumpy bits. I did size zero and up to size 6 in utero and arrived looking Junoesque, as my father sweetly put it. I look absolutely ridiculous in today's fashionably wispy clothes. Having always coveted the 'two peas on a breadboard' look [small breasts] I had to accept mine were cauliflowers and as such needed support, which meant bras designed by Isambard Kingdom Brunel and such edifices look ridiculous covered in a whisper of chiffon. Nowadays, for me, buying trousers is a truly hideous and soul destroying experience. I like trousers that come to my waist because I still have one, of sorts. Where have all the hour glass figures gone? Most models seem to go straight from ribs to pelvis; it's all thin, but nothing goes in. I don't know how they manage to keep their trousers up, suspended as they are by a hope and a prayer somewhere between their navel and danger zone. I had the unfortunate experience of being behind one of these suspensions on a busy and steep escalator recently and I can tell you the wearer was not a model and well past size zero herself. So much of her ample buttock was on display, in front of my nose, that I had to remind myself to be charitable. Then there was the strange bisected central tattoo, to which I gave a moue.

I did an astounded double take the other day when a newspaper columnist admired a woman's 'chic' outfit. 'But she is wearing a 1970's curtain, bless her', I thought. I look at the women who are repeatedly in the papers and have serious money to spend on serious clothes and .. well … for the most part I am confused. Exquisitely expensive clothes and masses of primping would, I would have thought, make you feel exquisite and comfortable, but I don't seem to see it. It all looks so uneasy, so wanting, so needing. Last month I was walking behind an attractive young woman - late twenties, lovely face, neat little figure, expensive clothes. Her choice of colour was nothing out of the ordinary but I thought her ensemble was nothing short of mind boggling. Completely inconsistent layers reduced what was, I am sure, a perfect hour glass figure [with exquisite skin] to a shapeless mess; structured, tailored and beautiful one minute hotly followed by baggy, bulging and distracting the next. Why would she want to detract so markedly from what was already so lovely? The very simplest and cleanest lines would have made her drop dead gorgeous and would have stopped anyone in their tracks to stare at her, but as it was no-one was paying her any attention at all. I could not understand it. It bothered me and I have been pondering on it ever since. I wondered why I was so perturbed then I realised I had already hit upon the answer I was looking for ..... distracting. It was another representation of the world we live in today, one of consistently inconsistent distraction. I think most of the so-called high fashion of today is a sign of the distracted muddle we live in, hiding and sometimes smothering the beauty of our being. Too much distracting time wasted on our outer appearance to the expense and detriment of our inner lives. Too much 'me' and not enough 'be'. We keep being told that 'less is more' and it is, but few seem to grasp it. A beautiful young face, or a beautiful old face, needs attention not detraction. I remember standing in an art gallery staring and smiling appreciatively at a photograph of an old man in a chunky navy polo-neck. The absolute simplicity of his jumper perfectly framed and enhanced the beauty of his old, wise, merry, wrinkled face.

I think clothing says so much about our state of mind and because of that I am depressed by what I see worn on the streets of most towns and cities in Britain today. Seas of shapeless clothing. Clouds of tired and tatty greys or blacks. It all spells a national sadness to me and to a certain extent a loss of hope. A sea of casual clothes is relaxed, informal and says 'open to change' but it is the lack of shape, definition and mostly lack of colour that worries me. I also think we have thrown the baby out with the bath water with our casual clothes and I am dispirited when so little effort is made at formal functions because I think this is a more worrying sign of the times. I have been to funerals where the some of the mourners wore black fleece jackets and jeans, yet the occupant of the coffin would, I know, have worn a smart dark suit to such an occasion. I attended a wedding which was *not* a casual affair. The bridegroom was elegantly kitted out and looked dashing and the bride was a shimmering white foamy form of loveliness. Their families were tailored and the women had stunning hats but there were some guests that had made no effort at all. I thought it was sad and really rather rude because it was not their day; it was the young newly married couples' day and, most especially, it was the bride's day. She had made such an effort, her family too, and footed the bill. I mark standards by what you would do for the Queen, should you be invited to Buckingham Palace. I reckon you would don a hat and forego the everyday cardigan. So if you will do it then, why would you not do it for a family or friend's wedding? If you can't be bothered [and that is what it is saying, let's be frank] to make an effort for someone else on their most special day, I am not sure you deserve an invite. Do let's smarten up folks. Picture this .... off you go to London to see Prince William, bless his cottons, marry his sweetheart. Out he comes, from wherever, in an anorak. The Horse Guards are in jeans and old sweatshirts; the horses haven't been groomed. What would you think? A poor show, I bet, but what are you wearing to your cousin's/best friend's wedding? Let's have a bit of local pageantry, a pitch up of some style. Let us make an effort, please do, because we are sending out a very personal message about ourselves with every item of clothing we choose to put on. En masse, as a country, we are sending out a message to the rest of the world and frankly it does not look good. It looks sad. It looks sloppy. It speaks of lowered standards and this attitude is infiltrating every aspect of our lives.

It would be nice to see a return to clothes with shape because I think that would say we have gained some confidence, especially among the young, who seem to swing from one extreme to the other. Either the clothes are minimal, almost sprayed on, leaving not a pubic hair to the imagination, or they are designed to 'house' the occupant [sex indecipherable] plus pet, snacks, personal metal ware, a weapon, a supply of condoms [hopefully] and still leave enough excess fabric at wrist and heel to polish a car, if the fabric was clean enough [doubtful]. What are we saying here? Sprayed-on micro clothes I understand. I am not saying I like them but youthful hormones and all that - all quite normal. It is the walking dirty clothes basket in shades of charcoal that I find so sad. It does not say rebellion to me, it says 'lacking in confidence' and 'I don't know who I am or where I am going'. To me it very much says 'I am not beautiful'. You would have thought that with all our caring and sharing the young would feel so much more confident nowadays but that does not seem to be the case.

Boys, I am hoping you read 'skills' as well as 'future'. Life is going to get much tougher so you will need every edge over the competition, especially in the workplace. Casual clothes are perfect for casual times but professional work now [and, more importantly] in the future is NOT casual so make some effort to dress well. Please don't think your clothes do not matter because, unwittingly, you are giving away a raft of information about yourself. Consciously people are making an assessment of you by your appearance and subconsciously they will react to your choice of colour and style. I believe any assessment of suitability is made within minutes [the very first few minutes], so your first few seconds of visual impact at an interview could have a major outcome on your future. Look well put together and you spell reliability, even if you are a perfect little shit. If you do not have a clue about clothes pay attention to someone who is well dressed and copy their look. Gary Lineker has grasped good tailoring but I would avoid his schoolgirl outfit. Try and see a tailor if you can afford it. If pennies are tight go and find a kindly tailor and ask him to tell you what to look for in a well fitting off the peg suit. If you lack the confidence to do that, then check out photographs of the older male members of the royal family because they see the best tailors and their suits fit and sit perfectly. It does not matter if you don't like their clothes, focus your attention on the cut because that is what counts. A well cut suit makes you feel good and it gets you instant attention because it makes you look serious and therefore people take you seriously. Please read that sentence again and take notice. Suit collars are supposed to LIE FLAT against shirts at the back of the neck [shirt collars also should lie flat against the neck]. Some suits rise up and are so badly fitted around the neck and shoulders that you could insert a coat hanger in them while being worn. Cheap fabric looks cheap and that's that. Shiny cheap suits are a really sad sight, buy one good quality natural fibre one and take care of it. A small amount [quarter to half inch] of contrast coloured shirt cuff showing at the wrist compliments the cut off from suit to skin whatever colour your skin is, but especially if it is dark. I know everyone is favouring ditching the glimpse of shirt at the wrist but a sliver of contrast fabric makes the suit look better - end of story. Check your rear view in the mirror, the front of your suit may look crease free but the back may look as if half a dozen ferrets are dozing in your lining. You need contrast, I don't give a monkey's what the fashionistas say, and contrast means exactly that. Most men cannot get away with layering dark on dark colours, it drains their faces, and dark skinned men definitely can't. Look at traditional clothing all over the world, you will virtually always see contrast somewhere, even if it is only a tiny amount. A small amount of contrast light colour is usually worn at the neck or somewhere to break great amounts of dark colour, it just looks better that way. If you always wear a black or charcoal grey suit and a grey shirt you look fit for a mortuary not fit for life, plus you are saying you are doubly depressed [see colour]. White shirts look great against dark suits but only if you are a healthy colour, or you have dark skin. White shirts on white faces can really drain you so wear a shirt that reflects some colour up into your face, for goodness sake, and avoid big statement ties, either big or a statement, as it draws attention away from your face and downwards [mind you, that might be your objective]. Remember that dark suits [black, dark grey, navy or indigo] are reassuring and pack more of a punch if you are presenting something or lecturing, whereas a dark brown suit would say too much earth and people may tire of listening to you. Beige or a light brown suit would be saying 'I know I am standing on stage lecturing, but really I don't want you to notice me' [read 'colour' if you haven't already]. Spend some money on good shoes for work because the look of a good suit can be ruined by shoes with thick rubbery soles and heels. Go for a classic style, keep them polished and well heeled and wear dark socks. Red socks and black shoes - dicey - I would give you a wide berth. Look at up-dating your glasses if you are still wearing the same style from ten years ago. If you are using coloured lenses please read 'colour' and then 'health' and I am serious about this because I am uneasy about continual, one colour, visual saturation. Remember your choice of jewellery can be very revealing [more later]. And darlings .... darlings, who pray, told you hair gel was sexy? I have never met a woman yet who said she enjoyed running her hands through hedgehog hair and the current trend of colouring hair has got out of hand - some men are looking like heavy smoking badgers auditioning for the role of Tin Tin. It is beyond me. You are only young and gorgeous for a very short time, do make the most of it. Try clean and natural, it is devilishly attractive.

I think it is easy for men because if you get a really classic wardrobe put together it will do for years and years. I have a picture of Steve McQueen wearing a well cut dark suit, white shirt, dark tie and a honey coloured mackintosh [contrast colours]. I am well aware Mr. McQueen could look drop dead gorgeous in a dirty coal sack but this photo was taken at least thirty years ago. In that outfit he would have looked stylish, not to mention serious, on any city street today. I have to say I had a bit of a crush on Steve. I was working as a nurse in London on the day he died. I was devastated and wore a black arm band for the day, but the only one to hand was a black blood pressure cuff, the old fashioned type, with dangling rubber bits. My colleagues whooped with hilarity but I was undeterred. The divine man was an actor and a pilot and I am rather hoping we shall be in the same display team when I get to heaven [see angels]. Can't see myself tucking my knickers into my frock in front of him .... still he might be in knickers and frock too, and quite gorgeous he will look.

What do clothes say to me? Let me tell you a story before I start. A few years ago I sat on a train next to a lovely lady with a serene smile. We struck up a conversation and she told me how everything was going perfectly in her life, how lucky she was and how everything everywhere was hunky dory. I would have been delighted for her but the problem was every word that was coming out of her mouth was directly at odds with everything she had put on her body [including nail polish] which was saying I am angry, angry, angry and I have a major first [and probably] second chakra issue. I could tell you exactly what it was about all her items that alerted me, but that lady might read this book and I do not think I have a right to expose her emotions to such a blatant attack, but if you have read the colour section and marry that to what I am about to say you will learn to read clothes yourself. What really astounded me about this lady was her shoes, which I only saw when she got up to get off the train. They were decorated with enormous hearts. Hearts …. and shoes are on your feet - think about it. This lady was in a muddle. Angels like sorting out muddles. I wouldn't be at all surprised if an angelic spanner was being aimed at her as we spoke. Hope it was not a health spanner.

Ok, let's start with headwear. I look at very old photographs of long gone folk around these parts and every single person of every age wore a hat or a bonnet and they all looked adorable. In those days everyone was taught their tribes' idea of God, most believed it and that was that. Being that you bung a hat on your head and the crown chakra is your direct energetic link to the divine it seems to me, therefore, that the abandonment of hat wearing [in Britain, anyway] came about at a time when we started challenging the teachings of the religion of our specific tribe. I suppose you could say this started roughly in the late fifties and early sixties. From then on most went hatless, except my mother, but we haven't got time to go into that, even if it is funny. Then baseball caps suddenly started popping up everywhere pointing every which way, much like weathervanes. I thought this was fascinating and wondered if people were covering their seventh chakra [and sixth] hence shutting down old ideas of God, while opening up to Mammon [the worship of money] especially as it became fashionable to drop waistlines, thus exposing the second chakra area of lower abdomens. Is this a little wacky for you? Apologies … but .. I reckon, come the recession you will see those infuriating low waistlines *ascend*.

The most important thing to me about headwear is how often it is worn and what the colour is. Making allowances for wintry weather, hair loss and lovely old country boys in tweedy hats and caps, I am inclined to pay attention to any type of headwear that is worn a lot that covers the crown chakra. I am aware that I am stepping on religious territory and I most certainly do not wish to offend. I am just saying I would be more attentive and listen more carefully. Some teenagers and young men wear knitted headgear and I would worry if black was worn a lot and even more if it was red and black [it may be just a phase but pay attention in case in turns into something nasty]. Watch for any decoration or written statements on the hats, you may need to take them literally. I don't suppose you can regulate what psychiatric patients wear in hospital, if they can get into one these days, but I would recommend that they avoid headwear and that their surroundings [or their clothes - even better] are in gently healing colours, such as pale pink, light green, light blue and the very palest yellow [and let's all fervently pray they are seeing a nutritionist and getting their bowels sorted out]. Allowing for hair loss I am always attentive and slightly wary of anyone in a dark hat when it is not cold, wet or winter. Like trousers, I wear hats a lot and you certainly need to be attentive to me. [Joke.]

I think most people would agree that a very general rule of thumb is that structured clothes say structured person and fluid clothes say creative or artistic person. Recently there has been a trend of wearing underwear as outer wear and I am struck at how almost 'little girly' feminine some of the items of clothing are. I thought it was an interesting development in this day and age and it struck me that the message appeared to say 'take care of me' which seemed extraordinary. I wondered if I had got it completely wrong and it was just that women felt so confident they could wear the merest whisper of a dress and still feel able to take on the world but I am coming round to the conclusion that my original thought might be spot on and that women are indeed looking for someone to take care of them. We are living in uncertain and potentially threatening times and there is an undercurrent of a swing back to gender defined roles. Could this signify the return of the caveman? Are there any left? Of course, rugby is making *such* a comeback.

Unstructured clothes such as floppy and far too long jeans with layers of mismatched tops say 'muddle' to me, and/or 'I don't know where I am going, yet' and/or 'I don't wish to conform' but this is also tribal gear so that one muddler can instantly recognise another muddler and feel comfortable. There is nothing wrong with muddle, I did muddle for years, but I did it smartly dressed which confused everyone including myself. Muddle means you haven't made up your mind which path to follow with urgency and commitment and you are not going to be helped by someone cross-questioning you on the subject of work or future or the state of your shredded and filthy hems. Muddlers need listening to, could do with a spot of orange and navy and need lots of loving non-judgmental attention, assuming they are middle-aged. Early muddlers need to witness discipline and have a certain degree of enforced discipline but they also need listening to with very acute ears. Have I told you I am going to cover listening under 'listening'? Well I have now. Buy yourself a beer, or something very like it, you will need it.

It goes without saying that women wearing trousers a lot have a leaning towards being yang [male] than yin [female]. I think it would be fair to say that these days women lead more yang working lives and therefore wearing trousers makes life easier but then I wear trousers all the time, so I would say that wouldn't I? The colour of trousers is always a point of interest, because I link them with first and second chakra and the ability to ground oneself but also the ability to move forward. The continual use of black trousers for a women would indicate to me that a major block needed to be cleared. It might be a first chakra issue of grief or one of the four lessons of second chakra, either way I would be concerned about health in the long term. I would be fascinated to know if women prone to wearing trousers a lot are more liable to get right sided breast cancer than women who wear skirts [and might get left sided breast cancer]. I noticed a trouser wearing friend, who got right sided breast cancer, reduced her right sided body movement after surgery, a very normal reaction to pain and discomfort. By doing so she needed to use the left side [female side] of her body more, which would in turn activate the right side of the brain. Just an observation I found interesting.

Tentatively I am going to bring in the exposure of chest skin, in either the male but more obviously the female. This is usually read as a sexual sign, but I don't think it is. People do tend to reveal what they think is their best feature [especially if they think their face is not] but even allowing for that I think chest exposure in a man or woman is a distraction from the face and in particular the mouth. I would therefore recommend, when you are in the company of a low cut top [male or female], that you pay particular attention to what is verbally coming out of the mouth because it may be at odds with the skin exposure and you may get a lot of mixed messages. While you are at it, monitor the body language carefully because an exposure of heaving mammaries with tightly crossed legs and arms folded across the lower abdomen says 'I am not quite sure what I am doing'. This might well turn out, long term, to be a rather expensive date.

Jumpers, shirts and tops in general cover the heart, lungs and breasts so the colour is important. If you are wearing black or grey over your heart area all the time please try and gently ask yourself why. I have already talked about the wearing of green under the colour section but I do want to reiterate the darker the green worn the more the emphasis on the heart, so if you are talking to a dark green shirt frame your words with care. I do bang on about colours worn all the time, but I note I will pull out a darkish green jumper if I am feeling sad or vulnerable. If pale pink is worn, particularly on the upper half of the body, know that a healing is taking place and don't boss the wearer around. Leave them to do things at their own pace. Turquoise tops [the higher and nearer the throat the more relevant - therefore polo-necks are very relevant] indicate that its owner is starting to 'ground' themselves [especially if they are wearing brown shoes] and flex their authority in the vocal department, so be alert to it as you may need to take cover.

Please take notice of anything written on t-shirts or sweats. I am inclined to take messages literally. People do not chose slogans or patterns at random, they are telling you something about themselves, usually subconsciously and when someone is trying to tell you something you need to pay attention. The busier the pattern or slogan the more you need to listen. A shy studious bookworm girl is unlikely to buy a glittery t-shirt with 'party animal' on it. A woman with 'Queen of Shopping' printed across her chest is unlikely to be a cheap date. Me wearing a t-shirt with 'I love karaoke' on it is about as likely as one of my dogs singing like Maria Callas. An obsession with ghouls, heavy metal bands, skulls and such like, usually going hand-in-hand with black and some red would alert me to the meaning of those colours but I would also be alert to first [particularly] third and sixth chakras. Watch the diet and the colon.

Animals featured on clothing say either a great love for and/or a wish for the quality of the animal depicted. A t-shirt depicting a roaring wolf with blood dripping from its teeth says much the same to me as unhappy and agitated attack-type dogs on a leash - that there is a gaping hole at third chakra level and a huge amount of second chakra work to be done. We are talking love here, or the lack of it. In fact we are always talking lack of love. Simple really.

A few years back I noticed a pattern creeping into many items of clothing and even household furniture and goods. It was a sort of continuous circle. This is not a very good description but the best I can do. While out shopping

I was constantly stopping and staring in amazement at how often it was being used. In my bones I felt it heralded a change and though I could not put my finger exactly on what the change was the circular pattern or logo had a primitive feel to it and seemed to say 'a return to earth' in some way. Now labels are coming off and I have noticed a flavour of a twenty first century take on old work-wear and even peasant clothing creeping in. Again it says to me a 'return to earth' and all things related. I am hugely encouraged by it because I don't think it is a passing trend and it signifies a collective shift forward, while simultaneously connecting with our past. All good news.

Pay particular attention to stripes and checks. I am still working out the intricacies of both and I need a lot more information on checks, but it does seem that vertical stripes are less restricting than horizontal ones. Any type of stripe and check says there is an element of restriction to me and depending on depth, width and colour may go as far as to say 'I feel imprisoned'. I have listened carefully and my observations are that the thinner stripes represent the wearer feeling hemmed in by external causes. Therefore a woman feeling trapped in a marriage is more likely to go for the finer stripes, the colour obviously would give much more information. Thicker stripes appear to be the wearer knowing that they feel trapped for some reason but also recognising an internal need for restraint - for limiting action. I would always think about the restraint being linked to an intimate relationship firstly, sexual secondly but it might also encompass restraint when it comes to booze, food, drugs, gambling and anything else that can get you into trouble, if taken to excess. It seems to be that the bolder the stripes the more restraint is felt to be needed. If there is a thick black stripe I'm on double alert. When it comes to stripes and checks I am of course talking about them when they are worn a great deal. I am sometimes to be seen in a rather fetching matelot style indigo and white thin striped top myself, but only in high summer, and this does not mean that I am feeling virginal but imprisoned by a visionary sailor. You need to look at the colours in the stripes or checks, then go back through the chakras and work out what the colour combination means. Someone recently showed me a photograph of a woman and asked what I deduced from her outfit. The upper body was visible only and was covered in a dark green jumper with fine turquoise stripes and there was a slightly baffling bit of whirling embroidery or pattern over the chest area. I surmised that this person was armouring her heart [dark green] and felt trapped by being unable to speak out [turquoise stripes] and was in a heart led turmoil about it [whirling embroidery]. Apparently it was a very accurate description. I had more to say about her jewellery, but I will cover that subject later.

Last year I sat at a café watching a couple and their youngish daughter who was seated between them. The mother [in pink top and black skirt] was trying to concentrate on the child while absolutely yearning for some interaction or contact with the father, so much so that her whole body moved forward when she looked pleadingly at him. The father sat, cross legged, facing away from the wife and child. He was wearing a thick mid to dark blue and white striped sweatshirt. He was utterly disconnected from his family, spending most of his time staring out into the distance away from them [he did not feel angry to me, just not present]. The child 'appeared' oblivious and was concentrating on her drawing, which I could not see, unfortunately, because that picture may well have told an interesting story about what was going on at home. A home where attention and communication were almost certainly missing.

I have always wondered about city men in pin-stripe suits, perhaps they would rather be playing golf. It is interesting that pin-stripes became almost a tribal uniform in the city and beyond for many male office workers. Perhaps an element of striped restriction was necessary to keep them at their desks when for thousands of years they have been citizens of the earth or the sword. It may have changed now that we are more health and happiness conscious but for many years if I ventured into the City of London I was distressed at the high level of pin-stripe suits that went with either bloodlessly pale faces or extremely florid ones.

Watch out for the colour purple in striped clothing because it suggests there is a restriction coming about from a sense of connection or commitment to divine order. Someone I know quite well and who is very spiritually aware was going through an extraordinarily difficult and sad situation where she felt trapped and spiritually bound to see something through. At the end of a long phone call she said she was going out. I told her to wrap up warm against the cold and it was no surprise to me to hear her say she was putting on her new purple and black striped long socks. Black/grief, purple/spiritual, stripes = restriction/imprisoning, socks/feet = moving forward.

I am still collecting information about patterned clothing. I find it quite difficult to analyse unless the colour combination spells out a message. Men are keen on patterned jumpers but not so keen on my gentle probing of their feelings, which is a pity because it makes learning more difficult for me. Patterns themselves do not always say something specific to me but sometimes they do if there is a definitive shape. If the pattern is very busy or chaotic I am inclined to keep quiet, especially if the colours are chaotic too. I have noticed that as people become introspective and calmer they tend to shy away from patterns and their clothing and accessories become quieter.

While making huge allowances for the hunting, shooting and fishing fraternity, I am inclined to take combat fatigues at their word. Combat fabric, even if dressed up in high fashion would make me very quiet and I would listen very carefully. It says anger to me, with a strong heart element, but the beige mixed in with it would say 'I don't want to be confrontational'. I find it a worrying dress code from a health point of view and I am bothered to see so many children in it. I note also that there has been a trend to produce combat fabric in black and grey and I would link this with sadness.

It is a sweeping generalization but women in animal prints have a reputation for enjoying horizontal activity so it was with much amusement that I returned from a trip from Namibia with not one, but two cheetah print chiffon scarves - the very devil in me - it'll be black lace corsets next. Horizontal activity has, I hear, been around for quite awhile, but don't tell the teenagers, you will so disappoint them. Joking aside, large cat print makes me think 'a transition from first to second chakra hiccup'. Furry animal print cloth is lovely and I have some myself, recently parting with a worn out pair of velvet trousers that were dark brown and vaguely very small leopard print [such an interesting phase I went through]. However, if animal print clothing and certain second chakra issues were going hand-in-hand I would advise some balancing with other colours, perhaps ones that are not a first choice - in fact, definitely ones that are not a first choice. I would also throw in some pink. Animal fur is tricky and emotive. I just have not had enough experience nor opportunity to talk to women who wear a lot of fur in order to get a rounded picture. Taking aside cold climates and cultural differences I am still inclined to think fur is strongly linked to first chakra, the father or father figure influence and the tribal mindset. As I have already pointed out tribes are still tribes whether they be Amazonian Indian or Gstaad jet set and each will have their own tribal rules. I am extremely wary and would be disinclined to do business with someone wearing snakeskin print, doubly so if the snakeskin was dyed red. Snakes are snakes. However, if the snakeskin was on shoes I would wonder about someone not fully revealing themselves emotionally, perhaps with a tendency to be too nice when they need to do a bit of snake like snapping and biting. I wish the fashion industry would not produce real snakeskin shoes, these animals are becoming endangered and have a perfect right to be on this planet whether we like them or not. I have read appalling stories about how these animals are skinned alive [this goes for animal fur too], I don't want to think about it because it makes me feel sick, sick, sick. Please be aware that, if the story is true, you are placing a screaming negative energy on your feet or any other part of your body and I would ask that you enquire just how that fur was obtained on that cuddly toy you are about to buy for a child.

I am alert to excessive boot wearing of any style and what that might say about the wearer. It may be a cover up or an unconscious defensive [or otherwise] weapon. Boots, especially if they are heavy and bulky, heavily pointed or heavily laced often say 'angry' to me, but the heavily laced variety would make me think of an element of restraint or restriction - either the having or the needing of it. I would think about first chakra issues and depending on the style I would think along the lines of 'I am angry at my father or father figure'. I would then pay attention to the ovaries, particularly, colon and head area and I would be worried if the boots were red and black [watch for black shoes/red laces]. Please change these colours quickly if you have any health problems, especially abdominal.

Shoes say a lot about how someone views their facial looks. The colour is always interesting and I would take the repetitive wearing of black shoes seriously in relation to how someone sees their future. You might remember what I said about the wearing of red shoes in 'colour' - be wary. Running shoes [as in 'I don't want to be here'] would say exactly that to me, especially teamed with a suit, or it might say rebellion, which is fine at twenty but at sixty it indicates you have some first chakra clearing work to do. The colour and state of running shoes [trainers] is always interesting. When I first got arthritis, wearing any shoes other than ones that looked like gigantic canal barges was out of the question. I could not even get into, let alone out of, Wellington boots for several years so winter dog walking was a muddy messy business. I love wearing skirts when the weather is warm and the dog walks are dry and now my joints are better I can wear quite attractive shoes again but I have always favoured flat shoes and I suppose that says a lot about me. Too much overactive thinking needed to be compensated for by flat grounding/earthing shoes and as I have already said I often chose dark brown ones, though that has changed now. When I trained and worked as a reflexologist I became fascinated with the amount of information feet and toes told me about a person's personality. I noted that flattish feet needed light blue to raise the thinking from too much contact with the ground and high arches needed brown to pull the thinking down to ground level. I wondered if this would help children who adopt either a tiptoe walk or that upward heel bounce gait so often favoured by young boys.

Interestingly, well interesting to me anyway, many years ago I bought a divine pair of strappy heeled sandals in pale yellow. Designer they were and right out of my price range normally, but I found these in a charity shop for a fiver. I was thrilled. They looked fabulous on my pretty good legs [in those days]. Several years later a girlfriend was helping me sort through my groaning wardrobe and said, 'What lovely shoes, I have never seen you wear them, why not?', I shot back,'I can't run in them'. My friend wasn't paying attention and changed the subject, chatting gaily on, but I was paying attention and I was in complete confusion.'What on earth had made me say that?', I agonised. 'From what did I need to run?' Further, shortly after my partner and I started living together, I went out and bought an outrageous pair of vertiginous heeled, black, sparkly diamante mules. I couldn't wear them anywhere but in the house, preferably sitting down because my joints were too painful and unreliable but I loved them and so did my beloved. Why did I buy them? Was I done running? Was it because I had found the man of my dreams? Had I arrived at my sacred contract? Read on, read on. I'm bound to drive you to drink eventually.

CELEBRITIES

Although it is slightly on the wane, I am still bothered by our excessive devotion to the celebrity cult, not least because we seem to have such double standards. Celebrity wayward behaviour is often 'lit up', applauded and even financially rewarded yet the same behaviour within a family is unlikely to get a round of applause, it would almost certainly be the cause of much worry and distress. Instead of checking, reining in [or even better, ignoring] what appears to me to be generally unhappy and sometimes almost suicidal celebrity behaviour, we encourage them. What does this say about us and our society? It feels like a twenty-first century take on the Coliseum to me.

Celebrities have their place, they are here to give us dreams and that is healthy but we seem to elevate beyond reason these days. It would not be so bad if they remained inside a few celebrity magazines that I can avoid but they are absolutely everywhere and just when I just want balanced and comprehensive international news, from any source, I am given intimate details of the lives of models, sportsmen, actors or singers and now, I can hardly bear it, I have to know about footballer's girlfriends. An endless stream of over exposed skin, mammary glands, shopping bags and tedious behaviour. Then, to add insult to injury, publicity courting celebrities bemoan media harassment … publicly. What do they expect? Put some bloody clothes on and get a quiet life. Every day I sigh at my newspaper or newsreader and ask for global news with a plea of, 'Anything happening in Chile? Canada? Malaysia? Australia? Anywhere?'. Now we have celebrity newsreaders, *dressed to death.* I can't take them seriously. Even when they are reporting grave news I fully expect them to suddenly jump up and do a song and dance routine. Is that why they are now standing up to read the news? Is this the warming up exercise?

Nowadays, super rich celebrities and singers encourage us to donate our money to good causes. At concerts, in between strutting the stage, they instruct us to hand over our money and the crowd roars its approval. I am baffled. Why don't the crowd roar, 'Show us your money?'. Why do we have to be noisily entertained in order to hand over our money? Frankly, I would pay not to be noisily entertained, but that is just dinosaur me. I know many celebrities give huge donations to charity, but so do many ordinary people. If you balanced income against donations you would almost certainly find there are thousands of people all over this country who give equally as much as those who are famous. These quiet givers rarely get recognition. I know some celebrities have raised huge sums for Africa and done wonderful things there, but what about poorer countries in South America, or Asia? I suppose it is a necessary raising of consciousness and for the best, but still I am uneasy with it, much as I have always been uneasy with the idea of charity balls. Have a fabulously expensive ball and enjoy it, please do, and give your money to charity, but not at the same time. My view infuriated my mother. 'Oh Amanda, why do you have to be so difficult?', she would sigh. I don't know why she saw my attitude as being difficult. To me dancing or drinking champagne in silken attire while simultaneously coughing up for charity just seemed at odds and made me feel uncomfortable, especially if the noisy enjoyment was going to ease hunger and/or the sick and dying. Can't we give quietly? Then we would be free to dance ecstatically for ourselves alone with no emaciated figure hovering in the dark recesses of our guilty minds. Now we have kisses sold for charity. I look at the pictures, read the blurb and struggle to get a wider perspective and a sixth chakra view of it, but I can't …….. I just see repercussions.

Why do fans scream at celebrities? I mean really scream. Perhaps it is a healthy release of emotion, or then again, perhaps not. In my very tender youth I loved one of the Beatles but I never wanted to scream at him and the idea of queuing anywhere to see and to scream at him would have baffled me even at the age of twelve and besides, I liked The Monkeys better by then. Next, Scott Walker, so fickle was I. It was Leonard Cohen by the time I was seventeen, deeply mournful [I was not paying attention in those days] and screaming at him would have been *most* inappropriate.

We love celebrities because they get so much attention and all those popping flashbulbs make them appear to be in a halo of light. We want some of that attention and some of that light so we struggle to get close to it, reach out to it, queue for hours to get a glimpse of it. If we can't get close to stardom personally we do it by ridiculous association [my brother's girlfriend's best friend stroked George Clooney's pet pig, or my sister-in-law's first cousin's aunt patted the Queen's corgi and has the teeth marks to prove it]. If we can't get a personal touch we will do it by flicking through a glossy magazine full of glossy celebs. We want to pop some of that magic into our empty third chakra and feel second-hand good about ourselves, but celebrity magic does what it says on the tin, it disappears, like the white rabbit or dove. We are left with an empty hat. An empty third chakra. Why not make yourself into a celebrity? Celebrate the real magic that is YOU. Then you get to keep the hat, the rabbit, the dove, the silk scarf, the wand *and* you know the trick. We all have magic … we do, we do. If you are sitting there thinking, 'I don't shine at anything', you are wrong. There will be one thing you do really well - it might be listening, or keeping the hamster, or naming clouds. Pursue your listening talent. Be an hamster expert [do some more research]. Move from clouds to weather patterns and amaze folk with your knowledge. Don't look at stick thin, rich celebrities and feel a failure. Many celebrities make ludicrous demands of those around them, which is basically saying 'I am afraid'. To demand a red carpet or tell people not to look you in the eye is not an order that comes from love - it comes from *fear*. Many celebrities have strange, if not downright sad lives and most are lousy listeners because they just want attention, attention, attention [exhausting to be with, I should imagine]. They probably know next to nothing about keeping hamsters and couldn't tell a mackerel sky from a ….. erm … nimbus? Cloudulous nimbus?

Sometimes you see a completely unknown celebrity. They walk past you or sit in a nearby café and you know you have never, ever seen them before but they just exude celebrity status. They are comfortable in their own skin, not ostentatiously dressed but look groomed and they have an air of magic and you can't take your eyes of them. You can be one of them - yes you can. You just need to return to yourself, retake your inner power and be guided by your inner compass.

I don't want to sound as if celebrities are the scourge of society, they most categorically are not. They are archetypes and therefore they are here to teach us. All through history we have needed to have our heroes, though I think now we are in an awful muddle about what the meaning of hero is. I am watching and reading about one celebrity, George Clooney, with great interest. I am wondering if he might be in danger of turning into a little bit of a hero himself. He has that upper lip, which is a bit of a worry, and then there is his chin. I looked it up in my Oriental face reading book but the Chinese don't seem to go in for Clooney chins, so I am left to wonder. I used to watch that soap ER because it made me giggle. Clooney was a paediatric doctor in it; I didn't like the cut of his jib - too much of a loose cannon. I was a Mark girl myself. Mark was dull but reliable. He looked like the kind of chap who would remember your birthday whereas our Cloones looked like he could hardly remember breakfast let alone who he spent the night with. Of course he behaved like an absolute shower toward that nice young nurse and eventually he disappeared off somewhere watery. Seattle I think it might have been. Just the place for a shower. Nursey followed him with her double bump. 'Don't do it girl', I yelled at the telly, choking on my ice cream and waving an admonishing spoon. 'Go back to Chic-a-Goo [Chicago] and find yourself a nice fireman' [fireman = hero in my book; matches seem to get the better of me and burning buildings, well … no thanks]. Nursey didn't listen to me. I feared the worse. That was the last of George on ER and I felt thoroughly relieved but I notice has been busy since then doing rather interesting things and I am wondering if he is heading on a Washington trajectory. Do you think he has still got his pot-bellied pig? A pig on the White House lawn. I like the idea.

CURIOSITY

I am fascinated by peoples' lack of curiosity. When I meet someone, I want to know all about them and, if I find someone who has visited another country, I want to know all - tell me, tell me do. What did you do? How did you do it? How did you travel and what did it look like, feel like, dress like, smell like? What did you see and do and eat? For the most part I find it hard to get people to give information or tell stories, especially about themselves. From women you can get any amount of information about their baby's feeding habits, children's schooling, children's gap years or working life, then it becomes the grandbaby's feeding habits, schooling and so on and so forth. My polite but glazed expression never seems to staunch the flow, but ask a woman about her holiday and she will tell you it was nice. Two weeks in a foreign land = nice. Extraordinary. Men have improved a bit, I have to say. I spent my youth despairing of young men and their lack of conversation; sitting in pubs wilting under fire from a chain delivery of second-hand jokes designed to keep everyone at a distance. I remember going to America in 1976 and being astounded to meet young men who actually talked to me and listened to me, it took me months to get over the shock. Younger men do talk more these days [what a relief!] but even now you can greet a visiting man you have not seen for a while and he will bore you to sobs with what road he took to get where he is now and how many gear changes it required to beat his personal best, but rarely will he comment on anything seen en route. I try not to ask men how they feel about something …. anything ….. because they tend to look at me as if I am mad.

My partner and me like to travel and tend to head for distant parts with not too many tourists. Our return has often been met with an 'oh', and that is it. I am amazed by this lack of curiosity. I sometimes wonder that because we love to travel off the beaten track that others think their holiday in Cornwall or Scotland is not of interest, but it is fascinating to me. We share our amazement with friends of ours who are equally curious and the very best company. They are not international but local travellers. They can have a weekend in Norfolk or Sussex and come back jam-packed with fascinating stories, observations and recommendations. They have both had extraordinary lives but can return from dinner parties where their dining companions are none the wiser about any aspects of their entertaining lives because they have not enquired. I am truly and utterly amazed. A most excellent osteopath recently commented to me that people don't chat these days because they are too afraid. I thought about this and decided he was exactly right. I was hugely excited by his observation because this is one of the problems and lessons of second chakra. I think people are getting more and more envious and afraid that other people are overtaking them, whereas in fact if you can only embrace others and embrace their getting and their achievements you move forward yourself and are much more likely to find yourself getting and achieving too.

I can chat for Britain in short bursts. Perhaps I am too forward and should cultivate some reticence but I shall find it hard to change. We recently had a fabulous day out on a countryside 'food for free' course. On our return I could not wait to tell anyone who would listen what a wonderful, educational and fun day it had been [I really should charge for free advertising]. My curiosity has been the saving grace of my education, taking off from where my schooling had bludgeoned it into submission. It has led to some beautiful encounters, both in this country and abroad. Heaven help anyone who knows a place I wish to visit because I will pump them dry for information and that way I have found out about little treasures, secret gems, stunning sights and how to see them. Perhaps I should have worked for a travel company.

I wish people would be more forthcoming about their lives, because I find them absolutely riveting. I love to talk to old country folk about the changes they have witnessed in their lifetime. Given half a chance the oldies will tell me spellbinding stories and if they are male they usually pull my leg unmercifully in the process. A couple of years back I went to a party where the ages ranged from tiddly tots to eighty year olds. I had my beady eye on one elderly gentleman who looked like he could supply a whole book of good stories, but try as hard as I could I was unable to talk to him because of the deafening disco music that is, apparently, essential to a 'good time' party. I am wondering if there will come a time when we are not afraid to talk to each other, where we can have parties where conversation is king and manic music induced hurling about of limbs is done in another area. Preferably on a platform in the North Sea.

CHINA

In 1982 I went to work in Hong Kong. Having been there for a bit I took off with a colleague for a few days of hiking about on surrounding islands and into the New Territory. It was all blissfully peaceful and rural and we had a happy time staying at a Catholic and then a Buddhist monastery, where we slept on mats in a long dormitory amid many chattering women. While tramping down a beachside path one day, I happened upon a long low building and crept up to peer in through a door. Inside were twenty or thirty girls with their backs to me, all busily sewing clothes at their machines.

There was a dirt floor and one light bulb hanging from the ceiling. Wires were suspended everywhere but especially at 'trip' height. It would have been closed in a nanosecond by Health and Safety in Britain. I went very still and very quiet, as I do when I am confronted with something of great magnitude. 'We are stuffed', I thought.

I was not unaware of our very own history of sweated labour in Britain. I also knew factory workers in many countries abroad were paid what we would see as a pittance and worked without paid holidays, sick pay, maternity benefits or any of the other 'perks' we consider 'normal' or 'our rights'. What silenced me was the realization that this particular spectacle before me was the tiniest fraction of what was happening all over the world, but particularly South East Asia, not to mention the gigantic land mass of China that was somewhere over my left shoulder. Britain was to become a service economy assured Margaret Thatcher, but for how long I wondered? How long before Shanghai became the monetary capital of the world, filled with pin-stripe suited Chinese stockbrokers and bankers? I thought how fast the women were when using an abacus in the food markets of Hong Kong, arithmetic being a part of their daily life. I thought of the cut price clothes in Stanley Market where I had recently bought a cotton jumper for £3. They were £30 in London, out of my price range and in those days only found in the smart trend-setting shops. I wondered what it was about these people that made them cutting edge and cutting price. I pondered on the streams of immaculately, spotlessly dressed young girls heading punctually for their office jobs every morning, many from Aberdeen Harbour where, presumably, they lived on boats. As a child I remembered my father, who had spent a lot of time in Singapore and Hong Kong years earlier, telling me, with a tone of respect that I noted, that the Chinese were natural business men and women. It was in their blood, and they were hard workers.

It is a long time since I worked in London, maybe things have changed, but my memory is of Chinese immigrants who took work very seriously and kept a low profile. When they chose to fight it was among themselves, with breathtakingly simple and lethal dexterity and an unusual choice of weaponry. I am thinking of a small handful of Chinese patients we had in Casualty on an emergency basis - we nurses were thoughtful after those experiences. Chop suey took on a whole new meaning. So did hat pins.

Having had my eyes well and truly opened to the threat to Britain, I returned home from Hong Kong in 1983 clutching my savings. I moved to the country, got a hospital job on an Intensive Care Unit and commenced an even more penurious life as a first time tiny home owner, working six days a week. Watching my trusty little black and white portable television night after night, I would listen to politicians drone infuriatingly on and on about negotiations with the European Union. 'It's China you need to worry about, *you morons*', I would yell at the box, knowing full well in the twenty-four hours since the last tedious outpouring from the six o'clock news, that hundreds, probably thousands, of factories had been opened in the East. Not much negotiating there I daresay, or union involvement. The workers got a job for which they were profoundly grateful and they worked hard or they were fired, full stop. No, it is not the workers' rights that our forefathers' and foremothers' campaigned for, but it is, unfortunately, reality. We are indeed a global village now. Twenty-three years on from my Hong Kong epiphany, the government has finally cottoned on to the threat from China, India and everywhere else, but they are so rooted in second chakra power battles to get re-elected and maintain control that they will fail to deliver the bitter pill that this country needs and China knows it. It is her turn now.

There are, I read, sixty million people with no electricity in China. Can you imagine how hard they would work for the luxury of turning on a light switch or a hair dryer? Some of the lucky others get 150 watts per head, as opposed to the USA which furnishes 3000 watts for every citizen. I dry my hair now with the sobering thought that if I was in China my partner would not be able to switch on the kettle at the same time. Would 150 watts power an electric kettle? I don't know, I don't think so. I often wonder, as I flick a light switch, how long I will be able to do so with such casual insouciance.

In 2005 I was astounded to hear from a young public schoolboy that Mandarin had not been discussed with him, let alone offered as an option, even though he wanted to do 'A' level languages. 'Surely, surely we cannot, as a country, have been so slow on the uptake?', I thought, only to read a couple of months later that a college somewhere in Brighton, I think, had begun to make Mandarin a priority. A college? One college? Now I read that Mandarin lessons are quite the thing among the Chelsea set in London for their young children, but still I am dumbfounded. What took so long? What do our leaders see when they travel abroad? What do they hear? Have they no curiosity? Do they travel on the Beijing buses that are, I hear, not run on fossil fuel? Shall we be twenty years behind a Beijing bus?

One last point. China is not stupid, she is, in fact, pretty ruthless and will arm herself to the teeth, to the hilt, with whatever arms she thinks she needs and she will have thousands and thousands of soldiers. Those soldiers are schooled from infants in daily displays of unquestioning patriotism. Although we are seeing a swing to a more tribal mindset in Britain we still have a rather apathetic approach to patriotism, unless it involves football or some other sport and we treat our armed forces with contempt. Whatever your views on China, their patriotism is sobering. I am not suggesting we will ever end up fighting them, the Chinese are far too canny for that sort of carry on but they need vast quantities of raw materials, energy and water for their rapidly 'developing' country [hilarious term for a country that was so cultured when we were still daubing ourselves in woad] and they will make sure they get them. To everyone's cost. I am always amused by the thought that the two most sought after tourist destinations in China are the Great Wall [defence] and the terracotta warriors. If I had children I would be watching China with a mighty careful eye.

COMMITMENT

'Until one is committed, there is the chance to draw back, always ineffectiveness. Concerning all acts of initiative [and creation] there is one elementary truth, the ignorance of which kills countless ideas and plans - that the moment one definitely commits oneself, then providence moves too.

All sorts of things occur to help one that would not otherwise have occurred. A whole stream of events issues from the decision, raising in one's favour all manner of unforeseen incidents and meetings and material assistance which no man could have dreamed would come his way.

Whatever you can do or dream you can, begin it. Boldness has genius, magic and power in it. Begin it now!'

These words of immense wisdom were penned by an eighteenth century German writer and philosopher called Goethe. I didn't know him personally, more is the pity. I think you pronounce his name 'goater' but don't quote me.

COOKING

You have to learn, if you don't know how to. Seasoned hands, excuse the pun, skip this bit, I want you youngsters to listen up. Now boys, especially, it is not difficult to cook and you have no excuse with Jamie Oliver and all that. If you are off to University you need only a handful of implements of destructive capabilities - a small kettle and a large wok with a glass lid. The latter will cook most things and I have been using one for more years than I care to remember. If you want to really push the boat out you could get a cheap enamel roasting dish with lid. Then you need a wooden spoon or two, a couple of sharp knives, one long, one small [Ikea is mustard for knives] and a bowl - metal is good [Ikea again] it will last for years, washes up with ease and when you settle down you can give it to the dog. I like a bowl with a bit of history. I suppose you might need a bread board. We have a most excellent circular board of absolutely enormous proportions with a raised edge and metal handles but still my partner is capable of getting crumbs everywhere. He is 'King of the Crumbs' is my beloved but he is a savagely good and inventive cook [I lift not a finger in the kitchen all weekend, unless he is working, I just pour and entertain] so I turn a blind eye to all the crumbs and there is only a hint of a sigh from me at the pink cupboards when he has been hell-bent on beetroot.

Now children, most things start with onions in my book. Slap some butter in a wok, slurp the beer and chop the onbion ... onion even. Add squished garlic. Chop up any softish vegetables you can get your hands on and hurl them into the pan. Chuck in mince, a little bit of salt [it is not good for you, you know, get out of the habit now while you still have trim and shapely ankles] and pepper. Lots of black pepper. Stir, put the lid on and pour another beer. In a short while you will have mince and veg. What more could you ask for? Wholesome and heart warming. Now you are an expert, remember practice makes perfect, so do it again soon before you lose confidence and this time you can throw in some ginger or cumin, you spicey devil you. Now you are up to speed, go out and buy a cookery book that is short on words and big on pictures of the end product [so you know what to aim for]. I can't bear those cookery books where the recipe is over three pages and ingredients have to be sourced internationally. I am exhausted before I have gone past a mushroom I can't pronounce. I loved 'Cooking in a Bedsitter' by Katharine Whitehorn. No pictures, of course, but you have to make allowances for her outstanding brevity. I love brevity except when I am doing the talking. You would have a hell of a job finding her book now though, because the cover says 3'6.

I enjoy cookery books but it is the pictures I really like because they give me the gist of the meal without boring the pants off me. I read half a recipe and then lose interest and I rarely weigh anything in the kitchen. It is a complete mystery to me how things come out edible. My partner says I am the fastest cook he has ever come across, but that is only because I have a short attention span and if it takes longer than forty five minutes to put a meal on the table it has to be a seriously good roast, so worth the extra effort, or I am on my third glass of wine and haven't a clue what time it is anyway because the clock looks blurred.

My cooking is probably saved by having an aga. I wanted one for as long as I can remember. My mother was mystified by my passion until she heard you don't have to clean the ovens, then she quickly got my drift. My first aga arrived when I was forty-five and it was love from the word go. I called her Missie. Navy, four doored, costing a breathtaking amount of money and worth every cent. She has two cupboards above her, left and right, and in between three silver towel rails. From early autumn to late spring, Missie disappears cheerfully behind a welter of drying clothes, sheets and human or dog blankets. At 6pm[ish] she reappears and is ready for the off. We get on well. She is my kind of girl. Warm and approachable, multi-tasking and she never complains. Well that's not strictly true, she doesn't complain but she can be a tad temperamental at times and will steadfastly refuse to be relit after some servicing. She doesn't always seem to like having her bits fiddled with and who can blame her? One of the wonderful things about agas is that bubbling things can be hurled from one oven to the next, either to speed things up or slow things down. It is all most excellent. If the wood-burning stove in the sitting room is lit by 4pm[ish] and Missie is beaming in the kitchen then we can do without central heating unless it is ferociously cold. Missie is not cheap to run but I haven't worked out how much our electricity bill would be if I had to use a drier all the time and put the central heating on more. Probably evens stevens. However, Missie is, dare I say it, gas fired and I haven't had the heart to break it to her. One day soon I will have to push the animals out of the way, sit down on the Ikea mat and say the dreaded words, just so that she will understand. Forewarned is forearmed so they say. As I stroke Missie's doors I shall whisper, 'Mr. Putin ……. it's 'im wots in charge of the pipe, darlin, but do try not t'worry'.

One lesser known fact about agas, to the unitiated, is you can cook and do pilates together. Such a graceful backward arc I manage, to reach my wine with my legs at improbable angles to avoid stepping on a dog or cat.

Now remember this most important fact. Maybe two facts now I come to think about it. One, being able to cook puts you well ahead of the competition for lurve, boys and girls. Two, if someone really loves you they will not be rude about your burnt offering on a plate. Think Bridget Jones and blue soup. Over the years I have eaten many a meal I did not enjoy but was delighted to be given it by someone I loved dearly, because their company and kindness was all that mattered. If you have tried hard and someone is rude about your food GET RID OF THEM. These people you do not need in your life. One final word, don't attempt soufflés for company, they are nervous breakdown material.

CRICKET

I worked at a boys school once. I would join the little treasures at a cricket match and say, 'How's it going chaps?'. They would sombrely inform me of the proceedings. I was absolutely none the wiser. I would sit down gingerly on an unreliable deckchair, sip my tea and smile at the charming and bucolic scene before me. A glorious spectacle and it mattered not one jot that I had not an inkling of what was happening …… until I spotted, with a sigh, a boy with a grassy arse. The very devil of a stain to remove.

I always felt angels and cricketers had one thing in common - white. It was easy on the eye, gentle and undemanding, except in the wash. Even as a child with my picture books I could not be doing with that sort of 1920's period depicting angels with coloured wings. Preposterous idea! Like British Airways and their ghastly jazzed up tail-fins. I cannot be doing with all this experimentation, if it works leave it alone, dammit. I can't remember when cricketers first appeared like jazzed up tail-fins but I blame the Australians - anarchic bunch of trouble makers. They have quite enough colour on their parakeets they do not need it on their cricket pitches. Get a grip. Now I see a cricketer, Flintknife or some such, in BLUE on grass! There is a rule you know …'blue and green should never be seen without a colour in between'. I break this rule but I know what I am doing. I don't interfere with cricket and they should not interfere with colour. It is terribly upsetting. They looked so smart and pretty in white, and that is modern for you, anything pretty AND smart is doomed. It finished my father. He adored watching the 'crichit' as he called it but he never got over the shock of seeing them dressed like a bunch of demented canaries.

Now, because the cricketers got silly, everyone has joined in. Quite the other day I saw a picture of a tennis player in what looked like sprayed on leather. She had a perfectly good set of leather already - skin. All she needed was something smart and cool to offset it - white cotton. I don't know where it will all end. I'm upset. What time is it anyway? Oh ………….. the yardarm is half a leg short of the Plimsoll line, it'll have to be tea. Still, Betty's of Harrogate Spiced Christmas Tea. My fave!

$\mathcal{D}$ Is for DIGESTION

Are you over fifty? Sixty? More? Are you as physically strong as you were when you were thirty? No? If you find that your muscles are not as strong as they used to be why would your digestive system be as strong as it used to be when you were thirty? It isn't. Everything ages, including your stomach and intestines. If you are hurling down the same food as you ate when you were thirty, at the same rate, perhaps you could just remind yourself that your tired old stomach and bowel might be thinking, 'Oh no, not another lot to digest and sort when I have barely finished the last meal … I so wanted a rest'. I am not suggesting starvation, indeed no, or even fasting, but I do suggest that you think about easily digested soups and juicing every now and then, just to give your hard working old intestines a break.

$\mathcal{D}$RAINS

Drain or radiator, which one are you? If you can be honest enough to recognise that you are a drain please take a pat on the back and then pootle off to do some home study [there are plenty of helpful books about and I will list some at the rear of the book] to find out why you cannot generate enough energy yourself that you have to drain others. I am not talking about 'rushing about' energy here but third chakra positive self-image energy. Don't think all drains are doormats, oh no, bullies drain too and they drain faster.

If you are a radiator you may have to wipe that smile off your face. Radiators are lovely and warming and people like them a lot but radiators 'cost', sometimes need 'bleeding' and occasionally 'leak'. I am talking energetic third chakra 'cost, bleeding and leaking'. Chronic fatigue type 'cost, bleeding and leaking'. Radiate yourself first and if you have some heat left over, then radiate others. I know what I am talking about, I was a leaking radiator for years and my plumbing still needs attention.

DOUBT

If in doubt do nothing. If in doubt do nothing, say nothing and promise nothing ………. but make sure you don't *use* doubt as a method of always doing nothing. When doubt has passed, act purposefully.

DECISIONS

I am sure it was Caroline Myss who first introduced me to the idea of a lovely image that always makes me smile. There I am, sitting on the sofa, chewing my nails and wondering what to do with my life while my unseen angels are leaning in a bored manner against the door frame of my living room, smoking cigarettes, filing their nails and watching celestial television. Every once in a while one angel will ask the other angel, 'Has Amanda made a decision yet about what she is going to do?'. 'Nope', will come the bored reply. Months, possibly years later, I DECIDE. Hallelujah! The angels nudged each other, stub out their fags, turn off the box and move in behind me, orchestrating with magic wands.

I hasten to add I may not have made the right decision, in which case it seems to me their magic wands close doors smartly in my face [rather too smartly as I recall]. This is probably for my protection but should I make the right decision … well ….. things happen. Perhaps some unseen force is waiting for you to make a decision too.

DEPRESSION

I don't do depression. I do other things and I occasionally have a 'down day' but I have, unfortunately, spent too many years up close and personal to serious depression. I think the new agey belief that 'depression is anger turned in on oneself' is definitely worth bearing in mind but to my mind depression is far more about sadness. Sadness, regret and sometimes guilt.

My mother's manic depression was probably around when I was born, only then it was little, like me, and liked to sleep a lot. As the years wore on it needed less sleep and it grew. Sometime during my tender years her depression reared up and started walking and talking and came out in the shape of a mini breakdown over a pink hat. My father sought help. Kindly doctors gave sedatives, different for day and night. Doctors were God in those days and you did as you were told, so when my night-owl father came to bed to find his wife snoring peacefully he did not question the prescriptions, even when she suddenly reared up at midnight, as she always did, and said, 'Omigod, I haven't taken my sleeping pills!', and took not one, but the prescribed two. How she functioned at all the next day is still a complete mystery to me. A catastrophic financial mishap [emotional trauma] in her early fifties pitched her into full scale manic depression and the pills that had been prescribed and changed over the years now came thick and fast, also treating a burgeoning number of small medical problems [possibly side effects from the original medication] that had no intention of going away. It was a long and difficult road to her death, even allowing for the lithium treatment which evened out the ups and downs somewhat. Depression, like alcoholism, is a nightmare for the participant but also for the onlookers who love and care. When I go down memory lane I try to avert my face to the worst of it and focus my eyes on the happy times only, for my mother could be the very best of company and great fun for about three months of the year. On a good year.

For my mother the full slide into manic depression coincided with the start of my nurse training. Apart from watching my mother chop vegetables, cook sound nutritious meals daily and her encouraging me to eat my greens I knew nothing about nutrition and I gained pathetically little more knowledge during my student years. I don't know if nutrition is now taught comprehensively to nurses but it needs to be, it needs to be given the highest level of attention. If nurses are still not being taught about what food does to the body my advice to them is to learn themselves because, in the face of healthcare now being big business, nothing will challenge the money making giants but a united thought form put out by enough nurses that want to see a change. Trauma [you can encompass accidents, surgery, or even bereavement] can wipe out certain body nutrients in *minutes* [B vitamins especially] and my guess is that hospital food will not replace them, assuming you are well enough to eat. I have long held a gut feeling that monumental amounts of certain minerals and vitamins given, as fast as possible, to severe nerve injuries could probably produce healing results. I have not a single shred of knowledge or evidence to back this up, but during my life my gut feelings have been right over and over again.

Since my mother's death I have thought and read a lot about depression, healing, food and absorption. I have known several other depressives and of course I have been profoundly ill myself with Rheumatoid Arthritis. Casting my eye back over the years to when I was a small child I noted my mother's medical and surgical history, then I followed through with all her varying medical complaints until the day she died. I have come to the conclusion that my mother was massively *cellular* deficient in B vitamins and magnesium [these two being critical and the low magnesium made loud noises unbearable to her] and also calcium [it might have been going in but not absorbed or absorbed to combat her acid diet only but was not getting to her bones], possibly potassium, vitamin C and zinc [she had lost her sense of smell and taste completely before she died and this is often a sign of low zinc]. My mother's diet was quite good because she was always disciplined in cooking good old fashioned meals from scratch with plenty of fresh vegetables, but I now think the state of her gut was so poor that she was not accessing the nutrients she was ingesting and I have inherited, or acquired, the same problem.

In the last few years of her life I lost count of how many times I sat in a car park while my mother attended her various medical, psychiatric and surgical appointments at various hospitals, clinics and other places. Taking her to the local hospital for blood tests was also a regular occurrence. Looking back it seems to me that those endless blood tests were not picking up some basic fault lines. It makes me wonder what are blood tests telling you? Are they telling you what is happening in the blood but not what is happening in a cell in your knee, or thumb, or perhaps, more importantly, the brain? I don't know and while I am in the 'I don't know' ball park I am wondering if long birthing labours use up a huge amount of magnesium. Could this be a link with postnatal depression? I look back on my years as a midwife and chew my lip. How would that affect a breast-fed baby? Colic?

When my mother was alive I had never heard of Adelle Davis, more is the profoundly sad and regretful pity. Had I been armed with a copy of 'Let's Get Well' my mother would never have heard the end of it. I would have marched into her kitchen, emptied her food cupboards, commandeered her pots and pans and supervised her every mouthful and I daresay Mum would have been scowling at me every inch of the way. In the years after her death I began to wonder just how profoundly mineral and vitamin deficiencies affect our emotional wellbeing. To put slightly more of a finger on something I do not know - do certain deficiencies lead to specific mental problems? Is a specific deficiency as catastrophic for our emotions as it is for our physical state, such as a deficiency of vitamin D leading to rickets or someone getting scurvy because of a lack of vitamin C? Which comes first - the emotion or the deficiency? It is a tricky one but I would lay money on emotion coming first.

I looked back at our emotional family history, plenty of major ups and downs. A third chakra energetic deficiency, but that would be common to most. However, it struck me that my mother and me shared a common thread, we were both worriers and had a 'nervy' disposition. I was better at hiding my nerves than she was, in fact I was a pro, but I was also better at identifying a problem and pro-actively dealing with it. Nerves affect the gut and that is why we say, 'My stomach is in knots'. Daily low level anxiety, coming in just below the radar, is bound to affect your digestion. This will have a knock on effect on your absorption and is therefore going to make you mineral and vitamin deficient at some level. I had years of 'just below the radar' anxiety, so much so that when I didn't need to be anxious I found it hellishly difficult to break the habit. I have often been overwhelmed by feelings of responsibility and this would have affected my pancreas and its functioning. Worriers and people of nervy dispositions nearly always need more B vitamins, low levels of which mean sleep can be of poor quality. I think this is relevant to many but particularly to the elderly and snorers. Both my parents snored for Britain, so did I, when overtired, but since I started taking B vitamins I sleep quite quietly and so does my now B vitamin saturated ex-snoring partner. The B vitamins are not stored so you need to take them in every day and I have been told that you need adequate B6 in order to absorb magnesium [I seem to recall B6 is needed for the pancreas and also has a specific link with sleep]. I wonder a lot about B vitamins in food these days [particularly in relation to storage] and I strongly suspect it is much, much less than it was before the war. I have also read much about the low levels of magnesium in the soil, particularly since 1945. I was once told that magnesium was so low in the soil from the Kent coast right through to Somerset that daily supplementation ought to be a consideration for most. I have no idea if this is correct but I would not be surprised.

I was sad to hear recently that many cricketers have been suffering from depression [see, I knew it, they should stick to wearing *white*]. I wondered if the general lack of magnesium and B vitamins in our modern diet, coupled with today's high levels of sporting expectation and pressure, plus the length of the matches [leaving not much time for body repair] meant that some players used up an already low supply and that had an affect on their mental health. Most depressives do not eat well and some eat abysmally. My mother enjoyed a drink but did not have a problem with it, even so, only a modest intake of booze uses up a lot of B's and magnesium, amongst other things. I wondered if my mother's manic phases of activity used up her hugely depleted vitamin and mineral store and when it was running on empty the depression came back. I can remember standing in her kitchen staring at her and saying, 'It's not good, is it Ma?'. She turned to me with a haunted expression and said, 'It's coming back, I can feel it starting'. Sure enough, she was back in full depression within days, either in bed or sitting on the sofa all day, every day, in a still state but a wretched state. Looking back I now wonder was she *sitting so still* because the body needed to restore its levels of deficient minerals/vitamins? Was this her body's *only* way of controlling the limited supply it had - by keeping her body still? I don't know, but I suspect so.

My mother suffered from years and years of chronic constipation. She would take the laxatives her doctor recommended but resolutely ignored my father when he told her to drink more. During my childhood my father had a couple of stints working at the Ministry of Defence [MOD] in London [he hated it, poor man]. He would commute by train and returning home in the evening would be incredulous to find my mother had drunk nothing since the pot of tea they shared at breakfast, my father drinking the lion's share. Later in life I tried to get her to drink a litre of water a day but I was not successful and in the ensuing years I have noticed that sometimes [but more often than not] the people who will not drink water are fearful of the future. Lack of water seems to act like an emotional holding pattern, a bit like some colours. I don't know why this is but I suspect it has something to do with our cellular vibratory rate. In the wacky world, constipation is linked to 'holding on to emotions' and this makes sense to me. Years of constipation and taking laxatives will produce an unhealthy bowel lining, often referred to as a leaky gut [I have one myself]. Leaky gut sounds strange to me; I never heard an operating surgeon, holding some tubing aloft, exclaim 'LOOK at THAT BOWEL! More holes than a tea strainer!' [this is a joke - please be calm if you suffer from a tea strainer gut]. Some [or one] of the B vitamins is made in the lower bowel [can't remember which] and if a bowel is leaky and creaky, holding on to either vast amounts of stored poop or three sheep's droppings, the chances are B vitamin production is not going to be in productive full swing - yet you need B vitamins daily. My partner is home studying a degree in nutritional medicine and he brings books on the subject to bed; books so vast they could underpin a house. Night after night he regales me with ever more confusing stories of the delicate balance of relations between one mineral and one vitamin, or one vitamin to another. If one vitamin is too up, another is down; how one mineral can't possibly manage without another and goes into a sulk. 'Sounds like a bloody family to me', says I. Now I read that my carefully spaced out supplements are wrong because my breakfast vitamin won't 'do' without my lunchtime vitamin. 'Can't my breakfast vitamin flaming well wait?!', I wail. Apparently not. All that we read points us to the absolute imperative of carefully planned and well thought out balanced meals, so that three times a day everything goes in together but in its most natural state, which is food. If it is imperative for adults, think how much more imperative it is for a growing child.

I am not sure that counselling would have helped my mother's sadness, this was something so personal to her and something only she could find a way of living with. I couldn't help her, though we talked for hours and hours. My rather new age spiritual beliefs confused her and she did not seem to gather strength from her Christianity. I wish I could have helped more but I could not change the past. My gut [third chakra] feeling that she needed more physical exercise was right, the problem being by then she was so arthritic that I don't know if she could have even managed swimming. She knew she needed massage and had some treatments, but not enough. Since her death and since meeting my partner I understand the enormity of the power of healing that stretching and working the meridians and acupuncture points gives and how strong muscular contracting and relaxing, through exercise, will have a similar effect. By having just a straight massage some acupuncture points are pressed, though haphazardly. Shiatsu will press all the acupuncture points and is wonderful for emotional and physical wellbeing and many of my partner's clients have remarked that they feel strangely lighter and less dense after a treatment and many of the horses he works on are completely transformed after a session [he gets many a kiss from a grateful mare - I try not to be jealous]. Certainly a shiatsu treatment transforms my state of health [for some weeks] but I still have much work to do on cleansing my body and strengthening my third chakra. For everyone, not in the best of health, exercise builds an appetite and thirst, so with good 'clean' nutritious food and water going in health should start to improve. I look back now and realise I should have given my mother a liquid vitamin and mineral supplement at the very least and insisted on colonic irrigation ……. but reflecting on the latter I am not sure my mother was ready to let go. Perhaps, for her, it was easier to let go of life than emotions.

DEFENCE

I have pondered about putting this section into this book but decided that as I am going to air my views under 'future' I might as well air my views on defence. It's contentious in some quarters but in my view we have not as a nation, or more importantly as a mass consciousness, reached a point where we can do without a defence force. I think we are heading painfully in the right direction but we are probably a century or two away from laying down our arms for good. It is a chakra business and until we have, in large enough numbers, got to grip with the lessons of second and third chakra [internal power and control as opposed to external power and control] it is going to be necessary to have an army, navy and air force bristling with technology and things that go bang. Laying down our arms for good is a fourth heart chakra business and wonderful it will be when it happens but I don't think we are anywhere near ready yet. Decisions coming from fourth chakra need a solid, firm and full third chakra to rest upon. Our country is starting to work on its 'collective' third chakra but our government is woefully dragging behind the masses. Other countries, hauling themselves out of tribal first chakra beliefs, will sub- consciously assess our chakra status and see muddle. You cannot lay down your guns until you have a country at peace with itself and this country is not, in fact it is going through galvanic change and unrest. For a country to be at peace with itself you need a sufficient number of its countrymen and women to be thinking peacefully. I don't see it, or hear it. I am tremendously fortunate to live in a peaceful rural area but I know I must continually and rigorously patrol my thoughts so that I aim for peace in my brain [emphasis on 'aim', because I can tell you I miss frequently]. As I have pointed out in 'attitude' if you think peacefully it means you do not tend to attract violence. I don't often, these days, physically witness anger, but when I do I know I need to stop and do some internal work, for we carry our unresolved anger within ourselves and then external anger finds us. I think this may be a tricky concept to adjust to for some people. I made light of it in 'attitude' but I am actually very serious about it; quite literally 'what you are and what you think, is what you get'. When trouble finds me, in whatever shape or form it takes, even witnessing two angry drivers shouting at each other, I absolutely know I have not had peace in my head and heart for the last few hours or days, so it is up to me to find my anger and deal with it.

I am constantly amazed that we are a nation at war on two fronts, yet this rarely hits the headlines. I worry that by making the fighting almost a side-issue on the news we are losing a sense of perspective. Have we become battle weary sitting on our sofas? Although my views on the current deployment of our troops is not mainstream I think it is strange that we do not see the real outcome of war yet watch a continual diet of warfare on television. It is relentless and it is making me switch the box off. We return home from work to peak time television and a diet of fighting, shouting, hating, grabbing, getting, plotting and violence. We have to correct this and get some balance. This is how is has to be before we can put down our weapons. Enough of us have to have peace in our hearts, heads and in our everyday lives. Peace, therefore, is an inside job. We have to get a grip of second chakra lessons, start living a little more in third chakra so that we can respect, at least, if not exactly love our next door neighbour, whatever colour or creed. This is testing ground for all of us, not least me. This country is so out of balance at the moment it seems to me to be bordering on insane. We can't feed ourselves, heat ourselves and we are up to our eyeballs in debt. We are absolutely obsessed with youth culture but the older among us are the stabilising force, the experienced hand, the soothers. I don't see soothing elderly folk these days, probably because they have been so marginalised and ignored. Our wise geriatrics can witness and permit youthful energy to let off necessary steam while reminding the young of the necessary basics - duty, honesty, honest labour, diligence, love that has been tried and tested and an appreciation of things that money cannot buy. These concepts bring stability and peace in enough measure for a country to be at peace with itself, but we are a country obsessed with 'now', instant gratification and mine's bigger than yours. This has to stop if we want a peaceful world.

I have always been for the return of national service - to serve one's nation. Seems reasonable to me. My national service, if you like, was years of nursing. No matter my emotions for the job, and I had plenty, I am a better person for the experience. It taught me discipline, compassion, presence, voice projection, professional courtesy when dealing with the public and how to work fast and efficiently as a team - every single one a plus point for future employment of any type. I did not need a stint in the armed forces - listening to my father's stories was enough. For the young of today a year spent in the service of the country they call home would be invaluable experience not to mention an inculcation of much needed discipline - such a dirty word these days. The option could be a year in the defence force, or hospital based work or perhaps even farming [assuming our poor dispirited and battered farmers were game enough to take the youth of today on]. I am really bothered that too many youngsters are able to watch violence on a screen [and actually chose to do so] but cannot cope with the reality of broken bodies.

Whatever the current use of our armed forces it is government that sends our soldiers citizens [for they are both] to war - soldiers are at Westminster's bidding. Over the years I have listened to many of the opinion that we can do without defence and even more who are scathing about our police force. Whilst there are a few in the armed forces and the police whose actions are reprehensible there are thousands and thousands more who work hard and heroically in jobs I could not do. I worked for a few years in a mid-London

Accident and Emergency Department. I got thoroughly bored with being sworn at and called exquisitely unpleasant things repeatedly, hour after hour, come day shift or night shift, but especially the latter, by boorish drunks and drug addicts. The latter would often smear their blood onto razor blades and needles and place sunny side up in their jean pockets knowing full well we would have to strip them and search their clothing when they were brought in unconscious by ambulance. We learnt to strip and search carefully, never to turn our backs on tricky customers and to dodge fists. It is difficult to deal with this sort of behaviour on a regular basis without becoming hardened to some extent. I cannot imagine how it must be for the police to deal with this on the streets on a daily basis as they do, what a bloody waste of their time. In the same way I can only try to imagine how a young eighteen year old would feel, having joined the army knowing fighting may be called for, to actually feel bullets whizzing past his ears and see a fellow soldier and probable friend blown to bits in front of him. I would feel terrified and angry, no matter how well I had been trained [and while I am in the fighting area, would a soldier in such a situation use up all his B vitamins and/or magnesium? I should say so. Would his diet put them back in? I would doubt it. Might this make him ill long term? What do you think?].

My father, who served in the Royal Air Force, battled with his superior officers to get protection for the station he commanded in times of civil unrest in the sixties. It was s l o w arriving to say the least. Before he got the protection for the station that he continually and urgently requested he was issued, from the MOD, personal protection in the form of a rather large revolver [it looked historic, verging an antique to me], but not a holster to put it in. Perhaps the gun and the holster came from two different departments and expecting communication and co-operation between the two was expecting too much. My father raised his eyebrows with a sigh and shoved the unwieldy weapon down his underpants, because it would not fit in a pocket. My mother, nerves in shreds, shrieked at me several times, 'He's going to shoot his balls off'. I gravely assessed the situation [aged fourteen] and came to the conclusion that at my parents' great age [late forties] balls were not imperative. When he left the RAF my father told me endless stories of incompetence during the Second World War when it came to delivering to the forces the equipment and ammunition they needed. I read the news today and it seems nothing changes. My view is no man or woman should be permitted into Westminster without having done a stint of national service in the forces and that goes for anyone working for the MOD too. Like farming and education, defence is too crucial to the structure of the country not to be basically understood. I don't believe reading documents gives government ministers the insight needed, a mile walking in the forces moccasins is required. [This comes from the native American saying 'never judge a man until you have walked a mile in his moccasins - just in case you didn't know - and isn't it interesting to see just *who* is *walking* a mile in the forces moccasins these days? I am certainly paying attention to that.]

Taking aside the complete lack of integrity [third chakra], to poorly equip and not care for our fighting forces is an extraordinarily stupid and dangerous thing to do, especially in this day and age. It is to send out a message to the armed forces that 'you are expendable'. Thin ice. Very, very thin ice. We are not in first chakra now. This message has a poisonous drip-drip effect and long term it could be catastrophic. I have watched this poison drip through the National Health Service where once, should they become sick, staff were treated first and with great care but no longer, they now know they are expendable. There is a difference between thinking and fully knowing you are expendable because fully knowing has dropped down through the chakras and has settled in to the lower abdomen where we all, but especially the army, keep our weapons. To send someone to war with poor equipment is to say, 'I don't care about you'. To be on the receiving end of an 'I don't care about you' attitude, whether it be in a marriage, a hospital ward or a regiment is to invite a reply of, 'Well, stuff you then, I'm off'. How then will they recruit?

I am greatly bothered about the slashing of regiments and making one big blob of an army, even allowing for modern warfare. Government today seems to like big, big blobs even better [European Union] and would like big police forces and big hospitals but regiments, like small police forces and small hospitals, are like families with their own language, history, traditions and support network and by breaking them up you inevitably lose a sense of belonging. It may save money short term but long term I doubt it will make for a cohesive structure. The bigger any organisation gets the wider the gap between the chief and the indian, between the general and the foot soldier [prime minister and voter] and the bigger the gap the less the high and supposedly mighty have a grasp of events at ground level. Chiefs become isolated and indians unheard. A breeding ground for disillusionment and a perfect environment for bullies. I have watched this first hand in the NHS. The disaffection affects all and the experienced leave, or are pushed, taking with them vital information that only years of service can accumulate, leaving younger staff to wonder whether long service is an option at all, let alone an attractive one.

It is one of the duties of government to keep its people safe; protecting grannies from having their purses snatched right through to giving as much protection as possible to soldiers on active duty. The appalling purse snatcher needs appropriate and swift punishment and the soldier should be wearing, carrying and trained in the very best. It is the right thing to do. It is the *only* thing to do. It is honourable. It's third chakra standards. Protect the granny and give the soldier his boots, the best boots money can buy. Defence is very expensive but as it is no good weeping over your burnt out house and wishing you had kept up your household insurance policy, in the same way it is no good trying to make up a defence force that has been repeatedly slashed and demoralised when the enemy is at the door. What enemy? Who knows? We live in uncertain times where events are not just moving fast but seem to me to be at warp speed. A major terrorist attack is more than possible. Countries will fight for water as global warming increases - maybe even fight within nations [our north has much more water than our overpopulated and over consuming south]. Civil unrest in this country is a distinct possibility and mass migration due to sudden catastrophic climate change is verging on a certainty. Hopefully we will not be shooting a flood of starving immigrants but the country will need a defence force [and a strong police force] to control and maintain order on our streets in the event of sudden mayhem. I am extremely worried about sudden mayhem. My grandfather used to tell my mother that a hungry man [not starving - too late] was a dangerous man. Think what a hungry drug addict will do to get a fix. This country has had fifty years of comfortably stuffed food shelves in supermarkets but in the event of sudden mayhem if we suddenly found empty food shelves and could not feed our families then things could get very nasty very quickly. There is a saying that 'we are only three days off anarchy' and I believe it ….. just how long could you last on the contents of your kitchen cupboards if the shops were empty? Despite the dramatic change in our weather patterns and the catastrophic flooding in New Orleans our government was still ill-prepared for our recent torrential rain and off we go again with foot and mouth disease.

Come sudden trouble within this country, for whatever reason, you had better be prepared. Personally and nationally. In my book that means personally paying attention and having a fully equipped and well maintained defence force. We live in troubled times. Read your history books, everything is cyclical and so far human nature has changed not one jot over thousands of years. Please do not think because we have television, central heating, mobile phones, computer games and pink fluffy bed socks that these in some way civilise us. They do not. Handling a television remote control or pushing a shopping trolley is a human, barely a breath away from an animal. There is still a wolf in most dogs and there is a murderous human in most of us if food, shelter and family are seriously threatened.

I can't remember where the saying 'guns before butter' came from. It is a bit over the top, but a fully equipped defence force is a necessity until we have seriously shifted through the chakras and moved into the next dimension because it is damn dangerous standing in whatever bit of second chakra you are presently stuck in and speaking through fourth chakra [love and compassion] while negotiating with anybody armed and stuck firmly in fearful first chakra. The first chakra person usually wins the argument but loses the point. How do they do this? Easy, first chakra person pulls out his gun and shoots you.

DRAMA QUEEN

I have observed that unchecked drama queens often get given a real life drama and not one of their choosing.

DRUGS

I used to smoke ordinary cigarettes and I enjoyed it. I have tried marijuana and hashish but I fell asleep, so I couldn't see the point. My drug of choice these days is booze and my idea of heaven is a candlelit bath on a winter's evening with a scotch at my elbow and time to ponder the deeper meaning of life. Either that or a bottle of red wine shared with my beloved while one of us cooks and the other dissects the day's happenings. I know my limit of booze almost to the drop and it is not a huge amount. I know I need to take extra minerals and vitamins if I drink alcohol and I normally drink extra water [with a drop of apple cider vinegar] before I have an evening drink, but I know if I push my limit my body will reproach me and I will feel agonies of guilt.

Recreational drugs are changing. I hear they are becoming stronger and more addictive. I don't know much about them but what I do know is alcohol, cigarettes and recreational drugs change your biochemistry and if you partake in them you need to shove in what your drug of choice removes. If you don't you will find your body breaking down eventually. As most bodies break down as we get older anyway, you don't really want to exacerbate and speed up the process if you can help it. I have heard the arguments that rock stars are still going strong at sixty after years of drug abuse and in some cases this is true, but sixty year old rock stars usually have two things going for them: the level of minerals and vitamins in their childhood food was probably considerably better than it is for the rock stars just emerging to jump about on stage now and many of the oldies in the rock business have made quite a bit of cash. Money cushions you. If you are not stressing yourself on how to pay the rent, mortgage or bills, life is easier, no question. Long term emotional stress [or rather your body's reaction to it] can adversely affect your biochemistry and/or your digestion. Shove in drugs, or whatever, on top and you double the trouble. I often wonder if our present day actions affect our sperm, ova, DNA and therefore our future children, grandchildren and onwards. I don't know, but possibly. You only have to talk to homeopaths about miasms to get some idea of what problems can carry through the generations.

Everyone these days is bombarded with chemicals but I worry most for the little ones among us. Babies crawl at low air level, shove plastic toys in their mouth, cuddle soft toys made of man-made fabrics soaked in man-made dyes. They must inhale chemicals all the time, everywhere. I live in the country and what I can't find in local charity shops I buy from catalogues [some of which stink of chemical dyes to my ever increasing nasal sensitivities], so for me 'shopping' means food and essential supplies for the house. The odd forays into large stores has me instantly complaining about the smell of chemicals, presumably because I do it so infrequently I am more aware of the onslaught to my senses. I was sitting in a car showroom recently while my partner got some details about a vehicle and he noted my eyes went from white to scarlet in a matter of minutes while I was noticing the intense smell of I knew not what. A few weeks later I had to move away from a carpet that was designer cladding half a wall in a famous art gallery because I could not bear the smell of what I presumed was fire retardant chemicals. It made me wonder about babies crawling across carpets. Now, I am not well, I'm still hauling my health back into shape and probably have less ability to cope with the ordinary mundane chemical overload we are bombarded with, but I can't help wondering what this onslaught is doing to those who live, work or frequently frequent places where chemicals abound. My guess is long term health problems, more allergies, an inability to fight infections and increased problems with fertility. It is not so much the possibility of avian bird flu arriving in this country that I worry about, it is the poor shape we are in to fight the invading organism. A flu or plague will arrive some day, that's for sure, but can we individually ward it off? I doubt it. In our house we keep a ready stock of the necessary extra minerals and vitamins should some flu type thing arrive suddenly and I have also started adding these to our hens' diet. My partner thinks I am a bit over the top but I would be devastated if Doris, Phoebe, Hattie, Bunty Binmont and the rest of the girls keeled over at the first whiff of an international bug. Good job I am childless because my children would be going to school daily armed with a rucksack of pills and potions. I am not alarmist, I am alarmingly pro-active, that's all.

As 99.9% of the population have no idea what state of health they really are in and what their drug of choice is likely to do to their biochemistry, they are in effect gambling. That the drug of choice will change their biochemistry is a given, even food does that, but whether it will have a seriously detrimental affect you will not know until you get sick. How fast you get sick and whether you heal depends much on how strong your constitution is plus what you emotionally and physically inherited from your parents. It also depends on what your diet has been like [possibly, even your mother's diet when you were in utero], how you ate that diet [fast, slow, on the move] and how nervy, sensitive and/or stressed you are. All of life is a risk, of course, but please bear the following points in mind if you are dabbling with drugs. One, you are taking a gamble with your health - gamble with money and you may be able to replace it but your health may be a different matter. Two, you will not value your health until you have lost it. Three, only when you hit 'chronic' illness [over six months] will you find how inadequate Western medicine is. Four, the National Health Service is doomed in its present form and soon we will be paying through the nose for our medical and nursing care and it is therefore crucial that you put your health as a primary priority. This is called self reliance .... this is chakra and spiritual awareness.

One more point. If you constantly need to be 'out of your head' you are sending a potent message to the universe. I have found the universe listens attentively and takes messages seriously. Be very careful it does not take your need/request literally.

$\mathcal{D}$OG

Do dogs go to heaven? Of course they do, ridiculous question! Though I did read somewhere that there are no insects upstairs. I am still mulling that one over .... no bees? Can't be right.

Dog is, of course, God spelt backwards. I have not a shadow of a doubt that dogs are here to teach us unconditional love and how to live in the moment. My many dogs, past and present, have been the teachers I have liked the best. Brogan, about whom I have written, was my most sensitive teacher. Looking back I can see he was telling me to change my life and take better care of my health. I abjectly failed to get the lesson because I thought his problems were all about him but Brogan was more like me than I care to admit and these days, if I am permitted or it is appropriate, I urge people to pay attention to their choice of dog and particularly the dog's behaviour while asking, 'Am I being taught something or am I having something highlighted about me?'. This is highly sensitive questioning so be gentle with yourself. Right now my littlest dog is highlighting the dark emotional holes in my third chakra, my middle dog is teaching me about poor digestion

[I can't work out the lesson] and my oldest dog is giving me a master class on split level fear.

I read that dogs are being trained to sniff out cancer and I was wondering if we could train them to sniff out other impending medical problems? Whiffing dogs in doctor's surgeries, what a woofing good idea!

I have rescued most of my dogs and I have a bit of advice if you are thinking of doing likewise. Don't rescue on a Saturday and go to work on a Monday. I worked when I had mine, but I did night-duty and they got their normal walks and snored on my bed as I ploughed through the night in the hospital. I had two small dogs to keep each other company, a cat that the dogs did not much care for and a tiny dog flap for emergency night time pees. I took on a new rescue dog during my annual leave and the moment it arrived home the leaving process would begin. I would walk outside the front door, count to five and come back in again. Then an hour later I would repeat the process and count to twenty and so on. I would always say the same thing before I left the front door. Then I would go and sit in my car for five minutes. A couple of days later I would go to a shop, but only be gone for ten minutes. Gradually I would build up to half an hour, then an hour, then more. While all this was going on the new and old dog would have extremely long lead walks all around the area we lived with plenty of sniffing time. This enabled the new family member to build up a visual and sniffy picture of the area around home, so that it could find its way back should a calamity happen, while the whole process plum tuckered us all out so that restful sleep was ensured.

Dogs give much and ask little in return; a warm bed, love, food and at the very least one decent walk a day. Please think before you buy a working dog because they need huge amounts of exercise and stimulation and it is so cruel not to give an animal the life it needs. I was reduced to tears by a tale of an old English sheepdog locked in a tiny bathroom for ten hours a day while its owner's worked. It went mad. Dogs are pack animals and need another to talk dog to. My dogs silently communicate to each other all the time, it is a total fascination to me. Occasionally you get a dog that genuinely prefers to have just its human owner as companion but most like to doggy chat and if you have to leave one while you work please try and get it a pal to keep it company.

I take the feeding of all our animals seriously. I know dried food is recommended by some vets but would you want to eat it day after day? Would you feed it to your children? If you have a sick dog look at changing the diet. Dogs are hunter and opportunistic gatherers and we have massively interfered with their natural looks; travel across Asia and most dogs look like dingos. To say that all dogs need the same balanced diet is to say that all humans need the same balanced diet, but I have found all humans are different with differing needs, it must surely to the same for dogs. Many years ago [probably thirty or more] I remember asking a vet why I heard of so many dogs that were having epileptic fits. He thought they were over stimulated, a constant barrage of daily human noise, interlaced with alarms, low flying aircraft and loud music. Pity the poor dog subjected to relentless high voltage music. They have, I believe, hearing that is several hundred times better than ours [sometimes I wonder if really loud noise causes them pain]. Fifteen years ago one of my much loved whippets had an epileptic type fit in old-age. I knew nothing about nutrition then, but now I wonder if I had given him magnesium would I have prevented, or at the very least delayed, another attack? I look back now and realise I should have given him Brewer's Yeast as I do for my dogs now on a daily basis. On the day he died he had a massive fit and immediately after, or perhaps during, his old and yellowing teeth went completely black. Did he bleed into them? Did he removed much needed minerals in an effort to stay alive? Do I feel guilty? Yes, why the bloody hell did I not thoroughly research after the first fit, instead of just making a meandering effort to improve his diet? I think teeth talk like the rest of the body. Post glandular fever, when I returned to work far too early and as a result had multiple small niggling infections to deal with for the following two years, I told my dentist my teeth went from white to slightly transparent when I was feeling unwell. He told me I was completely and utterly wrong because it was not possible. A year or two later I shared a house with someone who had a year or more of post-viral problems and tiredness. She assured me that during that time her teeth did exactly the same as mine and also mirrored her health.

I have often heard the remark 'I don't know why people are cruel to animals'. I do. If, as a baby, you witness violence to anyone or anything from your pram, it will seem to be normal behaviour. However, when you reach adulthood you will make a choice - to repeat the cycle or stop it. I believe our actions are noted, every single one. If you cannot be kind to an animal then show how courageous you can be - give the animal away to someone who will love it. All courage is rewarded eventually. All kindness is noted. What you give out you get back. That goes for cruelty too. If you have been cruel, be alert for the boomerang.

E Is for EMOTIONS

This is where you find out where you are losing power. Don't lift the bonnet, I'm not talking engines. I have given this subject a lot of thought and my conclusion is that emotions and feelings are utterly different. Feelings are the signposts on the road of life, emotions are the people you stop and ask for directions. [Aha! That's why men won't stop and ask for directions - it's too emotional.]

There is a saying that there are only two emotions, love and fear; that everything said and every action taken that does not obviously stem from love stems from fear. From the hurtful comment, to the vicious act, to racial taunting, murder and war, these are all fear based actions performed by individuals or nations. This fear stems from *the perception* of loss of personal power.

Why, you may be asking, is it important to know the difference between emotions and feelings? Well, the answer is this ... well honed, tried, trusted and acted upon feelings keep you out of trouble, whilst out of control energy loss through emotions makes life difficult, rampages through your wallet, disrupts relationships and can make you ill. Your feelings hold your power, your emotions take your power away. Your feelings are your earthly link to your spiritual eternal self and therefore your earthly connection to whatever you perceive as the divine, whereas your emotions, buffeting you busily around, keep you from returning to base, to third chakra, to self-love, to your peaceful eternal state. A state it is possible to reach on earth during a lifetime. We have all heard someone say, 'I had a gut feeling I should not have ....', you fill in the blanks. Our third chakra gut instincts operate, I believe, out of self-love and self-interest so to ignore them is counter productive, to say the very least. Our emotions are driven by fear of loss of power and being alone. We are frightened of being taken advantage of [power loss] sexually or in business deals. We are frightened of being ignored [power loss] at home, at school, at work, or in our love affairs and we are frightened of being overtaken [power loss] by a more beautiful sibling, a more intelligent friend, a better dressed colleague, a better paid business partner or a neighbour who wins the lottery. Ultimately we are frightened of being left alone. It starts with the fear of living alone, though this is being increasingly tackled. Then 'doing' alone, but this too is also being challenged by many who are singly self-employed - often creators, repairers and therapists - and an increasing number of people who travel alone. There is the obvious and understandable fear of aloneness from bereavement. Finally there is the ultimate fear of being spiritually alone, 'the dark night of the soul', an expression that is rather glibly bandied about. I don't think the 'dark night' is in our realm of understanding; it is for the intensely spiritually advanced who are physically present but who have pretty much left our world behind. I can only imagine how terrifying it must be for anyone to face the final spiritual challenge - the void.

Our job here on earth is to find our pure and loving divine spark and in order to do this we have to learn how we are controlled by our fearful emotions. Is there a point in returning to base to find your divine spark? Yes, because life gets easier, your health improves, you find love, you don't have financial worries and you find life deeply fulfilling. Is your divine spark easy to find? No, absolutely blooming not ... well, not in my experience anyway. Let's go back to third chakra again because that is where your feelings reside, in your gut, your second brain. Your feelings are your guidance and will tell you, 'This is wrong', while your emotional self says, 'No it isn't'. Sometimes this two way conversation is just a bore but sometimes it is truly character building, like thinking, 'I feel shouldn't be doing this', on the morning of your wedding, but doing it anyway. While your feelings know this marriage is not going to be made in heaven and will in fact end up funding a solicitor's expensive holiday, your emotional self says any amount to the contrary. 'He/she will change' [oooops!], it says, or, 'My friends are all married', or ,'I will get left on the shelf', or [cutting it fine], 'The guests are at the church'.

Now, let's fetch some tools. I like tools. Tools mean action. Naughty emotions need tools to sort them out. Let's try an example .... you are at work and have just been on the receiving end of a really hurtful comment and you are in emotional meltdown. The moment you are able to do so, disappear into the loo and lock the whole world out. Sit down, think about the hurtful comment and ask yourself [*this is crucial*], 'Where does my body hurt?'. This will be at a chakra point and if the pain is intense you are haemorrhaging energy - this is not good news. Everyone is unique and complicated, a hurtful comment that flattens one person might be water off a duck's back to another, but we all have our Achilles heel. An energetic 'hit' may affect more than one chakra, or may provoke a total body 'breakdown' because the body is storing [filing] too many hurts and the filing cabinet is full to bursting. The following is not comprehensive, my intention is to widen your sixth chakra perspective to what is happening when you are under energetic attack so then you can learn to help yourself. I will list the targets so it is easier to read.

1. Hurtful remarks about your family, your nationality, your religion, or even your pets [all first chakra], may cause an overall total body reaction [seeing 'red'] from head to toe, or locally cause you pain in the area you sit on, make your buttock muscles tense, knees or legs hurt. You may want to kick out or punch because raw anger is a natural human response in retaliation to any sort of threat, verbal or otherwise, to one's tribe.

2. Cutting remarks about your work performance, your finances, your boyfriend/girlfriend, your sex appeal or lack of it or anything that hits second chakra may make you feel disembowelled, cause pain across your hips and abdomen or lower back [you may get the energetic 'hit' at the time but the back 'goes' a day or so later]. It is possible [I don't know] that it might tighten internal scar tissue. It could affect your bowels [shortly after a cutting or frightening remark you may find you need to open your bowels or your bowels clamp down and you cannot defecate] but possibly more likely your bladder. Apologies for repeating myself but when someone is told an unpalatable truth they often feel the need to urinate [and/or defecate if the unpalatable truth has frightened them].

3. Fear from loss of freedom or third chakra hurtful comments about your personal performance or abilities, your looks and/or bullying in relation to boundaries can make you nauseous, reject food, or cause physical pain or tightening under your ribcage and across your upper abdomen. It may also rattle your already present gallstones, make your hiatus hernia do a song and dance routine or fire up your duodenal ulcer, if you have one.

4. Fourth heart chakra pain might come if someone made a harsh comment about someone, or something, you have loved and lost. I would expect this to cause a pulling or crushing feeling to the heart. A really fearful situation will always affect the heart [pounding], lungs [rapid fearful breathing] and adrenal glands [a blast of adrenaline].

5 and **6.** If your neck is red, your throat sore or burning, or your jaw aches, you have taken an energetic hit to your fifth chakra - probably because you are unable for some reason to catch the missile [hurtful comment] and chuck it back. If you have a lump in your throat you are preventing your heart chakra from having its say by putting up a road block to prevent your heart energy reaching your head. A developing frontal headache may be as a result of tightening your shoulders and neck in fear, in which case it may be a fifth chakra issue, or it may be you have had a great idea rejected and taken a hit on your sixth [wider perspective] chakra. Are you frowning?

When you have located the pain, discomfort or heat and you know the chakra, think back. When did this area hurt last? Was it recently? Are you holding or storing a whole filing cabinet of hurts? Back track through the years and see if you can pinpoint the original comment or action that energetically caused the wound. It will be from your childhood. Look closely at who did the hurting and how you forgive. If forgiveness is too tall an order, stop finger pointing because you are just wasting time. Make self-awareness, self-healing and self-kindness your utmost priority. Use colour, try Bach Flower Remedies, make a daily list of your attributes, whatever, just start the repair work. You can't do this sitting on the loo, so hold the thought and when you leave work take it home for some serious mulling over and then action. Meanwhile, take a deep breath and return to face your colleagues. If Mr. or Mrs. Hurtful Comment are about you have two options, you can think, 'Peace be with you', or you can pull out your imaginary pistols and shoot them full of holes. It might help to know this - when I was a teenager someone close made an extremely unpleasant comment to me, about me. It was a third chakra hit. I was very upset for far too long; the reason being that of all my *many* failings, the one being lobbed at me was *entirely* inaccurate. It took me nearly twenty-five years to fully understand that they were describing themselves and not me at all.

OK, try another one. This one is more for the boys. When the souped-up red car pulls sharply in front of your car, carving you up in a flurry of farting exhaust and you honk your horn, the reply to which is the driver winding down his window screaming abuse and shoving two fingers in the air ……. stop reacting … if you can. Loosen your white knuckled grip on the steering wheel, don't reciprocate with more expletives and induce calm. Pull over as soon as you can and ask yourself, 'Where does this hurt?', or …. 'Where is the heat?'. The emotion will be somewhere located in a chakra. You are losing energy, you have an energetic wound here. You need to fix it - heal it. Who last carved you up, not necessarily in a car? Who was the first person to carve you up and then be rude about it? This is the starting point, each perceived carving up from childhood on will add fuel to the fire, a file to the filing cabinet, so by the time you are thirty or forty, you will be a volcano with a lid on [blood pressure, blood pressure] and you will be attracting every carver-upper in the neighbourhood because that's how the universe works; that's how it draws your attention to your problems - it shoves them in your face. Clever but unpleasant. Mr. Farty Exhaust will come along and blow the lid off and you may find yourself, uncharacteristically, out of your car threatening grievous bodily harm while waving a car jack because your filing cabinet of stored 'carving-ups' is overloaded and you cannot take another file.

Now you are completely calm and sitting in a lay-by working out where your chakra energetic wound is located. When you have found the wound you can set about healing it. Do the repair work suggested two paragraphs ago but remember, please, you need to keep a balanced view of your wound by examining your capability of inflicting wounds ...... so, how have you carved someone else up? Driving? Verbally? Have you ever shoved 'mine is bigger and better than yours' in someone's face? Patronised someone less intelligent? I am sure you can think of more, I definitely can. Now you can release the steering wheel, flex fingers and think, 'Ok, I get the message ... peace be with you brother', or you can shoot the car full of imaginary holes with your imaginary pistol. Personally I would go with, 'Peace be with you brother', through gritted teeth, because my aim is hopeless when I am angry.

Try and think of chakras one to six as dart-boards. You are a target until you have cleared everything - numbers, felt, metal, errrr .. [you can see I don't play, can't you?] off the face of the dart-board and have replaced all the clutter with a perfectly balanced spinning wheel in the appropriate chakra colour. Once that coloured wheel is spinning beautifully you are no longer a target. You will not get the hits because the dart-board has gone. Are you with me? There will be more challenges ahead but they are different, internal, quieter. They will humble you, they may make you cry, but they will bring deep understanding and joy. We have to make this journey, each and every one of us. It is becoming imperative because this planet is on collision course to self-destruct unless enough of us start reclaiming our power. With that reclamation comes a different way of living. You may think that silently saying, 'Peace be with you', to someone who just gave you an unpleasant life lesson, is a piddle in the ocean of pesticides, plastic bags, tribal hatreds [fear, fear, fear] and nuclear weapons but please allow me to remind you .... out of tiny acorns mighty oaks do grow.

Start today, there is not a minute to waste. You need lots of practice and today's infuriations give you plenty to practice on because the media give us so much to be infuriated about and that is before you get to work and your colleagues, or boss, wind you up. If enough of us start really working on where we are losing power, healing our wounds and living a different life we will move mountains. We will shift government thinking because our opinions will be out there, growing and expanding like a huge white cloud in a united mass thought form of ....'Let's take responsibility for ourselves - let's behave with kindness, compassion, dignity, honesty, integrity and reverence'. Phew! Looks good to me!

I am learning, slowly and painfully, to become less emotional and more in touch with the safety of my feelings. I still get energetic hits which leave me emotionally out of kilter; many are thoroughly unpleasant and I don't like them one little bit but they are necessary because my second chakra is still in poor shape, my third is full of holes and my fifth is still partially blocked. I watch mouthy youngsters on the telly [The Apprentice - I'm quite literally gob-smacked] and think, 'How the hell do they do and say that?!!'. I could not do it, but I can do other things. I can write this book.

I had a gentle 'aha' moment on losing power this very morning. It was very, very subtle and I had to really think about it. I was walking the dogs early and, as I walked, I suddenly remembered an incident when I was nursing. An ambulance crew brought in a gentleman in his mid-fifties, as I recall, immaculately dressed in a dark suit, white shirt, black tie and polished black shoes. He was smart but I remember looking at his old fashioned glasses and thinking he was stuck in a bit of a 1950's fashion time warp. He was deathly pale and weak and dehydrated. It was so long ago that I cannot remember whether he was brought in from his home or the office where he worked, but I think it was his office. The ambulance crew said he was bleeding from his groin but the man had been unwilling to remove his trousers, so us nurses did. He had no genitals left, just a huge raw cancerous mass that looked like minced meat which extended up to his navel. It was bleeding a lot and he was leaking urine but it was impossible to say where it was coming from. I whispered to him, 'How long have you had this, sir?', but he would barely answer. His only concern was his mother with whom he lived. She was about 90. He was so worried that he would be unable to look after her that he had kept silent about the growing mass. We nursed him as best we could and transferred him to the ward. We must have called social services to provide care for the mother - I can't recall exactly because I was so upset I have blotted it out. I did not follow him up. I think he died. As I walked and recalled this event, the sight of him so clear in my mind, I monitored my distress and loss of power. My forehead did not hurt exactly but there was a lot of heat and discomfort and I was frowning intensely. I was losing power from my sixth chakra and my eyes had tears. I could not embrace a bigger picture of his journey because I was then, and still am now [obviously], wrapped up in my own distress because of my relationship with my mother. I am not sure how I heal this. The answer will come. I will ask for it, because I could have nursed him better if I had not been so overwhelmed with emotion. I cannot do more for this particular lovely gentleman, but there will be others for whom I can be of service and my service will be greater and clearer if I am not consumed by swirling emotion.

You might be interested to note that the cancerous mass had started in the groin. This is borderline territory between first and second chakra. By putting the care of his mother first and not seeking medical attention for himself this man had been trapped by first chakra tribal duty which had not allowed him to empower himself in second chakra and he was dying because of it. Perhaps if he had made the full transition he would have been able to care for his mother while maintaining his own power and staying alive.

EDUCATION

For as long as I can remember, politicians have been making education a priority. Buckets of tax-payers' money are thrown at schools annually but the results have been extraordinarily inadequate in some quarters. It's either failing children or the superbright clutching a rather unbelievable array of trophies. That it is possible these days for a child to leave school illiterate is simply unbelievable, the child quite possibly blighted for life. It is abuse. The newspapers shriek again and again, 'Illiterate, innumerate youngsters!!', and the politicians respond by announcing yet more unnecessary changes and more priority buckets. It goes on year after tedious year and for the life of me I could not understand why until I realised it was yet another chakra business because education, in its broadest terms, is about empowering and this is third chakra territory. Taking teachers aside [poor things - I would give them all medals for attendance, never mind staying the course] why would politicians have any real interest in empowering an entire generation? They wouldn't and anyway they can't. Agenda laden politicians cannot empower because agendas are the priority of second chakra and you cannot fully empower another individual while having an agenda. You have to be on more than nodding terms with your own third chakra in order to empower another. To give without any thought other than to elevate another human being. This is the realm of the true compliment, the *true* compliment that holds the *truth*; the recognition of excellence in another and the wish to acknowledge that excellence, to validate it. Sadly, I don't see much evidence of third chakra in politics today and with so little sunny third chakra input to be found, how would it be possible to empower anyone, let alone the nations' children? You might be able to lob the odd compliment but that would be about it, because you cannot give what you have not got. To fully empower the nation's children would be to send each child out into adulthood educated to a basic standard and fully equipped to tackle life in every sphere. No government, as yet, will fully empower all the children because the end result is that the government votes itself out of a job. An empowered generation would dismantle Westminster.

My late father, born in 1920, was bright but certainly not from a wealthy family. He got a scholarship to a private school and had an unbelievably uplifting, well-rounded and thorough education. My education, by comparison, was derisory. I never had a whiff of the classics that my father and his classmates took for granted. How could that possibly be? My first stint of book-burning boarding school imprisonment must have taught me something, I just can't think what. I remember spending most of my days there thinking, 'Help, get me out! Help!'. The school closed down rather suddenly … hooray! Celebrations were not long-lasting. I ended up in Northern Ireland at another school which had day girls and boarders and terrifyingly high teaching and examination standards [grammar school]. Academically I was so well and truly behind I was considered quite thick, verging on gormless, probably reassuring everyone at the school that everything they had always thought about the English was absolutely correct. I spent two years there and recall constant hunger and constant study.

Both schools, however, taught me a great deal about education. The first school taught me that, in any school, discipline must be in reasonable proportion to praise otherwise you just get dejection, rejection and 'shut down'. I spent three years at that school in 'shut down', rejecting ludicrously over the top discipline, getting virtually no praise and needing more contact with my parents [no phone, ever. Our letters home - we were not allowed to seal them - were read and destroyed if we failed to make satisfactory noises about the school]. The second school taught me that spirited teaching will always win the day. My parents, when taken on a tour of the building, were thrilled to find a dazzling new language laboratory. Weekly, us schoolgirls would file in, sit down in our cubicles, put on our headsets and watch the French teacher mouthing at us over the static din. Eventually she would gather we could not hear her, instruct us to open our books and read while she went in search of the engineer. Even as a tender young teenager my priority was to grasp enough of the language so that I could go to France, order a meal and a bed for the night in stutter-free French without breaking into a sweat. Instead we learnt to conjugate. Naturally, as teenagers we thought conjugal [in relation to sex, obviously] was a far more interesting subject. Fortunately we had plenty of time to discuss this in the non-operational language laboratory, as the teacher was more without than within. This teacher was kind enough to write and inform me, having left school, that I had been the only one in my class to pass French 'O' level. This was to be my first personal experience of a major miracle. Still, those wasted hours spent in a silly cubicle left me with an indelible distrust of technology when it comes to teaching. 'Why can't she just do simple things in class, say what she is doing in French and get us to repeat it?', I wondered. 'Why can't she take us for a walk round the grounds and point at things in French?', I agonised. 'Why can't we have some bloody fun?!' I thought French films [for *children* - settle down please] and French cartoons would be a good idea and a quick way of learning the basics of a language - grammar could come later. I gather you can buy foreign language cartoons for children these days but I don't know if they have managed to find their way into schools ……….. no rush, I only left school thirty-seven years ago. I do understand that by not teaching all British children to speak French, Spanish or German, the English language became globally dominant. Clever, but having achieved the objective surely it is time to move on.

History never gave me goose bumps at school but I once stood in a farmhouse kitchen open mouthed and electrified as a Hampshire housewife waved a wooden spoon and re-enacted the Trojan War for me as she cooked. This woman also worked in an office - wasted! She was a storyteller bar none. What a service she would have done the country by touring the schools and inspiring. I love history now, put David Starkey on the box and I am spellbound. Darling John Romer [where is he?] brings the ancients alive. Richard Holmes is the only person who can rouse me from deep coma when it comes to battles, as he manfully rides across the fields of France. I was not so enthralled with history at school where, having grasped the stone age, we bypassed metal and failed to light the dark ages. We pounced on the Minoans and Alfred's cakes, in no particular order, but pretty much ignored the middle ages [shame, loved the frocks] and pitched, full tilt, into the Tudors. I didn't mind. It was all darkly devious with terrifying characters in astounding clothes. The women were a complete and utter fascination to me and my love affair with Holbein began. His Lady Guildford [1527 - postcard size - all I can afford] sits in front of me as I type, she of the knowing and oh so modern half smile, what a girl! I reckon she was a scheming Miss, but, back to school ..... there I was, in raptures, with Queen Liz I, when I was dragged, kicking and screaming, into the Stuarts. We managed the Jacobite rebellion, touched on Mary, skipped George I to IV and blundered into Brunel - as if I gave a monkeys. Bridges? Boys stuff! I wanted draughty castles and wimples.

Is it still the same? What is wrong with continuity? Why can't we start with the dinosaurs when we are tiddly-tots and work our way through each historic period term by term steadfastly building a solid bedrock of knowledge? We really should leave school knowing which Richard came where - it is so basic. Our history is everything to us. Knowledge of our past triumphs and disasters, both private-emotional and national-historical gives us a course to steer by, a safer road map to our future. I read that some government ministers don't think history is that important a teaching subject ..... someone is blind and deaf to the present pike sharpening.

I think the vast amount of taxpayer's money hurled at school buildings is completely ludicrous and wasteful. Schools do not have to be fantastically expensive, huge, glass erections, stuffed with techno stuff and looking like some modern airport terminal. It's is a load of old cobblers. You need labs for some lessons but not most. From my childhood until this year [I am still attending courses] I have been taught in extremely basic classrooms. My learning was not improved by, or dependent on, the building, or the room I sat in - it was all down to my willingness to learn and how well I was taught. Most people have a great fondness for old stone and old wood and I think buildings with a bit of history evoke more loyalty. Nooks, crannies and wooden floorboards that have been trampled by countless previous generations of students leave their mark on a memory. I can remember the old wooden staircase at my first boarding school with clarity, yet I struggle to recall any aspect of the modern building of my second boarding school. Perhaps it is my age, but I remember with nostalgia the Nightingale wards of my student nurse days, with their enormous pipes covered in countless layers of paint, the cockroaches to be dodged at night and the ward's extremely high ceilings that practically created their own micro-climate [mostly draughty]. I have no such nostalgia for the modern hospitals I have worked in where the wards all looked the same, each equally dull. I am for school grounds and sports fields, smart uniforms and 'be thankful for the food on your plate and eat what you are bloody well given' [complainants could have a free seven day holiday living with a farming family in Rajasthan or Tamil Nadu - you can take the cost of the flight out of my tax, I'd be delighted]. I am for nostalgia. It invokes loyalty. The two, hand-in-hand, are a mighty prod to wealthy buttocks who need stimulating to philanthropy.

Children can and do learn in tents and huts. On our world travels we have been mighty humbled by adorable beaming barefoot children learning and achieving to extraordinary standards in the most rudimentary buildings and were struck by their upright postures and loose limbed movement. These youngsters made their own entertainment in wild areas where poisonous snakes are a hazard, swinging from trees and hurling themselves, shrieking and giggling, into rivers - yet they could not rely on ambulances or local hospitals. We have been stunned by how many small children teach themselves a foreign language just by talking to tourists. On our return home we look out for beaming schoolchildren - bit thin on the ground. We see grumpy, unhappy schoolchildren with appalling posture and stiff gait. It makes us wonder who has got it right, because the countries we travel to are not known for their free education, child protection, workers' rights, job opportunities and state benefits. The children in those countries will be on familiar terms with death from an early age and may well have lost siblings. Though this is tragic it does give a sense of urgency to life, of grabbing every possible opportunity and chance at learning in case there is no tomorrow. Where did we go so wrong with our fantastically expensive education? I think it all points to simplicity, that children everywhere need outdoor playtime, a basic school building that is warm and dry and a real will to learn from a teacher who is respected and valued by the community. This will return, but it will take an economic nose-dive to achieve.

I would like to see uniform back on the streets. The armed forces are nowhere to be seen these days, except on the television news. I think this is really unhealthy. Teachers no longer wear black gowns and nurses wear scruffy theatre greens. By bringing back, but maybe updating, easily identifiable uniforms and having groups of professionals [especially teachers] wearing those uniforms while being entertained at No 10 and Buckingham Palace, children would get some visual evidence of a society in some degree of balance. Instead what is continually reinforced is everyone kow-towing to money, celebrity, entertainer, or all three. We must get some balance back. Teachers are so deserving of our respect. Nowadays, a television surgeon would get considerably more respect than the real thing and a footballer is God compared to a vet. Wake up in your comfy, cosy bed at three o'clock in the morning and you won't find the TV star, or footballer [or supermodel] battling to save a life but, across the land in the dead of night, you will find doctors and vets doing just that and they will have already worked all day.

Building a solid bedrock of knowledge is empowering. I make a joke about my history teaching, but continuity gives a sounder sense of where events are leading to. I was really bothered recently when told that a young teenager was asked to write an empathic essay on a terrorist event, yet after gentle questioning it was apparent that the teenager had virtually no grasp on the facts surrounding the event, never mind the bigger historical picture. We have got so very touchy-feely and so distanced from fact that we are failing to see the wood for the trees, the event from the emotion, the hysteria from the reality. All this touchy-feely carry on [and I include 'hug a hoody'] is coming from fourth chakra. Jesus taught from fourth chakra but Jesus, as far as I can make out, was operating out of seven *fully* loaded chakras. We most categorically are NOT operating out of fully loaded chakras and if you pour kind hearted and well meant touchy-feely energy from the heart chakra without the solid bedrock of a fully loaded first, second and third chakra [particularly second and third] you won't be able to cope when the hoody or the extremely unruly schoolchild goes ape, with or without a weapon. I have watched this first hand when a new colleague arrived with a touchy-feely and rather lofty approach, but, when unable to take the pressure from thugs, responded as a thug. It takes a considerable loading into your internal power base to hold your ground and your control when things get nasty. The loading requires self-discipline birthed from imposed discipline. These days, in this country, we are desperately lacking in discipline, despite the fact that we have the most extraordinarily disciplined sovereign. Perhaps we should put her in charge of education.

EXAMINATIONS

You have to work hard and pass your exams, boys and girls, for a very simple reason - the harder you work, the more exams you get. The more exams you get, the better chances your job prospects are. The better your job prospects are, the more money you are likely to earn. And what does money mean, my cherubs? Money means freedom. Let's make that .... MONEY MEANS £REEDOM. However, if you are like me and examinations give you the screaming heebie-jeebies, try another tack - multiple skills, hard work, reliability and .... smiling.

EARTHWORMS

They are thing of wonder to me because I see worms as the lifeblood of the planet. Silently, slowly, industriously and globally they work, oxygenating the soil beneath our feet. How can such a little, soft and slimy thing do such staggeringly important work and go unpraised? As far as I know, we don't have an ode to an earthworm, do we? Wormy statues? Oscars for worms? No, but we have squidged worms.

I have a confession to make, I am a chronic rescuer and my baseline is rescuing worms. Wet winter walks along tarmac roads become a mission of seemingly impossible dimensions, because rain seems to bring out the suicidal tendencies in worms and I do not like picking them up. The live ones can be rescued with a twig or the sharp end of a blunt penknife and placed gently somewhere damp and safe, when I can find a damp and safe place. Dry worms must first be watered [I sometimes carry an atomiser, but don't tell anyone] otherwise they will dehydrate and die. All the while, during this delicate procedure, cars have to be listened for and avoided and the inquisitive noses of my dogs, fascinated with their owner's neurosis, kept at bay. Then there is the horror of the tractor passing and what to do with the half squidged worms, one end still wiggling? Surgery is sometimes required with a sharp penknife but I am never quite sure which way is 'up' on a worm. I am reminded of a man I once met who bred worms for a living and reacted with horror when I asked, 'How do you transport the worms, scoop them up and shove them in a box?'. 'Absolutely not!', he shrieked, 'They have to be very gently handled or they would foam and die.' *Foaming worms* .... doesn't bear thinking about.

My partner looks on with bemused sighs, but for me worm rescuing is a tiring but absolutely necessary business and I will not be deterred. I am slightly worried, however, that when I pop my clogs I am going to be met at the Pearly Gates by a heaving mass of smiling and gratefully rescued worms. I am not terribly looking forward to it. One worm hug is one too many.

EYE POSITIONING

I am absolutely, categorically not trained in this, so I hope and pray I am giving you the right information. If you want to study it properly get a book on neuro-linguistic programming [NLP]. Here is what I know about eye positioning. This goes for someone who is right handed, reverse it for left handers.

You look up and to the right when you are trying to imagine [construct] a thing, place, event, person.
You look up and to the left when you are trying to remember a thing, place, event, person.
You look across to the right when you construct words or sounds [through hearing].
You look across to the left when you remember words or sounds [through hearing].
You look down and to the right when you contact your feelings [including taste and smell].
You look down and to the left when you talk to yourself or listen to an inner dialogue.

If you want to test this out ask a right-handed person, 'What colour is the kitchen of the first house you ever lived in?'. The chances are their eyes will go up left as they try to remember, unless they are deeply kinaesthetic. This observing of eye positioning is just another tool in the body language tool box. Please note that a question such as, 'Everything all right at school today, darling?', needs to be asked at relatively close quarters and attention paid to eye positioning. Otherwise you might not pick up that bullying is taking place.

While I am in this area I will mention that people receive information in three different ways - visual, auditory or kinaesthetic. I am deeply visual. It's a struggle if someone is giving me complex instructions, I need drawings, diagrams or something written down. I continually ask my partner to describe, in immense detail, someone he has met; this drives him nuts but has taught him to pay attention. I listen and hear well, but only when physically talking to another person. My partner hears information much better than I do, so I will ask him to fill me in on the details of some radio programme [Melvyn Bragg's, probably] where I have failed to keep up. We both love art and music, but I *need* art and he *needs* music. My desk is surrounded by pictures and I work in silence. He works to music, which would drive me to distraction unless it was very gentle and quiet, but I am learning to disassociate my brain from the music and concentrate on the job in hand. This is good training for me. I am more likely to say, 'I *see* what you mean', whereas my partner is more likely to say, 'I *hear* what you are saying'. Kinaesthetic people [they are often artistic and creative] are more likely to use empathic words like, 'I understand that ...' and 'I feel such and such ...'. they also tend to look downwards as they contact their innermost feelings [downward tilting of the head, while in deep thought, is also an Aquarian trait, interestingly]. If you are trying to teach someone it is helpful to find out which way they best receive information. An accurate historical film might be a fast learning curve to a visual student, whereas a long lecture may not.

ℇUROPEAN UNION

What happened to the Common Market? Hmmm? When did the subtle transition from Common Market to European Union happen? How come I missed it? I must have been in the sluice, emptying bedpans.

Take twelve countries with exquisitely different and ancient cultures, languages and foreign interests, unite them and expect them to work harmoniously together. Whose idea was THAT? 'Winston Churchill', I hear you shout, or even, 'Napoleon!' [*slightly* different work ethic there, I reckon]. Yeah, well, that was then and this is now. Now we have twenty five countries working harmoniously together. Give me a break. Take twelve, never mind twenty five, members of one family and expect them to even vaguely co-operate and you are talking miracles. Not done with their European nonsense they then introduce a united currency and think one set of interest rates would be a good idea. Learned economists across Europe have written endless drivel about how good this will be for the participating countries. I read what they write and wonder, 'Am I going mad or are they way past madness?'. I opt for the latter and tell my partner, 'I give the Euro ten years, then they will all want their national currency back'. I over-estimated.

In order for us to all co-operate and not make nasty wars we take twenty-five countries, get rid of border controls and allow a tidal flood of immigration our infrastructure cannot cope with, hand out dole money here to work-shy Brits and get Poles to build our houses. It would be laughable if it wasn't downright lunacy. We can't afford pensions but we can afford to throw billions at Brussels. This helps businesses apparently but I have noticed that since biblical times business seems to manage quite nicely without interfering politicians. I still don't believe that the European Union has benefited us, I want concrete black and white evidence of it, because I think whatever gains may have been made by a few the psychological damage done to this country has been far greater. We, the people, have been disempowered and we know it. We are impotent and we know it [we are not, actually, but I am coming on to that]. It is a breeding ground for depression or fury. To me this is a very serious state of affairs and ultimately, whichever way it goes, it will cost us dear. I am hoping for fury because if it is depression, we are really stuffed.

The National Health Service was created to prevent the really desperate sight of poverty and sickness walking hand-in-hand. The European Union was created out of a genuine wish not to return to the slaughter of all out war. Both organisations sprung from noble intentions; an elevated idea, you might say, birthed from a sixth chakra vision of a better future but raised in the egotistical land of second chakra. The problem with the NHS and the EU is that they are funded by a tax paying public that can neither steer nor apply brakes and both are run by human beings. Ultimately human nature will out. Within any huge tax funded organisation, for every couple of hundred or so workers who are trying for a life of modest income and maximum service to others there will be one who doesn't give a bollocks and, because of just that, Mr. Bollocksy is usually in charge. There he sits [sometimes she] behind a desk in an elevated office [at yours and my expense] now needing to justify the job and becoming, if not already, an expert at three things - meetings, meddling and money wasting. If the expensive, meddling, unnecessary meeting can be held in a classy hotel or an expensive resort, so much the better. Who is paying? Who cares? This is a second chakra party masquerading as fourth chakra caring.

I live in a village, 'a world in miniature' as my father used to call it. Taking council tax aside, it would be interesting to see all my neighbours being forced to physically hand over a chunk of their salary or pension to the Parish Council for it to decide how much each household may have back and how they might spend it. I daresay before long there would be a noisy, angry gathering in our small market square. Somehow, because we do not hand over our money personally to our unelected officials in Brussels, our government does that so nimbly for us, and it goes to an organisation in a country few of us have actually visited, we apathetically let our money leave us. Though I try to remain in sixth chakra calm awareness I fear I fail miserably when the television shows me an EU meeting of giants in Strasbourg. Instantly my second chakra starts totting up the cost. A salary [I fear we are not talking minimum wage] for every person present at the meeting; a more than comfortable pension for all; an office per person with office furniture; a secretary or two; a computer or three; travel and a very lengthy expense account; an even lengthier lunch, telephones, telephone bills, mountains of paper, coffee, tea, loo rolls, someone to service the photocopier, clean the office, clean the windows and vacuum the carpet ……… and steadily my second chakra stokes the boiler of my blood pressure and my sixth chakra goes from peaceful indigo to fiery rage filled red. We have people in this country who cannot get the cancer restraining drugs they need to keep them alive but we can afford to support this ridiculous carry on. Now we have the EU constitution being thrust upon us. We are being *bullied* into a *union* [both second chakra] most of us do not want. Forced marriages usually end in tears and occasionally bloodshed.

I see the European Union billowing out like a giant mushroom [I hesitate to say mushroom cloud .. but it is on my mind] casting dark shadows over this country and eventually, proving too weighty for its stalk [think tax payers], it implodes. The best we can hope for. Better than tumbrels. Because it is wrong to think the EU is held together with a treaty; it is not, it is held together by a collective thought form. At the moment, that thought form is apathetic because we have become used to being unheard; those that govern us have trained us to expect to be ignored. However, the EU has federal intentions and that means, in case you are not sure, that they intend to fully govern us. It's a takeover. Getting out of this enforced union could result in a massive financial [possibly bankrupting] fine, or, much worse, war. The future looks bleak to me, but we can change events. We have to drag our eyes from the television soap operas, magazines, shops and work drudgery.

We have to think, on a daily basis, 'Enough is enough'. We have to concentrate because a united thought form will stop the slide.

Meanwhile, back home at the Ponderosa, big business gets bigger, small business gets squashed, tiny happy schools are closed and Scotland talks of independence. Good idea. Scottish taxpayers funding more zero business orientated expensive windbags. Marvellous. Hope they can afford it, though judging by the £400,000,000 [eight taxpayers noughts! Would you Adam and Eve it?] new parliamentary building ['Looks like they will need the SAS to clean the windows, darling', I tell my partner] I very much doubt they will contain such almighty starting-block hubris.

_E_FFORT

I was brought up on 'if at first you don't succeed, try, try and try again'. This was probably the most unhelpful advice I was ever given.

I am all for trying your best and if you stumble at the first hurdle have another bash. However, should you land on your butt at the second or third attempt my personal advice is this - you may well be barking up the wrong tree or you may be barking up the right tree at the wrong time. Persevere, if your passion dictates, but don't exhaust yourself in the process.

During the character building journey that has been my life, I have come to understand that effort is absolutely essential BUT if you are in a position of multiple failures, continuous doors being slammed in your face or non-stop rejections, just stop a minute and have a very long think. Reassess. Look at what you are doing from different angles. Ask agenda-free friends what they think. Then ask them to ask you what you think and get them to watch your body language as you reply, especially when it comes to tricky subjects like power, money or what you really, really want from life. If you are jamming your hands across second chakra in a protective gesture while you are talking of going self-employed, starting up a business or taking a gap year to sail round the coast of Britain on a tea tray, then you are likely to fail. Be brutally honest with yourself. Is this thing you want so badly right for you? Are you doing it for you or for someone else? Do you have the power, physical or emotional, to sustain it? What are the pros and cons of the object of your desire and does one outweigh the other? Is this the right time for you to pursue something? Would it be better in a few months or years? Perhaps you need a bit more experience in a specific field or a bit more experience of life. Perhaps you need some rest and recuperation. You may even need a period of fun. Failing any of those, do you need to see a psychiatrist?

When you are trying to open a door that will not budge, you usually start to fiddle with the handle. Then you lean against the door. Then push with all your might. Now comes one of three scenarios: the door resolutely will not open, you crash through the door in a skidding heap and flurry or [really annoying] someone else comes along and turns the door handle you have been wrestling with for minutes and the door magically opens. You can take this image to anything in life from trying to *get that man*, to trying to *get that job*, to trying to *close that deal*. You need to step back and take back your power. Leaning against a door means you are not centred, you are literally leaning at an angle, all wanting and needing and usually pushing what you think you want and need away. Stand back, take some deep breaths and ask yourself for what and why are you pushing against an object that will not budge? Do we have a naughty little agenda? Centre yourself, be still and wait. Try the door some time later, it may open smoothly for you. I once tried, repeatedly and determinedly, to contact someone, with no luck. I am so profoundly grateful now that I could not get through to them because my sticky agenda would have made a mess of things. Now, when I phone someone three times and they are engaged or out, I leave it for a day, or more, or completely. When I am pushing a metaphorical non-budging door I always like to think there are four eighteen stone angels on the other side holding the door in place and as I walk away I hear them sigh with relief.

*E*FFICIENT

I was told over and over again during my nursing years that I was 'so efficient'. I never understood what people meant, other than they meant it as a compliment. Efficiency was just the way to get the job done in my eyes. It was only when I left hospital work that I realised how inefficient business can be. One thing, out of thousands, that working in the NHS taught me, was that the British public had immense stores of good natured patience if you periodically faced them, explained and apologised for the wait and made them a cuppa; but let them sit for hours and hours waiting, while staff say nothing, do not apologise and pretty soon you have a near riot on your hands. This was not just common sense to me, or efficiency, but basic courtesy. It strikes me that business has a lot to learn from this most basic form of courteous good public relations. While I am in the business of being struck I would like to strike 'leave it with me' [leave - that's exactly right] and 'I'll get back to you' [they frequently don't] out of the business lexicon. It is especially silly to leave women fuming from unreturned calls, because women talk to each other and swap horror stories. At this very moment I am busy telling anyone who will listen which computer not to buy because their after sales service is time consuming, unhelpful and unsympathetic. What absolutely daft public relations! Look after me and my computer and I will tell everyone, 'Fantastic, helpful, friendly - buy their goods, I recommend them!'. It's not rocket science [sorry, rocket engineering] it's completely free advertising stemming from courteous efficiency and good business practice. Rudeness and inefficiency is so non-productive, if not downright destructive.

When I first came to East Anglia, twenty five years ago, the shop assistants in many large stores and supermarkets were country slow. 'Why doesn't the management send them to a big London store for a week to teach them to speed up?', I wondered. These days they need to send shop assistants to America to learn how to serve with speed, knowledge, efficiency and courtesy. My partner was dumbfounded when he bought some jeans in New York. The moment we entered the enormous shop [where the jeans were stacked from floor to ceiling - literally, tall ladders were required to fetch stock] two assistants approached with a smile. They were charming, well trained, fast, knew every inch of their stock, suggested exactly the right style for him [a pair he would not have chosen, but looked wonderful] and they generally made the whole experience fun and a pleasure. I often cringe and wonder what Americans must think when they come here and wander into one of our big shops.

ℰLECTRICITY

Dull old life it would be without it but I have recently attended a lecture from a company selling equipment that neutralises the negative effect of electro-magnetic energy on the human body. I did not buy one of their gizmos but I might well have done if I had small children because I have, over the years, heard stories that make me uneasy. If you have a history of unexplained headaches or general unwellness, try removing any electrical equipment [like clock] from your bedside because you may be hypersensitive to its emissions. Much more importantly, if you have distressed babies or children, especially at night, do the same thing and check that they are not sleeping anywhere near electrical points or equipment and that goes for cots or beds positioned against an internal wall where there is an outside burglar alarm.

Nowadays, we fill our homes with gadgets and gizmos but have given our bodies little time to adapt to such major change. When I lived in my cottage, where space was very tight, one of my elderly dogs loved to sleep in front of the fire which put him, albeit at floor level, directly between me and the telly. I noticed, with concern, that when I used my hand-held television remote control to change channels, his body would twitch slightly, so I stopped using it when he was lying in its range [it was the same dog that later went on to have fits]. I'm not keen on microwave cookers, my ex-colleagues used one to heat up their food in the middle of the night and I would drive them nuts by standing in the doorway to the staff room, two protective index fingers to my either side of my lower abdomen asking if they were trying to nuke my ovaries. The infuriation and hilarity this spectacle induced can only really be comprehended by those who worked with me, as I was, in their eyes, a dog-mad, child-free, trainee [if not full blown] eccentric with largely redundant ovaries anyway. I am not seriously suggesting microwaves nuke your ovaries, or anything else, but I am saying the only cooking that works for me is the old fashioned conventional type and I prefer quickly steamed vegetables because they are far more nutritious than boiled veg. I am getting twitchy about using Teflon coated cooking pans and the first time I used my personal computer my body did not like it; I felt reverberations right through to my spine, but quite how long it would take me to write this book on my manual typewriter is anybody's guess. I am also uneasy about the fluoridation of the drinking water because I am wondering if this is having a negative effect on our bowel flora [for 'flora' read 'good bacteria' not delphiniums]. I read worrying reports alleging that fluoride in drinking water strips out our B vitamins.

ENVY

In times past I have spent far too much time being envious of others. If you keep envy company, be comforted by the fact that life can change dramatically for everyone. As the years have rolled by and events unfolded I would not now have the lives of those I have most envied in the past.

Most are envious of lottery winners but buckets of money can destroy families and friendships while presenting dozens of 'hangers-on' who do not really love you. Sudden wealth can be a minefield of people with agendas and does not guarantee health or love. Fame may look attractive to some but it means little privacy, a media itching to catch you looking dishevelled, misquote your every word and age can be brutal to the once beautiful. Huge houses mean huge maintenance, besides, you can only sit in one chair and in one room at a time. Beautiful clothes do not make you feel beautiful inside, only your mind and heart can do that. If it is relationships you envy, and God knows I have been there, don't waste time thinking about or staring at others because partnerships can be wonderful but often they are destructive and families can be the very best of things or the very worst of things. Be your own best friend and best partner. Look within and work on yourself because the faster you clean out your mental debris and set your goals the faster you are going to get where you want to be and have what you want to have.

$\mathcal{F}$ Is for FUN

Please get some fun on a regular basis. If you cannot remember when you last whooped and giggled like a child, it is time to do something constructive. Go to an amusement park, if that is your thing. Go to the seaside, have an ice-cream and run barefoot across the sand. You should be able do this alone and still enjoy it. If you steadfastly cannot enjoy yourself while alone and fun requires someone to hold your adult hand, you have some serious internal work to do on yourself. Fun gurgles up your internal drainpipe, it is, therefore, another 'inside job'. You can attach yourself to someone else's cheery drainpipe but you may clog it up.

Take a walk with a jolly dog because they always know how to have fun, but I would avoid sniffing lamp posts …. still each to his own. Go and see a funny film. Do it … you know your body needs it.

$\mathcal{F}$ENG SHUI

Recently a friend told me she wanted to feng shui her house. I advised her to feng shui her brain because it was cheaper and possibly just as effective. She thought this was amusing and worth a try. I am looking forward to seeing her with a pot plant sticking out behind an ear, energising her south west corner. Not sure about the water feature though.

$\mathcal{F}$IBS

I tell a lot of fibs. I tell more fibs now than I ever did because as each day passes I see less and less reason to hurt another person's feelings. If you show up at my front door wearing only a large lampshade with a fringe that j u s t covers your bits and ask me if I like your outfit, I am going to tell you an almighty fib. 'Fabulous', I shall say, though I might not encourage you to come in, sit down and relax in case your lampshade rides up. If you do not like someone's clothes you can tell yourself but don't tell them, because that is a form of control and we know that all controllers are basically insecure and unhappy .... or politicians. The same goes for houses; try and find something positive to comment on, the light, the colour, the shape of a room or the view and resolutely ignore the bits you think should go in the skip.

I need advance preparation before I tell my partner a porkie so that I can hide my feet. I am stuffed if I tell the tiniest, weeniest fib to him if my feet are visible [or even under bed linen] because he watches my toes. My big toe lifts ever so slightly if I am being ever so slightly dishonest, a movement he cannot resist pointing out with enthusiasm. I am infuriated until the summer when he is barefoot and trying to convince me the glass of wine with the least content is mine, whereas I know he has switched them and his big toe is confirming his perfidy. I point and pounce on this elevation with shrieks of hilarity and glass retrieval. Autumn brings blessed relief with the arrival of thick socks, sensible footwear and a period of relatively unchecked small porkieland.

However, I am concerned with the amount of large lies that go unchecked these days and although we let them pass I think this has the affect of a slow seepage of poison. We expect nothing less than lies from our politicians and to my mind this is a very serious state of affairs. We shrug at the high and mighty telling outright lies and even living lies which requires sustained and indiscriminate lying to everyone, including loved ones. It bothers me tremendously, not least because I lived a lie for six months and to conceal it, I had to be mighty evasive. When that failed, I had to tell lies and I hated it and hated myself for the lies I told. I am fortunate to be a nobody but I wondered if I would have behaved differently had I been in a position of authority. I sincerely hope I would have held fast to my heart but stepped away from my 'position'. I don't think you can have it both ways. In the long run it has a drip-down incapacitating effect.

$\mathcal{F}$ARMING

I wonder how it could have come to this, that we are unable to feed our nation and must rely to such an alarming degree on imported food. Do we learn nothing from our history books? Obviously not. Such complacency. I am told global corn stocks are dangerously low yet not a hint of global panic. Extraordinary. Now we have laudable fair trade for foreigners yet terrorise our local farmers. I listen to their stories and wonder they have the heart to continue their toil of our land in the face of endless restrictions from government and bullying from buyers. Our farmers feed us - *feed us* - they are, therefore, far more important to this country than our blundering, pig-ignorant [literally] politicians.

A country that is not basically self-sufficient in food is courting disaster. It is too much of a risk to take with something you cannot do without for more than a few hours or days. In my mind it's beyond insane that in Britain we do not own all of our own water but that we cannot feed ourselves is truly frightening. Come an unforeseen emergency you cannot just conjure up food, it takes months or a year to get a crop. It astounds me that Westminster, stuffed to the gunnels with so called intellectuals, is as blind to the danger as it was in 1939. It is, to me, yet another symptom of our growing national weakness - to be so reliant when we need, in every possible sphere, to be self-reliant and self-sufficient. Your reliance IS your weakness, as we find to our cost personally, within relationships, and nationally with oil. I know food is not just business, it is huge business, but you can't eat money and massive basic food importation [I am not talking about luxuries] looks like another 'get rich quick' scheme with the possibility that somewhere down the line you, your children or grandchildren may starve. There is, or was, a native American Indian tribe [can't remember the name] that made decisions after taking into consideration the impact the decision would have on the next seven generations. How wise was that? Is it any wonder that spirit guides are so often Red Indians? I daresay 'Sensible Hunting Bear' and 'Moose Dances With Organic Cornfield' have been ringing the celestial phone line to No 10 Downing Street for years. Engaged .... too busy talking to food and oil exporters.

Over the centuries so called civilisations have produced cities and many of these city folk have sneered at the peasants. Not only is this arrogant it is also profoundly stupid, because you cannot eat stone, brick, tarmac or glass and dense populations pass on deadly germs quickly and efficiently. We must be the first generation ever in the entire history of planet Earth where so many have so totally lost contact with the soil. It may prove to be a disastrous loss. I think it is desperately sad and dangerous that so many children have minimal contact with nature, so little understanding and respect of something as life giving as farming. Next time you are in a supermarket try finding something to eat that did not involve soil or water. This is a grounding exercise and keeps you in touch with what is absolutely essential and a good antidote to the newspaper section at the entrance to the supermarket, where good ink and good trees are wasted on bad news. I recycle our newspapers in our compost bins but I worry about the chemicals in the coloured pictures. Still, the sight of certain people who irritate me being defaced by damp teabags and smelly vegetable peelings cheers me up no end. This is shocking spiritual impoverishment on my part. I vow to do better.

Try to be a little farmer and grow your own vegetables if you can. They taste better, it saves money and you will not be worrying about pesticides. You can grow an incredible amount in a small space, even in pots, even on a balcony. It is hugely satisfying and I am much looking forward to rootling around in our vegetable patch next year now my joints are better and digging is once more a pleasure. We have just reconfigured our veg patch with new raised beds, as the last lot of timber rotted. We plan to grow more green vegetables and try our potatoes in a stacking system of car tyres, when we can locate some. Spuds take up so much room and this will be space saving and, hopefully, cut down on the weeding. Are there many unhappy chemicals in car tyres [I ask myself, sighing]?

I thought about being a farmer once. I went to Canberra and bought a mirror with a hand painted frame that looked like a gorgeous outback dawn. I asked the shop owner what else she thought I should be doing, apart from visiting the main museum, the gallery and walking over the politicians [there is a grassy mound over the Australian parliamentary building that voters can walk on, which is not quite as big as the mound I would like to put over Westminster but still, it might be a start]. The owner of the shop thought I looked like a Harley Davidson sort of girl.'*I should say so*', said I. Organised. I hurried back to my hotel, sauntered through the lobby and told the two receptionists, with whom I had shared some humour, that I was just off to change and my Harley would be around shortly. They giggled mightily, because in those days Harleys were not much in evidence. They ceased to giggle when my Harley roared up and so did I, because it took me three attempts to get my leg over it - great *beast* of a machine. We were off and it was fabulous. Later, as we took a liquid break, my driver, Peter as I recall, told me all about his family and varied career. 'So what do you do now', I asked, 'ride Harleys all day?'. Sounded good to me. 'Certainly not', he replied, 'I am a worm farmer'. Small silence while I tried to look intelligent. 'Fishing!', I cried, hopefully. Nope - compost. Peter bred the little wiggly wigglers and sold them to the Australian equivalent of a district council for composting the biodegradeable rubbish. 'What a rollicking good idea', I said, imagining setting myself up as a worm farmer in Suffolk and my local council's response [not promising in those days, but distinctly promising now]. A farmer! I could become a farmer ... *I shall have arrived!* People will take me seriously. Not exactly large and exhausting stock to take care of and I liked the idea of a set of farmer's overalls but not in that nasty shade of green that my farmer friend Alan wears. No, no, I shall have some bespoke overalls in a tasteful shade of pale sage green with 'Lady Farmers Do It With Worms' embroidered in purple on my back. I could even have a 'waving worm' painted on the side of a Landrover .... no, best not ..... someone might misconstrue. Meanwhile, back in Tidbinbilla I think it was, Peter was pointing out koalas ....

$\mathcal{F}$IVE

There is a most perspicacious gentleman called Gary Chapman who has written a book [details at the back of this book] showing that people love in 5 different ways. PHYSICAL love [this is not just sexual, but includes loving touch]. Love shown in ACTS OF SERVICE. Giving QUALITY TIME love. Giving PRESENTS [from a paper toy made by a child to expensive gifts] with love. Using loving WORDS OF AFFIRMATION. I urge you to rush out and buy this book, it is absolutely marvellous. If you are in a close relationship and you and your beloved show love differently, things may not be entirely smooth in your life. Fortunately, me and my chap both have the same primary love language, physical [though we interact with all of them] but we need to touch each other and be in close physical proximity a lot. I have a girlfriend who will listen and give sound advice at any time of the day or night. Though she likes presents, she really is not bothered. What she really needs is love shown back to her in the same way that she gives it - by me giving her quality listening time, at any time. I have another friend who gives love, primarily, by giving presents. Lots of little things and not necessarily at Christmas and birthdays. Little gifts given back to her mean more than words of affirmation, though she likes them too. My cats love acts of service [food and make it snappy] but my dogs like physical hugs, hotly followed by acts of service [walkies/food]. My mother was a physical/acts of service person [she loved hugs and grub cooked for her] and my father was a physical/quality time person, who gave me bear hugs that I remember with longing and hours and hours of philosophical meanderings that I miss. Do try to get your hands on this book, it is a treasure and such an eye opener to better understanding and harmonious relationships.

FIELD

We are incredibly fortunate to have had the chance to buy some land. I cannot remember a time when I did not long for a field or two; a chance to plant trees and watch them soar. I have always wanted to be in a position to give nature something back. We took expert seed and sowing advice and then laid down one acre as a wild flower meadow, changing it from the wheat or barley field it had been when it belonged to a local farmer. From year one it has been a source of intense joy for us and a wildlife haven. An old English hedgerow has been planted with lots of dog roses and wild honeysuckle that I grew from a few cuttings. Native and fruit trees have been planted, though the two Eucalyptus have caused some consternation [I had them in pots, lunacy I know, and when they inevitably outgrew their home I could not bear to throw them out]. I am not too choosy about absolutely everything being native or wild in the field, if it is food for insects in it goes, because I think they need all the help they can get. This single acre is awash with colour every summer and a haven for bees, butterflies, moths, unidentified buzzy things and, in summer, there are so many grasshoppers that you have to walk slowly around the cut grass paths so as not to tread on them. We were amazed at the sight of so much life so soon. Give nature an inch of a chance and my, how fast she repays you with glory!

We have a resident tawny owl, a newly arrived little owl and a woodpecker hammering at a very dead tree we refuse to cut down. We left piles of logs scattered about the edges of the field in the hope they would provide a refuge for something and just a week ago I found a female stag beetle in the field. Huge excitement! I used to see them all the time as a child, but not now. A single common orchid popped up this year. A grass snake was spotted and finger wagged at [they eat tadpoles and frogs]. The field is cut once a year as late as possible and this gives the house martins and swallows a chance to do plenty of feeding, swooping endlessly over the field and fattening up on tiny insects before they start on their incredible and heroic journey back to Africa. The goldfinches, such a lovely sight, arrive in a small flock and finish off the late seed heads, so they would not get their tea if we cut the field too early. We should cut twice a year, we are losing some wildflowers because the grass is forcing them out, but it is hard to cut just as the plants are showing promise. I shall have to be braver next year but meanwhile I shall get busy this winter, replacing lost stock.

A fox deposits his calling cards and a couple of muntjac deer seem to have moved in though I worry about them nibbling our newly planted fruit trees. If they eat the fruit it will be all out war. Charlie the Pheasant has found a wife and Daphne and Trevor Duck pop in and out. Trevor cleared off when Daphne proudly launched fifteen ducklings on to the pond. Cute beyond belief! Daffers then had me worn out with twice daily road escort patrol when she wanted to take her babies for a trip to the river, but be back to us in time for lunch or supper. As soon as she and her babies took to the river for good Trevor reappeared with a new shy bride, Demelza, *the two timing hound-dog.* They quack politely for food. What to do? Refuse them? Can't … haven't the willpower.

In the summer we take our picnics, or a mug of tea out to the field and listen in rapture to the buzzing, whirring and chirping of several thousand insects. The field is a lot of work as nettles and brambles threaten continually to invade, but the expense of purchase, sowing and maintenance is nothing to the feeling that in some very small way we have given nature a breathing space. If you have only a tiny garden you can also give something back. Honey bees are in huge trouble, millions and millions have died across America and may be in trouble over here. Is this relevant to you? Do you like eating fruit? Bees pollinate the flowers that produce the fruit. There are honey bees in middle of London and if you just put a pot of red clover or lavender on your windowsill you are giving them breakfast. The more you do the more you will be rewarded. Remember this is still England and the insects need English plants [yes, I do know where most plants originate from] because exotic grasses don't provide much food. Extremely tidy gardens and great expanses of decking are not wildlife havens. Grass lawns provide food for starlings, blackbirds and thrushes whereas concrete and stones do not, unless they are hiding snails. Modern houses do not provide the nooks and crannies for birds to nest so nest boxes are *crucial*, especially for *sparrows* who nest in groups. Specially designed sparrow boxes need to be put fairly high up on a house, ours is far to low and used by blue tits but fortunately we are surrounded by very old houses that are sparrow nest friendly. In ten years, having created an untidy old fashioned cottage garden, our bird population has soared. I have pretty much stopped bird feeding in winter, unless it is ferociously cold, concentrating now on early spring and summer when babies are being made. The different feeders are emptied so fast by ravenous birds that I refill them every other day. Since doing this I have found the fledglings are stronger and more able to evade our cats, presumably because the parents don't have to work so hard at gathering food for themselves and their young. Still, even with my feeding I was amazed at how many birds I saw with beaks absolutely stuffed with insects and caterpillars this spring and summer. Our two cats are natural hunters but I have found my new collars have cut the bird loss down to less than a handful per year. I make the collars out of black knicker elastic and attach multiple bells [from a local fabric ship, 15p each]. It makes the cats sound like wandering minstrels but alerts the birds early. Sadly, I can't attach one of these collars to our local sparrowhawks, both of which account for the death of so many songbirds. I believe they are capable of killing three a day. I hate seeing them swoop on my little sparrows and carry them off. It ruins my week.

Ponds attract insects, insects attract bats [and you can put a few bat boxes on your house near the roof, three boxes is good, apparently]. Insects are as precious as elephants. We may not think their dying off and eventual extinction is that important but they are only small living things at one end of the chain and we are at the other. We have a choice and we pursue our choices ruthlessly. The small creatures do not have a choice and have to try and survive around our brutality. Without care it will be our turn for extinction. We have no right to keep destroying their habitat. Our legacy will be a global exhibition of extreme second chakra bullying that will last, detrimentally, for hundreds, maybe thousands of years.

The media frets about the endangered polar bear [and so do I] but we do not pay enough attention to what is happening on our own doorstep. Hedgerows are cut in early autumn, removing all the berries that birds will need for the coming winter. We have already slaughtered most of our verges and the life that depended on them. There is little colour, only grasses which are always cut at a time of maximum disruption to insects. Only the other day I was nearly reduced to tears to see some local verges had been cut in July. Incomprehensible. The few wild plants they contained had been cut down just as the butterflies were landing on the flowers to feed and breed. Now those butterflies will have to look elsewhere or starve. A woman once told me as a child in East Anglia she would run into roadside verges chock full of wildflowers and clap her hands in order to watch a cloud of butterflies rise up. That sight has gone now but it could be reclaimed with a bit of forward thinking from local councils and a Westminster that was balanced enough to have some representatives with a deep understanding of the soil. A soil that will, within thirty to fifty years, contain the remains of those who govern us now.

'Only after the last tree has been cut down, only after the last river has been poisoned, only after the last fish has been caught, only then will you find that money cannot be eaten'. A Cree Indian prophecy.

*F*OOTBALL

I just never got it; it was an alien mystery to me. Men rushed about on a patch of grass and fans screamed. I was unmoved. Years and years ago I worked, for a short time, at the Football Association in London, amid really lovely people who were football mad. There was such a nice chap who worked downstairs, doing something important, can't remember. Football was this man's life and we once had an intense debate about the importance of 'the game' but I was none the wiser. Then last year my partner took me to an out of town computer shop that was the size of an aircraft hanger. I am not keen on these establishments but I made a mental note to 'try harder' as I walked through the door. I tried hard for five minutes, but that was enough and I was off wandering the aisles disconsolately looking for something that vaguely interested me. Nothing doing. Ten bored minutes later I whispered in my beloved's ear, 'Where's the plant section?'. He ignored me [he has heard this one before], his attention being held deeply by some square plastic thing. I resorted to my usual tactic of finding a comfortable office chair for sale, sitting in it and people-watching. Half an hour later, to my relief, my partner appeared laden with plastic and instructed me to follow him to the sales area. I dutifully removed my butt from one comfortable chair to another while he entered into deep computer-talk about mysterious things with the salesman. With a sigh, I recommenced my people-watching from a chair that swivelled, thus allowing me to do an arc. When I had swung right round, my eye was caught by the occupants of a nearby desk. Seated either side of the desk was a nice young pale grey salesman talking to a voluble buyer in black and white. The nice pale grey man patiently listened and listened and then slowly looked over at me and gave me a gentle, tired but sweet smile. I smiled back at him and suddenly my heart broke, my jaw dropped, my eyes cast up and about me and I understood football. As my gaze returned to the nice pale grey man, I thought, 'Once, he was a warrior'. As I stared, I thought of thousands of his forbears who were warriors, farmers, craftsmen. Their tribe and their intention crystal clear, with vivid lives that were sometimes brutal and short. Their battles were with the soil, the elements, or maybe bloody and man to man. I stared about me at the huge soulless electrically lit and powered landscape. I could not see sky or a tree. As my chair swung me left and right I observed the 'once warriors' doing battle in this alien landscape and suddenly serried ranks of male togetherness screaming for their tribe on the football pitch made perfect sense. I refocused my gaze on my lovely pale grey 'once warrior' salesman and beamed some rainbow colours at him while fervently wishing him to be showered with happiness and if that be football, may his life be one long winning game.

$\mathcal{F}$AT

Let's keep it simple. Eating fat makes you fat. Eating sugar, which turns into fat, makes you fat. Eating more carbohydrates [or more anything] than you are burning off makes you fat - and there you have it. What do I do when I am unhappy? I head straight for the fridge and I am NOT looking for a stick of celery. No Sireee. The craving of fatty foods is interesting. From my personal experience I think the craving for creamy food points to a calcium problem - the calcium is going in but the up-take is going wrong. This may be because magnesium is too low or not being absorbed [you need professional help with taking magnesium supplements because there are several types, you may need a specific one and it can take time - I have been told months - to re-establish and stabilise the levels in every cell in your body]. I have noticed that creamy sauces, once a 'must have' for me are no longer a favourite since I have sorted out my magnesium levels. Enormous fatty meals do not make people feisty and ready for a fight [unless stoked by a lot of alcohol]. Fatty food comforts - like pouring oil on troubled water - therefore, I would suggest that the craving for fat is for the relief of anger, which is a cover for fear. Watch out for the green and black colour combination.

NOW, for the interesting part. Where do you store your fat? We are talking emotions here. Let's get me out of the way so we can pick on everyone else. Where do I store my fat? On my tummy and on my botty. Why for? It is on my tummy because I have been worse than useless at protecting my second chakra [and with it my stomach/intestines], erecting boundaries [third chakra] and all that goes with a flat picket fence. I store it on my bottom because it makes a nice comfortable cushion to sit on and that's all you are getting out of my confessional. Let us now, dear hearts, turn our attention to the others …. what a relief!

Fat will go where we emotionally tell it to go and, in particular, it will protect chakras. Evenly distributed fat covering most of the body, even to extremes, is telling the whole world to clear off. It is, in my opinion, a picket fence, a sign that says, 'I am much more sensitive than people realise'. It may well also say, 'I have been hurt and I am not letting that happen again'. It is, quite literally, a protective blanket from the painful and dangerous world that these sensitive souls inhabit. Now, you may think that is a load of rubbish and that you know some evenly distributed fat people who are as sensitive as speeding steam rollers, but I think you would be quite wrong. We all have a different levels of tolerance to hurtful situations; one person's fear is another person's challenge. A hurtful remark to an adult can be shrugged off, but a child may register it differently and put on a protective layer. Excess weight can go hand-in-hand with a jolly personality, but you may be interested to read 'smile' later in the book.

If you are evenly overweight and want to do something about it, look at your wardrobe. The colours you chose to wear will give you an idea where any emotion or hurt is stemming from. If you need to dig deeper, look at the things or comments that make you either angry or sad, this may be your 'flashback' point or phrase. Who knows what finger-wagging nagging went on when you were a child and how you reacted to it. It does not have to be nagging or a one-off vicious comment [or worse], being ignored or ridiculed is just as painful. A lot of extra weight can be a way of keeping sexual partners at bay, so you may need to do some honest self-questioning. Of course, eating sensibly helps to lose weight, but in my opinion when weight has been a problem for many years you have to heal the hurt to keep the weight off permanently. If the hurt is a self-esteem issue [third chakra] you may find that losing the weight makes you feel good about yourself and so you heal the hurt anyway. When you [and only you] feel it is time to lose weight and you don't want to trawl through painful memories with yourself [or anyone else for that matter, thank you very much] then just use the colour section to work out which colour will help you move forward and then, repeat *then*, start changing your food regime. Don't look at and/or compare yourself to others or, heaven forbid, compare yourself to people in magazines. I comfort myself with the thought that glossy people in glossy magazines are only about three to six inches tall, that's why they look so small and neat. In real life they would probably be my size. Then I have a glass of wine and all is right with the world.

Fat on the neck can signify two things; I had a rubber tyre round the front of my neck as a baby [I was, in fact, indistinguishable from Michelin Man and I consider my parent's love for me as nothing short of an heroic gesture. I did eventually blossom, aged two, into a blonde bombshell but it was short lived. Indeed, some unkind souls, surveying photos of me at that age, have remarked it was downhill all the way. *Their names have been noted*]. That fat spare tyre on my neck was an early warning sign of future trouble because that is how the body talks to us, with fat, hair [downy or otherwise], lumps, bumps, ridges, moles and marks highlighting potential problem areas. My lumpy neck was not helped by my loving parents force-feeding me right through childhood. I only wanted very tiny quantities of food, so tiny that my parents took fright and insisted I eat every scrap of food they doled onto my plate. Mealtimes, for me, became hell-times. It is possible, even at that very young age, I instinctively knew I was having problems digesting food. In adults, fat deposits on the front of the neck would alert me to fifth chakras issues, possibly failing to speak up for oneself, maybe poor at singing or speaking in public. There is a strong link between second chakra and fifth, so I would be alert to thyroid gland and everything in the lower abdomen. Fat on back of neck can indicate stubborn tendencies, inflexibility, possibly a controlling nature but I would also bear in mind the bladder [second chakra], because this is bladder meridian territory. This meridian is something of a bladder bugbear for me.

Fat on the chest [men especially] is protecting heart and lungs. It may point to a broken heart at some stage of the proceedings [even as a tiny baby] and possibly a fearful connection, which would point to lungs, and often goes hand-in-hand with tense muscular armouring of the upper body. If your shoulders are like concrete please remember you are using large quantities of minerals and vitamins on a daily basis to keep those muscles locked; you will be depriving the rest of your body if you are not bunging those minerals and vits back in. Find the emotional block [see 'emotions' and get some clues from 'colour'], learn how to breathe abdominally, free the muscles and so ease the blood supply. Feed your body what it needs. Large breasts on women [that are wholly and fully their own] often show a wish to nurture. It may not be related to breast feeding or nurturing a baby, although I think it probably is a fairly strong indicator in young women. In older women it may signify an unfulfilled wish to receive or give nurturing which can take many forms; healing, feeding, cooking, comforting, even planting and gardening all count as nurturing in my book and you can long to nurture [and be nurtured by] animals just as strongly as the desire to nurture babies. Fat on the upper back can be, quite literally, protecting the upper back from stabbing. Watch the politicians for this one. Of course a person has to think or know the stabbing is coming before the fat can be laid down, so if the assassination [I am not talking literal assassination] is not expected, as it were, the back would not necessarily be protected. This area is rearguard heart protection and fat deposition here could possibly be coupled with an attitude of 'they are out to get me'. As we instinctively comfort someone in times of sadness by putting a protective arm across the upper back and holding a shoulder, fat laid down across the upper back would make me think this kind of loving had been absent in childhood.

Fat on the upper abdomen [predominantly male] is mainly a third chakra/self esteem protective layer. The bigger the abdomen the larger the *hurt*, which probably requires a great deal of *comfort* food. It can also be a defence mechanism against being overloaded with responsibility. It might be business concerns but more likely being weighed down with family responsibility or feeling responsible for family members who are overly dependant. I might also incorporate a feeling of responsibility toward a cause [maybe political, or in that arena] or a burden of living up to someone else's expectations [watch the shoulders]. As an added point, any of these will put an emotional strain on the pancreas and liver. This is not good news. Fat on the lower abdomen [predominantly female] protects the second chakra so it may be laid down in response to either sex, money [usually loss or lack], tricky relationships or loss of external power. I think women are much better at protecting themselves in this area today and that may be why waistlines have dropped, therefore the fashionable waistline drop is a healthy sign even if it is not always a beautiful sight. Fat deposited in this area is often very difficult for women to shift, especially after pregnancy, but then a women is very vulnerable during her pregnancy. That emotional vulnerability may be as difficult to shift as the fat.

I will just interrupt myself at this juncture and point out one salient point; as I get older I turn more and more into my mother - it is a bit of a worry. Please note that in relevance to fat and to health [and, I believe, disease] we learn how to think from our parents. We may lob their ideas into the dustbin during our youthful years but often, about paunch time, those ideas clamber out of the bin and into our brains. Our thinking patterns are dominated by our emotions, not alas, our feelings. Fearful thoughts and inadequacies gained from the crib and beyond will have time to expand when nights are no longer spent in alcohol-fuelled hormone chasing and the realities of uncertain work, certain bills and family life take centre stage. This is often when fat deposition in a specific area materializes.

Fat around hips and thighs, usually seen in women, to me indicates a first and third chakra issue. Heavy fat deposition in this area is a tricky one and I have not had much chance to talk to women about the emotional factor that surrounds it, but I would be wondering about the relationship between a child [girls especially] and parents but particularly the father. Maybe the absence of a father or a physically present but emotionally absent father [possibly emotionally absent to female children rather than males]. I would wonder if the energy of the child had been concentrated in the head/brain area or perhaps upper torso in detriment to the lower body.

Most of us would like to be slim, I am no exception, but as the years slide by I am making peace with my body. To be honest, I worry far more about the content of my thinking than my physical shape. I know if my thinking is straight, my body will be joyful and those extra pounds will not make me ill, whereas, if my thinking is wrong, I am in big trouble. If losing weight is a preoccupation with you it may help to read the 'health' section.

FRIENDS

A huge relief [most of the time] and an absolute necessity sometimes. I remind my young friends, those just about to leave home for the first time [especially those attending college or university] to make friends slowly. Take a good look at your new companions and listen carefully. Pick out kind people and don't latch on to the first group of people [or person] you come across. That way, six months down the line, when you are comfortable in your new surroundings and have fully found your feet, you are not stuck with a group of people you find you have nothing in common with.

Two things about friendships: they take effort, not much, but a little and often. Men are particularly bad at picking up the phone to say, 'Hello', or dropping a card in the post to say, 'Thinking of you'. In fact they often have to be reminded of birthdays, unless it is their own. I think this is a shame because I love talking to men on the phone. I love hearing a man's opinion on any subject, even when he is completely and utterly wrong. The other thing about friendships is this; as the years go by, friends drop by the wayside. Don't worry. You, or they, may have emotionally moved on. New friends will come, but only if you really want new friends [try and be honest with yourself on this one]. I wouldn't say I make new friends every day, I don't, but I certainly make new acquaintances every week and this year has been a bumper crop of fascinating new people met in all sorts of different places.

Try and make friends of all ages. It is healthy. It gives you a sense of perspective and avoids the possibility of a lonely old age when your aged friends are filling up the graveyard. Having young friends keeps you in touch with change and means they will have a friendly older face to give comfort when the world looks bleak. You will be in much demand in the ensuing years as the current crop of teenagers hit the reality of work. I anticipate much depression for them and the very early arrival of midlife crises.

*F*UTURE

I went to a wacky lecture recently given by a man I have been following for many years, for whom I have measured respect. I asked him whether we were heading for a cliff edge fall or a slow downward economic and social slide. He made a downward staircase motion. It was not enough. I wanted specifics. A time frame, dates even. 'Where do I put my money when the banks go belly-up?' He gave me the answer I had already formulated, which was, 'Your greatest place of safety is in the softness of your heart'. *I know that, dammit, I just don't want to know that.* I want second chakra safety, I do, I do. Bricks and building societies - all stuff and nonsense come crunch time, of course. I know perfectly well you cannot have second chakra safety unless you have a toehold in fourth chakra .... *hell's teeth.* My spirituality slumped in its chair anticipating the horizon and one giant leap of faith. I don't like sports.

In my world, the belief is that humans are changing into a slightly different species. We are going from carbon base to crystalline base - I think I have got that right. Are carbon and crystals geology or are we doing physics here? I haven't a clue, but I do understand that you used to put crystals in radios. Now, if you think about it we are all receiving now. Our little antennae are picking up all sorts of new and strange information and we are accepting it. We have 'do it yourself' spirituality and the advance of alternative medicine. Seventy to eighty years ago you followed your tribe's religion and that was that. Alternative medicine was confined to dock leaves on nettle stings and most people, if asked, would hazard a guess that acupuncture was a nasty hole in a bicycle tyre, while a tiny minority thought it was something in China and should damn well stay there. Nowadays, everyone knows someone who has looked like a hedgehog. We have accepted it into mainstream healing though we prefer a sleepy anaesthetic for gall-bladder removal. In another twenty years, I reckon, the idea of having your gall-stones removed surgically will be greeted with hilarity. It is even possible that the idea of seeing a doctor about gall-stones will be equally amusing. There are hundreds of things we now accept as 'normal' that would have got you ostracised from society not so long ago. Even I am accepted ...... sometimes. Travel, television and computers have widened our horizons and perspective. There is a 'fluidity' that is much more accepting of all sorts of 'unusual' things, including distant healing and thought form transference [I was just thinking of you when you phoned - or - I just knew something was wrong/had happened, I felt it]. This fluidity will expand and accelerate. In order for this to happen we will have to become less dense and I think we are all changing our cell vibratory rate in order to achieve this state.

Right, that is the wacky stuff. Let's get down to basics. I don't know if we can make the transition we are going through at the moment peacefully, I sincerely hope we can, but my second chakra suspects not. I anticipate an economic slide and social unrest. The gap has widened too far and those at the bottom will have their say and those breathlessly squeezed in the middle will have their day. Financially things are already beginning to bite and though I anticipate this to get worse very quickly, I suspect most people have a few more years grace [I hope]. Already we are seeing the results of deaf, blind and reactive government. In the 1970's most of us gathered oil producing countries could be a tad tricky, but car driving, house heating, plastic buying oil junkies we became and no-one in government made long term plans for energy consumption. Now we have a major problem on our hands. Recently we have seen agitation over second home ownership in lovely rural areas and pretty seaside towns, where high house prices are forcing locals on the defensive. I am quietly surprised the agitators have taken so long when a few in Wales were suggesting, 'come home to a real fire' [arson attacks on second homes] back in the seventies. Is it *possible* that Westminster did not anticipate the discontent of those unable to buy homes?

Economically I look at things very simply and I have been derided and sneered at for years and years for doing so, but I am getting to old to care and I notice my simple homespun philosophy seems to stand the test of time. Low interest rates have allowed unproductive businesses to limp along while lulling everyone into a false sense of security. The wild borrowing and spending has resulted in us becoming a debt-ridden nation, which makes us weak and vulnerable. The public, on a slow and very small scale, has started to realise this and to do something to rectify the situation on a personal basis. The government, however, has yet to catch on and put its own house in order. Business, the banks and institutions that hold our money make large allowances for large debt; a mindset that does not make me sleep easy at night. In my mind there is a pot of money in this whole country that goes round and round and round. That pot does not get any bigger until we can pull a tourist in and relieve them of their money, make something here and flog it abroad, or get some foreigner or foreign company to invest in this country. That pot of money has got very big for a small amount of people but it has not dripped down that much to the rest of the population. The City of London has made a gigantic fortune but everything is cyclical, this will change and it looks like it is on the turn now. A lot of money has been acquired releasing equity from personal homes - I thought this was lunacy because interest rates were bound to rise eventually [because they always do, eventually] and most people end up hitting a crisis of health, relationships or work/finances at some stage of their life. Rising house prices meant some people made a lot of money, which will be at the expense of everyone long term because the next generation will not be able to afford the four bedroom houses that now sell for ludicrous sums of money, never mind pay the running and heating costs. Meanwhile, us Brits haemorrhage our money out of the country buying foreign clothes, goods, cars and then remove more of our money on foreign travel just as we make less and less here to sell abroad with which to bring money back in. The biggest employer in the country is small business, yet small business is hounded by government, despite silken words spun out at the despatch box. Our basic standard of education is appalling and well behind other nations, particularly India and China, which is a potential disaster for a 'service' dependent economy. Many of our children have unrealistic living and work aspirations, cannot comprehend frugality and think house ownership is an entitlement. We are over taxed. The tax payers are getting restless. Hundreds of thousands of workers' salaries are paid by tax payers. Hundreds of thousands of welfare cheques are paid by tax payers, so if the economy suddenly nosedived an awful lot of salaries, pensions and welfare cheques could fail to materialise. We fly food in from abroad while snubbing our own farmers. We are overcrowded, over-consuming of energy we cannot provide ourselves, controlled by the EU, our infrastructure is groaning and our transport system is a mess. Many of our railway stations, trains and public loos stink and are a national disgrace. We are not good at service, or selling in shops. We are becoming more and more unhealthy, which will put a huge strain on welfare and the already struggling NHS. How's the future looking to you?

I am quite optimistic. I have been through my deep and gloomy blue period and have emerged into hope-filled sunny uplands because I think the British are a bit special and are waking up and walking away from all the nonsense, bit by tiny bit. A farm shop here, a snort of derision at an overpaid celebrity there. People are starting to understand the importance of saving. At Christmas they are sending chickens and goats to Africa. They are happy watching blue tits nesting on the telly and they are aspiring to beach huts ………….. *beach huts.* Perhaps 'chic' repositions itself economically, but I think it goes deeper than that. People are returning to basics and reaching for something that feeds their souls. My adorable young hairdressers discuss with me the joys of vegetable growing and happy nights spent in with loved ones - a stunning volte-face [complete change of attitude] to the heavy duty partying of yesteryear. I walk into busy bookshops and see a nation reconnecting with words, everyone, it seems [even me], is a writer these days. My partner's Ipod downloads music from all over the world, everyone, it seems [except me], is a musician these days. Such creativity - it is wonderful. Nature is being treasured again. Fear-channelled purchasing of designer anything is being challenged, at last! Bar-b-ques on the beach are found to be more restful than high voltage dinner parties where competition is rife. Human interaction is best, it always has been ……… in fact from my receding position I am beginning to view it as positively holy, because each interaction I have with someone, or something, is a chance to empower or to decimate.

I am not saying things are not going to be rough but poverty is relative. For me it would be no basic shelter but more importantly no food and no medicine [that means vitamins/minerals for me]. Strange to think we live in a country where there is too much food and medicine and it is killing us. At times of economic uncertainty, or even economic bust, what really matters in life becomes self-evident. Love matters. Kindness matters. Home, food, family and wellness matters. However, we have a problem in that first chakra values and rules have been overlooked, there has been way too much indulgence and not enough instilled discipline [in both families and government] and without this instilled first chakra discipline, third chakra self-imposed discipline becomes a much more difficult challenge. This does not bode well for our long term economy and we are beginning to pay the price. Our outlook is hugely uncertain and therefore my advice would be to take pro-active action RIGHT NOW. Cut up all but one credit card, staple your wallets shut and pay off your debts as soon as possible. Glittery t-shirts, Ipods, strappy sandals and CD's will not put food on the table if and when push comes to shove. Don't fully trust the banks or anyone who is holding your money. Keep some cash where you can access it quickly [maybe a local Post Office, if you have one] so you can feed your family if the economy takes a sudden nasty, deep dip. Read 'skills' later in the book. Watch the political and economic horizon like a hawk and keep abreast of what business is doing: that means reading the business section of the newspapers and talking to anyone who is in business. Count the shopping bags people are carrying in towns and cities - it is always a good indicator of the economy and whether people are spending. Don't be an ostrich. If things start to get shaky keep a supply of water in your house and some non-perishable food [rice, tinned beans, etc.,] plus pet food. Start making friends with your neighbours, because crime will certainly rise and you will all need to be on the look-out for one another. You may think I am being ridiculously alarmist, you are entitled to your views, but I look at it as being prepared and self-sufficient. Read your history books and NEVER ASSUME things will stay the same, let alone get better. The wacky books I read have been predicting a crisis *years* before the newspapers started saying, 'Oh dear, trouble might be coming'. [The wackies understand this is a spiritual shift which will encompass an economic and/or climate shift.] The imbalance in debt, welfare and public sector jobs can be contained while interest rates and inflation remain relatively low but this is changing fast. We are reverting to tribalism to re-establish first chakra values that were turfed out [or more accurately - not learnt] by the 'loads of money' second chakra culture. In pursuit of the tribal cause, Scotland will doubtless break free [as it perceives it], Wales too and Cornwall may follow. Problem is, tribalism may have socialism at its core but the application of tribal rules is usually very right wing. I do so hope the public are paying attention to that. I don't think the politicians understand what they are unleashing, but that is their problem.

The universe brings important lessons in threes. I have learnt to pay serious attention when I get a third [in quick succession] wake-up call. Although I have been gravely concerned since 1992 [when I begged my mother to buy land - she would not listen], it was about three years ago [2003] that I had three chance encounters with three different men and their political opinions made me very jumpy. The men were salt of the earth workers, each in completely different jobs, yet all of them were virtually foaming at the mouth with anger at our current state of government and taxation. I have heard anger before, when Margaret Thatcher was Prime Minister, but this anger felt different to me - it felt more dangerous. We are not, at present, governed by consent, unless you call having a vote every four years consent. I don't and I have long favoured the Swiss method of mini-referendums on most matters. It appears debate in the Commons and in the Cabinet is dwindling. The opposition looks and sounds weak. It may only take one person to voice our widespread discontent loudly and convincingly and you could see a massive political pole shift. The big cities may be liberal and/or soft focus labour but out in the sticks, where what's left of our food growth is based, all I hear is right wing views with no party to vote for. It worries me because, it seems, in history, civil wars define a nation and we are at a defining moment. I am not suggesting civil war, but I am suggesting a huge potential for strife. The vociferously vocal minority groups, in fact everyone, would be well advised to read their history books, look up, wake up, smell the coffee, watch the horizon and make preparations.

If you want a tiny glimpse at the far future read 'reincarnation', then you will need to get hold of the book. What Jenny Cockell says makes perfect sense, because we are starting to kill the seas now. You could say that our future is in our hands but I think our future is first in our state of mind. Forget government, at present it is not for us, it is for itself. Maybe another Winston Churchill, Abraham Lincoln or Gandhi is coming, but don't count on it. We have to go within and concentrate on us. We need to empower ourselves one by one. If we can do this with well-loaded first and second chakras, empowered third chakras AND peace in our hearts, we will move mountains.

As I said to my father around 1989 [he looked quizzically at me] we only have one problem and it is easy to fix. We don't have a problem with food or water or energy, there is plenty of it. We don't even have a problem with globalisation or foreign travel. We only have one major problem to deal with and that is global over-population. Every cute baby grows up deserving a loving home, health, work and happiness, but right now there are too many cute babies being born who will consume, consume and consume during their lifetime, yet the planet has limited resources. Reduce the amount of people and everyone works, roads clear, beaches empty, hospital beds await, heat does not need to be rationed, local food tastes good, people smile and everyone wins. It is not a big deal - you just stop paying people to have children. You can try paying them not to produce, but personally I would advocate heavily taxing the second child. Governments will not do this, so meanwhile, back in the real world, things will get much worse. A few sticking plasters will be popped on here and there. The EU will strangle us. The seas will empty of fish. The energy will come from nuclear reactors and the waste will be a headache for thousands of years. All over the world we will lose millions of animal species and humans will depopulate themselves the unpleasant way with chemical overload, infertility, disease, starvation and war. Shame. It does not have to be like this, but it looks like this is how it will be.

G Is for GOD

Does anybody know what God looks like? I have to say an old man in a long frock with a white beard doesn't do it for me. A judgmental God? Why would God need to judge when earthly spiritual progression always seems to lead to becoming non-judgmental? God the father? Father? What happened to Mrs. God? Perhaps she is busy washing his frocks, trimming his beard and keeping heaven neat and tidy. If God is judgmental and male I feel quite sorry for him; he has had to witness thousands of generations of his children behaving like *raving maniacs*. He was there for the birth and witnessed the first steps. He has winced at His childrens' language, despaired of the hairstyles, clothes, lovers and job-hopping …… and that was just the quiet members of the brood. His other children have tortured, slaughtered babies [and anything else they didn't like the look of], lied, thieved, burned, bombed and when they have paused from their busy endeavours of making life hell for other humans and animals, they have now polluted their Father's garden earth. Children! Who'd have 'em? If I was God I would be beyond tearing my hair out, I would be on Prozac, at the very least.

The best description I have ever come across was that 'God was beautiful but indescribable'. I rather liked that idea. What if God was neutral? What if God was waiting patiently, very patiently, for us humans to grow up? What if God was waiting for us humans to finally wake up and say, 'We are all God's children and now we are grown up we need to take complete responsibility for ourselves as individuals. We need to stop fighting each other and fight our egos instead. We need to regulate our numbers so that we do not overcrowd our precious planet and its limited resources. We need to be nice to ourselves and nice to our fellow man, whatever race or creed. We need to live simple non-destructive lives, protect every single plant and animal, because they have as much right to be here as humans. We need to enjoy our lives on this wondrously diverse planet we call home' ……. and having acknowledged that we need to do it …… do it. I reckon God would heave a sigh of immense relief and say 'AT LAST!'.

Sometimes, I ponder on such a scenario, when the whole planet is peopled with spiritually mature, humble, kind and loving humans. I wonder if God will look down on us and think, 'Result!'. God might then wander off to some distant galaxy, with a smile and a twinkle in His eye. He might point at something and watch it go BANG!!! Then, standing back, finger to mouth, think, 'Off we go again ……. let's see how long it takes them this time'.

Meanwhile, Mrs. God, smoothing her white hair and straightening her pinny, sighs in her heavenly garden and thinks, 'I'm still trying to housetrain the last lot of dinosaurs and now we are going to get the next batch'.

GIFTS

Gift giving should not be that important but I think it is. To give a gift that is received with genuine pleasure is a measure of how well the giver understands the recipient; no matter if the gift be hand picked flowers from the garden or something a tad more expensive. It is in the nature of the giving, but most of all it is about paying attention.

GODDESSES

There is a lovely little book called 'Goddesses in Every Woman' by Jean Shinoda Bolen. I decided I was a mixture of Artemis and Hestia. Slightly contrary but that's me, contrary through and through. It was followed by 'Gods in Every Man' which is definitely worth a read, so you chaps can confirm to yourself that you are indeed an Apollo while we ladies murmur, 'Cronus, more like it'.

GOVERNMENT MONEY

It is NOT government money. It is OUR money. They take it, they spend it and they waste it. It is called taxation - or theft, depending on how you look at it. It looks increasingly like theft to me.

GOVERNMENT

Politicians are our servants. They seem to forget this and so do we. We pay them. Because we pay them and provide them with an extremely comfortable pension you would think they would listen to our wishes and instructions. Nope. Our servants are running the household to suit themselves and we let them get away with it. While we are out at work they are flogging off part of the garden, selling the family silver, helping themselves to the scotch and making deals [that we will pay for] with people we don't know. Is this a 'Carry On' script? No, it's a reality horror film.

I have voted for the Conservative party all my life. Apparently that makes me a turgid reactionary who lacks compassion. I ask my partner for his opinion...... he thinks I am very compassionate person but with political views slightly to the right of Attila the Hun. This is nonsense, of course, but I have always been deeply suspicious of socialism since I was at school and made to run about on a playing field. I am not sporty but I was chosen, for some hilarious and completely inexplicable reason, to run against a gazelle [I think this is called pacing or being a pacer]. There we were, on the starting block, me and her, because the hideous teacher did not believe I still had a period after three successful weeks of games evasion. Bang! Off we shot, for a short while, until I staggered to a halt, red, sweaty and panting like a sheepdog, while she, the gazelle, galloped gracefully into the misty distance. 'There you go', thought I, 'there will always be someone who can run faster and better than me. Now, if only they would let me gallop gracefully to the misty distance of the library or art room, where maybe I could shine, we could all win together while separately doing our different things'. I decided that this meant choice and in those days the governing socialists were not at all keen on choice. Now we have new socialists, apparently, who are deeply committed, so they say, to giving as much choice as possible while removing it faster than we can say, 'That hospital, or this school please'.

I rarely meet anyone, except the deeply religious, who is not a capitalist at heart. It is natural. You want to get on and make money, buy nice things and have some choice in how you educate your nippers. If you suddenly get your hands on buckets of money a slightly larger house, or even a stately pile, is usually on cards, whatever your background or upbringing, and most people like getting a gong from the Queen. We are gradually, if grudgingly, accepting this concept and that is why all the parties are heading for the centre ground because this part of the second chakra lesson has been learnt. Now, at this point of our spiritual development [pause ... while I pop on my rose-tinted spectacles] it would be lovely if we could find a governmental head honcho who is on good terms with third chakra who can plainly state the facts and set out the scenario for the next lesson - disciplined self-governing, self-reliance, self-responsibility, emphasis, just in case you have not gathered, on self. Problem is, third chakra head honchos are a bit thin on the ground and anyway, we are supposed to do the next bit ourselves. Us voters. It is up to us, individually, to 'be the change we want to see in the world' [as Mahatma Gandhi so wisely instructed]. As we, collectively, pull our socks up we can demand dramatic change in our government. We are not quite ready yet, but I think we are warming up nicely. It is the over-heating I worry about.

My father always used to say to me, 'A country gets the police force it deserves, ducky', which is probably right and I daresay a country gets the government it deserves. I am appallingly ignorant about the why's and wherefore's of government but it seems to me that governing this country, or any country for that matter, boils down to them giving us the vote, for starters, then providing a decent infrastructure [roads, rail, water, sewerage, that sort of thing], basic education and health care, a justice system that protects its *law-abiding* citizens and their property, defence of the realm, a currency and reasonable taxation. Have I left anything out? I don't think so. Eight things. Why is it so difficult? It seems to me that it is difficult because at the moment we have a second chakra 'gimme money' policy springing from the more distributive 'let's look after the tribe' attitude of first chakra and a concentration, a thickening, if you will, of 'grubbing about' second chakra external power play. This is all spiritually necessary but a thoroughly unedifying spectacle. The point of these tedious shenanigans is to get us voters to press pause on our hamster wheels, get off and demand better leadership. This is a third chakra demand because we will have reached a point of understanding that 'we deserve better than this'. That we are worth it [remember the advertisement that ran the line 'because I'm worth it' - such interesting timing and fascinating that it annoyed many older women ... sixth chakra curtain opening]. The only spoke in the hamster wheel is that we won't get off until things get really, really unpleasant but fortunately we have a government that has been hell-bent on making it as unpleasant as possible for the large majority of the population, especially the law-abiding tax payers. Depending on how you look at it, this is either an awfully silly thing to do at this stage of the proceedings to a public that has had a good taste of freedom - or - it is exactly what needs to happen at this stage of the proceedings, so that the public will take that freedom a step further.

I am getting tired of shouting at politicians on the box. Nowadays, I relocate my brain to something sensible and soothing, like the washing up. I have always voted, but I don't know if I can bring myself to vote at the next election because, at present, I cannot see a leader who is sufficiently 'collected' and 'within' himself to be able to see clearly, make some thoroughly difficult and unpleasant changes, while leaving what works alone. We are finally emerging from a long period of political middle of the road, caring, sharing, playing with babies and casual clothes. This was, apparently, to show connection to the public - it never worked for me. I have had a bellyful of ridiculous political party slogans, undelivered promises and meaningless sweaty speeches and now I am hoping for some grown-up politics and personal honesty. There is nothing wrong with wanting to be Prime Minister but we all know the work leaves little time for family life, so to be hell-bent on the top job while wittering on about the importance of one's family seems rather dishonest to me. I am not much interested in a politician's family anyway and I am not keen on this buy-one-get-one-free business; it's like buying a packet of washing powder in 1960 and getting a free plastic daffodil. In my view political spouses should be a little seen and never heard. Better still, bog off completely. I have no time for politicians who tell me they change nappies at night. *So what?* Let's keep children out of it. There are enough things to trip up political leaders without toys and plastic building blocks littering their floor. I was not thrilled to hear toddlers were being brought to work at the Treasury; I was about as appreciative of that news as my ventilated patient on Intensive Care would have been had I, as a nurse, brought in to work a toddler of mine - to play with the tubes. I cannot be doing with political chumminess. I do not find chummy at all reassuring. In my own life I have observed that people don't take chummy seriously. Politically you can't make decisions on national security one minute and be chummy the next, because you have to drop your boundaries to be chummy - big mistake and there is no withdrawal. I thought Margaret Thatcher was on a downhill slide the moment she chummily took some television interviewer upstairs in No 10 and showed how she just popped some tissue paper into her blouse bows to keep them looking perky. 'Ooopsy daisy', I thought. Sooner or later the media, not to mention colleagues, are going to be sharpening their knives, so it is best that they only have your policies to slice up, not your nappies, casual shoes, bows, kitchen, wife and anything else you rashly threw in. Anyway chummy says needy to me .... and I should know.

I heard a retired foreign leader on the radio comment that, 'Governments do not represent the people, they never have'. I did not agree. Sometimes they do and sometimes they don't, everything is cyclical and governments *reflect* the people. We have allowed our leaders to get away with some disgraceful behaviour in the last few years but then we have allowed ourselves to do much the same. Our leadership has mirrored back to us our own lax behaviour. Our lack of self-discipline and failure to preserve and cherish our freedom has allowed our government to take more and more liberties and erode our freedom of speech. Our apathetic approach to pilfering and lying, our greed for money and yet more material goods has been mirrored back to us by an increasingly pilfering and lying government obsessed with money and prestige. I don't think we can expect government to change us; we have to change first because in order for government to change us we would have to retreat back to the swingeing laws of first chakra, of tribalism …. but then many in the new age movement think that is exactly what is going to happen. This thought keeps me awake at night and challenges my third chakra 'trust' to its extreme limits. I wonder about the future and how all this middle of the road politics leaves a widening gap left and right. Left has had its day because we have all been seen for what we really are - upwardly mobile to some degree or rather, given half a chance - it is the extreme right that worries me. An extreme [any extremist is operating out of fear] right wing leader making noises about a crack down on immigration, fairer taxation, swingeing laws against thieving etc., would be attractive to many but could result in just another round of bullying - bullying that could get deadly eventually. Dead journalists for starters and I reckon I would not be looking too sharp either.

This century is squaring up to be a time of massive and possibly brutal change for us all. The United States does not look so frightening any more, is being challenged from all over the globe and is having to look outward [sixth chakra] at the bigger picture [perhaps the baseball caps will come off]. Britain is being economically challenged by countries that do not have welfare states or much in the way of worker's rights. We in Britain have a staggeringly high population, far too many employed or living at tax-payers expense and we import most of our food, learning nothing, zilch, zero, from our history books. Oil producing countries have everyone by the short and curlies, global warming is on everyone's lips and there is panic everywhere about energy, water and debt. Extraordinary. Didn't our leaders see this problem coming? Obviously not. Or did I miss an agenda? I listen to [and read about] politicians daily but I see no-one on the political front who can instigate the dramatic and brutal changes that this country needs to stave off disaster with the very possible exception of one politician [but even he needs a frontal lobotomy for his views on Europe]. As a result of this paucity of leadership potential I spend much of my time reminding myself to breath deeply and calmly and remember that nationally this void is a spiritual necessity for chakra growth. I don't get restful sleep, especially as someone has flogged off the nation's gold. Was the nation asked? No. Our gold [and I reckon it was ours - not his] has virtually gone but now the super-rich movers and shakers are buying gold by the bucket load. It makes me jittery.

I worry that the Government cannot put the brakes on its enlargement and even if it starts hitting the brake pedal now it will be too little and way too late. Our huge and distant government, while murmuring platitudes, seems to have little concept of the problems faced by its ordinary citizens. The political world seems like the NHS managerial world where I watched a creeping enlargement. Managers, with no experience of ward work or caring for sick people, started appearing out of nowhere taking on work that previously senior nurses had done. Senior nurses worked up through the wards and understood one basic and simple fact - the point of a hospital is to get patients better. Patients were usually in beds on wards and that is where the nurses needed to be too because patients usually could not do much for themselves. Most managers I met seemed unable to grasp this concept. Once installed in an office, with all the necessary and expensive office paraphernalia, they seemed to need to justify their jobs by calling multiple meetings. Nurses, midwives and anybody else busy at the rock face of patient care were dragged away from the wards [worse - dragged from their homes on their days off and supposed to be thrilled] to attend meetings which rarely started on time and usually lasted an hour - two if there was more than one managerial windbag holding court. I would sit, Miss Popularity herself [you can imagine], steaming. The essence of the meeting could invariably be boiled down to a basic ten minutes, maybe less. Instead of which staff had to sit and fidget and were finally released back to the wards an hour or two later to complete the work of caring for patients, only now they had considerably less time to do it in and the waiting patients were understandably pissed off. I would leave every meeting trying to calm down while thinking, 'This is just the NHS, then there are all the unnecessary meetings at Westminster and then there is that mother of all humbug meetings - the European Union, God give me strength'.

At present the whole institution of Westminster looks, to me, to be a living, heaving, breathing fight for external second chakra power. Our politburo style of governance is breathtakingly controlling [fear based], snaking into every facet of our life and squeezing. While it controls, bullies, over-taxes, frightens and monitors us, it is actually, tragically, fighting itself and in my view to death. I am getting heartily sick of it all but the problem is where the government leaves off, big business takes over the bullying and controlling and big business has more clout and it moves much faster. Big business *bludgeons* me as I sit, in impotent sighing desperation, holding the phone for what seems like an eternity trying to sort out a household bill with recorded voices. The sheer relief when I hear a human at the other end of the phone almost reduces me to tears. Such is the *extraordinary* degree of second chakra bullying from big bosses who are creaming enormous profits, salaries and pensions while I waste too many minutes of my day on the receiving end of extremely expensive but extremely poor service. Unfortunately nothing will be done to control it because government is also bullying. They are all in the same second chakra territory and I see no potential leader who can stand up, take a cool sixth chakra look at what is coming and make the changes. I don't know who to vote for. They all frighten me and that makes me hate them all. I especially hate the Conservative Party for slapping me so savagely in the face. For that, of course, I have absolutely no-one to blame but myself. I probably should not vote - it just encourages them. There is only one way out, to retreat and reduce consumption - then they can all go hang.

I want to know why I am forced to pay VAT on products that are a necessity. I am clobbered when buying a loo brush. Why? I pay again when I get my car repaired. Why? Why am I *forced* to pay the Chancellor of the Exchequer if I need to take my sick dog to the vet? It is beyond decency, it is GROTESQUE. Where is the compassion in that nasty little ruse? Even tampons are taxed - I don't give a continental damn who introduced VAT on tampons and vet bills, someone with any form of third chakra honour code would sweep away VAT completely, or at least reinstate it as the original tax on value goods that we can choose not to buy. I resent being so bullied and having no-one to plead my case. I wish Government would wake up, slim down, move faster, concentrate on controlling the worst excesses of big business and stop picking on us little ones. Pick, pick, pick, bully, bully, bully. Nasty. I see banana skins coming.

Why don't we halve the number of MP's and double their salary? They would have to work harder, of course, but I note quite a few of them write books [amongst *other* time consuming activities] and judging by the amount of time it is taking me to write this book it leads me to suspect MP's are not hard at the day job. The Prime Minister does not get paid enough - don't shout at me please. I would offer half a million a year and a full time chef [ridiculous idea that the PM has to send out for a pizza - for God's sake, someone get him a cook!]. The job needs total concentration, not half concentration and half grubbing about looking for future job opportunities when the inevitable boot has hit their backside. Is there a catch to this largesse? *I should say.* I would like to see every single member of parliament being forced to do nine gestational months of national service [followed by the paparazzi - I'll just dust off my camera] before they are allowed to enter Westminster. Two months working on a ward in a hospital [geriatrics would be good], two months teaching in an inner city school, two months with the forces [at the sharp end, mind you] and then three months running a small corner shop in the Midlands and I mean running it, not just working in it. That should give them a healthy reality check.

Most people now accept that long term welfare has a debilitating effect and despite the inundation of foreign workers from all over Europe [and beyond] coming here and finding work all our political parties are too terrified to pull the plug on benefits [extraordinary word], but it just has to be done, and quickly, no matter how unpleasant. Anyone who has visited India or China will know what we are up against economically. That is just two countries, out of many, where you don't eat if you don't work. My 'slightly to the right of Attila the Hun' political views have witnessed up close how desperately depressed people can get when they are continually drawing benefits and not working. It becomes a vicious downward spiral as self-respect and, more importantly, work confidence ebb away; then the diet suffers and the downward spiral increases aided by a mineral and vitamin deficiency. In these times of fast-paced change you need to keep your hand in at some sort of work - it is crucial. I have always been against handing people money over and above a few months. You must have a safety net, it is the duty of a civilised society to break a work/financial fall and support during a recovery period but after a few months hand-outs should be food and clothing coupons only, otherwise there is little incentive to clamber back to the work principle and it is absolutely wrong to expect the working tax payers to carry an increasingly heavy load. Now, as the interest rates rise and the economic reality of the future begins to bite, it is national suicide to be carrying large numbers of non-workers [who are able to work] because the tax payer's bill for the public sector wages and pensions is already way out of hand. I am bored witless by the argument that you need more and more workers to pay for an ageing population. To suggest we cannot afford pensions without a higher population is a load of rubbish coming from successive governments that have hurled billions of our money at any number of ridiculous causes [sent God knows how much money to other countries - and now we have the Olympics bill to swallow] and then taxed our savings and pensions - outrageous. Not done with thieving our piggy-banks they then clobber the poorest by taxing them too. No-one should pay tax until they have earned twelve grand a year, it is indecent to tax earnings under that because the basic cost of living is so high.

Quite apart from over-population I have always thoroughly resented paying for other peoples' children. Other people have argued back that their children will pay my old age pension. Yeah? Well, I am not banking on it, that is why both my partner and me have taken on training in work that will carry us into old age. I sincerely hope I get my state pension but I am not hopeful. If I work until I am ninety I will be taxed and, presumably, will still have to pay for other peoples' child benefits - there is no cut off point. I don't have any children but no-one ever offered me a refund or a whippet allowance. I resent this. I nearly choked on my lunch when, as a particularly hard-up nurse, I heard a colleague mention she always spent her child benefits at a well known chemist on something nice for herself - perfume, perhaps, or nail polish. On hearing this I damn near needed resuscitating as my sandwich blocked my throat and my sense of humour at the same time. I was outraged that I paid for her bloody nail polish when I had no car, no social life and barely managed my mortgage and bills. I don't mind anyone who is genuinely struggling financially to raise children being given food and clothing vouchers - in fact I applaud it - but not nail polish. We need to get a grip in this country and stop being so sloppy and soft. We will have to have a network of hotel type [dare I say hostel?] accommodation, paid for initially by the tax-payers, that allows workers to migrate from Monday to Friday to where the work is. It will not suit many but we have for centuries had to follow the work and the future will see this returning - big time. During my childhood our roads seemed to be built by the Irish, who returned home to their families when they could, not, I reckon, when they wanted. Life is cyclical [we start out in nappies and often end up in them] so is economics and much of what makes up a nation - it just dresses differently. I was fantastically fortunate to be raised in a middle-class family during the post war years when people had had enough of violence. Children were cherished as the replacement to thousands slaughtered during the war years. We were safe to wander and play on our own. We knew when we reached adulthood we could find some sort of work fairly easily .... but those halcyon days were a *blip*, not a constant.

The brakes have to be slammed on over immigration. It is an emergency because our infrastructure can't take more people plus water and energy shortages are going to be a feature of future life. We have to pull out of the European Union because we have lost control of our laws, our borders, our fishing industry and the EU is constricting, slow moving and expensive at a time when we need just the opposite. If global warming steps up a pace the government running this country will have to move very fast indeed - it can't if it has to wait for Europe to 'permit this' or 'allow that'. I can't see any of this happening, it looks like bunker mentality to me at present and we all know how that story ends. Still, revolution before evolution means I am spiritually optimistic about the future while being deeply gloomy about the environment.

Meanwhile, as Lord Hailsham observed, we have an elected dictatorship. It is interesting to watch how the court at Westminster becomes more and more controlling and less and less accessible to the public it does not wish to meet, as the monarchy becomes more accessible and even, if I might make so bold, perhaps a tad more in touch with the people. Fascinating, but let us hold hard and dear to our democracy and that goes for me too - I must vote, I must, no matter that the parties are all *pants*. Let us read our history books, history repeats itself because human nature does not change. Humans want external power, whether they are dressed in a toga, doublet and hose or a bullet-proof jaguar speedily passing the tedious masses that have paid for it. Fasten your seat belts, it is going to be a bumpy ride.

GOD'S GOVERNMENT

Of course it is possible that this has all been planned. What if ...... what if there was another scenario entirely. What if all this was *meant* to happen .... imagine this. In ye olden days God called a meeting. In trundles all the happy little angels trailing their harps and wisps of cloud. 'Now settle down chaps', because God looks like Bill Nighy and sounds like a softly spoken Captain Mainwaring. 'I want to draw your attention to this drawing behind me', and the angels look at a long line of hills and vales with various civilisations up one minute and down the next. 'Now', says God, 'we have had a good run of this last hill here marked The West and it is time it slipped down into a valley. The next little ascending hill I have planned will be marked The East, because it is their turn now. What I need you volunteers to do is to go down here, here, here, here and here', waving a pointer all over Europe, Britain and America, 'get yourself elected into high office and generally start making a hash of things. Lots of interference, bureaucracy and red tape, that sort of thing. Rules and regulations, the more the merrier. Taxation, lots of that. No parking signs, speed cameras, I am sure you get the picture'. Lots of little hands go up, offering to cause mayhem. Two little eager beavers at the back, one strumming his harp and the other strumming his calculator offer to finish off what an earlier volunteer, who looked remarkably like Edward Heath, would start. God smiled and said, 'Off you go my little treasures, get busy'.

That would be an interesting thought, wouldn't it? Well, then, our dead leaders, when they get back to heaven, would be judged by God, not by us and presumably God would be delighted. 'You did well my darlings, you hashed it up good and proper. Now off you go and play with the other angels'. Off they go, those cherubic, rosy buttocked ex-leaders and head for the playground where all the other little angels [who were on the receiving end of their hashing - me included] are waiting for them. What happened next? Censored. Not passed for viewers of a delicate nature.

GUILT

It's a messy business is guilt. I have watched guilt, in its different forms, derail many a life. I have also observed, over the years, that divorce carries enormous guilt trips. I am not against divorce, far from it, but lax parental behaviour driven by divorce guilt has messed up far too many childrens' heads.

Whatever your guilt may be - acknowledge it firstly. Then *forgive yourself* second. After that, leave it be. We *all* make mistakes. We are *human*.

$\mathcal{H}$ Is for HEAVEN

Some years back, someone, who seemed to be in the know, told me that there are colleges in heaven. It took me months to get over the shock. On receipt of this bombshell I drove home in a cold sweat. 'Exams! *You have to be joking?* .... I won't go. Games! Hideous hockey!! Red faced St.Trinian girls racing at you, screaming like banshees and they will be even faster with wings. I won't go. I won't'. I think I went through the entire grieving process, complete denial, fury, then I tried plea bargaining. 'I'll do extra English Lit. if you absolutely promise I don't have to vault a flaming horse or do Maths'. I got no response from God so he definitely is not an old man with a white beard because I can just imagine what He would have had to say .... with his red marker pen.

Heaven is always portrayed as a garden. Who does the weeding? I am worried that when I have finished my day in college I will have to tackle the ground elder and nettles. It all sounds rather tiring and I was so hoping for a rest. Somewhere I read that heaven is always the temperature of an English summer's day, bathed in a pinky glow and the flowers are permanently in full bloom. It sounds like a naffing bore. I like a bit of winter, a good howling gale and what about snowdrops? Are you telling me I have to go to college every day in a pinky glow surrounded by constantly flowering peonies - is that it? What's the alternative?

Having finally decided I was going to have to accept the heavenly college option [with or without good grace] I picked up another book that said when you get to heaven you become a spherical ball. I started giggling. It seemed to me that that idea stuffed the college option because how would I turn the pages of my textbook? Further to the spherical ball option was, that, on arrival in heaven, you are put in a holding pen while you learn to negotiate movement as a ball. Apparently, as a ball you don't move towards something, you ball-like think about something and it ball-like moves towards you. I loved this idea. There's me, a new arrival in the holding pen, but also in the holding pen is Thelma the African hippopotamus who died just about the same time as me. I think about Thelma ...... fatal! A collision of two balls, only 'Thelma-ball' is considerably bigger than 'me-ball'. Presumably there are paramedics in the holding pen to patch up the balls, though I'm not quite sure how you paramedic without hands. There must be teachers [aha - seconded from a college!] to instruct new balls in the art of movement by thinking, which must be trickier than learning to drive [in which case my mother - a deceased erratic driver - may well still be in the holding pen]. I wondered if you had to pass an exam, heaven forbid, to show your ball-driving proficiency before you were let into heaven, because careless ball-drivers could knock the heads off constantly flowering peonies - and we can't have that.

I have been wondering about the ball theory. Many years ago I watched a programme where an American soldier was interviewed. He said he was shot in Vietnam but did not die. He had an out of body experience and saw his dead buddies, only they were balls of light. He wasn't sure how he recognised them, he just knew who they were. So maybe the ball theory is correct, only the balls obviously have their headlights on. Recently I saw a programme about a monastery and a spherical object seemed to appear around the monk's throat. Actually I think there was more than one spherical thingy, if I recall correctly. Of course the wackies think the 'movement as thought' theory is what happens here on earth and I am inclined to agree. The idea is that you attract what you think about, so I must remember to keep hippopotamus thoughts fairly low on my radar screen. They are lovable and I simply adore them but I am not sure I want them in my garden knocking the heads off my occasionally flowering peonies.

Would being a ball be interesting? No mouth or other end, so no grub. No eating, but then no washing up. No curling up with a good book and a mug of tea - tragic - but then no shopping, so that's good. No feet, so no dog walking - tragic - but then whippet balls could roll themselves around on the grass for exercise. Grass? Presumably not. Rivers? River balls ….. doesn't work for me. Tree balls? Oh no, no, it's no good, I prefer it here.

$\mathcal{H}$ELL

My idea of hell is too many people too all the time. I would go stark raving round the bend living in a large commune or a huge family. I am not quite sure how I survived boarding school. Perhaps I didn't. Perhaps I have been permanently damaged. Perhaps I am a bit barking. Explains a lot.

HORSES

It is interesting how humans treat horses, isn't it? Human slavery has been abolished, mostly, but we subject horses to the equivalent. They are bought and sold on a whim, without so much as a by your leave to their happiness. We treat them as if they have no feelings and are perfect idiots, until they come from the finishing post exhaling tornadoes of steam from their nostrils and we say, 'Well done, well done, who is a clever chap?!'. Then we go and collect our winnings. Why can't a horse also be for life and not just for Christmas? Poor old Dobbin wakes up and says, 'Morning!', to his chums and next thing he knows he is being herded into the back of a box and taken away, never to see his best mates again and never to be told why. It is a wonder they are not all complete basket cases. I would be if you treated me like that.

Now we have coats for horses. I have coats for my dogs in mid-freezing winter because they can do without as long as they keep moving, but if I start chatting they start chattering. There is no doubt that some horses definitely need a coat in mid-winter, especially at night and if they are clipped, but many do not and I see them coated-up on warm spring and autumn days - it is ridiculous. I don't know how horses get their quota of Vitamin D when they are either in a stable, where the sun don't shine, or out in a field but covered in a coat. Have you seen those coats that go up and all over their faces? I would go stark raving bonkers in one of those. Imagine putting a rider in a burqa. They wouldn't like it, but at least they could take it off. They are horses, animals, for God's sake, not Barbie Dolls. Animals will do things like rolling around in smelly mud because it is a huge pleasure to them and is probably a form of natural physiotherapy - relaxing muscles and realigning their spine. The mud may well furnish them with minerals that they absorb through their skin while keeping buzzy bitey things at bay. I know if I am frustrated or angry mosquito bites [and even nettle stings] are more inflamed and painful, this is because the anger and frustration quickly uses up my B vitamins, which act as an anti-inflammatory. Is this the same for frustrated and angry horses? I don't know but I wouldn't be surprised. As the skin is the biggest eliminatory organ for humans and horses alike, it must be crucial, surely, to allow that skin to be in its most natural state for as many hours in the day as possible. My dogs love to roll about on grass and they also love to find and dab Eau de Fox Poo behind their ears. I understand they are dogs, not humans, and Chanel No 5 teamed with a pink silk scarf would not be their idea of heaven on a stick. I absolutely hate having to wash the Eau de Fox Poo off the dogs' necks, and anywhere else they may have liberally spread it, because they always start shaking and showering me with smelly water, but there you go, animals are hard work and so are horses covered in mud. My partner, who treats horses nearly every day and loves them dearly, despairs of the coats. 'Let's have some DFH ..... Dignity For Horses', he says.

I wish horses had more access to old English hedgerows and proper old verges so they could self medicate themselves on natural plants if they were poorly. If I had a sickly horse, I would look for a really old hedgerow to walk the horse along, watch what plants it was reaching for and then research the mineral or vitamin content of that plant whilst avoiding the obvious poisonous plants. Good old hawthorn is a remedy used by any self-respecting herbalist for heart conditions and I have seen horses negotiate the plant's thorns with dexterity. Pity the horse that knows it is ill but is corralled in and cannot reach its natural medicine. Someone told me recently that sunflower hearts are wonderful for horses with brittle hooves. Sunflower hearts are not exactly hedgerow plants around here, but there must be something in the hearts that is also found in a native wild plant. I wonder also how some horses manage to regulate their vitamin levels when they are fenced in with no shade at all during high summer [I am thinking about vitamin E and burning, for starters]. Go on safari and watch how all the animals head for shade from any tree or bush to escape the midday sun. I know that if I have too much sun, or if I am stressed, I rapidly use up minerals and vitamins and soon my body is sending me distress signals for urgent replacements. Could it be the same for a horse? Why would it not be? Different gut maybe, but stress is stress.

I have learnt to look at myself carefully when I have a problem with one of my dogs. If you have a problem horse, just remember you are the owner, the rider [your auras will connect or even merge as you ride], the one interacting with the animal. Any problem you have with the horse may have a connecting element to you. What colours are you wearing? Why did you choose that particular horse or pony? Look within and calm down. Try *being* with your animal rather than *doing* with your animal, you may find it is trying to communicate with you in the only language it has.

ℋATE

One belief is that the person you hate the most has characteristics you possess but deny. Occasionally, when feeling brave, I mull this one over. I will pull one hateful person out, usually a politician but not always, and debate whether, in different circumstances, I was capable of behaving as they have done. Sometimes I am overly keen on my deep deliberations.

A while back I decided I was going to have to do some serious work on this subject and as I was alone for a week I thought this would be a good time to tackle a big think. I pulled out some scotch and two of my most favourite hate figures. I thought about giving you the names but I decided it was thoroughly below the belt [second chakra]. Suffice to say one is a male international political figure and the other is a female pop singer. Both used to make my lip curl. I thought I knew exactly why they made me so angry but as I scraped away my feelings about them I found I was in for a shock. Underneath the outrage I found a layer of fear. Nothing unusual about that, the underlay of any carpet emotion is fear, but I found that it was not them personally that made me see red [first chakra], it was their role as a parent [first chakra] and my perception of that role as a daughter. It was all about humiliation. It was a total revelation to me and I was absolutely astounded.

Having delved into my hidden depths I am not saying I like these two people enough to invite them round for tea, but I do now recognise their important role in pushing my buttons. I am, of course, here to press someone's buttons too. This book may infuriate someone somewhere and, if so, I invite you to ponder on what it is about me or the book that triggers an emotion in you, where that emotion is situated and who helped put it there. Excavate. You may be amazed, as I was.

ℋERO

Let's just recap because it is high bloody time. The dictionary definition of hero is, 'a person admired for nobility, COURAGE and outstanding achievement'. To me that means footballer no, fireman, yes, rugby player [even Jonny Wilkinson - sorry Jonny] no, lifeboatman, yes. Anyone jumping up and down in a sports arena, 'Well done, well done', heroic no. Exceptions ….. well Ellen Whatsername who sailed round the world on her own was hugely brave, I have to say, and I have great respect for sportsmen and women who compete despite a physical disability.

I shall share a story with you. A couple of years ago there were appalling floods in New Zealand. These floods were not mentioned at all in our newspaper or on television - extraordinary. I was told a tale of a farmer and his farmhand who were swept away in a raging torrent of water. Hanging on for hours to a fallen tree the ageing farmer started to wilt and was developing hypothermia so the farmhand grabbed a passing dead sheep, as you do, managed somehow, despite the roaring water, to skin it and put the fleece over his freezing boss. They were both eventually spotted and saved. The hospital doctors said the fleece had definitely saved the farmer's life. When told this tale I was speechless with admiration because this was heroic to me, but a year later I was to be speechless again to hear of a Kiwi farmer, not in the first flush of youth [sorry Nick], who had a nasty accident with one of those mini-tractor, quad bike thingies. Having broken his arm and feeling mighty queer he walked a considerable distance home, washed and put on his best suit [because you do, when you go to town] before driving himself and his injuries to his local hospital [distances are great in New Zealand]. At the hospital there was a bit of a panic and he was airlifted to the capital's hospital because he had indeed sustained internal injuries as well as a broken arm and he spent several weeks as an in-patient. I call that fortitude with more than a dab of courage and I am quite sure if said farmer had been tripped up on any sort of playing pitch at all he would have considered it entirely unnecessary to roll around on the ground hugging his knees, wincing and generally poncing about.

There is a belief that courage is the greatest of all the virtues, for without it you cannot practice the other virtues consistently. It would certainly be true that you cannot be honest all the time without courage. It certainly takes courage to be honest where honesty is required but, in my book, it takes even more courage to recognise that, nine times out of ten, when you are being brutally honest you are also being brutal, possibly controlling and you are stemming from a point of fear. I ponder on this subject a lot because I think life requires courage on a daily basis, not just to take on the major life altering events or don a flak-jacket in war but the courage to do the right thing. The courage needed for the daily grind of being kind, which can be utterly exhausting. It takes courage to be kind to someone who you know is lonely but is also ragingly dull. It takes courage to be understanding to the red-faced driver who is screaming obscenities at you for your minor act of carelessness - screaming at you because he is terrified to scream at the person he needs to scream at, whereas you are a soft and easy target. It takes courage to stop and listen to your badly behaved teenager who is as terrified of life as you are, but has yet to learn to say, 'I'm really frightened, please hold me', because you haven't learned to say it either. It takes courage to come home exhausted and still make the time to walk the dog because it has waited all day for the freedom walk that it so loves and lives for. It takes enormous courage to say to a friend, or a partner, or spouse, 'This relationship is not working for me, we have to sort it or leave it'. It takes monumental courage to admit that self-love is absent and start providing it in the form of self-care, instead of care for everyone else. It takes a very special courage to look your greatest fears in the face [and I am not talking spiders and bungee jumping] and make a promise to overcome them and to keep that promise. All these are third chakra territory - tough terrain, but such rewards.

What is your biggest fear? It is an interesting descending staircase of options for each individual but the bottom line is usually the fear of being completely alone. Sure scares the hell out of me and I do 'alone' well.

I love to see courage in others because it is such an inspiration to me but I get irritated when the words 'brave' and 'courageous' are over-used on television in regard to some sporting event or ridiculous entertainment programme. I have never, mercifully, been in a war situation but I have witnessed many unsung acts of heroism performed during the day and in the middle of the night by exhausted doctors, nurses, midwives and other hospital staff. They have missed meals, sleep and home-time, put their sometimes grieving or turbulent emotional lives on hold and given those extra hours, gone that extra mile, given that extra bit of themselves in kindness to a frightened and seriously ill patient. No large audience for them, no posturing in front of flashing cameras, no fat publicity cheque, no round of applause, just a hand on the shoulder from a colleague to say, 'You did well', and a fatigued soaked knowing that they behaved with skill, kindness, integrity and courage. I salute you all ..... 'Well Done, Well Done'.

HENS

Here is Hattie the chicken, bless her tiny little cottons. You cannot imagine how much fun hens are to have about, crapping in exactly the right spot on the path for an unsuspecting foot and pulling up your favourite snowdrop bulbs, the little popsies. You get eggs of course, when they feel like it. 'Come on girls', I coo encouragingly, 'this isn't a holiday camp, you know'. I am ignored but I forgive them because on sunny afternoons I can take my tea break in their little meadow and be endlessly amused by their antics. My cake is purloined in a trice by Maisie-Daisie and her best pal Hattie. Maisie came from a rescue centre and quickly flowered into a glossy black beauty. Hattie is a tiny black Araucana bantam who lays me blue eggs once in a blue moon. Gertie [white] flaps frantically around the pond chasing butterflies and, unwisely, bees. I bought the two M's so I could sing, 'Come into the garden, Maud', and so she does, bringing her sister Miriam with her. They are Marans, big muscular black and white girls and they lay lovely brown eggs.

Lulu Costalot, a small Rhode Island Red, gets preferential treatment for everything. 'Your carriage awaits, Modom', I tell her every morning as she is gently picked up and taken to the feeding frenzy where she gets first pick of interesting morsels. Lulu had an accident, three operations and now has a bent leg but despite this she manages to hop about, though chasing daddy-long-legs is now out of the question. Toffee-coloured Felicity was named after my adopted aunty who was heavily important in the WRAF. I knew the name choice was unwise shortly after she arrived because it was obvious she was going to be a chip off the old block. A few days of settling in and she felt comfortable enough to begin eyeing up the fenced in vegetable patch. 'No', I instructed her, simply but firmly. She raised an eyebrow at me [a regrettable move] and decided to bide her time, while I marked her card. A few hours later, when she thought I was busy in the kitchen, she started the runway assessment. The first couple of warm-up runs were not quite long enough for a clear take-off and ended in a squawk, a thump and flurry of feathers at the fence. The third run was more successful but I was on the ball by then and watching. She returned to her 'chocks away' position and then reversed back until she was perilously close to tipping backwards into the pond. She fixed her beady eyes on the tender pea shoots on the other side of the fence, tested her flaps, dipped several times and then she was ungainly off, with me flying out of the kitchen yelling, 'You are NOT cleared for take off, Felicity, abort, abort, abort!'. Up and over the fence she sailed. Hateful measures had to be taken. Wing feather clipping. Horrible. I know they grow back, but still.

You don't need a hen chap to get eggs. I did have a cockerel once, rescued because he was for the chop. He had one eye but exceptional feathers which I rather coveted. The problem was that time was of no moment to Nigel and he cock-a-doodle-dooed morning, noon and bloody night. The neighbours were not impressed and he had to go. I was enormously fortunate to find him a kind home and Nigel's new owners even did a swap. I got a whippet! What a brilliant deal!

I have been extremely lucky, unlike many friends, as I have only lost one chicken to a fox, but that was one too many. Poor Lavender, she was, if I might whisper it, not very bright, but bright enough to know that she could squeeze her minute frame through any narrow fence you care to mention. She was a bantam old game something and lavender in hue, hence the name, but tiny, absolutely tiny and her demise was my fault entirely because I should not have brought her home with me, it wasn't safe. She was fond of disappearing through the fence into the front garden and finding somewhere quiet to lay. I always found her but one day I turned the place upside down to no avail. Giving up at nightfall, I restarted the search the next day. Nothing. Nor the next day. Several weeks later I felt sure she had met a sticky end and my fears were confirmed when one of the dogs brought me an egg and went off to fetch another. I searched through undergrowth and finally found a well hidden nest. Poor Lavender had chosen the most dangerous place to nest up, right in the corner of the front garden, hidden behind a wooden post and smack up against the rustic fence. The rustic fence that had been so neat and tidy and was now missing a large chunk of is rusticity. A fox had ripped through it, leaving a tell-tale hair, and taken our Lav in her prime. Chickens don't shriek and run from a fox, sadly, most will sit stock-still, petrified. I felt I had let her down badly.

In 1998 Lulabelle came to live with me because she was all wrong. She should have been a Bantam Barred Wyandotte [thin black and white horizontal stripes] but her mother must have fancied a hooting male lothario because Lulabelle looked like a baby owl to me. She had a slightly crossed beak and talked incessantly, so we got on well. She followed me absolutely everywhere and would come into the garden and help me weed, chatting away with her rasping lilt and cooing with delight at small tasty worms. She was my angel and I was devastated when she died. I struggled to maintain my composure as we buried her. I planted a rose over her grave and shall, one day, erect a headstone to mark some very fine hens indeed, who lie alongside her.

My chickens don't mind the cold but hate the long drawn out wet winters and go off colour, with pale cockscombs, no egg laying and are generally huddled and thoroughly fed up. I am interested that people tell you never to feed chickens on meat. Our chickens will fight each other to scoff remnants of a dead mouse deposited by our cats and all summer they will eat any insects and worms they come across. I have read many stories of hens cornering and killing mice and then eating them. I thought about this and on a really viciously cold, wet day I offered my hens some raw beef mince and they nearly took my fingers off trying to get at it, so they occasionally get a morsel of mince during the coldest days and we now have much healthier and happier winter hens with pillar-box red cockscombs and all year round eggs, though admittedly just a trickle in midwinter. In my early days of hen keeping I lost about three to sneezy winter infections [this was well before avian bird flu was even heard of]. When a fourth succumbed and was positively rattling as she breathed, I took no chances and rammed 1000mgs of Vitamin C down her tiny throat and offered her some raw mince which she took enthusiastically if desperately slowly. She recovered so spectacularly, in just a few hours, that I am now alert to the merest whiff of a chicken sneeze and the offender gets Vitamin C, either as a whole tablet or ground into dust and rolled in raw mince or a small amount of raw beef mince and mashed up kiwi fruit [very high in Vitamin C]. I think animals have very different personalities, like humans, therefore their dietary requirements must differ, like ours. I heard recently about a farmer who had eradicated tuberculosis [TB] in his cattle and nearby badgers by improving both their diets [I think he added selenium to the cattle food and added to it food left out for the badgers]. At a lecture we attended last year a leading herbalist told us rates of TB soar following periods of severe malnutrition. TB is on the rise everywhere. Are we well fed but malnourished? I am dumbfounded, as we start another round of foot and mouth, that preventative dietary measures are not sought for cattle. Why is that?

One last memorial address to Hermione. I fancied having a white hen and my local rescue centre hadn't got one so I pootled off to a local chicken breeder who said she only had one and if I took her I had to take her three babies too. I took one look and squawked with delight at the appealing sight. Without a thought I took the lot and then panicked totally in the car going home at the prospect of three tiny babies growing into three strapping crowing cockerels. What then? My neighbours would not like it. Lengthen necks? Don't be ridiculous! Lady luck shone down on me, three girlies, what a blessing! Identical brownish twins Jenny Penny I and II and their sister

Jenny Penny Henny. My new white hen was a seething mass of maternal hormones, clucking here and clucking there and should anything threaten her babies she would swoop down, bundle them up and take off at speed with three pairs of little legs dangling from under her wings. An adorable sight! Though I say Hermione was white she never quite pulled 'white' off, always looking as if she had been busy baking in the kitchen and had wiped her pastry laden hands down her front. Her cockscomb looked like a squashed beret and her feathers refused to lie flat. She always came when I called her, rushing over for titbits, but never once did she take the morsel for herself, always summoning her daughters with frantic clucking even when they were fully grown. Those ungrateful girls always snaffled the goodies while Mum looked on, crestfallen at her genetically driven generosity. 'Aw', she would sigh as her fat brood scoffed the last tasty crumb. I got wise to this but, to ensure she was isolated sufficiently to actually get some treats, meant logistical planning of tiring dimensions. My partner would watch my antics with much sighing and shaking of his head. I would not be deterred. She lived with me for many happy years and spent her last few hours in a fluffy pink towel nest in the not too hot sun, by the pond. I buried her with tears in my eyes, next to Lulabelle. I still miss them both. Such characters. Such fun. I have been greatly blessed.

There is a little literary treasure called 'Counting My Hens' and I urge you to rush out and buy it forthwith [details at rear]. Written by the Duchess of Chatsworth - no that's not right, hang on .... Devonshire. Duchess of Devonshire who lives in Derbyshire, doesn't make sense does it? Anyway, Her Grace, or whatever, likes chickens, whippets and Derry boots - *she is my kind of girl*. My partner took me to Chatsworth for my birthday a few years back. We had such a happy day. It is a lovely house but, as usual, all I could think of, as we went from room to room, was of all the dusting. I gather Graces don't dust much but still how, pray, do you house train a puppy in a house *that* size? Impossible! She deserves a medal if she has managed it. I have such happy images of her hurtling at terrific speed along endless portrait-filled corridors, in flowing nightwear, fabric curlers and tilted tiara, clutching a squirming, leaking, puppy in her arms. I daresay this image is entirely inaccurate but it amuses me no end.

HEALTH

I am telling you straight, you will not value your health until you have lost it. Then, if you are lucky enough to reclaim it, you will value it above all things. It is slowly becoming accepted that illness has a physical AND an emotional presence. I have read endless books that tell you how to cure your illness with positive thinking and even more books that show you how to improve your physical body. I believe you need to understand both aspects and that is what I am hoping this book will do; bring the two elements together, but also point you towards greater writers with bigger brains than mine.

We are an increasingly unhealthy nation. We often pay more attention to our cars than our bodies. Please understand this one crucially important fact - your whole body is CONNECTED. An infected cut on your thumb [or toe], a swollen, mucky, newly pierced-ear that is taking too long to heal, or repeated throat or chest infections point to a LOWERED IMMUNE SYSTEM, which, in turn, points to poor diet and/or a poor digestive system. Antibiotics, so appallingly overused with devastating consequences, will probably return your thumb, toe, ear, throat or chest to normal - for now - but in the process it will remove some, or all, of your intestinal bowel flora, which you need [so take a course of probiotics after each dose of antibiotics and watch your tongue], and will do absolutely nothing to improve your diet, digestion or immune system long term. If you carry on as before you can expect another infection somewhere down the line - let's hope it is just a small one. We are *designed to heal* but our healing is dependent on a calm emotional state, a good diet and a healthy gut. If you break into a sweat when you eat, your body is talking but are you listening? It may be saying, 'I don't like this food', or it may be pleading, 'I can't cope [or digest] this food'. Pay attention and show your bodily vehicle some respect. We all need to wise up because the NHS is toast and soon we will all be paying for our medical care. It is up to you to look after yourself and it's best if you begin right away. Let's start with your mug.

Tomorrow, when you are out and about keep a sharp look out for faces that look healthy. Observe closely ….. what colours do you see? Or, what colours do you not see? Now, boys and girls [girls, no make-up please] take a long cool appraising look at your mug in a well lit mirror in natural daylight. Look closely at the overall colour wash. I cannot BELIEVE how many pale washed out faces I see these days in all ages but especially in the old and the very young. Take a good look at your grandparents and your small children and see if they are pale. They may or may not be anaemic but I wish they would go to their doctor and check. I remember telling two ashen-faced colleagues for months on end that they were anaemic. They completely ignored me [always unwise] but when they finally were tested they were both extremely low in iron. I don't think I said, 'I told you so' ...... well .. I might have done ... just a little bit. There are lots of ways of tackling a spot of anaemia, my favourite is extremely rare rump steak and common red wine, but spinach or watercress is good, dried apricots too, as long as you sleep alone or you can blame the dog. You could drink nettle tea as it is very high in iron. I don't like it and I won't drink it, so do as I say not do as I do. Taking iron tablets as a supplement is tricky and allegedly can deplete your stores of vitamin E - disastrous if you are a gorgeous floozy and worried about your frown lines and even worse if you are menopausal. Now .... if you are pale AND tired, see your doctor and get tested. If blood tests fill you with horror, see a nutritionist. Ask at your local health food shop, they should be able to recommend one and remember - nutritionists are about nutrition ...... not supplements. I am all for supplements, believe me, I could not cope without mine, but I have been extremely ill. If you are not extremely poorly, supplements should be the fill in until you get your overall nutrition and digestion sorted out.

Next, look for any other overall colour in your face. Take a very close look at your skin and see if there is a colour just below the top surface layer. Relax your face completely, starting with your forehead and scalp and then work downwards to your neck. Check the colour again. Now screw your face up tight. Is there one colour in one area and another colour in the tightened up bits? Is it slightly yellow, buff coloured or green? You could have a sluggish liver or sluggish digestion or both and both can be helped by eating a bitter salad before your main meal because it alerts your pancreas to chuck out some digestive enzymes. Try watercress and chicory drizzled with olive oil - delish - or you can take a course of herbal bitters [centaury] emphasis on 'a course of' [be careful about taking herbs for months and months, or even years on end, without really professional advice - see a herbalist]. Sluggish livers don't appreciate booze but don't panic - bowels, think bowels, in fact always think bowels. What are yours doing? I don't want the details, I had more than enough of poop during my nursing years. I will cover bowels and poop in a minute but I should point out that I will use the word gut and bowel interchangeably, which is naughty of me.

Your gut is your alimentary tract and encompasses everything from your mouth to out. Your bowels [small and large intestine] starts from the bottom end of your stomach to out. Your entire gut is important in food digestion and absorption because things start happening in the mouth with your saliva, that is why it is important to chew your food well. Do some research, check out your diet and don't follow that crazy trend of regularly taking Milk Thistle and then going on a boozey bender. Ridiculous idea. Grow up. You think your liver isn't intelligent and rolling its eyes at that trick? Nothing wrong with a boozy bender now and then, when you are young and perky and so is your liver, but multiple boozey benders mean you are not dealing with the emotion that requires 'out of it' and that goes for multiple druggy benders too. You are saying you are unhappy enough not to want to be here for a while - not sensible - hope your angels have ear plugs and have mislaid their spanners.

Ok, back to your skin …. does it have an overall dark burgundy red or blue hue? If so please get your blood pressure checked on a regular basis. Better still, buy a blood pressure machine yourself [thirty to fifty quid] and ask your doctor what range your blood pressure should be. Write the readings down carefully and put them in a safe place, then check it weekly. WEEKLY. Blood pressure can change from minute to minute, from sitting to running upstairs but a reading taken when you are at rest is the one you are after. I think we should all grow up and be responsible adults about our health and everyone over fifty should have their own machine and check their own blood pressure regularly. If your blood pressure goes up a bit and stays up a bit there are dozens of things you can do to get it down [see a qualified and experienced nutritionist] before you need to start taking drugs BUT there is a difference between 'up a bit' and 'up a lot' and the difference could be a danger zone. *Don't mess with high blood pressure.* If you need the drugs to get your blood pressure down, take them, but look closely at underlying causes like your diet, fluid intake, salt intake, fat intake, booze intake, smoke intake, emotional intake. If your blood pressure is up because you are living with a nag, of either gender, or you are furious with yourself about something but will not admit it, pills will not cure the situation. See a shrink or get a divorce.

If your face is pale and with a slight blueish tinge, see a doctor. If it is pale grey see a doctor and/or cheer up, get out of black or grey clothes and fill your house with colour. See 'Bach' and I am not talking music, but that helps too. THINK PINK. Your face should have a pale pinky glow and your lips should be pink and well hydrated. If you are dark skinned your skin should be clear and soft and the inside of your mouth and eyelids pink and healthy looking. If you have a faint network of just visible veins anywhere on your face keep an eye on your blood pressure and try very, very gentle massage. Your underlying facial muscles may be tight and putting stress on the capillaries. Press your fingertips gently down to the bone of your skull all over your face - it should not hurt anywhere. Hurting indicates congestion. Don't rub your cheeks with vigour, just gently persuade your muscles to relax. Do this regularly. You can get broken capillaries on your cheeks from lots of healthy outdoor living, particularly if you live in an area where the wind doth blow, but cheeks represent the lungs and lungs also represent fear. Did you have a fearful time as a child? Do you have rational fears? Irrational fears? Are you a silent worrier who is shallow breathing? Is your tummy going up and down properly as you breathe?

Spots. I do not hold with the theory that teenagers get spots, I have known many who do not. What teenagers have in common is snacking on rubbish or eating vast amounts of carbohydrates decorated with anything that resembles colourful glue. Diet, bowels, diet and that applies to adults too. Nowadays teenagers have far too much money to spend and inevitably they will buy things to eat and drink that are unwholesome. Alcohol uses up vitamin A [amongst other things] and can result in spots, spots, spots. Drugs will also use up minerals and vitamins that will need to be replaced at the speed they are being vacuumed up or you can expect trouble and anti-social behaviour. 'An apple a day keeps the doctor away' ..... probably not, because it will be covered in pesticide, or some such, but it is full of potassium, calcium and magnesium. Thoroughly wholesome but buy organic if you can. For those of you who have never had the happy opportunity to pick an unsprayed apple straight from a tree, the apple skin is completely dry, not covered in that ghastly grease like the ones in the shops. Your diet may be reasonable but you may have problems digesting it, or you may be short of hydrochloric acid [I am assuming - always dangerous - that you read 'bicarbonate'] or digestive enzymes. Take note of persistent spots because your large or small intestine is trying to tell you something and certainly the body is throwing off unwanted material. You may not be able to deal well with wheat. An iridologist can tell you if wheat or dairy is not your bowel's idea of heaven on a spoon. What does your poop look like? Does it smell awful? Think undigested food. Poop is heavily relevant to good skin, so get heavily checking the contents of your loo. Boils and carbuncles not attached to large art galleries are the body shouting, 'Help!'. Think bowels, for starters, then think diet, then emotions. Spots can sometimes indicate a hormonal imbalance, especially for girls if the spots are around the lower jaw. See a doctor first, check your diet and then look at the colours and jewellery [coming up later] you wear for clues to emotions.

Your hair is a big indicator of your health. Dry hair may indicate a lack of moisture or oil. You don't see much dandruff these days suggesting people are getting more vitamin A but we are seeing much more baldness. We have just come back from Southern India where teeth were perfect and baldness rare, but then food goes from field to table in a matter of hours [especially nuts]. If you are losing your hair do look at your levels of B vits because they sky rocket at times of stress. My darling chap had his hair fall out during a particularly stressful period in his thirties. Just make sure you eat well but also think about your neck [tense muscles, poor blood supply] and an all round improvement to your nutritional intake. And don't forget to tummy breathe, breathe, breathe.

Now look at your forehead. Excessively furrowed brows can mean a male or female who is excessively yang, as in yin and yang [yin/female, yang/male]. Nothing wrong with that of course just don't argue with them, unless you are feeling brave. A faint flush of burgundy across the forehead should be taken seriously, check your blood pressure and cast your mind over your family history. The forehead is associated with the circulation and nervous system in Oriental face reading. Do you have furrows above your nose and between your eyebrows? Think yangy liver. Check your wardrobe for tell tale 'I am cross' colours. There is nothing wrong with being cross, in my experience you have good reason to be, just find the culprit and yell at them, not everyone else. Make sure your neck is nice and supple too as muscular tension or bony problems in this area can result in problems all over body but especially the head area, the shoulders, arms, wrists, hands and fingers. Are you bending over paperwork or computers all day and straining upper back and neck muscles? Can you slide your hands under your lower back when you lie down? If you can, re-read 'Alexander Technique' because if one part of your spine is out it knocks the rest out of kilter, including your neck. I have a hell of a time with my concrete neck but my theory is my neck is connected to my gall bladder [the gall bladder meridian runs across the back of the shoulder and up the neck] and when I get cross [something gets my gall] my neck plays up. When this happens I always blame the politicians for winding me up and never my ultra creamy and utterly delicious rice pudding.

Now look at your eyes - don't look at mine. Two years before I suddenly got Rheumatoid Arthritis I developed a reddened patch in the white of my left eye. My poor body was silently yelling at me every morning as I cleaned my teeth in front of the mirror but I was not fluent in its language. I understood it signified something and had it fully investigated by an eye surgeon, but he could find no answer for it. I now know that the first red patch signified my small intestine was bellowing for help and later my spleen and liver sent red distress signals. Continuously reddened eyes could say scotch but it could say that more specific vitamins are required [do some research], it might point to a serious digestive problem that needs proper investigation [see an experienced nutritionist or go to a nutritional teaching establishment for comprehensive blood and urine testing - not cheap but well worth it], or it might point to your neck which might not be as swively as it used to be [think blood supply to the eye]. Clear bright eyes are what you are aiming for. Look at the skin around the eyes, what colours do you see? The area just below the eye represents the kidneys, therefore bags under the eyes point to your body probably having kidney and urinary output problems. Is your diet too acid? Are you eating too much salt? Do you need more potassium rich food? What is your blood pressure? Dark brown patches under the eyes have been a bit of a puzzle to me and I have endlessly discussed this with my partner. He will not be swayed and says this area categorically represents kidneys - yet the colour brown represents intestines. In Oriental medicine the colours for kidney or urinary problems [usually long standing] are blue or blue-black [sometimes presenting as pale grey initially], but in iridology we would be alerted to the colour yellow. I have examined eyes that had no worrying sign of gut or kidney problems yet the client presented with dark brown skin under the eyes. I am now inclined to read this as an emotional stagnation, which relates to the kidneys but also second and third chakra. Your small kidneys do continuous work of staggering proportions making pee, removing waste and balancing your body so if your have dark patches under your eyes you might want to look at your work ethic, your removal of waste emotion and your level of emotional balance. We talk about being 'pissed off', why would that be? We could say 'mucoused off' or 'ear waxed off', but we don't. Look at the skin in the corner of your eye by the bridge of the nose. Purpley-blue or purpley-brown denotes deep down tiredness [are you snoring?] and you are probably exhausting your adrenal glands [which sit on top of your kidneys]. Exhausted adrenals are seriously bad news and you can expect health problems later in life, or worse, any minute now. Please do something about it immediately, don't wait until you have a serious problem and cannot pay the mortgage. See a therapist, a nutritionist, get more relaxed and get much, much more sleep. Take a few days off and do nothing but sleep, day and night until that colour has gone from purpley-brown to pink. I have a hell of a job keeping on top of my purpley-brown patch and have to force myself get a kip during the day because I feel guilty kipping when my partner is working. He thinks I am completely ridiculous and I am inclined to agree but I am good at guilt, it is one of my few specialities. Hot milk, or even cold milk [calcium = sleepy bye byes], before bed has been an age-old sleep remedy, or chamomile [you cannot not like it because it hardly tastes of anything]. Hot milk and cocoa gives you calcium and magnesium [cocoa is very high in magnesium]. I am amazed how many children I see with a faint blue under and around their eyes and I wonder how they will manage, health wise, as adults. Don't the parents see it? The children are chronically tired. What kind of a start in life is that? Irritable, I should think.

Your eyes are so precious - find out what they need. The elderly can develop all sorts of distressing eye and sight problems. I very much hope they have read 'digestion' and have taken note. Don't waste a moment if you are having problems with your eyesight, see a doctor immediately but then research, research, research. Read 'Adelle', if you haven't already. If your eyes [and hearing] are going downhill it almost certainly will have something to do with your digestion or diet, unless you do not want to look at the future or you are living with a wittery old nag. As I have already said, your digestive tract gets tired as you get older and therefore will not work as efficiently at absorbing nutrients. Make a list of all your bodily niggling complaints, no matter how small and then list your parents' health problems. See if the niggles build up to a picture of a large digestive upset or a need for a specific mineral or vitamin. You may be eating well but your body is unable to access the nutrients [this was what happened to me], in which case you will need a specific dietary and supplement repair plan. We are all individuals with differing needs and different histories. My eyesight for reading deteriorates rapidly [within hours] if I do not take my daily Vitamin B Complex. Once, being in a rush to catch a train, I forgot my morning supplement and later I was struggling to read even the large [but blurred] signs on the London underground. I took a double dose of B Complex as soon as I got home and my eyesight returned to normal. Recently I have been on a probiotic spree and since starting the course I have noticed my specs, which I use as a hair band, tend to stay on my head more than on my nose because my sight has improved. Perhaps I am now able to make my own B's in my gut. I must say the probiotic course is rather expensive but cheaper than prescription glasses and anyway it should be 'a course of ' rather than a daily fixture. Now we are making our own yoghurt [that's the royal 'we' … he makes, I eat] which is full of helpful bacteria for my tummy and for increasing B vitamins. If my neck stiffens my requirement for vitamin A quadruples [and I get a build up of mucous deposits in the corner of my eye]. I don't know exactly why this is, though I think it has something to do with my liver and gut or possibly my pissed off bladder [this is under investigation]. I have multiple contraction furrows [see 'iridology] in my eyes and I therefore use up B vitamins quickly. My mother had cataracts so I am keeping a beady eye on my eyes. Nothing so far but one of my dogs [the thieving monkey one - and that is probably very relevant] started developing faint opacities in both eyes a couple of years ago which Brewer's Yeast seems to be keeping at bay. I am not saying it works on my dog - I am saying it seems to work. When I forget to give her the Brewer's she starts thieving and eating unmentionables and this is, I believe, how some dogs tell us their diet is insufficient. For years I was teased about wearing dark glasses during the winter, no matter that I pleaded winter sun blinded me, particularly as I drove a car. I was massively Vitamin A deficient [be careful with Vitamin A, it is stored in the liver unlike some other vitamins and therefore you can overdose] and, now I have rectified this with regular supplementation, I rarely need dark glasses except in very high summer. I also get far fewer colds. However, low B2 can also make your eyes light-sensitive, so if you are sitting irritably in dim light because it is all you can take, think diet, digestion, diet. Gritty, sore, watering eyes and cracks in the corner of the mouth can also point to low B2 [don't take B's in isolation, take a combined complex or better still, eat better].

Now check your nose. Look out for broken blood vessels, single or multiple, on the nose but especially behind the nostril and note which side it is. For some strange reason, when I am gardening or reading I unconsciously tighten my face by somehow pulling my nose down a bit. It is very odd and I don't know why I do it, but when I realise I am doing it I look in the mirror and the small vessels on my nostrils are showing slightly. If I completely relax my nose and then massage the skin the veins disappear. In Chinese medicine the nose represents the heart, but don't panic, rush out to find the nearest defribrillator and glue yourself to it - just be aware that you need to be aware. If you are middle-aged or over get your blood pressure checked frequently [every six months is a joke] and don't be stupid about your diet. It is amazing how many middle-aged and elderly people think a daily intake of pastry or cheese, or both, is healthy and sugar is even better. If you are constantly reaching for sweeties try taking a course of chromium supplements and see if that stops your sugar craving. If you have a history of diabetes in the family and you keep sweeties here, there and even in the car, definitely get some chromium. My partner talked to a client recently who could not make the connection between the well known variety of chocolate type sweets he ate daily [a whole bag of them] and his family history of diabetes. Extraordinary. He looked quite shocked when my partner filled him in on the facts because he suddenly realised acquiring diabetes would have severely jeopardised his job. If your handkerchief is full of unpleasantness when you blow your hooter, it is a pointer to poor mucous membrane and a lack of vitamin A [especially if you are getting spotting or small specks of blood - emphasis on small]. The mucous membrane up your snoz is the first line of defence against naughty bacteria [and their friends], so that membrane needs to be in tip-top condition. Zinc is essential for smelling. For years I was confused when out on joint dog walks with friends who exclaimed, 'What a stink! Fox urine!'. I had no idea what they were talking about until I found out I was zinc deficient. Now I can smell the foxy pee from yards away. You need zinc to digest your food so if you are low on it you can't smell and you can't digest - what a muddle! If you lose your appetite I would recommend a course of zinc [have some oysters!]. My dog went off his food, but after a small bit of zinc he was ravenous again.

I keep talking about emotions and diet but they are both as crucial as each other. Try and look at emotional pain from the past and acknowledge just that, if you can, that it is 'past'. You cannot undo the past, only accept it and make the future full of fun and above all, full of kindness. What you put out is what you get back. If you are getting long in the tooth and on the final run in, make sure you have a happy time on the downhill slope. Whatever you think about the state of this country it is beautiful and offers much to do, learn, see and enjoy for not too much money. Do what it takes to get a happy heart. What colours are you wearing? Do you wear grey, beige, stripes or checks frequently? Why? Get some bright pink, get a new friend and be a good friend to them. Have some fun ... go on, you know you want to.

Now, back to your mug and your lips. Lipstick creeping up whistle-mark lines can be a sign of low B2, think diet and bowels and the same goes for the age related disappearing upper lip. Your lips should be a nice rich pink and plump, even when they are thin, if you get my drift. If you are dark-skinned check the inside of your lips for pinkness. Lips represent sexuality but also bowel and there is a theory that large fleshy lips mean a lax bowel with related problems, so you might be a sex god who suffers from wind. Could be a problem. Dry lips mean you are dehydrated. DRY LIPS MEAN YOU ARE DEHYDRATED. Hello? Concentrate please. Do you drink water? Are you covering your food with salt? You might be zinc deficient. If you are dehydrated you are probably tired. Are you wilting at two or three in the afternoon? Drink a pint of water and see how it can perk you up. Coffee and tea make you pee [well, I can't stop when I drink tea] and they do not count as fluid, not in my book anyway, unless it is something like peppermint or green tea. If you hate plain water I can assure you it does not take long to become addicted to it. Drink one litre every single day, between meals, for six weeks and you are hooked. Although some schools have finally cottoned on I still don't think dehydration is taken seriously enough, especially among the older generation. Quite apart from the fact that it makes you more wrinkly [complete waste of time slapping on expensive face creams if you won't drink water] I think it makes you age faster internally too. It strikes me that we are made up mostly of water and every cell is mostly water. If you only put a dribble of water in each day then your intelligent body will take it and use it for the most important organs [the ones that keep you alive] but anything in your body that you can do without has to go thirsty. This is only my opinion and I may be using some artistic licence but still, I reckon I am right.

Look at the area above your lips. If it is ever so slightly blue tinged you may have problems with your digestion and be gulping down wind with your chips. Babies often go lilac coloured between upper lip and nostril if they are full of wind. Slow down your eating or, if you are game, ask someone to throw you over their shoulder and pat your back until you burp. Make sure you pick someone physically strong with a sense of humour. Now, have a good look at the skin all around your mouth. From mouth to chin represents the lower abdomen and all organs therein [think reproductive organs, ladies] but also bowel and bladder. Sometimes the skin is quite pale pinky but the area surrounding the lips is yellowy [liver, possibly gall-bladder, check your emotions and then diet]. If there is a very slight dark blueish tinge make sure you are tummy breathing properly and get checked for any bowel spasm [pain or wind, poop alternating between watery and then formed, or explosive liquid poop are clues]. Jaws hold a lot of tension, affect how the mouth and lips look and can have a knock on effect on the whole spine. Look to see if you are tight on the right side or left for a clue to male or female emotional issues. If your mouth is tight, relax your jaw, check out your emotions and your wardrobe. You could see a cranio-sacral therapist or try somato-emotional release. Tight jaws often go with tight necks and I think there is a connection with a troubled gut and gall-bladder. I have already mentioned it, but your gall-bladder meridian runs behind your shoulder, up your neck towards your ear - give it a prod and a probe for 'ouch' factor. Then work backwards to who first got on your gall and made you tense your jaw or clench your teeth [how are your teeth by the way?]. Do the same for the bladder meridian [runs up the back of the neck over the crown to the forehead] and see who pissed you off and don't dismiss a low grade bladder infection if the back of your neck is giving you gip and you feel hot and bothered. See your doctor. If anything feels tight try wearing turquoise, but maybe not across your jaw .... still, you might start a whole new trend.

Tongues. I have done tongues separately. Why? Because I couldn't think of much to say under T.

Toothypegs. Get your teeth checked as often as you can. You only have one set so look after them. Rotten teeth may mean bacterial infection and that means you are swallowing the bacteria continually. It does your body no favours and can affect the heart. Bleeding gums can be SERIOUS - see a doctor - but it can mean you are low in vitamin C. Check your toothbrush after you have cleaned your teeth for pinkness and check that your gums are not receding. Receding gums need vitamin C and a close look at diet and digestion. I take 1000mgs of vitamin C every two to three days and I would definitely take it every day if I lived in a big polluted city or if my job meant I was inhaling chemicals of some description [sometimes I am overwhelmed by the smell emanating from new magazines or catalogues and some shops have me reeling]. If you are seventy, eighty or more and poorly you may need more than 1000mgs of vitamin C daily to help you get better, a lot more - take a good multi-vitamin with it. If you smoke you use up a large amount of Vitamin C daily so put it back in. Emotionally, teeth and gum problems can represent your 'bite on life'. Each tooth is linked with areas or organs in the body, so for instance the front teeth, top and bottom, are linked to the suprarenal [adrenal] gland, bladder area, kidneys, parts of the lower spine, hips, back of the knee, eye and frontal sinus. Remember, female issues will be on the left side and male issues on the right and that the whole body is connected; you cannot look at things in isolation..

I am greatly bothered by this current craze for ironmongery in faces. You may have a ring or stud in an acupuncture point and God knows what you are doing to your body long term. Same goes for multiple earrings. There are multiple acupuncture points on the ears [ears represent kidneys and you don't want to mess with them]. I was walking behind a young woman once and I just intuitively knew there was something seriously wrong in her head area but I could not pinpoint it. Later we got talking and she told me she was flying home soon to see doctors because she was being treated for a major eye problem and her eyesight was deteriorating very seriously and rapidly but the doctors were not sure what had caused the problem in the first place. I told her I had a strong gut feeling [third chakra] it was something to do with the nose ring she was wearing, which astounded her because she had had the ring put in while travelling in Asia [where they should have plenty of experience] but when it went in there had been quite a problem with intense nerve type pain and infection. I couldn't follow this up and I am not saying I was right - I am just asking that you be aware you may be causing yourself a problem by puncturing your face. If you want to make holes in your mug just ask advice from an acupuncturist first. Also be aware that repetitive ear infections can point to low vitamin A levels [and a lowered immune system] and tinnitus can be indicative of low B vits and/or manganese but you might need your neck muscles seen to as well.

One large spot or a discolouration somewhere on the face [or anywhere on the body] may be on an acupuncture point [or meridian line - between two acupuncture points] and may be highlighting an internal problem. If you often get a single spot or small rash or maybe even a bump or tiny cyst on the same spot do some research. Get a book that shows acupuncture points and meridian lines and prod your body to see if you have any sore points [you shouldn't have any]. If necessary, see a shiatsu practitioner or acupuncturist. I really do believe that this is how the body talks to us, by highlighting problems areas with spots, marks or rashes - and the same goes for your pets.

Look at the lower part of your neck [front] and if you think it looks a bit lumpy and you are tired/falling asleep in the armchair, your eyes look a bit poppy, you are putting on weight or emotionally overwrought, get your thyroid function checked. ALWAYS see a doctor about this but know that there are natural remedies you can take. My thyroid wobbles a bit at times and when it does I have Miso soup with dried seaweed for a few days, or take a liquid seaweed remedy and wear a kingfisher blue scarf. *Check out the connection between vitamin E and the thyroid or the uptake of iodine.*

Now if you are feeling brave you can strip off and check yourself out in a long mirror. I have a scotch before I do this because I always think I look slimmer and healthier when some fire water has bolstered my ego. I look at my moles and lumps and bumps and things and panic, because you can take the nurse out of the hospital but you cannot take the paranoia out of the nurse. Nurses do not get headaches, they get subarachnoid haemorrhages - big ones. Strip off on a regular basis and watch out for moles, rashes, spots and veins. Check your back regularly, especially if you live alone. I am amazed how often women are advised to 'check your breasts' but not 'check your back'. Precancerous or even cancerous moles can pop up anywhere and a back gives plenty of room and scope. I would look out for anything out of the ordinary, even downy hair growth because that is how the body highlights weak areas. I have noticed over many years that my animals grow tiny cysts over acupuncture points indicating an underlying problem. One of my dogs is developing a fatty cyst on her underbelly and I am wondering if this is her body depositing excess fat where it is safe. I have no idea if this is correct but I think bodies are much more clever than their tenants - animals and humans alike.

Your body should not hurt. Listen to pain. Calcium is an old remedy for pain relief. If you are getting a lot of bony or jointy pain you may have a calcium imbalance - it might be going in but not properly accessed; used up to correct an acid diet; magnesium might be low. Now, get in the bath and with soapy fingers massage your whole body. Do each hand and then work up your arms. The small and large intestine meridians run down both arms [small intestine down back of arm to little finger - large intestine down front of arm to thumb - more information on fingers in 'jewellery']. Therefore arm pain might not be *just* arm pain but may also point to your gut. Watch for body language; a man casually scratching/rubbing his left [female] upper arm [large intestine meridian] with his right [male] hand would alert me to his feeling either protective or threatened over second chakra issues [scratching or itching *small* intestine meridian - third chakra issues]. Tennis elbow, check your gut/emotions, left or right? We elbow people out of the way. Your tummy should be soft and pain free; gently prod and check. Digestion should be *silent* to your ears, gurgling and wind everyday is not normal. Pay attention, especially if the wind requires a hurricane to clear the air and make it breathable again. If this is a regular occurance your gut is in deep distress, do something about it. Look at your diet and how you eat it. If you have a poorly bowel try to imagine what sort of diet you would want if you were really sick. That may be just the diet your bowel is asking for to get better [but skip the jelly and ice cream bit, I know this is a hospital favourite and I had to give it to patients frequently but it always seemed like sheer lunacy to offer a sick body a double whammy of sugar]. There is a saying that 'what you crave is what is doing you harm'. If you stop ingesting your craving and then get headaches or feel generally unwell, then your craving is almost certainly not doing you any favours. Try skipping all wheat products for a few days then have some bread. How does it make you feel? Do the same for dairy products.

Are you still soaped up in the bath? If so, move down and check your legs. Inflamed bite marks from naughty buzzy bitey things point to low B vits and probably magnesium too. Knees are connected to your gut so an unhappy tummy equals unhappy knees. Kidney and bladder meridians run round here [watch for pissed off scratching/rubbing body language]. Knees are full of emotions and sometimes won't, like mine, bend. To what or to whom do you not wish to bend your knee? Do you have any rashes? Rashes are the skin talking when you won't. Are you inclined to be rash about anything? Do you have a lot of broken veins on your upper or lower legs? Massage beneath them, but gently, gently. The underlying area should feel soft. Are you feeling tight muscles or just an overall tightness? It shouldn't be. Check that your tummy is pain free and/or get your back checked by a good body working therapist. You may need to improve your diet and/or take some supplements and/or chill out [I hate that expression]. I have two small patches of thread veins that come up when I need magnesium; a bit of that, a massage and they disappear again. I have fearful problems with my gut and absorption. It probably has something to do with me hating the expression 'chill out' and it has absolutely everything to do with emotions I cannot, as yet, get to the bottom of. I plan to scrub my basement emotions clean if it is the last thing I do, and it probably will be .. on bended knee. I check my eyes [iris] frequently to monitor my healing process [lots of improvement so that is a great encouragement] and I am hoping once I have healed my gut I will no longer need to take supplements because I will be able to absorb what I need from my food. There is no end to my wishful thinking.

Have a look at your nails. They should be pink. White or dipping spoon-shaped nails can indicate iron deficiency. Highly arched and rounded nails can point to the lungs but also vitamin B12. White spots indicate a zinc imbalance [I am fascinated by which fingernail - see jewellery - gets the white spot]. As I have said you need zinc in your stomach to properly digest food. Boys of all ages need zinc for their diddlies. Teenage boys, especially, need it when they are taking exams because, if it comes to an internal fight for zinc, I reckon balls win over brains, but balls don't tend to pass Maths GCSE. Chuck a boiled whelk [high in zinc] at your teenage grunting chap, he will doubtless catch it if not eat it. Nails need protein to grow and it is amazing how little protein people eat in a day. Hours and hours go by before you deign to shove some protein in your gob, meanwhile your poor body is struggling to cope. Low protein may show as white bands across the nails. Low protein, calcium and vitamin A can make nails brittle, but brittle nails can also denote low hydrochloric acid and/or an inability to process protein - how's your poop, are you tired? Soft nails *need* investigation. Re-read 'bicarbonate'. Low B vitamins show up as ridges on nails.

Check your heels. Dryness and/or cracked heels shows pelvic area problems. This can be gut or bone but it is usually problems relating to bowels. Do something about it and I don't mean slap some cream on. See a reflexologist and/or nutritionist to sort out the underlying problem. The cracks will go but it will take time and can take years if you are well past twenty-one. Stick at it and make your third chakra proud. Look at your shoes, especially the heels, see how you wear them down. Do they look like a listing ship? See an Alexander Technique teacher who will show you how to stand up, stand tall, stand proud and look damn good. Don't leave fungal foot [or nail] problems, see a nutritionist, get some probiotics for your gut and try wearing pure cotton or pure silk socks [not as expensive as they sound and you can buy them from a mail order company - some little tootsies need lots of fresh air!]. I have seen a very long term but low grade fungal foot problem make a spectacular recovery [sheets of skin coming off and lovely pink perfect skin underneath] after a course of blood and bowel cleansing herbs (details at rear of book).

See an osteopath or chiropractor if you have small aches and pains before they become big aches and pains. You may need fascial [that's fascial - not facial] connective tissue release. This is very subtle and you may need to track a practitioner down. There is an excellent one in East Anglia who also practises in London [see back of book]. Remember all *aches* and *pains* have an emotional starting point. Do you ache for something? Are you pained about something? Different emotions, different chakras. Also, the bowel affects your lower back, oh yes it does. Mucky bowel = slacky back. Slacky tummy too and I should know.

Let's head to the smallest room. Widdle! No, on second thoughts, let's do not do widdle. I'll do it later under 'U', give you something to look forward to. Poop! Vegetarians normally have their bowels open more than meat eaters. Everyone, whatever your diet, should poop once a day at the very least. You spotted the 'should' didn't you? I have every excuse to 'should on you' on this one. You do not want poop hanging about. Get rid of it, quick smart and it should be sausage shaped with a pointy end. Ideally it will look a little fluffy, be mid to dark brown and float a little bit, not sink like a stone, be mucousy or leave skid marks - these need dietary attention. Light coloured stools can be indicative of gall-bladder problems; research, research, because it is not *just* about fatty diets or non-fatty diets. Gall-bladders store bile [and anger] and bile helps keep you regular, so if you have had your gall-bladder removed you need to take care with your food and elimination. Diarrhoea obviously indicates bowel problems, often connected to nerves and fear. Alternate diarrhoea and normal bowel movements can mean bowel spasm and a hold-up which will not do your bowel any favours long term. A truly mucky bowel can make you very ill indeed [and tired] and will have a knock on effect on all your other closely packed together bits and bobs, including your reproductive organs [ladies please note, if you have problems with infertility and pregnancy look at your diet and bowel habits very, very seriously]. We hold a huge amount of emotion in our lower abdomens because this is where we store our second chakra and all its hideously ghastly and painful lessons. I once talked to a really lovely lady with mind blowing constipation. I could not believe what she was telling me but I did believe her constant connected references to 'shit' and 'husband' [second chakra for both]. Go figure, as they say, but figure back to Daddy because that is where it will have started, remembering that less than perfect Daddys probably also have had less than perfect Daddys and all through the generations they are all trying to do the best they can with the limited knowledge they have of themselves at the time. Also remember [as Wayne Dyer so hilariously points out] that while you are having therapy to get over whomsoever, someone somewhere may be having therapy to get over you.

Just raise your level of awareness and learn to listen and observe your 'body language'. Don't ignore small niggling problems because they may be a pointer to something deeper and eventually more worrying. Try to be 'pro-active' about your health rather than 'reactive' when things may have got out of hand. Pro-active people have easier lives because they are pro-active about everything, not just their health. This is called being wise.

ℋEALING

I believe in miracles. I think that when a miracle occurs something profound takes place internally. The trigger may be external but the transition is internal. A miracle healing can take place in seconds but you have to be ready for that transition, for it will change your future life, sometimes completely. Deep down you will know this. Miraculous healing brings you back towards your internal spiritual self, closer to the divine spark within. It brings you to a place and a vibration where others are not ready to be, causing relationships to change and some to falter. I don't know anything about physics but we all know that our cells vibrate, in fact our whole bodies vibrate. I think, as we spiritually progress, our vibrational rate speeds up and a lightness occurs. Some years back I was walking in the countryside when I had an extraordinary sensation of being weightless. At the time I knew this experience was meant to teach me something. It only lasted for a few minutes but I felt in a state of grace for some days afterwards. It did not last because I was, and still am, a naughty little monkey trying to be good but rarely succeeding. What the experience did do was to get me thinking about vibrational rates. I wondered about that saintly nun that floated about by the ceiling [can't remember her name]. Was she periodically in a weightless state? I wondered about Jesus when he walked on water; was it because he was in a permanent grace-filled weightless state? Shirley Maclaine's books, as I recall, have tales of Buddhist monks who levitate weightlessly. Is the ego heavy? Energetically heavy? Is that what keeps us grounded?

Miracles aside there are two crucial elements to healing a serious illness. The first is you have to absolutely want to heal. I know this sounds crazy but it is the most important question to ask. It probably is not a question you can ask yourself, better to have someone else ask you, someone you love and totally trust. They can listen and observe your body language. The first question needs to be, 'Do you want to heal?'. The next question is, 'Are you afraid of being completely well?'. If you asked me the first question my answer is an unequivocal, 'Yes'. If you asked me the second question, I would hesitate [always, always, always pay attention to hesitation] before replying, 'Yes' [but my hesitation is definitely shortening]. Why do I fear complete wellness? Because I fear it would change me and therefore change my life and my relationships. By becoming completely well I would change my vibrational rate and that might put pressure on my relationship with my most beloved partner, unless he can change his vibrational rate at the same time. Do you think I am completely away with the fairies? I am not, I can assure you. Changing one's vibrational rate does not mean donning long white robes, John the Baptist sandals and shaving off hair. It means either a big or a little widening of sixth chakra perspective, opening of fourth heart chakra and repairing holes in whatever chakras are pock-marked. These things don't necessarily change your personality but they empower you, they change the way you look at things, they still and calm you and by doing so they make you less reactive. Sometimes they can make you need to spend time alone.

You may be thinking, 'Well, I recovered from a major illness and it has not affected my life that much'. It might not have affected your life that much but every illness brings a greater degree of awareness and compassion for others - even if it is a head cold; even if it is only one thought of, 'This is awful, poor so and so with their ghastly illness'. The greater the illness the more time there is for introspection, but also the chance to see/experience humanity at its frailest and to be treated/nursed with or without compassion from professionals and loved ones alike. I have been introspecting since childhood and my working life has given me a chance to be 'up close and personal' to frail humans. I knew from the start that my own illness was something much more profound than a body breakdown. I was being reconfigured internally. Now, my grounded first and partially repaired second and third chakras battle with my upper chakras on a daily basis. I have a foot in both camps and I can see both sides of the coin but I am just not ready to make the switch over. It frightens the living daylights out of me purely because I will be stepping into the unknown. Strange that, because I love to explore and will happily globe trot on my own. Have rucksack - will travel, but internal journeys are much, much more scary. Chakra hopping can really rock the boat. The trek from head [thought] to heart [love] is through very difficult terrain.

For a healing to take place you need 'a place of safety'. My partner brought with him *a place of safety* for me to slowly heal and I did likewise for him. This place of safety has absolutely nothing to do with anything material, it is a place or person where you can explore personal honesty down to its bare and uncomfortable bones and then start the journey of reclaiming your personal authentic power. Your environment and the people around you need to offer you unconditional acceptance so you can voice your fears and have them *validated.* To offer agenda-free unconditional acceptance is tremendously challenging for some; these people you do not need around you while you are in a critical phase of healing. It is not remotely helpful to have people with agendas around you while you are in an emotionally or physically weak state. If you are very ill, you need to be able to voice your innermost fears. If you cannot do this because you know your fears will frighten loved ones, you will remain silent. This will not aid healing. If you voice your fear and get an, 'Oh, don't think like that', or worse, 'You can't think like that', response, the response is coming from a point of fear and you have not been heard. The response needs to be, '*Why* do you think like that?'. Now you have been heard. Now you can get to the bottom of your fear and hopefully clear the decks - unless of course the fear you have voiced frightens the one who hears it. Are you with me?

I want to make one more point about holding the hand of one who is dying. Ask them how they want their hand held because sometimes your hand over theirs is felt as restraining. It might be more comforting to put your hand under theirs, loving but supporting their departure.

HOUSES

I suppose you make a home but today we seem to build houses only. Our newish house greets you with a staircase. I can't understand it. When and if we can be bothered we will enlarge the front of the house so that people can be greeted at the door. At the moment I have to open the door and reverse several feet or stand behind the door and hope guests can hear me. A hallway, with cupboards for coats and clutter, is such a blessing for a home.

I look with eager anticipation at very modern new houses but I am virtually always disappointed. Inside they seem to look like empty art galleries or dentist's waiting rooms. Outside so often looks like an updated version of our local hospital, which is eye wateringly unattractive, but did at least have pretty little garden courtyards ... once. These seem to have shrunk, or disappeared, as the hospital expanded, which is a pity because sick people need to look at lovely things. I am not knocking all 'modern'. Sydney Opera House held me spellbound as did the Guggenheim Museum in New York with its gloriously seductive curves, but I rarely see anything built in the last seventy odd years in Britain, large or small, that makes me stop and gaze with awe and wonder. My dinosaur eye is equally delighted by the enchanting country cottage and the clapboard fisherman's house, the medieval church and the soaring cathedral, the stately pile and the elegant London town house, but somehow, I think it must have been just after the First World War, we seemed to lose our sense of beauty in buildings. Why was that? My partner assures me it was due to financial shortage after the war, but I don't agree, I think the eye for beauty was lost.

I recently re-visited that little gem of a London museum [just behind Selfridges], The Wallace Collection, because I had not been for twenty years or more. Before going in, I stood and admired the buildings in Manchester Square. Queen Anne period they looked to me [I am not, sadly, an expert], but certainly two hundred years old, or more. They are so classy and discreet in their simple elegant lines. As desirable today as when they were built and as versatile; from home to embassy, from shop to restaurant, office to brothel, these buildings could adapt with grace, and probably have. I pondered on some of the recent erections in London. Not too versatile, not suitable for a brothel anyway, I decided. Interesting that we still flock in our millions to beautiful buildings and cathedrals all over Britain and murmur appreciatively at picturesque cottages but still we persist in erecting ugly buildings that we would not choose to visit let alone decorate greeting cards or calendars.

1 Is for ILLUSION

It's an illusion. All of it. Life, love, relationships, the lot. Intellectually I understand this, I really do, but I will not fully embrace it because I fear what it will do to me and where it will take me. I fear being wholly alone. To fully 'know' that all is an illusion is to spiritually break free and I won't go there - not yet ……… not yet. I stand on the river bank staring at the barrier to a new and wonderful consciousness. Not so much crossing the Rubicon for me but crossing my bloody diaphragm and taking residence in my heart chakra. I won't go. I won't. I stand the wrong side of the river bank like a badly behaved toddler, twitching my knicker elastic and mewling, 'It isn't fair', or my other favourite … 'Why?'. It's pathetic and I must grow up because I am worried they will turn on the tap, turn the river into a raging torrent and push me in. Or will they?

*1*RIDOLOGY

Another ology, but what a subject! Such a staggering wealth of information we totally ignore as we stare lovingly into each others eyes. A veritable library of knowledge staring back at us each morning as we blearily brush our teeth before the start of the day.

Iridology is the study of the iris and named after Iris [the Greek goddess of the rainbow] because under magnification you can see all the colours of the rainbow in the iris. About twenty-three years ago I was amazed and enchanted while attending a private lecture on iridology but had not the wherewithal [money, basically] to study the subject. A few weeks ago at an international iridology symposium I approached a man I thought might have been that very same lecturer. It was. I told him he had been my inspiration and I had finally trained in the subject. We were both thrilled and he gave me a hug. Shucks …. I love happy endings!

Although iridology has been around for a very long time - those Egyptians again [they got into everything, didn't they?] and possibly the Mayans or the Incas, but the father of iridology is recognised as Ignatz Von Peczely [Hungarian, born 1826]. Peczely had a saying, 'Hic signum ubi ulcis' [hope

I spelt that right], meaning, 'here is the sign but where is the disease?', which every iridologist is taught to bear in mind when confronted with a sign, or signs, in an iris, which could spell trouble but clearly are doing no such thing in the presenting client. As I was taught, over and over, during my training, the point of iridology is to educate a client in their strengths as much as their potential weak points. What I love about iridology is that it not only gives clues to physical strengths and weaknesses but it covers emotional strengths and weaknesses too.

The first time an iridologist examined my eyes, her first to me question was, 'Was your father a heavy smoker?', to which I replied, 'How on earth did you know to ask me that?'. It was in my eyes and had I known, as a teenager, about the loosening of fibres over the lung section of both my irides [iris in plural] I would have thought much more seriously about not smoking myself. I did not know and smoked for far too long. Had I also known about my other constitutional strengths and weaknesses, my nutritional requirements and potential problems with my gut, my life might have taken a very different course .... but then there might have been no book for me to write.

I am drawn to art and I have lost track of the amount of times I have visited the National Portrait Gallery in London. Since training as an iridologist, staring at old portraits takes on even more depth and significance. A few years back we visited New York and scuttled to the Metropolitan Museum of Art as fast as our legs could get us there. I was fascinated at the colour of irides in the portraits, especially in the 20th century collection. I scanned portrait after portrait for mixed biliary [hazel] constitutions and only spotted one. The gallery was full of clear blue and a few brown irides. I saw quite a few clear pale green but I did not see the darkish brown and green so common today. I commented on this to my partner, who argued artistic licence, but I was not convinced. Too many different artists for that much licence. It seems to me to be irrefutable proof that our eyes are changing and our guts are struggling to adapt.

Within our library of books I have a bible of iridology with hundreds of colour studies of eyes by the late and great Bernard Jensen who made a lifetime study of the subject. The book retails at just under £250 - just in case you think iridology is not a serious subject. If you enjoy the following and want to learn more you cannot do better than Peter Jackson-Main's book 'Practical Iridology' [about £12 - details at the back of this book]. It is beautifully illustrated, so you can easily spot your iris type and full of helpful advice on how to live to optimum health with your iris constitution, but meanwhile here is an ultra-brief whistle stop layman's tour of the subject.

There are three main iris types and we talk about them as being 'constitutions'. The three are:- lymphatic [blue or grey], haematogenic [brown], and mixed biliary [hazel]. The following is a brief description of who's who and what's what.

Lymphatic's - pertaining to the lymphatic system, the recycling of body fluids. Lymphatic irides originate from the northern hemisphere where folk have to generate their own body heat because the sun is on semi-permanent holiday in the southern hemisphere. The fibres are usually very clearly visible [unlike a haematogenic brown iris]. This constitution reacts quickly and vigorously to incoming bugs, spiking sudden temperatures, getting sore throats, swollen glands and producing industrial quantities of mucous which they wheeze and sneeze about. Lymphatics are not so good at throwing off waste products [sweating in saunas is good for them - probably why saunas became so popular in blue eyed northern countries]. They have a tendency to acidity [which may affect the kidneys], rheumatics and arthritis. Look closely at children or blue eyed models in glossy magazines because they often have a dark ring around the very outer edge of their iris [next to the white bit]. This is called, unattractively, a 'scurf rim' and means the skin [and possibly the lymphatic system, depending on the depth of the ring] may have problems throwing off unwanted material efficiently [allowing for the fact that the skin is the largest eliminatory organ in the body]. Emotionally this ring can mean they may be throwing up a barrier to their outside world. I never see these dark iris rings in old portraits, but then our world is so very different now.

Haematogenic's ['haem' meaning blood] come from the south, where they have a decent climate and they don't need to dress in a duvet for six months of the year. Usually the fibres cannot be seen, instead the iris presents as a velvety carpet of pigmentation cleverly designed to filter out all that sunshine. This velvety carpet is harder to read for an iridologist but still reveals a great deal. There are, of course always exceptions to the rule but generally haematogenics are not as reactive as lymphatic types and are often slower to show illness. They have a tendency to blood disorders, particularly high blood pressure, stasis and circulatory problems [cold hands and feet in winter]. Their digestion, particularly of fats, needs careful attention. They often lean to diabetes especially if they leave their ancestral homeland abandoning their highly spiced food, to which they were ideally suited, come to sunny England and eat a lot of soggy pies, chips and chocolate to which their tummies are highly unsuited.

Mixed Biliary [biliary pertaining to liver] are green or hazel eyes. Fibres can usually be seen and brownish pigment may be heavier over the inner [towards the pupil] aspect of the iris which represents the digestive tract. Thick brown pigmentation radiating upwards in the iris above the top of the pupil can indicate someone who is a worrier, thinker and prone to a lot of dreaming. Health problems can often occur around the waist area - stomach, liver, gall-bladder, pancreas, spleen but also large and small bowel. Digestion and absorption may be a problem so therefore your choice of grub and how you eat it needs to be taken very seriously indeed or you may find a tendency to the dreaded wind, for starters. Eat sensibly and slowly, protect your liver and keep your bowels regular. Watch out for bicycle spokes of brown radiating out from the middle of the eye and note your liver is talking to you in its own and very special way.

Following the three constitutions there are five dispositions and five diatheses giving even more information about the type of person you are and your physiological function, but I will leave it to you to follow these up if you want to. Peter's book [already mentioned] explains them well.

The shape of your pupils tell many stories. Ideally they should be nicely rounded with no flattened bits because flattened bits indicate problems with your spine. A very enlarged pupil may mean you are mighty attracted to the dishpot sitting opposite you, or you have been smoking naughties, or a lion just got into the passenger seat of your safari vehicle, or you are stressed out of your eyeballs but appear as fresh and calm as a daisy. Dishpots, naughties and lions I cannot really advise you about, but if you are stressed out while appearing daisy fresh please see a nutritionist or herbalist and take affirmative calming down action before your adrenal glands go on strike. The first one third [from the pupil edge] of the iris is the digestive area. Then there is a wavy, roughly circular structure called the collarette, or autonomic nerve wreath. The structure and shape of this will tell an iridologist a great deal about you as a person and how you digest food. The final, outer part of the iris, is the ciliary body and encompasses all your other bits from nose to toe, skin to bones, liver to bladder, all of which sit somewhere on a clock face, i.e. your spleen is in the left eye at 4.15 and your liver/gall-bladder is in your right eye at 7.45. Your brain is at the top of your iris and your leg, from upper thigh to foot is at the time you think a walk to the pub for a pint would be an excellent idea [6pm] in both eyes.

All babies are born with blue eyes, pigmentation developing over the first few weeks of life. Fibres, when seen, look like silk [tightly packed together], linen [less so], hessian [looser] or net [very loose]. One is not better than another, they all have their merits as long as you understand what they mean and how to live with your particular iris fibre type. Silk fibred peopled can carry enormous workloads but usually will not stop until they drop, whereas net fibred people often instinctively know they cannot overdo things and may have the sense to cut work down to manageable proportions. Can eyes change colour? Fundamentally no, but pigmentation laid down in front of the anterior border layer [foremost of the four layers] can change a bit, though there is debate about this. My partner had emphatically green/brown hazel eyes when we met but sadly we did not take a photograph before he was well into a recommended regime of bowel cleansing and a radical change of diet. He is now displaying a lot of blue fibres where the brownish hue has broken up and faded, but without photographic proof this means little. My eyes are also changing but very slowly. Hopeless for an impatient Aries! There can be many different colour deposits in the anterior border layer, each one pointing or highlighting different organs or areas of the body. A certain type of yellow points to kidneys and a specific shade of orange highlights the pancreas. Traumatic events, both emotional and physical can leave marks in the iris [[particularly the inner pupil border - the only place in the body where cells from the central nervous system are visible] and there has been some extraordinary research into this, led by an Italian ear, nose and throat surgeon [Dr. Daniele Lo Rito] throwing up thought provoking spiritual questions. I attended one of his lectures a couple of years ago. His research findings made my jaw drop.

If you look very closely you may see circular rings in your irides. These rings [there is usually more than one] are called contraction 'furrows' [because they look like furrows in a field]. Not everyone has them but if you do it points to stress and indicates a high rate of vitamin and mineral consumption. You can see these in very, very young children which would indicate their nutrition needs to be of high quality. If you have these furrows you are likely to be quietly anxious, probably good at hiding your fears and someone who appears to be able to cope with whatever life throws at you.

Just make sure you put those minerals and vitamins back in as fast as you use them up. Don't confuse these furrows with a scurf rim [already discussed] or a complete white ring around the very edge of the iris which is known as a lipemic ring [or sodium ring]. This indicates a problem with digesting fats and/or a sodium imbalance. A white ring around the top of your iris is called an arcus senilis and has long been recognised by the medical profession as a pointer to potential problems. Emotionally, a lipemic ring can point to stubbornness. If you have one of these rings in your eyes get your stubborn bottom to a nutritionist because you don't want fat laid down where you can't see it. Fatty deposits are trouble enough where you can see them but thoroughly naughty when hidden from view. Please concentrate .... I am NOT saying you are laying down fatty internal deposits if you have a white ring around the edge of your iris, what I AM saying is *you may have a predisposition toward doing so*. Self-knowledge means you are forewarned, therefore forearmed, and you will understand that half a pound of Camembert for lunch may not be your stomach's idea of a fun day out, even if your ego is eyeing up the cheese, salivating mightily and tail wagging. [Digesting fats; research lecithin/inositol/choline.]

While we are in the area, look out for a ring of little white dots [like a rosary] around the edge of the iris. This does not mean you have a vocation to be a nun but it also [but less than the lipemic or sodium ring] points to problems with fat digestion [dairy products may not be ideal for you in daily doses] and emotionally you will not be the first to start a row because you like harmony, which may, in the long run, see you running yourself ragged trying to maintain equilibrium in a topsy-turvy world.

One fine day every child in every school will have Alexander Technique lessons and see an iridologist so they can get individual advice [relating specifically to their body and its functioning] on how to stay healthy. This will save the NHS, if we still have one, billions. It's no good barking at a young boy hovering nervously at the edge of a rugby scrum to, 'Get stuck in lad', if that child has net fibres [connective tissue weakness] because he is far more liable to injury [specifically dislocation injuries - and he will know this instinctively], than a child with silk linen fibres, but the games teacher will think he is a wimp. This child will not be suited to contact sports; swimming would be ideal. If your daughter is a silk fibred [increasingly rare these days] workaholic you may need to drag her away from her studies/work and teach her to relax so her body can repair itself, while ensuring her diet does not go the way of most adolescents.

Let's just go briefly back to silk fibres [packed tightly together and more often seen in blue eyes]. It is interesting to note that silk fibres are not seen so often in the young nowadays. I reckon it is because our diet is a disgrace and even those who do eat well are under intense pressure from chemicals and the like. However [and this is what I love about iridology], it is also possible that we have had to become more flexible in our approach to life as we are bombarded with change almost on a daily basis. Silk fibred people have a tendency to rigid thinking and inflexibility. They can be very hard and judgmental about themselves and liable to push their bodies to an extreme work load limit. Could it be that our bodies are adapting to modern life by producing more loose fibres in our eyes so that we emotionally bend like a willow, not stand rigid like an oak?

When I started studying iridology all the students had access to a high magnification instrument and the first time we started examining each other's eyes we all went rather quiet. A whole new extraordinary and intimate landscape opened up before our eyes. I think we all felt rather humbled and honoured. I certainly did.

𝓘NTENTION

It is a bit of a buzz word these days but, nevertheless, I find it helpful when I am in a difficult situation to ask myself, 'What is my intention?'. It is surprising how often I find myself answering truthfully, 'Self-protection'. Self-protection, of course, stems from fear. Wayne Dyer has written a nice little book about this very subject. I like reading Wayne Dyer's books, but really I prefer listening to his tapes because he makes me laugh and ... he has a dead sexy voice .... *shouldn't be allowed*.

I like the idea of intention. My intention is to be the best me I can be, which is not easy when Ava Gardner got in ahead and filched my cheek bones and figure. If I am unclear about my intention I go out into the garden and look at the flowers who have one intention only - that is to be themselves. That way you don't get daffdaisies, primbutterpeonies, or bleedinhyacinths. No, a buttercup does not want to be a blousy old rose or a prim primula, it just wants to be a buttercup and that is exactly what it is. I want to be a smart, strong, wise, soft and good Amanda Mansell. Is this easy? No.

*I*NSULTS

Do try and remember that when someone has just chucked an insult at you, nine times out of ten they are talking about themselves. You are just an easy target and the person hurling the insult cannot face their own shortcomings. They have a problem they are, as yet, unwilling to deal with - you, however, have a boundary problem. Take a deep breath. Dust yourself down. Fish out some navy blue clothes, work on your self-esteem and get some carpentry repair work to your picket fence. Angry people unconsciously pick on others who are unconsciously angry too, whereas really peaceful people tend to have peaceful lives. Think about it, but think about it with some chocolate. You will need something sweet after the bitter.

*I*MPATIENCE

I came here to learn patience. Appropriately, I was born under the sign of Aries. Most Aries people want all things done the day before yesterday. The universe, noting me tapping my foot and exhaling steam from my nostrils, has obligingly made me wait for everything. I read that the reward for patience is patience. Such a smug and infuriating little homily … guaranteed to test my patience.

*I*NTERVIEWS

I am talking interviews with magazines and the like; I am agin them. You have no control, or precious little, over what is actually written about you once your interviewer has left and interviews given at twenty could make you squirm with embarrassment at forty. I once read an interview of a pretty and fairly harmless female actress. She was really viciously stitched up by the interviewer which I thought was unfair and I paid attention. The actress was not paying attention, in a bit of a muddle and needed picket fence repair work, but she did not come across as unkind, whereas the interviewer was thoroughly nasty. I made a mental note that should I ever become a pretty and fairly harmless actress and someone asked me for an interview, I should politely decline. Least said, soonest mended.

*I*NSTANT WEIGHT LOSS

Pull your breast bone up and your stomach goes in. This does work but you have to remember to keep doing it ….. but .. if you radically improve your diet and digestion your posture automatically improves and your breast bone goes up, stays up and there is no need to remember to do it at all. Infuriating isn't it?

J Is for JEWELLERY

I do not point out my observations on someone's personal choice of jewellery, I merely observe, learn [continuously] and then tread carefully around what I think *may* be a touchy subject. Just as clothing type and colour choice talks, so does jewellery. There are always exceptions, traditions, gifts and pieces of ornamentation handed down through families but I have observed that, as a general rule, the type, colour and positioning of jewellery makes an unconscious statement. In the newspaper recently a woman left court wearing a necklace so apt to the moment [it looked like a ball and chain] it even made me do a double take. My mother favoured a tight bracelet and necklace that she often requested I wear after she died. I cannot bear the constriction of the bracelet, so I don't wear it and I had the necklace loosened. My mother needed [I think felt comforted by] an element of tight restraint. I most certainly do not.

I am going to talk a little bit more about body language. Apologies for the repetition, but our whole body is connected, emotionally and physically. Each part of the face is linked to a different area or organ of the body and the same goes for fingers and toes. I am going to start with fingers because in most cultures rings are worn and I will briefly outline what to look out for when someone joins fingers. When it comes to describing the meaning of jewellery there are, no doubt, exceptions to the rule, there always are, but here are my observations for what they are worth. Each finger and toe represents a different aspect of the self. Remembering that the left side is female and right side male, so ....

The thumb [big toe] is the head, neck, spine, willpower and to some extent the character [but also large intestine]. A straight unbending thumb can mean rigid thinking whereas a very bent back thumb is seen as being a sign of the entertainer [bit of a worry in political thumbs].

The index finger [first toe] represents the ego and is the one used to point with [as in accusatory pointing]. Aggressive finger pointing is based on fear.

The third finger [second toe] represents sex [possibly a sacred contract linked to lineage] but also the immune system, a very interesting link, especially when it comes to reproduction.

The fourth finger [third toe] represents the heart and all intimate relationships [not necessarily sexual]. This is the wedding ring finger.

The little finger [baby toe] represents the inner child, or childhood.

With this information in mind it is an interesting exercise to hold up your hand, extend your fingers and take a good look at what shape your hand and fingers make [same with your feet]. I am sure the top inside edge of my thumbs have bent outwards a little since I was in my twenties, which makes me think I am less rigid in my thinking. My little fingers strain to get away from the rest and this is usually a sign of someone who tends not to indulge in tribal thinking [a flaming little rebel am I] but interestingly my right little finger is slightly bent and always affected by the arthritis, whereas my left is not. What does your hand say? Look for a finger or toe that leans towards another such as a sex finger that leans towards the wedding ring finger. I would read this literally and would suspect the owner of such fingers would lean towards monogamy. Bent fingers and toes can straighten when emotional blocks have been cleared [I have watched this happen]. I am fascinated that some toes are always raised up slightly [lack of grounding, or unwillingness to ground that particular toe?]. The top of the thumb and the big toe represents the top of the head [seventh chakra] and therefore the tip relates to the crown chakra and one's connection with one's perception of God. There is an old saying that the person with the first toe longer than the big toe is the boss of the house. I have delivered quite a lot of babies and they all had perfect, evenly matched little toes, so it is interesting to watch and see exactly when single toes stop growing and become shorter or ones become excessively long. Of course genetic family traits come through the generations but then so do family thought patterns, beliefs and behaviour.

For many years I have been paying attention to any small injury or burns to my fingers [or toes]. After the 'ouch' I stop and think, 'Is this on the left side or right side and what was I thinking at the exact time of the injury?'. There is nearly always a correlation between thought and specific finger or toe and the thought is usually not one of love, sweetness and light [definitely not when I burn myself]. However, I have found that I invariably bang or stub my big toe when I am thinking serious, large scale, repetitive rubbish - my 'drivel dialogue' as I call it. I take it as a universal plea to SHUT my brain UP because the big toe represents the head area. I tend to look at banging my thumb in the same light. I love hand sewing because I find it very soothing but I cannot tell you how many times I have stabbed my finger with a needle while sewing, then stopped, tracked back and thought about my angry thoughts as the needle went in. Try, if you can, to get into the habit of paying attention to small injuries because I believe that by paying attention to the small knocks and prangs in your life you massively reduce the risk of the universe bringing you a monumental injury to wake you up.

I pay attention to every detail of rings especially the colour of stones because the colour chosen is as significant as the colour of clothing, perhaps even more so in some people not given to changing the way they dress. It has become fashionable to wear thumb rings, a development I view with great interest. Thumb rings, as far as I know, have not been much in evidence since the Tudor period; a time when outspoken views could result in a head being swiftly removed from a neck. I am paying particular attention to the fact that thumb rings have now made a come-back because the ring envelops the lower half of the thumb which corresponds with the throat and neck [fifth chakra]. If a male or female client pitched up wearing a right thumb ring my thinking [but not my saying] would be that this person probably has a second chakra issue and feels *unable* to *speak out* about it. Whatever the issue is it will have a male [right thumb] bias and that may mean support or advice from me, being female, may not be helpful or even heard and I may have to frame my words with care. I would think along the same lines if the ring was placed on the left thumb substituting the male influence to female. It is interesting to observe body language because someone holding, encircling or stroking their thumb would be saying the same to me as if they were wearing a thumb ring. If someone was making a speech as they fingered their thumb it would make me wonder about what they were not saying. When talking to people watch for thumb movements, such as a thumb connecting to another finger. Thumb to third [wedding ring] finger might indicate the person was thinking about a partner or loved one. I would be alert to whether the thumb [willpower] was on top of the ring finger [subjugating] or beneath [yielding]. Making a T shape with thumb and ring finger might indicate a degree of propping up or support. Thumb to index finger would say willpower to ego, depending on the position the thumb might even be saying, 'Ego, shut up'.

A ring on the index finger indicates ego issues, possibly wishing to dominate, needing to tone down aggression or, conversely, needing to become more assertive. I am sure you know the one 'whenever you point your index finger at someone, in an accusatory manner, always remember that three fingers are pointing back at you'. The assertive issue, which may or may not encompass needing protection from a person, would depend on whether it was on the left or the right index finger. I am inclined to lean towards thinking a woman wearing a ring on her left index finger may need some 'bolstering' rather than outright protection in asserting herself with a significant man or men in her life. It is possible that this is not in response to being dominated, but may also be from having to deal with an emotionally evasive father figure or spouse. A ring worn on the right index finger may reveal a need to tone down assertion [this may change according to whether someone is right or left-handed].

Observe also for body language. If you spot someone who is right-handed using their right index finger to tap, point downwards, or scratch at something [even scratching a wine glass rim at a party] you can be pretty sure you are annoying them. My partner was advising a very dehydrated client to drink more water when he noticed they started scratching their gall-bladder meridian [gall-bladder and liver are associated with anger] on their upper leg with their right index finger. He realised he was wasting his breath and stopped talking.

A middle finger ring indicates an issue over sex or sexuality, not necessarily a negative issue, it might be a statement that sex is important to the wearer and again it would be interesting to note whether it was on the left or the right side and if the ring is a specific colour. There is a link with this finger and the immune system. I have a suspicion that the current trend to wearing rings on this finger may have much more to do with protection than I realise, it may well be connected to the massive increase in sexually transmitted diseases and rising infertility. I have noticed that, if very large rings are favoured, they are usually worn on this finger, or the fourth finger. I will cover large rings later on. Thumb to this finger in a gesture would be very interesting especially coming from a man. I would look at his partner with fascination. I am still studying a family/lineage/sacred contract link with this finger.

Fourth finger rings say relationships and commitment. Obviously this is the area of the wedding ring, but would have the same message if someone was not married and wearing a wedding ring on either left or right hand. I would pay attention if they were in multiples, or big. A young single man wearing a wedding type band on his right hand fourth finger might be a good bet for a stable relationship. When wedding rings come off, take this very seriously. Men often wear them on *chains around their neck* before discarding them completely. Watch out for skin condition at the ring site indicating possible irritation and the 'type' of wedding ring [thin, wide or some unusual design that may have a deeper meaning]. Ostentatious wedding bling rings are usually very big, but to me they also say a lot about the society we live in, where even our most intimate vows are 'up for sale' to the highest bidder in magazines.

Rings worn on little fingers protect the inner child. I wore rings [that could be interpreted as wedding rings] on both my little fingers [only] for years. I had a happy time as a small child but I often felt unheard and my slightly unusual ideas were frequently met with puzzlement or amusement which made me feel deeply uncomfortable and sometimes isolated. I also believe I arrived with a sacred contract that bound me in some way to my mother and I think these rings were a representation of that commitment [more under 'sacred contracts']. All my rings, plus my much favoured pearls, came off after my mother died. I then died my greying hair blonde, took up scuba diving and wore toe rings, which I viewed with amusement. Within a couple of weeks of meeting my future partner [I was wearing no rings at all at that time] I had slipped an old, unworn silver ring [that looked like a wedding band] onto the fourth finger of my right hand and because I was not paying attention it was several days before I realised what I had unconsciously done. I have only occasionally worn a ring on this finger. I find it interesting that men tend to wear signet rings on their little fingers [this may have relevance to their childhood, especially if they were sent unhappily to boarding school].

The size of a ring says a lot to me, the bigger it gets the louder the statement and I am inclined to view large rings as defensive, quite possibly *protective* statements, almost to the point of armoury if they are very big. The shape is interesting and I always note the colour. I have noted that a very large ring worn on the second finger [sex/immune system] of either hand frequently incorporates the colour turquoise [fifth chakra - speaking out]. I view rings worn on every finger, regardless of size, as having the same defensive message. A multiplicity of rings coupled with the wearing of red and black would make me pay very serious attention and I would focus on the lower abdomen for signs of health problems. I am also very attentive to black jewellery as it can have all the connotations of the colour black. I would listen very carefully and aim to hear every word [see 'listening'].

Imagery, stones and their colour in rings all say different things to me. There are countless different combinations but use the basic chakra colours as a guiding principle and work out from there. Turquoise jewellery is nearly always chosen to assist 'speaking out', green indicates heart led issues, dark blue stones are traditional for engagement rings but I would observe for size and be aware of sixth chakra connotations. Pearls do have an association with tears, so pay attention to large rings with pearls in them, even if the pearls are very small but in multiples. I am particularly fascinated with imagery relating to animals as they have such ancient meanings for us. Fast animals in motion, particularly birds, say much to me about the need for freedom [especially if the imagery is placed near the feet in toe rings, ankle bracelets, or tattoos and the left or right side placement is interesting]. Freedom may not be just physical but being granted freedom of thought, especially if the thought is in contrast to the prevailing tribal view. It takes an authentically strong partner or spouse to allow their significant other to have wildly contrasting views [even I am not good at this, but that is because I am always right, even when I am wrong ... and go into a sulk]. Butterflies are about metamorphosing and possibly an intuitive recognition of change, now or later, or possibly even sacrifice of some type - they would therefore make me wonder about a sacred contract and I would listen carefully. Tigers, or anything feline, would alert me to claws but would also say private because I think cat people often have a hidden side to them, either that or they can slink off and disappear in a second, even when they are standing in front of you; they are present but the connection has gone. Wolves says wilderness, but also family. Bears, not often seen, represent strength, as would a bull, but bears also hibernate and bulls get tetchy. I would look at the relationship with a father and/or male partner if the imagery was of a horse and worn by a woman. Turtles or tortoises spell spirituality to me or a connection with the sacred. Large fish and dolphins say freedom [but fish have other deeper connotations]. Skull and crossbones rings say 'sensitive' to me [regardless if worn by big hairy bikers] but then I have not had a skull and crossbones ring arriving in my face at speed. You may have had other experiences.

Earrings are a tad more difficult to read. They are often worn for tribal recognition; pearls for the county lady tribe, dangly or mismatching for the hippy chicks, silver statements for the artistic and bohemian and so on and so forth. I wondered a lot about long earrings but I have decided that as they frame the lower face they bring attention to the mouth perhaps in the hope that words will be heard. A convoluted shape in a pair of earrings would make me wonder about words used giving mixed messages. I would wonder about someone who has [or does] not feel they have been allowed to speak their mind, but I also think that the length and weight can be a grounding mechanism for someone who thinks a lot or who is extremely creative. I always note imagery and colour in earrings and I smile when I see hearts, but you will have to read on.

I am really not sure why someone would want to put half a dozen rings in their ears other than perhaps indicating that they were a leader of their 'tribe' or gang or family unit. Just as the grand dame of an old aristocratic family might wear the most pearls or diamond jewellery to denote her credentials as leader, I reckon the same goes for layers of heavy gold jewellery [though chains have a different, more obvious meaning]. Tongue rings can have a sexual connotation - but I am more inclined to view them as another form of thumb ring. It must take considerable commitment to have your tongue pierced, not just because of the thickness of it and the pain but because the tongue represents your ability [or not] to speak out *and be heard*. I am still struggling a bit with metal bungs in lips, chins and eyebrows. There is, obviously, a tradition in tribal cultures of piercing and shoving things in holes in faces, or earlobes. In some hunter gatherer societies there is a very strong connection with animal energies, even a reverence and a desire to emulate the look of the animal. There is also a belief in some countries in the East that long earlobes represent wisdom. I am slightly confused as to why youngsters today are choosing bungs and bullet-shaped objects to decorate their faces other than to shock or unnerve onlookers, because I do not see much evidence of reverence for much at all, let alone nature, though I may be wrong. I don't know enough people with bungs to ask them in depth why they are doing it and the few I have been able to ask don't seem to have any intriguing answers, other than they like they look of them. I take it they are stating they are a member of a recognisable tribe but what their tribe stands for confuses me - rebellion I suppose. Bullets are a mystery to me. I asked a sweet, young, male shop assistant about the very pointed missile sticking out under his lower lip. He didn't know why he had it. I wondered how he kissed his girlfriend without lacerating her face, then I wondered if there was an issue with tenderness - in the giving or, perhaps much more interestingly, in the receiving. I have already covered this but, please remember the face and ears have many acupuncture points. Bunging holes and metal objects in and around your face may be over stimulating these points, so, if you have to puncture yourself, try and be sensible and seek advice from an acupuncturist first, they may be able to tell you which areas are point free and safe.

Whether it is diamonds, gold or base metal, the more of it you are wearing the more attention you attract. The more attention you attract the more dominance you appear to have. Please note emphasis on 'appear' and that perpetually needing attention is a dangerous game. The universe watches and listens and may deliver 'attention' for you in a manner you most definitely did not want.

Heart-shaped jewellery says love to me. I know men buy heart-shaped things for the women they love but often when a woman is coming out of a relationship break-up or has been on her own for a while and feels ready to embark on another relationship she will often chose to wear something heart-shaped. This can be a heart-shaped neck pendant, belt-buckle, earrings or just hearts on clothing fabric. It is a signal that she is either ready for love again or moving towards getting ready. When you open up to the possibility of love colours also change. There may be a transition from grieving black to pale green, pink or peach or colours with pink in it such as light brown [though not beige]. The colours and hearts may extend from clothing to living space with a sudden need to buy pink towels and heart shaped cushions or ornaments. Hair can get longer as it is often cut short after the break-up [or distancing] of a relationship [not *just* the break-up between lovers] while the woman makes a statement about freedom. This is not to be confused with the severe cutting of a woman's hair after the death of a spouse, which is a signal of deep grief - a not wanting to be noticed, especially sexually, and a wish for period of withdrawal from the world. When a women opens up to the possibility of love the hair may lengthen and the speech may get softer and more receptive. You can often see similar changes when a woman gets pregnant.

Brooches are not worn much these days so I don't get a lot of opportunities to find out about them and the wearer. In the past they were very often a statement of your relationship or standing within a certain tribe. I would be interested if a brooch depicted a particular animal [I have already covered animal imagery] and I always note the colour. Huge brooches I would read as protective, possibly armoury and the left or right side positioning would be interesting. I wonder if they are positioned on acupuncture points? I must look into that. Before the last world war, women often wore high necks and large brooches pinned over their throat [fifth chakra]. Apart from a short period during the sixties this has not been fashionable ...... or needed, as the case may be. Belts are more common these days, they are often wide, decorated with *large* buckles and worn slung low over the hips as if to protect the second chakra, which is an interesting drop from the belt-buckle that covered third chakra of yesteryear. I wore a large brass buckle for many years with jeans. The buckle sat between second and third chakra level and depicted a little child sitting under a tree. I think the imagery said a lot about me as I am in heaven sitting under huge old trees and have been since I was very little. Much later, I bought a monster brass buckle which I wore with trousers and it sat a little higher, more over third chakra than second. I was doing major emotional work during the couple of years that I wore it regularly, but I have not worn it since because I find it uncomfortable now, even though I still think it is lovely to look at, because it is so unusual. It was definitely a protective buckle for me.

There has been a recent trend for women towards wearing a necklace or pendant over the breast bone. These are often quite large and sometimes made of shell. I think the shell may mean more than I realise, for hard outer shells cover soft interiors and the shell is quite an ancient tribal adornment. The pendant usually covers the thymus gland. I have a suspicion this has something to do with the awakening of a change in women's attitude to their role in life and how society perceives that role and I am also pondering if there is some sort of sexual connection. It is interesting that the pendant is often a blue, blue/green, turquoise colour [fifth chakra].

We call some necklaces, chokers [note the word]. Anything worn tight over the throat, be it pearls or trendy modern pieces, is unlikely to be chosen unless there was an issue with speaking out. It might be an inability to speak out or a need to refrain from speaking out [clues would be finger pointing and the choice of colour worn]. Chokers can make me think of being bound by tribal rules when it comes to restriction but I am wary if they are being used as a method of restraint, possibly to control a sharpish tongue. Chains are worn on both neck and wrist. I read them literally. I think they look lovely but they do represent an element of being bound or restrained. I wear a very thin loose gold neck chain most days. I think chains are chosen because the wearer feels they are restrained in some way or they feel a need for restraint. I note it is fashionable at the moment for young men to wear necklaces at the base of the neck that are made of leather or rope, often with a stone or natural object threaded or hung from it. I still see this as a slightly restraining element [vocal restraint] though it has a flavour of the return to the wild, which is reassuring as the wilderness brings wisdom and self-reliance in a way that technology does not. I note pendants on a necklace and their imagery; a timid person wearing an animal may be telling you of inner wishes unfulfilled. If the pendant has a sharp downward trajectory [same for earrings] this may mean a need for the owner to feel grounded and it would be exacerbated by the wearing of brown on the lower body. Very long chains or necklaces, whatever their style, that end at the solar plexus would indicate an element of restriction linked to third chakra, or possibly some other third chakra connection. Recently, I saw a bronze heart being worn on a long necklace. The outfit of the wearer told a story in itself but the bronze heart at the level of the solar plexus seemed to say to me that the woman was looking for love that would be grounding and would help repair her third chakra - but the bronze element made me wonder if money was fairly important. I might stick my neck out and say she would be looking for an older, reliable man with a bit of dosh.

Bracelets, whether they are metal, fabric or leather are another protective armour and this goes for men and woman. A woman wearing revealing low cut clothes with multiple bangles or bracelets on the right arm sends out a message of, 'I am available but do not try to dominate me'. The bigger the bangle [or bracelet] the louder the message and if it is huge or in serious *multiples* I would read it as a defensive/protective statement. Watch out for those new leather bracelets that look like the protection an archer wears - I would be inclined to read them literally. I am still mulling over chain bracelets. I would still read chain literally, but often they have a heart attached [as a clasp] and I would pay attention to that combination. I have wanted a single plain gold bangle for years and was delighted when my partner gave me one for Christmas. It was only when I put it on that I realised it looks like a very large wedding ring and I was amused that I chose to wear it on my left arm. Many years back I wore multiple bangles from Africa on my arms but it would make me feel most uncomfortable now. I have noticed my jewellery has become quieter as I have become more peaceful.

I am inclined to view large wristwatches in the same way as large bracelets - as protective statements. I know some watches are a status symbol but needing a status symbol is a sign of needing protection in itself. I am right-handed but when given a wristwatch for an early birthday [around eight years] I immediately, without thinking, put it on my right wrist much to my parents incomprehension. It may have been an early unconscious defensive statement against my father because I was starting to challenge first chakra thinking by then, but it may also be that I am primarily right brain orientated.

There will be dozens of reasons why people wear specific jewellery in specific places and the reasons will be very personal [possibly cultural] and some items will be of great sentimental value. Some people have issues about everything and wear no jewellery at all, but they may pull or hold specific fingers when stressed or adopt protective body language - like hand to the throat, or wrist/lower arm rubbing. I smiled recently at a picture of

Henry VIII vigorously pulling and twisting his fourth finger ring with his thumb [willpower] and forefinger [ego] in what appeared to be his male side, though sometimes these pictures are transposed when they appear in print. Perhaps if Anne Boleyn had known about digits [and she had a few herself] and their meaning she might have kept her head when all about were losing theirs. Finger placement is fascinating and reveals much, so pay attention to it. Jewellery colour means as much as clothing colour. I have dozens of different coloured hair bands [like fabric elastic bands] and one of them usually resides up on my wrist in case I suddenly get an urge to clean out the chicken house or weed the garden and need to get my hair out of the way. These bands infuriate my partner because they cut into the skin of my wrist but he observes he can tell what sort of mood I am in by my choice of colour of the band. One exhausted morning, last week, I found myself twining a bright red hair-band absent-mindedly around my right little finger. I stopped and wondered exactly what part of my male side, childhood issue, first chakra needed an energetic leg up. On consideration, I realised I had been dreading a specific appointment that would require an element of 'male warrior spirit' in order for me to stand my ground and the appointment had an element of first chakra 'survival' about it. Sorry not to be more specific, but this is personal.

I point out my observations in order to increase a level of awareness so that you can be more sensitive. We are all here on planet Earth just struggling to get it right. Let's be aware and try to be *kind,* but still ……….. should I attend a party and a sleepy eyed vixen enter the room in a skin tight leopard print outfit, plunging neckline and red rings on several fingers I would probably bristle, steer my partner smartly out of the back door and scuttle him home. Even the wise man ties up his camel in the desert at night.

JOB

My father used to say to me, 'Every job is ninety per cent routine, ducky, but it is the ten per cent that makes it worthwhile'. I have had jobs where that ten per cent was damned elusive. While seeking a 'ten per cent job' I have talked to many people and I have been given lots of extremely unhelpful advice. I have read even more frustratingly tedious exhortations to 'follow your dream' or 'do what you feel passionate about'. If I had followed my passionate dream from the teenage start of my working life I think I would have ended up living in a hedgerow and probably having to find my breakfast from it too. There are a few lucky souls who know exactly what they want to be when they grow up, then do it and love it and some get mightily financially rewarded, but they are rarities. We are all here to shine at something, but that something may not be recognised as significant by many and sometimes our shining does not bring in enough cash to pay the mortgage or rent, so for the rest of the population, back at the Ponderosa, you need a JOB.

My advice, for what it is worth, is this - get a trade. Find a trade that sort of suits you and will give you work any time and any place. Add to your trade as many skills as you can, by watching and learning from others. Don't stand idly in a working garage or stranger's kitchen, watch what people are doing with their spanner or spice. Now you have your trade or your job that is ok, not fabulous, but it pays the bills and puts food on the table, do your work to the best of your ability but spend your evenings and weekends doing what you feel passionate about. When you go back to work on Monday morning and as you start your labouring week, say a small prayer of gratitude that this work will give you the money to follow your passion tonight, or next Saturday. Keep saying thank you, through gritted teeth if necessary, until it becomes a habit. Read 'commitment' if you haven't already. If you keep steady, disciplined and committed then marvellous things can start to happen and you may find you can actually make a living out of your passion. Read on for 'money'. You may find you are unconsciously deflecting money away from you and this may put the kibosh on your passion.

$\mathcal{K}$ Is for KINDNESS

I have said it before but it is worth saying again - don't mistake kindness for weakness because if you do you may find you are in for a very rude awakening.

$\mathcal{K}$IDNEYS

I am hoping the current trend of bare midriffs is coming to a close. It is fine in India and other warm places but I see girls here with abdomens and backs exposed in deep midwinter. Usually the clothing covers the kidneys, but only just and the fabric is often thin. It is a dangerous practice and they may well find they gain weight because their bodies are not stupid and will lay down a layer of fat to heat and protect such important organs from the cold.

You cannot live without at least one kidney but can you point to yours? Most people get the positioning wrong. There are two small glands that sit at a jaunty angle atop your kidneys called adrenals. These have a multitude of functions but one is to supply adrenaline. You need a dribble of adrenaline just get dressed in the morning but having left the house should you be chased down the road by a large bad tempered dog, all teeth firing, you would need more than a dribble of adrenaline to get up a head of running steam. Now, these days, bad tempered dogs come in many different guises and many of us start the day envisaging a barking driver, snarling boss, whining colleague, yapping children, pleading friends and snoring, flea-bitten partner. I am sure, 'it was ever thus', as my Daddy used to say, but what was not ever thus is the amount of over stimulation we get now. It is relentless.

Most of us have too much stuff. Wardrobes bulge with clothes, cupboards burst with unused appliances, utensils sit for years and only come in useful three days after you gave them to charity. We fill our days with noise, clamour and doing - tidying, cleaning, insuring and maintaining our stuff. It is ridiculous if you stop and think about it. Barely a hundred years ago, many people had only one or two sets of clothing and everything slowed down when night fell because there was no electric lighting and other forms of lighting did not come cheap for the masses. A hundred years is absolutely nothing in the history of our evolution, just a blip. That blip gives our bodies little time to adapt to such a phenomenal change in lifestyle. I have given you a hell of a lecture on health and I don't want to drone on and on but kidneys work so hard, your adrenal glands are precious, so please give them, as well as yourself, some down time. I really do not think watching television is 'down' time, it is too stimulating and thought provoking, even when it is supposed to be light entertainment. If you are mostly solvent, and it is not hurting someone, it is ok to sit and stare at a wall or out of a window for a while each day, no matter what your over-achieving friends or relatives may have to say about it. Just feed your soul and rest your adrenals with a little silence and peace because adrenal gland is 'burn out' territory and you tamper with that at your peril. Don't muddle up ego and body - ego is in charge until the body goes on general strike and there ain't no union on this planet that will negotiate you out of that hole - you climb out by submission. Adrenals take a lot of punishment in a normal working lifetime, but they cannot take a lot of punishment plus a lot of worry and anxiety. Be careful, please, because if you do not protect your adrenal glands by hyper doing, doing, doing, you will be sorry, sorry, sorry.

$\mathcal{K}$GB

You knew where you were with the cold war. It was all in black and white, you know. Moscow was the enemy and the letters KGB sent shivers through your spine. There was a big, iron, grey curtain and everything behind it was snowy, cold and bugged. Should you venture behind the curtain you could rest assured that bulky men in black coats and unfortunate hats followed your every move. There was a lot of skulking about. Big grey files held untold secrets and were put away in big grey metal filing cabinets. Unmentionable things happened in horrid places. There were big black phones and small grey guns, snow-white snow and thunderous skies. It was them and us …… but we had George Smiley. Phew! Such a gentleman, so quiet and understated but always one step ahead of the nasty Russian with a ridiculous codename.

Nowadays Moscow is in Technicolor. It is too upsetting. The nasties are all over the place, everywhere, either dressed in frocks or jeans. George

Smiley has gone, we shan't see his like again and his replacements write their *memoirs* ...... George must be *spinning* in his grave! Within our very own shores we are watched and listened to by members of our very own British KGB [Kafkaesque Governmental Bodge-up] who don't know what to do with all their watching and listening information except to work out if they can tax it .... *I don't like modern.*

KALAHARI DESERT

Occasionally I worked with an anaesthetist from Namibia. On the very rare occasion that the night was not full of labouring mums requesting epidurals and this doctor was hovering I would make him a cup of tea and insist he tell me stories of the Kalahari. We were off and I would be agog with excitement. He would swoop me off in his small plane, fly me over the desert and back over dunes of beautiful changing colours. We would chase the lonesome gemsbok across the sands. I was in imaginary heaven while he, poor chap, got homesick. A couple of years ago I finally got my butt out to Namibia. At Bagatelle Game Ranch, with its fabulous red and orange sand dunes, they had a tribe of rescued abandoned pet meerkats that are now semi-wild. Yes, meerkats do have unpleasant habits but like dolphins we ignore these traits because they are cute, cute, cute. The littlest meerkats played with my boot laces and I fell very deeply in love.

My partner drove, as we headed for Sossusvlei to see those dunes that had so gripped my imagination. Later we flew over the dunes and chased a lonesome gemsbok. He was right, that doctor, it is all beautiful beyond words. It is so wonderfully silent there but at nightfall lizardy things come out and make noises like tapping stones. At Zebra River Lodge, a place that looks so ancient and stunningly strange, a snake joined me for a beer, which I thought was a thoroughly bold move on its part. We got on a boat with Cronje and saw 'Sally Wash Your Face' the seal at Walvis Bay. Sally got caught in netting and the fishermen managed to cut if off. Now she follows boats and, on command, washes her face with her flippers. I thought my heart would burst in adoration of her. Robbie the seal hopped aboard for lunch and, though wild, was remarkably sanguine about me cooing, cuddling, inspecting his toes and rustling his huge whiskers. I whispered in his ear that he was outrageously handsome. He looked at me with liquid agreeing eyes and then, with his nose, he pointed definitively at the lunch box ... typical male. Adorable Ernst took us on a tour and we watched him ripple the quicksand like a water bed [don't try this one at home folks]. We drove up, up, up to Huab and sat in the sunken stone, mineral rich, hot tub near the river bank, relaxing, until I noticed a very, very large round footprint in the sand by my elbow and said, 'Good heavens!', or words to that effect. I love elephants but I didn't want to share a mineral rich bath with one, even though I was wearing a very fetching swimming cossie at the time.

We watched hundreds of animals come to the water holes at night in Etosha National Park. A scorpion joined us but he was busy eyeing up the lunatic tourists wearing flip flops, seeing if he was in with a chance. On our way back we visited the cheetah sanctuary and marvelled at how Carla and her partner and others gave their lives in service to these glorious animals.

What a planet we live on! Namibia! Don't go, you will hate it.

L Is for LISTENING

I am going to talk about listening versus hearing in a minute but I had an interesting experience lately and I am going to share it with you. Are you sitting comfortably? Then I will begin. A very nice lady from our local radio station rang and asked if I would give a very short talk on iridology. I gulped and asked for time to think it over. I went to the kitchen, made tea and had a mini nervous breakdown as my ego boomeranged off the kitchen walls. *'I can't do it!* I'll be hopeless! I'll make a complete *tit* of myself! Oh God, what if someone asks me a question I can't answer?' When I had got a grip, I agreed be interviewed. My head, now ballooned with anticipation of a minor triumph, popped down to second chakra and sought out friends to impress. 'I'm going to be on the tranny! I'm terrified!', I shrieked at them with more than a dash of hysteria. 'Fabulous - we will be listening - don't worry - you will be great - we have every confidence in you', they all chorused, adorably. I have thoroughly nice friends. The following week I went on the tranny, teeth chattering with nerves. It was hardly an award-winning performance but rather 'sufficient unto the day'. I scuttled out of the studio as fast as my quaking knees would carry me and launched into town for some serious retail therapy at TK Maxx, on the excuse that I don't hit town often, I don't shop much, I deserved it and any other ridiculous excuse I could come up with. Loved ones rang and told me I was 'brilliant and marvellous' and my partner bought me a beautiful pressie. The day was mine! In the happy evening, having extracted every possible bit of interview glory, my partner wanted to talk through a business problem that was worrying him and as we talked about how to listen and support someone who was frightened it suddenly struck me that we both had had a different, yet similar experience at the same time. I had rung my fabulous friends and told them I was terrified of being on the radio and all of them had told me not to worry, but none of them had asked me what *specifically* was terrifying me and I was too clouded with emotion to see it clearly myself. My specific fear was that I would let iridology down. If I made a complete hash of the interview then I would have looked stupid, which would have given my ego a hammering, but much more worrying was what effect that might have on my fellow iridologists because I was, in a tiny local way, representing the profession and that thought scared the living daylights out of me. Iridology has been around a very long time but it is not yet well known. The next few years will see iridology talked of as reflexology is today, so any publicity it gets now needs to be professional and good.

On that day my partner and I learnt a powerful lesson. When we are confronted with someone who is in a fearful state it is more helpful to them to ask why specifically they are frightened and, if necessary, to keep gently digging and probing, rather than offering assurances, however heartfelt and well meant. By doing this you allow the person to explore their feelings [third chakra], consolidate their fear [second chakra] into a recognisable and hopefully manageable form and give voice [fifth chakra] to their concerns. All listening is showing a certain amount of love but in asking what someone is specifically afraid of you are giving that person concentrated hearing, therefore more love and you are saying, 'I hear you', while putting an invisible energetic hand on their lower back [second chakra]. This 'hand on lower back' is a supportive gesture - it's what people do when they are guiding someone they feel needs help. Rubbing the small of the back is also a supportive gesture, helping someone with an energetic power loss at second chakra, unlike the arm around the shoulder which covers the back and heart chakra which is a gesture given to someone who is sad or grief stricken.

Now, let's get back to hearing and listening ...the heart of darkness as it were. Are you a good listener? Most people think they are. I'd say about thirty per cent of the population are good listeners, if that. However, I rarely meet anyone who hears. Hearing can shake your foundations, that is why most people do not do it. I shall take a deep breath and announce that women are not great at hearing but men [especially if they are over forty] are ten times worse ..... sorry, but there you have it. Men may be exemplary at hearing every single word when it comes to information on anything from engines to complex mathematical equations but extremely basic 'off the cuff' comments from their spouses that are really saying, 'I don't like you one little bit', fall on deaf ears and then they wonder why they have very expensive divorces.

My partner is a good listener. When we met he would listen to me for hours, which is just as well because I have a great deal to say. I have said it now so we are on a re-run but he is still listening, bless him, he deserves an award. However, my beloved could not hear until I taught him; he now hears better than I can, which infuriates me. When he started hearing he got thoroughly depressed because he couldn't believe how much people disliked one another. 'Welcome to my hearing world', I responded, 'but don't worry too much because after a while you realise it doesn't matter, it's how we learn.'

What is the difference between listening and hearing? The answer is - the truth. We all listen all day long, turning on the telly or radio, listening on and off. During the 'off' we do other things or pursue our agendas but when we hear a knock at the front door we will know that we have a visitor. We are informed by the knock, we received information from a noise. You wouldn't believe how much information you can get from the noise that comes out of peoples' mouths, problem is, most of the time we don't believe it.

In order to hear well you need to follow three basic guidelines. The first is to switch off all your agendas and become a non-reactive hollow hearing instrument that allows everything said to you to filter through you. This is important because the more you can perfect non-reactive agenda-free hearing the more people will tell you, because you will make them feel safe. Did you get that? It's important. The second is to know that, generally speaking, people will not talk about things that are not running across their radar screen on a fairly regular basis or, to put it another way, what people think about the most is what they talk about the most. Thirdly, this is the most difficult part, you need to believe what they say. Having said that, I will throw a spanner in the works. On the opposite side of the coin you need to be hyper-aware of someone talking about they way they behave or operate. If you hear a man say, 'I am honest', or, 'I never lie', or, 'I am a gentleman', or, 'You can trust me', please observe for amber warning lights and listen for alarm bells because a genuinely honest, trustworthy gentleman would never make these statements. It would not occur to him to do so because he is intrinsically honest and trustworthy - he knows it, it is a done deal. A woman who says to you, 'I never flirt', and, 'I don't lie', is almost certainly going to be a problem, but watch the wording. 'I never flirt', is probably a lie and possibly a huge lie. Whereas, 'I can't flirt', or, 'I'm hopeless at flirting', is probably an honest assessment of one's lack of skill in the batting of eyelids department.

Now, I tell my dogs I will give them a damn good thrashing if they thieve the cat food again and my dogs give a delighted wag, ignore me, wait until I am out of sight and thieve the cat food. I tell my partner I will sink my teeth into his backside if he doesn't stop doing whatever it is that is winding me up, to which he gives a delighted wag, ignores me and carries on doing it. Everyone says things in jest that can slip through the net without alarm bells being rung. Most people blunder occasionally, usually from nerves, saying things they do not really mean, it's all quite normal human behaviour, but I am not talking about that, I am talking about the off the cuff remark that denotes fear and loathing to some degree or other. You will hear it in the everyday chit-chat on trains or buses, or from colleagues and acquaintances and these are the people I would start with before you move on to hearing loved ones, because you may not be ready for the shock. When listening to friends, colleagues and acquaintances make sure you hear all the casual, non-nervous, throw away remarks. Listen to what people say about their work or their spouses, it is a real eye opener because they won't say things that are not on their radar screen. A throw away remark gives you a *real insight* into how someone *really feels* about their work. It will also reveal the truth of a marriage. I remember once being told by someone that they were selfish. I didn't believe it, why would I? I didn't *want* to believe it ... but guess what? They were dead right, they were selfish and they should know because they knew themselves inside out and I didn't. I didn't even know myself inside out, let alone anyone else. Had I paid attention to that remark I might have saved myself a lot of bother. It taught me that if you 'hear' people they will tell you all about themselves .... all you have to do is believe them.

Try doing a spot of silent hearing today. It may take you a while to get the hang of it, weeks or months, it doesn't matter, just remember to be gentle on yourself because it is a thoroughly unsettling experience. Have a large gin because I plan to unsettle you some more when I get to 'love', but first .... Gene Pitney.

I am not remotely musical and I cannot play an instrument but I can tell Sibelius from Beethoven, The Supremes from Dire Straits, but that is about as far as it goes. I am a 'I know wot I loike' type of person and occasionally I surprise myself while shopping by singing along to the lyrics of Supertramp or Fleetwood Mac but only if they are blaring at me from the shop's loud speaker and the various bands can fill in the bits I cannot recall. I cannot recall any just now. My partner, on the other hand, is at the very rock face of music. From 1940 music hall artistes to the latest Arctic Marsupials, or some such, he can either sing along or, at the very least, he knows which beat is coming next and moves his body appropriately. I am hugely impressed by this as I have no rhythm at all and once, unwisely, took up flamenco dancing ..... we won't go into *that* humiliation.

One Saturday morning, my partner touched upon a difficult subject I thought I had long since dealt with. I suddenly found I was fighting back tears while getting a searing physical pain in my solar plexus that radiated up my neck settling into my left and right jaw. I noticed I had pulled my left [female] hand protectively over my upper abdomen [third chakra] while my right [male] hand was in a palm outward defensive posture, warding my partner off. I was amazed and so was he. The pain had settled in exactly the spot in my jaw where my arthritis periodically lingers, making it hellishly difficult to eat because I cannot get my molars to meet and, as I like my grub, this is a major problem. My partner immediately comforted me and I calmed down, but still, I realized I had a serious problem and I did not need comforting, I needed to be ……….. well … coaxed, needled, cross-questioned on this subject. I knew that my arthritis was a third chakra problem linked to suppressed anger with fifth chakra [jaw] involvement. I knew where the problem lay but I did not know the origin of the problem. I knew, theoretically, what might be emotionally driving my arthritis, but I did not know the point of entry of the wound, as it were. My reaction to the subject my partner had brought up was such an overwhelming one I decided I needed professional help to tackle it, someone who could question me but remain unemotional. My partner could not do this because he does not like to see me in tears, it upsets him.

Two weeks later I am driving home, very slowly, along country lanes from my second counselling session [where I had defined the nature of the 'energetic wound' as coming from an event where I felt victimised and invalidated - this is third chakra territory]. I was arguing with myself. Making excuses. Suddenly I heard an internal male voice say quite loudly and clearly, 'No, that was not acceptable behaviour from that person'. I was astounded and decided to pull over and listen up carefully. I restarted my argument and the voice repeated, 'No, it was not on'. I stared out of the car window wondering who the hell I was in conversation with, when suddenly Gene Pitney wailed into my ear, 'Something's got a hold of my heart, tearing my soul and my senses apart'. The car radio was not on. I was astounded because if you snapped your fingers in my face and demanded I sing a song … sing anything now, right now……….. I couldn't. Right now, with your snapping fingers ringing in my ears I am floundering to think of the lyrics to anything. Where, then, had I stored Gene Pitney? Why were the lyrics so incredibly apt to the moment? Something was indeed tearing at my heart because that is just what I had been discussing with my counsellor; fourth chakra [heart] forgiveness over my *perceived* 'victimisation' event.

Complete unconditional forgiveness, not second chakra forgiveness [which is putting your pistols down but knowing *exactly* which drawer of the kitchen dresser you put them in should you require them at a later date]. Fourth chakra forgiveness is big. BIG. It scares me because I know when I decide I will do it [for it is will, not can, of course I can] it will change me, utterly. There will be gains of wonderful proportions but there will be losses, there have to be. I know when I get there the losses won't matter, but from this side of the riverbank it looks jolly uncertain. Meanwhile, my third chakra is uncomfortably, unpleasantly unhappy and it is pressing against my diaphragmatic fourth chakra divide yelling, 'Time!' Meanwhile, during the four weeks that my four counselling sessions took in the morning I was, day after day, reaching for my big pale green sweater and pale pink scarf. 'Not that outfit, again, darling', my partner commented. 'I have to, I don't feel comfortable in anything else', I replied. Pink and green. I am sure you get my drift.

Have I crossed the river bank yet? Absolutely not. I am going to have some more swimming lessons first - anything to delay matters and by the way [just to change the hot and uncomfortable subject], counselling is great but have a goal and don't let the counselling become a holding pattern or an excuse to move forward.

Lastly, pay particular attention to songs in your head or the songs [humming or whistling] of others. I listen to my partner singing and I usually smile, but sometimes the lyrics he sings or hums make me stop what I am doing, go to him and pay him some serious attention. Listen carefully and hear the words.

*L*OVE

It's nice isn't it? It is extraordinary that such a nice thing should be so flaming difficult to get right, or even to get at all. If you were fantastically fortunate to have utterly normal and adoring parents and an uneventful life you will probably be all cosy and loved so you can skip the next bit, but for anyone else looking to be loved you need to know one simple thing - love, like charity, starts at home and home is you. Get you right, or as right as you can be and you will find you attract another right - Mr. or Miss Right, or Mr./Miss As Right As They Can Be At The Time. Just to confuse you completely, they are all Mr. or Miss Right, it is just that the less right you are the more unpleasant lessons Mr. or Miss Semi-Right bring with them.

Some years back [early nineties I think] I was watching Oprah on her show when she said, 'Love is not a feeling, it's behaviour'. I sat on the sofa staring at the telly while silently mouthing the phrase. I didn't understand it at all. I carried on silently repeating it for months. I sort of thought I understood it. Eventually, I got it. The penny dropped [so did my jaw] and it was not nice because I had to reassess, from my side and theirs, every relationship with anyone I had ever had. I had to ask myself some awkward questions about what did and what did not constitute 'loving behaviour' from them and from me. I was quite wobbly for months. Slowly, I began to make some sense of it all and, courtesy of Oprah's friend Maya Angelou, I made some measure of peace with myself by acknowledging her wise words, 'We do the best we can with the knowledge we have at the time - now we would do better'.

These days I have a handle on what love is. People who love you will show steadfast loving behaviour towards you. Their *actions* and their *touch* will be loving, *always.* You will have the odd blip, the odd row, the odd pinch or exasperated hand gesture but basically the behaviour and words are continually loving. If it is not, you have a problem. Your first hurdle is to acknowledge it. This can be very, very difficult in any relationship, but especially if the non-loving words, touch and actions are coming from a parent and even more difficult if it is spasmodic non-loving.

I have passed on 'love is not a feeling, it's behaviour' to many and I have been really surprised at how many people look at me blankly and then cannot repeat it, no matter how slowly and clearly I have said it. I have found this quite sad. We are all in such a muddle about love. True, unconditional love comes from fourth chakra and is incredibly rare. It only gives, it does not hold, restrain, judge or own because true fourth chakra love has no rules - it just loves. Most of planet Earth's humans are either mired in first chakra beliefs of what constitutes loving behaviour [I will only love you if you stay within our family/tribe, our family/tribal rules, our family/tribal religion - marriages must be made within those tribal limitations] and the rest are crashing around, literally, in the agenda-ridden minefield of second chakra [I cannot love you if you don't have some degree of money, power, looks, sex appeal - I might *stay* with you but I cannot really *love* you]. The best love option for us earthbound humans is third chakra love but you need some self-input before you can output, if you follow me. I am going to talk about 'input' in a minute.

If you are having problems in any relationship try asking yourself if your behaviour or their behaviour is/was loving. If it is not, always look for the fear factor, yours and theirs. Try and be honest. Behaviour encompasses words too, so are the words loving? Or honest? If someone says they adore their family but spend all their time at work, when it is not financially imperative, or else repeatedly doing something that is time consuming and away from the family home, then that someone is not being wholly honest about where the main love lies. We are back to hearing again. Too often we dismiss the truth because it is too painful, or fail to really hear the truth behind the disparaging remark or over the top teasing, but the remark would not be made if it was not on the radar screen, not thought about, not meant to some degree or other. So the next time you hear anyone making a rude remark about anyone else, take it seriously, no matter what the relationship between the two people is. If you are feeling brave you could point out to them the truth behind the words, but first make sure the back door is open in case you need to make a quick dash for it. We all want a nice love filled life and that starts with each and every one of us being brutally honest with ourselves. This is not easy or nice.

Here is a simple but really crucial love test, a first step to personal honesty. If you are single and you say you are looking for love, but not finding it, get your most reliable and kind best friend to ask you the following question [not now, but sometime later when you are not expecting it]. The question is, 'How much do you want to get married?'. Your friend can say, 'How much do you want a live-in partner?', if the word 'marriage' is a problem but partner HAS to mean 'live together - full time'. If your response is not, within a nanosecond, 100% affirmative with full eye contact, you are not yet ready for commitment. Any wavering, arm/hand closing gestures, moving of legs/feet or strangulated, protracted answers of ,'Well, y e e e s ... b u u t ….. means, 'I am not ready yet'. If you are right-handed and looking up to the right you are probably visually constructing something, possibly an unlikely future relationship with a libidinous film star. If you are looking up to the left it means you are visually remembering something, so you may be viewing an image of your last ghastly relationship and thinking, 'Not again ……. not blooming likely', and quite right too, you don't want another rehash of something that was beyond awful. You want to be loved. It is normal. It's just that saying it and meaning it are a whole different ball game. Saying it is just saying it. Meaning it is where the action is. To confuse you a bit - when you absolutely and completely mean something you will be quite still because there is always a *degree of stillness in deep truth.* There is nothing wrong with not being ready yet because your future beloved could be near or far, but also 'not quite ready yet'. Make the most of the time you have to get ready. Start liking yourself a lot because you will need plenty of third chakra self-like and self-love when lover boy or girl eventually turns up with their inevitable history of unpalatable past loves, quirky eating habits, dirty socks, noisy friends, interfering parents and credit card debt.

It is a sad but true fact of life that many of the people who need love most are often the most difficult to love. This is because without a degree of self-love you tend to run about trying to fill the void with love from another. This goes one of two ways - you will either repel [now or later] the other person because of your leaning and neediness or you will attract another who is quite like you, so now you have two people who don't really like themselves for the price of one. This is not a recipe for peaceful co-existence and can be expensive on paper hankies. Let's just go back to leaning for a second. It is interesting to watch the body language in relationships. You can start with looking at pictures of couples in magazines and newspapers. Are the couples united and together? See if a person is physically leaning towards the other. Is the other half of the couple reciprocating? There are, sadly, rather a lot of high profile couples who are far more in love with the camera than with each other. Loving couples [no matter how long they have been together] spend a lot of time looking at each other as they talk and the look will have softness [most of the time]. When you love you watch your beloved because you *always* want to *know* that they are *happy*. If you learn to look for imbalances in body language in other couples, then you will know when your own relationships are going wrong. This will strengthen your second and third chakra and open your sixth.

If you want a kind, loving and healthy relationship with another the work starts with you, so get yourself in shape whatever your body size. Preening and vanity are not self-love, they are fear and insecurity, so don't be mislead by that. How do you define love for oneself? Well I think it is kindness, being kind to yourself. No, not large boxes of choccies on the sofa or season tickets for favourite football teams, that is fun in your eyes, that is not being kind. I'm afraid kindness kicks off with that dreaded 'D' word. Stay in your seats ..... I'll just whisper it quietly .... discipline. Ghastly isn't it? Gets worse too, because it requires balls and we are not talking footie, we are talking courage. You have to have discipline to ensure you take care of your physical body and to train your thoughts to focus on sunny uplands and not go off awandering down dark alleys of people-pleasing, self-criticism and self-torture. This is where the 'input' is that I talked about earlier. Don't waste time trying to get other people to like you or to behave nicely towards you, they are only reflecting back to you the way you treat yourself. You are a walking mirror. Show yourself some serious respect and others will do likewise. I am going to run that one past you again because it is, like love, crucial. You are a walking mirror, people are reflecting back to you how you feel about and treat yourself. If you want respect you absolutely must have a measure of self-respect, this is a third chakra requirement. I hear any amount of teenagers wanting 'respect' who have no self-respect and what they really want is your fear - this is second chakra bullying of the nastiest kind.

Returning to courage, you need it to face some time alone and you will need a lot of courage to get rid of people in your life who are not kind to you, especially if they are apparent loved ones or family. Learn to hear their words, *all of them.* You may not have to make a sudden split or divorce people, just fill the hole in your third chakra [raising your vibratory rate] and the unloving will drift away. Neither the discipline nor the courage is easy and you may need to lie down in a darkened room with a peppermint-soaked lace handkerchief to your forehead before you read the next bit.

First and foremost start listening to yourself. You have to vigilantly monitor your thoughts from the moment you wake up. Put emergency brakes on your internal nagging and criticism. I have said it before but it is worth repeating, don't 'should' on yourself and while you are at it try not to 'should' on other people. I have made a conscious effort for several years to remove this word completely from my vocabulary and I have found it liberating, to say the least. I daresay everyone who is not now on the receiving end of my, 'You should do this', or, 'You should do that', is feeling liberated too. I have put 'should' into my rubbish bin marked 'Minding My Own Business', though my partner says I 'shoulded' on him the other morning. I told you he heard every word these days, didn't I? It's a nightmare. Next, assess just how happy or unhappy you are being on your own. I remember a startling occasion when I was living alone and busy telling everyone I wanted to be in a relationship. I was in my little cottage, it was a winter evening and I was on annual leave from the hospital. I could not afford to go away but I had spent the day doing some digging on my allotment, taking a long wintry dog walk, done a little painting and I was wearing my fetching new jumper bought for tuppence h'penny in a charity shop. My nice but frugal supper was in my tummy and my toes were competing with fireside space with my cat. My dogs were crashed out on their backs, paws in the air, snoring on the sofa. There was a good book by my side, a good film about to come on telly and I had a treat in my hand - a scotch. 'It doesn't get better than this', I announced with a satisfied sigh to the animals. Do you suppose my angels were listening? Do you think they heard every word? You better believe it. Why would I attract anything else when I was so satisfied with what I had got? I am not saying I didn't want more, I most certainly did, but not so badly that I focused on it most, if not all of the time. My commitment was not there. The total commitment arrived approximately one year before I met my partner and only wobbled slightly when I became extremely ill. So ….. just how happy or unhappy are you to be on your own? Let's get clear about that because I have had no end of girlfriends say to me, 'I'd like a part time boyfriend to take me out, someone to go with to the cinema or theatre'. Sounds nice doesn't it? But you don't learn anything having a nice time. Spiritual growth in the relationship department of second chakra is not about theatre tickets, red suspenders and a spot of 'how's your father' … well, not every day it isn't. The growth comes with all the messy bits of relationships that drive you round the twist, like his ghastly friends and her ghastly mother, unpaid bills, snoring, loo seats and, 'It's your turn to put the flaming rubbish out'. Growth comes from staying put and putting up *because* you love, or leaving with dignity and minimal damage because love *left*.

I truly believe you do not have to join things or go places to meet someone to love, all you have to do is stay exactly where you are and work on yourself. The more work you do on yourself the better that love will be when it shows up. Don't think this is an easy process, it isn't; it means shoving your grubby shortcomings under a microscope and then cleaning them up. Start by making absolutely sure you truly want a full time live-in partner. If you sail over that hurdle shouting, 'Yes!', then begin the process of finding love. Start approving of yourself *immediately*, there is no time to waste. If you do not approve of yourself you can expect someone to turn up and not approve of you either. It may start well, but sooner or later you will find that your internal self-inflicted nitpicking will be catching. Pretty soon there will be two of you at it, both aiming at the same exhausted target.

I remember when I was in my thirties, I read an article somewhere about a young woman full of boyfriend woes who had gone to visit her grandmother. Her grandmother's advice was this, 'Forget men. Concentrate on your work and getting your own home. When you are happy in your job and have a nice little place to go home to, the right man will come along'. I can remember reading that and passionately wishing some older and wiser woman had said that to me when I was twenty years of age. I think it is sound advice, but while you are establishing your work and home I do think you need to get clear in your head what you are looking for in a relationship and what type of person you want to be with. It is a good idea to write down what your ideal man or woman looks like because sitting down and actually physically writing a list means you are starting to take the subject seriously and love is a serious subject. On a piece of paper, list the most important attributes you want in that man or woman. What does your wish list include? Try and be practical as well as dreamy. Now, draw a line down the middle of the page and on the opposite side write down an equal number of your attributes; a list of what you have to offer that new and special person. How do the two lists look? Honestly? Girls [and I speak from experience] are good at drawing up a shopping list of things they want in a man but not so good at acknowledging what they have to offer, especially if they can't cook. A wish of 'I want to be looked after' is a favourite but usually only admitted after several glasses of wine to a very, very best friend and hotly denied the next sober day. Being looked after is lovely, but most men need grub sometime during the day in order to be able to look after a woman so, if you can't cook, you better put 'man who can cook' or 'financially loaded with resident chef' on your wish list. Likewise, if you are a man who cannot put up a shelf or mend anything you may need to put down 'a patient woman who can work a Black and Decker'. This may sound puny and small but self-recognition and honesty are huge and quite rare, in fact very rare. For me kindness, reliability, humour and shared interests are essential in a relationship but they may not be important to you. I also needed a partner who was good with machines [mine is brilliant and can fix/repair anything] because I hate complicated equipment and for me an ideal machine, of any description, would have two buttons only - 'off' and 'on'. Not too many of these about.

If you look at your side of the wish list and think things need improvement, first make a commitment to change whatever it is you want to change and then start with tiny movements. Don't do anything drastic or rash. The universe will hear your starter motor and will know if you are serious. Your angels, standing beside you, will be on full alert, watching, waiting and planning. Depending on how serious your commitment is they may be on the celestial phone to your future beloved's angels organising … 'The Meeting'. It might not be tomorrow, you may need to be patient but, meanwhile, urgently tackle the things you need to change about yourself and put health right up there on your list of priorities. You may not have been born with drop dead gorgeous looks but health gives a glow that is damned attractive and the better your diet and elimination the better your posture - that is a fact. Weak flabby muscles have not been properly *fed*. You don't need fabulous clothes, but clean is good, most people like it. Get stuck into the colour orange and check your boundaries, they may need sharpening. Even in the most healthy and loving relationships boundaries are essential because we don't want you doing doormat, do we? Bullies always make a bee-line for doormats. If you are in debt start correcting it in small but disciplined daily steps because by taking control of your second chakra finances you are less likely to meet someone with major money issues because that is how the deadly accurate universe works; be a spendthrift and you can bet your bottom dollar, if you have one left, that a penny-pinching purse-controller will pitch up and ask you for a date [and maybe even expect you to pay]. Then the fireworks begin. The spendthrift and white-knuckled purse holder [second chakra 'money' issues, for both] are operating from fear. The aim of the learning exercise is not to shout at one another, control the money or hide the new purchases but to find out where the fear stems from, on both sides, and replace the fear with love, on both sides. This is sixth chakra comprehension, third chakra instigation/follow through and second chakra repair - all together, it is spiritual progression. You can replace the spendthrift/purse controller with any scenario you like - lazy/workaholic …. my brain has gone dead, I can't think of another, but perhaps you can.

Next, start doing little things on your own. Take a walk, go to the cinema, visit a gallery. Don't be a wimp. You may suddenly find you are the best company you ever had and you will certainly have more things to talk about. I have a friend who assumes the world and his wife will be thinking she will be seen as a sad figure going to the cinema, theatre or whatever, alone. I think she is completely wrong. I always admire people who do things alone because often they look special - they have chutzpah. Make yourself into a 'place of safety' so that you enjoy coming home to you. When you have sorted out your thinking and created a warm, comfortable and loving internal landscape then that is what the world will reflect back to you. Now agenda-free people with a decent level of self-esteem start showing up in your life. These people are generally much nicer than people who do not like themselves.

Living alone gives you time to look at your strengths and weaknesses and to build up self-reliance. When you know you can handle anything life throws at you then you are going to make a solid, reliable mate but when you need to lean against someone you are not balanced and liable to emotionally fall over if they move away. Living alone can be a way of avoiding intimacy with another but likewise, relationships can be a way of avoiding intimacy with oneself. So too can a very hectic family life, too much time or concentration on work or a highly active social life. Living alone for too long can be a way of avoiding the next step of intimacy, which is being able to voice your very deepest fears and needs to your partner and to have that fear or need respectfully and compassionately heard. I have found this 'speaking out' part of a relationship a bit difficult, but bit by bit I am building a partnership with a man that I can be honest with and he with me. We both hope that by building an honest 'today' we can hope for an honest future together. This is what we hope and build for, but nothing is certain and I have no idea if we will still be together in ten or twenty years time.

Your age is immaterial when it comes to looking for love, in fact things may move faster if you are older because there will be a certain sense of urgency and you will definitely be more appreciative of love if you are wiser and a bit bruised. Love arrived late for me but age has made us both appreciate how delicate and precious our love is. Over the years I have watched many couples delicately and preciously loving their children, or animals, but failing to do the same for one another, yet the love between a couple is the primary relationship. It is the one left staring over the morning cornflakes when the children are gone. When I was a midwife, in my thirties, my colleagues asked me relentlessly, 'Are you courting yet?'. I would take a very deep breath, clench my fists and offer a strangulated, high pitched, 'Not yet!'. But let me tell you …. a few years, husbands, children, troubles and financial hardships later those self-same colleagues would hiss at me, 'You don't know how lucky you are on your own, doing as you please, when you please'. I would smirk off down the corridor. Like families, love relationships can be the best or the worst of things and I believe it's better to wait and get it right than have years of regret, a cold marital bed or an horrendous divorce.

I am repeating myself but I truly, honestly believe that you do not have to go anywhere to look for your man or your woman. Get your thinking straight and the right person will ring your doorbell, sit next to you on the train or plane, or collide into your shopping trolley at the supermarket. I am speaking from personal experience as I was once given just this advice.

Following one of my annual deep and meaningful conversations with an extraordinary and far-seeing huge male chimney sweep, I made the mistake of asking him about my loveless state. He thumped one massive fist into his opposite palm three times, while thundering so loudly it made my ornaments rattle. 'You are far too intelligent to be asking this sort of question', he roared, 'you are the block, you are the block, you are the block. You don't have to go anywhere or do anything but sort out your head and unlock your heart and then he will walk up the drive'. I knew he was right, though I did not want to admit it. Six months later the man I now adore walked up my drive. There are three morals to this tale, which I have deliberately foreshortened. The first is, never ever underestimate a very large man in a once white, but now coal black [literally] van. Two, try to look your best when you answer your doorbell because you never know who is ringing it [only kidding]. Three, real personal honesty can be hellishly evasive. Having said that, I am now of the opinion that my chimney-sweep was right, but only partially in my case. I think I was in the realm of a sacred contract with my partner and that contract had a pretty precise start date [more later].

I want to point out the dark side of Mr. or Miss Right, who might look to others like Mr. or Miss Not Right At All. Your family and pals may look uneasily at your new choice of mate. Instinctively they will know something doesn't feel right and they will be concerned because they want the best for you, but if your self-esteem is at rock bottom OR you have unresolved issues relating to your relationship with your mother or father then Mr. or Miss Not Right At All will come along to highlight your lack of self-esteem or whatever went wrong with Pa or Ma. This is how chakra strengthening lessons work and they may take the form of a relationship full of alienating, sniping, rows, fighting [gosh, singledom is starting to look good], or perhaps failing to show respect, to thank, to listen, forgetting birthdays, controlling or neglectful behaviour. These unpleasant happenings are how we learn to take our power back; by refusing to snipe back, by insisting birthdays are remembered, by seeing the fear behind the row, by having the self-respect to object to being controlled and, if necessary, packing your bags and walking right out of an abusive relationship. This is how you grow, by having someone come into your life and highlight all your dark cobwebby corners. Frankly, I would rather hold a torch to feather dust my corners myself and just have nice people in my life. As Caroline Myss and Wayne Dyer have pointed out so hilariously, your soul mate is most definitely *not* the dreamy beloved who shares your taste in exotic fruit, soft music and finishes your sentences. Oh no, soul mates are the ones who bug the hell out of you. A soul mate knows exactly which button to press to wind you up to finger jabbing, teeth grinding fury while your face flushes a fetching shade of cardinal red. How else would you grow up? By eating grapes on a hammock, listening to Bach, Barbra Streisand or Scissor Fingers [is that right?], with someone who agrees with every word you say? I think not. Hammock pals are comforters when it all gets too, too much. Soul mates prod you until you spiritually grow or collapse in a heap. Best to grow quickly because then you are no fun to prod - no fun at all. When you have grown nicely, Mr. or Miss Nicely will show up and you can have a lovely time with love.

*L*AUGHTER

I daresay every generation complains about the humour of the next generation but I find so little to laugh at on the television these days. There is so much coarseness, even cruelty, and so little gentle but witty cleverness. Thank God for Rabbi Lionel Blue who recently made us laugh uproariously for well over an hour while offending no-one [though offence, without malice behind it, can be hilarious]. I flew into Darwin some years back and immediately had all my Balinese booty confiscated. I was aghast. The next day I had to take a taxi to some out of town warehouse and the two gentleman who ran the place were so rude about me, my nationality and my Balinese bits and bobs that I nearly made myself physically sick laughing. When one man unwrapped one of my carved wooden thingies and an ant came out [ok two ants ..... ok several, but they were *very small*] they were met with such an hysterical hail of abuse that my knees buckled and I was literally hanging onto the desk to stop myself sliding onto the floor. My stomach hurt for days and I will love those two men until my dying day. Later, Peter the coach driver and Steve the pilot were equally rude about me, but they also told me hilarious stories that made my hair curl. Were the stories accurate? Who cares? This sort of humour was par for the course when I was a child, but we are humourless in Britain these days and I don't hold out much hope for Australia if it goes on being suburbanised. At least Darwin is outbackish. It's full of strange people - I simply loved it and felt right at home there.

I desperately miss not being able to relax into a funny programme. I always liken it to listening to a really good singer and being able to relax and enjoy their singing because you know they can push a word or beat to its limit but then effortlessly pick it up again. There are many who emulate Frank Sinatra but few who can manage to control a song the way he could. It is the same with most of today's humour - I am edgy. I have such happy early memories of relaxing family moments when each of us was rolling off our chairs roaring with laughter while watching or listening to a humorous television or radio programme. I miss Stanley Baxter and I do wish someone could persuade Robin Williams to take his place and do a Christmas special for the world to laugh at. I feel Mr. Williams is missing his sacred contract. He could poke fun at everyone and bring down mental barriers. He is a very funny man living in a time when humour is so desperately needed.

I find it difficult to comprehend why we are bludgeoned with poor taste humour on television but workplace humour is frowned upon, or worse. The forces used to be very keen on humour and my father could recount endless tales of tit-for-tat shenanigans that would have a whole RAF station giggling. I remember that the Canadians aircrews were mighty keen on reciprocal practical jokes aimed at their British counterparts; swiped mascots and moose heads clocked up a lot of air-miles in aircraft designed for more deadly passengers. Their antics, retold by my father over an evening gin, even had my mother tittering in the kitchen. 'Boys will be boys', she would sigh at me.

I suppose every generation has its own humour and what makes me giggle would not amuse youngsters today. Or would it? I was lucky enough, in the first half of my nursing life to laugh a lot - much of it silently, as we were trained not to laugh out loud in case a grieving relative was offended. Even in such a strict nursing environment practical jokes were the order of the day and in my training hospital a great deal of energy was expended on thinking up new ways to infuriate pompous senior members of staff. In several hospitals I worked in, Christmas leniency allowed for slightly lubricated and rather hairy rugby players, in wigs and pink tutus, to patrol the wards [doctors? I couldn't possibly comment] while tipsy voices took over the tannoy system and made impossible requests or announcements that had us nurses holding up the walls and weeping with hilarity. Ambulance drivers behaved impeccably, most of the time, the rest of the time was hugely enjoyed by all. Working in theatres was a minefield of naughtiness. I had a couple of hideous experiences, one of which was the very first time I was scrubbed for an operation. I was staring at rows and rows of what looked like impossible cutlery with ridiculous names while waiting for the surgeon [well known for his temper tantrums] and the start of a double hernia repair. I was completely and utterly terrified. Moments before the surgeon appeared, as I stood scrubbed, shakily ready and unable to retaliate because I dare not contaminate my gloved hands, a second anaesthetist, who was skulking aimlessly about, shot his hand up my theatre dress and tried to remove my knickers. I knew only too well that nurses knickers were collected for the flag pole outside the doctors mess and their fluttering indicated that more than a trophy had been taken. My only course of preventative action was to spread my legs as far as possible to stop the knickers from dropping further. I successfully suspended them at knee height moments before the surgeon kicked open the door and we were on the surgical off. I performed my scrub nurse duties magnificently while in the position of a giraffe at a water hole. After the successful operation I left the theatre walking as if on outstretched skis and readjusted myself. *It was now war.* The anaesthetist, an Australian of course [we had quite a few male Aussie docs and they behaved appallingly - we *simply* adored them], was sorely outnumbered by student nurses who screamed with hilarity at my tale and whooped with laughter planning revenge. Revenge was had ..... censored ... sorry.

Years later, at another hospital, hostilities broke out again, but this time the nurses were being lined up in the sights of policemen who would ring in the early hours of the morning declaring, 'This is *** ****** Police Station and it's war'. If coppers, cadging midnight coffee, on quiet patient and criminal nights were careless enough to leave their panda cars unlocked .. well ... they had it coming, we thought. A decoy was used to make the coffee and the rest of us would tiptoe out to extravagantly decorate the car, inside and out, with things pleasant and not so pleasant. Our grand finale was a metal bedpan tied, on a lengthy piece of string, to the exhaust. We would watch the panda car pull away, string unravel, bedpan fly up and as the bedpan came crashing noisily down we would run and hide. We always won the skirmishes because we knew which cupboards to hide in and they always forgave us our antics and brought us fresh doughnuts from the all night bakery, if they could. None of these antics interfered with the extremely high standards of nursing care. It also promoted a strong bond between working staff because humour always unites and the bond extended to those put upon police officers, which was just as well because they saved our bacon on numerous occasions when we were confronted by fists or weapons. Bless you and thank you, each and every one. I feel really sorry for the nurses of today. All work and no play. It stems from the top of course. You can always tell what the hierarchy is like, in any establishment, by the manner of the staff. We checked into The Taj Residency Hotel in Cochin [Ernakulam, India] and an hour later, as we were leaving to sight-see, I told the receptionist [called Cindrella - truly - and she was adorable, even without the 'e'], that the hotel had an outstanding manager. 'He *is* wonderful - how did you know?', she asked. 'Because he has infused the whole hotel with good service and happiness', I replied. In Britain, humourless government officials lacking second and third chakra power have infected the whole country and television has followed suit. Humour has become almost a dirty word but you need laughter in every walk of life and you especially need it in hospitals to counteract all the grim and sad reality of sickness and death.

*L*OOK

I met a woman recently who told me of a charming expression that she had learned as a child. Apparently it originated from up north but exactly where 'up north' was uncertain. The visited would fling open the front door and the visitors would say, 'We have come to look at you'. I just love it! How utterly charming and how utterly right. I fully intend to remind myself of this next time I fling open the front door to a visitor while thinking, 'The house is untidy'. The house is always untidy but my visitor has come to look at me, not the dust.

*L*ANGUAGE

I am hoping for a return to the British language. I am greatly in favour of regional accents but I am hugely depressed by the growing national habit of speaking as if one's mouth is full of food, dropping letters off the beginning and ends of words and peppering every single sentence with 'like'. Enough. please, enough. To get your point across and to be heard we need to hear the t of to, g of get, p and t of point and besides, speak clearly and you will gain power because people will automatically listen and pay attention to you. The media have to lead the way in this because even the younger members of the royal family are stuttering, like, y'know. It is enough to make Shakespeare weep.

$\mathcal{M}$ Is for MYSS

Dr. Caroline Myss [pronounced 'mace'] studied theology, is an author, a pioneer and international lecturer on energy medicine and human consciousness. She is the expert on chakras but also a medical intuitive. All she needs is your name, age and permission and she is off, like Starship Enterprise boldly going, via split infinitives, into the uncharted territories of your body where she will know what is wrong with you and why you got what you got. Nothing is hidden from her, not even your favourite brand of biscuits. She is a bit special, to say the very least. Let me give you a handful of her wise words ......'The universal jewel within the four major religions is that the Divine is locked into our biological system in seven stages of power that lead us to become more refined and transcendent in our personal power.'

Several years back a friend gave me a tape of one of Caroline's lectures. I stood in my kitchen stock-still and stunned, the only thing that moved was my finger as I pressed the buttons on my tape recording machine, going … stop, rewind, play …. stop rewind, play ….. stop, rewind, play. I can remember the feeling of overwhelming relief in that suddenly I was not alone and not completely loony. A thousand observations and feelings I felt sure about but could not fully explain and hundreds of completely incomprehensible things I had witnessed during my life, not least during my nursing years, fell into place and made sense of my world. I don't know why Caroline resonated with me like no other teacher, but resonate she did and I am so very grateful to her.

Dr. Myss, an author in her own right, teamed up with an American neurosurgeon, Norm Shealy, and they co-wrote 'The Creation of Health' [The Emotional, Psychological and Spiritual Responses that Promote Health and Healing], a book that merits the widest possible audience and certainly a must for anyone working in the therapeutic world. I have told any amount of people about this book but I am no longer surprised if it is not followed up because you have to be ready for it and sadly most are not. I do believe it is well past time that their work [and all the others working in the same field] became mainstream. We have to grow up about sickness. The time for just pill popping is over, we need to reach a level of maturity about our health and stop behaving like a bunch of badly behaved adolescents expecting someone else to 'fix' the physical mess we may have made of our bodies and to grasp some level of personal understanding of our emotional and spiritual problems. I think most people have accepted that a certain type of personality [type A, I think they call it] is more likely to have a heart attack. Well, it is time we moved on and embraced the many different 'types' from A to Z and that each one is likely to develop specific health problems. Over many years, I made my own health problems and that is why it is up to me to sort out my sickness because no-one else has my life experiences, my hurts, my happiness, my anger, my diet, my evacuations and my lifestyle. I have yet to meet a doctor who would be able to read me like Caroline can. She is not reading me because I am not brave enough. I will work me and my sickness out on my own, step by excruciating step.

Sacred contracts aside, and I think we are in this territory, if I needed a spur to write this book it was Caroline that provided the impetus. She is a teacher for 'our time' and we all need to listen to her. You can listen to her and dismiss what she says, she will not be offended because she understands you better than you do. Apart from nature it takes something special to impress me, usually it is creative work in some form or another, but I am hugely impressed with the Truth and that is what Caroline is about. I will list her books at the back of this book but she has made quite a few tapes of her lectures and she us still doing workshops in Britain. Hear her if you can, she has a huge sense of humour, unique vision and a warm and kind personality.

MONEY

Money is banknotes and coins but it is also a state of mind. Would you agree with that? No? Well, I think I am right about this. When I was a twenty year old woman, I passionately wish someone had told me .... YOU GET WHAT YOU THINK YOU ARE WORTH. This goes for everything in life, your lover, car, spouse, house, job and your bank balance. Took me years to work this one out.

I know all about managing on a shoe string and I know a little about having money but, I don't know anything about entrepreneurially making money [yet], so I'll just talk about the first two. Let's get down to basics. How much do you think you are worth? I am not *remotely* interested in your salary or your savings. I don't care what your house and car are valued at, I want to know what you think you are worth. Put a price tag on your personality.

Have you thought about it? How much? £2.50? £20,000,000? Oooops [for both!]. I have often asked clients or friends moaning about lack of funds this same question and there are several predictable responses. The first [major problem] is that the person who is asked does a fast hand clamp over their pubic bone [second chakra], their body concaves slightly, head turns away, their throat dries up and I proceed to back right off. The next response is astonishment at the question because the thought has never entered their head. The third is amusement with no eye contact and a lot of ermmmming and arrrrhhhhing. The fourth is some large sum of money, courtesy of the lottery, followed by guffaws of laughter. Occasionally you get a real pro who suggests a huge sum and I am nearly convinced except for the tiny movements of toe, thumb, finger, or swallowing. All of them are not serious about money and you need to get serious about money because money likes to be taken seriously.

Let me give you an example. Some years back a client was moaning about lack of funds so I stood them up in front of a mirror. Standing behind them I asked, 'How much do you think you are worth?'. Hadn't a clue, so I asked, 'How much would you like to win on the lottery?'. 'Oh, erm, three million.' Giggle, giggle. 'You are not serious, so I suggest you come down to an amount you feel comfortable with ... what do you think that would be?', I asked. 'Oh, er, one million', laugh, head toss, giggle, fidget, fidget. 'Ok, you are not serious, so come right down'. We got down to a fidgety and amusing five hundred thousand, followed by a second chakra covering two hundred thousand with swallowing that would make a python proud. Down, down, down and down we came until I got what I was looking for... at around three hundred pounds I got a flash of temper, hallelujah, but still we were twisting and turning, chin tilting and failing to make eye contact in the mirror. Eventually we got down to the very most bottom of the bottom line .... a fiver and tears, so I closed the subject rapidly. The interesting thing was that this person was always down to their last fiver. I explained to them that something absolutely momentous had just taken place, in that they had acknowledged just how bad their problem was. Now they knew what their basement looked like they could set about rectifying it in slow and small incremental steps. They were not impressed. People want quick fixes but I knew it was going to be a long journey because this is *healing* [this is not just second chakra repair, it is also the pathway to self-esteem and self-love.

Stay on the path and you leave people behind; deep down we all know this, that is what makes healing so difficult]. I watched their choice of colours for several months. Jammed. When you are ready to shift a block, whatever it is, you change your colours. Different cellular vibration requires matching colour vibration.

How is your basement? This exercise is really difficult to do on your own. You need someone to help you and to watch your body language, every last tiny detail. What you are aiming for is to find out just how comfortable you are with money and how much you want to attract into your life. There is an awful lot of personal dishonesty when it comes to money, in fact there is a lot of personal dishonesty when it comes to everything, especially relationships, and I think financial hardship is often the glue that holds rocky relationships together. Therefore, a sudden financial windfall can really rock the boat of an already unstable union.

We all want money, it is normal, but being in a state of denial is also normal, unfortunately. Most people say they want to win the lottery but do not understand the problems that come with a massive change in funds and income. Your whole life can be turned upside down because it changes the dynamics of relationships. It can bring family feuding, friendships snapping under the strain, resentful neighbours and hangers on appearing from nowhere. You may find yourself moving away somewhere and having to start a whole new life from scratch, new friends included. This may sound like good news but a few months down the line you could end up feeling lonely and disorientated and partially, if not fully, pining for the simplicity of the life you once led and understood. You need to get real about the emotions you attach to money so start by asking yourself how you would feel if your sister/brother, neighbour or pub pal won ten million on the lottery. Be honest. Would you expect them to give you something? If so, why? Would you still love them if they didn't give you anything? How would you feel if they started having exotic holidays, flash cars and a bought a mansion with a swimming pool and a private cinema? It would be unsettling, at the very least. You might not want to visit them but that's ok, because they might not want to see you either. You might clash with the décor or their new found friends. Big financial windfalls can be very disruptive; I have been saying for years that Premium Bond and lottery wins would be a thousand times more helpful and cohesive for this country if there were much, much lower wins and many more people winning - but we can't have helpful and cohesive can we? Far too sensible.

The ability to pull money into your life, and then keep it, is a profound second chakra lesson. I am going to take a deep breath and say it is even a spiritual lesson. Money is, after all, just paper and metal, we put the value on it. We seem to have a notion that having money and being spiritual don't marry but that is nonsense. Money is just another form of energy. If you can attract money you can do wonderful things with it but you cannot write out big cheques to your favourite charity if you are always just scraping through life yourself. Now, there will always be the odd person who is a lazy whatsit who comes into a bucket of money for bugger-all effort. Either ignore them or use your fury and indignation as a spur to move you into moneyland. Learn from the ones who get money but can't keep it; they get it, but don't think they are worthy of it so they let the money slip through their fingers until they reach a pitch, or bank balance, or level of debt they feel comfortable with. It's vibration again. I know this will sound a bit extreme but, debt attracts attention and, for some, any attention is better than no attention [same with being ill, you get attention and some people don't want to give that up ... while hotly denying such an outrageous, but true, statement]. If you are financially struggling can you change your vibration and attract money? Absolutely. Can you do it quickly? That depends how brutally honest you can be with yourself and how much work you are prepared to do to mend your chakras.

So how do you go about attracting money? You start examining your attitudes to it under a microscope. Understand this, if you are resentful of others who have money or nice things you need to stop it immediately. Moneyed people are in the money flow. They may be rubbish at other things in life like health, relationships, creativity, kindness, humility or even basic humanity but that is their problem and that is what they are here to work on. Believe me, their time will come, because angels have no respect for kings or billionaires, all are grist to their banana skin mill. Money does not necessarily bring you good friends, a happy marriage, healthy happy children or loving care in old age. Money does not protect you from sickness, the rich get cancer too and money CANNOT buy you authentic self-esteem, you have to earn that. Nevertheless, people with money are on the money flow train and you need to get on the train with them. No good standing on the platform staring at the people in the first class carriage and thinking, 'Bastards', because if you are doing this, even a teeny weeny bit, you are going nowhere. You have to stand on the platform, look in and think, 'I want that, that's for me, I deserve that, I am going to have that right now'. Now, do it [in your imagination]. Sit down in the cheaper train seat, close your eyes, take a deep breath and see yourself walking into the first class train carriage, sitting down and someone coming to serve you expensive food on a silver platter. What is your reaction? How comfortable do you feel? Where is the discomfort? Come on, be honest, which chakra is pulling, quaking, queasy, butterflying? Try another one. Get on the plane and turn left. Take a lovely stretched out seat and have the air hostess pour you champagne. Notice someone famous sitting a couple of seats away from you. Open up the duty free magazine, spot a fancy gold watch and think, 'Just the ticket for time keeping on my new yacht', and buy it. Write out the big cheque and hand it over. How are you feeling? Seriously? What's your body language telling you? What are you thinking? Are you thinking, 'This is a ridiculous waste of money, economy is fine for me'? What exactly is going through your mind? Because whatever negative thoughts are running through your mind are your financial blocks. Which chakra is it hitting? Your bottom area, first chakra? Who in your tribe/family would not approve of you coming into money? Would your tribe/family insist on you handing over all or part of the money? Is it hitting second chakra? Would a huge bucket of money affect your marriage? [oh boy, such a biggy, how honest can you be about this one?]. Is it making your third chakra wobble? Who first told you that you are a worthless piece of you know what? Or that you expect too much, you won't amount to anything, you won't earn much. These statements would either have been the trigger for, 'I'll show you!', or a victim's retreat and, for most, it is the latter. Don't beat yourself up about this, don't take over from where someone else started the process. Don't self-criticise, life is tough enough. Cut yourself some slack and have a gin and tonic. Tomorrow is another brand new day.

Whether you have no money at all, you are earning minimum wage and struggling, or just managing, whatever your money issue is, you will not break out of that until you start to challenge your financial blocks. Money has to reside *within you,* not be an energy form that lives *outside* of you. Your money is in your lower back, remember 'second chakra'? To hold the energy of money internally you need to first establish whether you have a poverty consciousness, whether you are in a holding pattern or actually pushing money away. First check your wardrobe and the colours you wear. How do you feel about wearing orange? Are you wearing restrictive stripes? Next, you have to hear your every word and every thought. Practice listening to other people first - it's easier. You will be amazed because people make holding pattern statements about money all the time or even downright derogatory remarks about money and/or people with money, but ask them if they want to win the lottery and they all say, 'Yesss!!!' . I was fascinated by a man I met a few years back. He was a really lovely bloke but he was also constantly broke. He made continual rude remarks about money and/or people with money. Once, I actually heard him say he hated money. Now, would you stick around someone who said they hated you? No, and it appeared money didn't stick around him either, so watch your thoughts and speech. If you are making negative noises about dosh, correct them. Work on changing your state of mind about money every single day. If your finances are in a parlous state you have probably distanced yourself from luxury, it just does not come anywhere near your radar screen. This is embracing a poverty consciousness so go out and buy a glossy magazine and, when you are on your own, go through it slowly. Look at the ads. Pick out one that shows a really expensive car [skip going green, you can do that later]. Drive that fabulous car. Change gears, press the accelerator, turn the wheel [who is watching you drive past and are they cheering for you or looking sulky?]. Keep going through the magazine and look at all the pictures. Find a holiday one. Feel that white sand under your feet and the breeze in the palm trees. Imagine yourself wearing that expensive jewellery - it does not matter a jot if you are a leather, pebble and feather necklace type of eco-girl. If the diamond jewellery makes you feel uncomfortable because you think you are ambushing the Kalahari bushmen's tribal lands, you will not get the money, but if you can clear the block and make the money, you can hand it over to Survival who have taken up the Kalahari bushmen's cause. Are you with me? This is where money makes you authentically powerful. Not because it buys you some completely daft diamond-studded toothbrush but because you can change the world profoundly when you have it, while at the same time living a quiet eco-friendly life and wearing a leather, pebble and feather necklace. Now you really rock, because you have grace. You are grounded and authentically loving and respecting mother Earth while at the same time respecting and elevating others.

You don't wear pebble necklaces? I know you - you are Mum. You have to sort out the kids first. You get a couple of grand and you split it between the nippers, leaving not a shred for yourself. You get five grand and split it between the nippers and have dinner out with hubby for the first time in years and think you have given yourself a treat. The nippers, all six foot of them, have taken the money no problem, because they think they are worth it. Am I hitting a button? Is that an ouchy nerve I touched? Here's the deal. Pick a sum your second chakra can deal with …. say one thousand pounds [go for less if that sum is making you nauseous or you have twitched your legs, fiddled with your fingers, thumb especially]. Ask the universe for exactly that sum and keep doing it until you get it. When it arrives you have to spend every single penny on yourself .... can you do it? NO, not a new washing machine .... blimey you are hard work, you are. We are talking luxuries that only you can use or have, you rascal you. Frocks and facials, you get my drift. This is big, ladies, so pay attention. This sends out a message that you deserve monetary recognition for all the nappy changing, washing, school runs and sleepless nights. If you can pass this test and spend the money on yourself you will have made a major breakthrough, cleared a second chakra hurdle, filled a second chakra hole. You can split the next windfall with the six foot nippers, better still, give them a loan and teach them the way of the world. My very first job earned me weekly wage of £11. I was seventeen and living with my parents. I came home clutching my first pay packet and my father put out his hand for £4 - for rent and board. 'You must understand, ducky, this is the way of the world. We have educated you and now you must learn to stand on your own two feet. You will learn to pay now to prepare you for the time when you have to pay for your own roof.' Later my father loaned me the money to buy my first car and I paid every penny back to him. This lesson taught me two things. The first was an immensely positive one, which was to stand on my own two feet as soon as possible. The second was a negative one in that I was not worthy of a small gift in recognition of a major turning point my life, maybe a week's pay packet grace, or the gift of a steering wheel. These things need to be balanced. My very personal view is that turning points need more recognition and celebration than most birthdays because turning points often require a spiritual shift or shift of perception. Birthdays come and go but first jobs mean fully embracing adulthood and first cars mean freedom coupled with huge responsibility because a badly driven car is a potential killer.

Now, let's go back to that sudden pot of dosh. 'Windfall? What windfall? Chance would be a fine thing!', I hear you mutter. Use a £1000 windfall only if you can get your brain round it and then drop it to second chakra, where the money pulling power lives. If you cannot envisage a grand make it something less, something you can get a handle on. Find out what your basement sum is. I don't care if it is only a fiver, a fiver is fine and a perfect place to start. Now, set your sights on twenty-five pounds. Cut out a picture of money and put it on your fridge door or anywhere else you can see it regularly. Start your day asking the universe for twenty-five quid and end your day exactly the same. Concentrate. Don't look up, stay focused and definitely don't start comparing yourself to anyone else, with or without money. That's them, this is you and you are all you have got, if you think about it. Decide how you will spend that twenty-five quid on something nice for yourself when it arrives. You must spend the first bit on yourself, you must, take my word for it because it's a celebration of a breakthrough, so acknowledge it. Sometimes you don't actually get handed twenty-five quid because the universe likes to work in cack-handed, convoluted ways so you may get someone offering to drive the kids to school for a week and that saves you the twenty-five quid, or someone might offer you a free hair do. It is the same thing. Just accept graciously because to refuse is to say you do not want the monetary value of the gift. When you have cracked the twenty-five quid, jack it up to fifty. If the fifty doesn't materialise after a few weeks or months, go down to thirty-five or forty, because that may be your comfort level. Nothing wrong with that, you are just recognising that somewhere along the line you have loaded in false information about money and what you are worth and, if the message was big, the correction will be big too, so go slowly and at your own pace. Do what you can to increase your income all the while because, by doing so, you are strengthening your second chakra power base. If you can generate some extra income like making jam or selling some garden plants, do it. I don't know what you do if you live in a city, you must be able to sell something that's legal; your call [but not your call-girl ...... still, pays well, I hear]. This is not about making and selling a pot of raspberry jam, this is about second chakra repair work and raising your third chakra [discipline] level of self-esteem. If you are at work, put in some overtime but watch out for gifts, or a tip [even a colleague buying you a sandwich is a gift] and be sure to thank the person who gave it to you and the universe, or God, or whomsoever you believe in, because *gratitude* is *vital.* Never, ever walk past a coin in the street. Pick it up and say thank you. Yes, I know they glue some down, the swines, I too have made a tit of myself. Keep this up every day and do the magazine exercise of imagining yourself having luxuries because they, and money, must become part of you, not outside of you. When you have cracked the fifty quid, increase it to one hundred and so on and so forth.

When you are ready, ask for a salary increase but make sure you know you are worth it. Salaries are a minefield. I hear no end of people who think they are the bees' knees because they earn a big salary, but that is being paid what *someone else* thinks you are worth. This territory can be extremely dangerous if you suddenly find yourself redundant in middle-age and you discover that you have a hole in your second chakra so cannot pull money in [or get another job earning the same salary]. Self-employed people, particularly craftsmen and women, are at the cutting brutal edge because they make, do or repair something and then have to charge for it while face to face with the buyer. For many this is hard. Imagine this ... paint a painting, no matter what your talent, and stand in a street in a city holding the painting in one hand and a price tag for the painting in the other. How much do you think you could sell your particular painting for? If it is a finger painting and you are asking £500 you are either a celebrity or in denial. I have to say I paint quite well but the idea of standing in a city street trying to flog one of my pictures fills my second chakra with diarrhoeaic dread. Imagine if I had to do it to put food on the table. Nightmare! I could sell fruit and veg, but then I didn't create them. Hope my angels are not listening ..... and planning. I will put on some loud music and confuse them ..... smokescreen, smokescreen.

Ok, enough of that. Does this principle of pulling money in work? Yes, but you have to be committed and watch out for any tendencies you have not to care for your money because money likes a safe pair of hands. Do you leave your wallet out where people can see it? Handbag? Do you always lock your car? Check your bank statements carefully? Shred financial documents? Take unnecessary risks with money or take risks that could cost you a lot of money in repairs/replacements/fines? These are all messages of carelessness. You also need to ask yourself where all your views on money came from. Usually they were heard from the pram such as 'Money does not grow on trees' [which is nonsense because farmers sell apples ... as long as they are in New Zealand, but don't get me started on *that* and besides, I am particularly fond of one hairy Kiwi apple farmer, what a gent!]. I am sure you can think of some more homespun financial homilies that set you off on the wrong track and these will have been reinforced right through childhood from one or other parent who couldn't pull in money either. Although this is changing now, I have found people are more willing to talk or brag about their sex lives than tell you how much money they earn or, more importantly, how much debt they are in. To me this says money is much more of an issue than sex to most people though you would never grasp that from watching television or reading a magazine. Any young man or woman who tells you they went out last night on the town and 'pulled', while failing to mention they 'pushed' their credit card debt up in the process, is in a dreadful muddle and hardly a safe pair of hands in either category. You cannot pull love and you push money around at your peril.

DEBT. Right, let's get down to it. You have to get out of it as fast as your little leggies will carry you. I have said it before but I am saying it again money means £reedom. Economically the future does not look good. A downturn will affect everyone, one way or another, some much worse than others. Wake up to this now please. Clear your debt as fast as you can then chip away at your mortgage.

I am, of course, hugely influenced by the fact that my parents lost pretty much everything when I was in my late teens and what that taught me was three things. Firstly, that everyone *needs* a home, a sanctuary, no matter how humble or small and you do not want to be renting, at the mercy of landlords and/or a topsy turvy economy, when you are old. I don't care what they do on the continent, that's them and this is you and me, here and now. Secondly, that borrowing money against the value of your home is a very dangerous thing to do at any age, but in your middle years it could be suicidal. Thirdly, if you suddenly find you get seriously ill, made redundant, hate your work, want to retrain, or fall out of love, your debt [including your mortgage] will be a millstone around your neck - 'mud on your wings'. Let me tell you about my money background.

You could say I picked the wrong trade because nursing was always excruciatingly badly paid but I look back with a level of pride in the work I did. I reckon I did my national service and then some, but I now realise I spent most of my life nursing sick people while also nursing a personal poverty consciousness. My mother was not the only person who said I could stretch a pound further than just about anyone and because I was so good at it, I trapped myself into it. When you are really good at something, you enjoy it, but I didn't realise the pleasure of 'making do and mend' prevented me from 'having'. I was always completely stunned how I continually just managed to cope on my wages. Occasionally there would be a small windfall, fifty or a hundred quid of unexpected money but it *always* came at around the same time as an unexpected car repair bill, or something similar, and the repair bill was invariably about fifty quid or a hundred. It was uncanny, I thought, not realising that I was calling the shots. Unconsciously, I had decided what I thought I was worth and that is what the universe gave me. I kept money at bay; money was outside of me and luxuries were something other people got.

Due my parent's housing hiccup, I desperately wanted, from an early age, a place of my own. A refuge, a place of safety, as I saw it. I worked abroad to pull together a deposit, saving money by staying in every evening as my colleagues went out having fun. I bought my first tiny one bedroom house when I was twenty nine [1983], having been gazumped on my first and at a time when small houses were going up in value £1000 a month [absolutely lunatic long term economics I thought, even then]. If I could have borrowed enough to buy a two bedroom house, I could have brought in a friend to rent a room but, in those days, building societies were blinkered and unrelenting; the sum was fixed against your salary and that was that. When I moved in, there was no extra cash to modernise or update the house. All I could afford was one second-hand armchair. I was given a few bits and bobs, a single bed that I used as a sofa and one very kind person gave me their old cooker. The tiny fridge, so old it would not have looked out of place as an exhibit in a museum, came with the house. The heating was a single calor gas stove and there was no washing machine, so drying clothes and bedding during the winter meant a damp house or taking it home to my mother in a rucksack on my moped; a car was out of the question. I had a small portable black and white television for entertainment. In winter, I went to bed at six p.m. with two hot water bottles, socks and a scarf. One of my friends still recalls, with hilarity, my chicken neck stew. Out of one 32p bag of frozen chicken necks, added to cheap veg, I made a stew to last three days. I did not resent the hardship because I thought I was lucky to have my own place.

In the early nineties, having moved twice and been caught out by the housing downturn, I was settled in another small, one bedroom terraced cottage and life was less than rosy. I was the wrong side of thirty, working full-time night duty at a local hospital, exhausted, unhappy and everything was wrong. I got a sudden jolt at work that shoved me to the edge and for which, in hindsight, I am grateful because it provided me with a massive second chakra and third chakra challenge. It was sink or swim. I wanted to be at home and I needed to paint because my spirit was dying. I sat down and thought, 'There is only one way out, I have to pay off my mortgage then I can stay at home and paint and do whatever small local jobs, cleaning, gardening or some such, come my way'. My salary was less than £800 a month, my mortgage was £350 [ish] and my car was geriatric. I slammed my wallet shut and started. Apart from work I did not leave my village for weeks at a time. Central heating was turned off and a small fire lit during very cold spells. I bought vegetables for each meal, sometimes counting out each Brussel sprout and buying a single carrot and single spud, so nothing was wasted. Later, I got an allotment; I used the library; everything I needed I got from charity shops, apart from underwear. I wrote long letters to friends, rarely used my phone and gave myself three monthly treats, Country Living magazine, one bottle of red wine and one video. I was hugely fortunate to have one holiday a year, four days in Dublin with extraordinarily kind friends. My flight ticket, booked three months in advance cost me £50 return and the trip was the highlight of my year. In my first month of saving I managed £120 and virtually every month it crept up. I got better and better at saving and found I was competing with myself to see how frugal I could be. I generated a little extra income by buying in small things and selling them on. In three years the interest rates had gone down, my salary went up and I was saving half my monthly pay packet. Every other month I trotted down to the building society and paid £1000 off my mortgage, which was slowly going down and down. I reckon I had about four years to go to full mortgage pay off. Then I got a windfall. Later I inherited money which I had never expected to get but, by then, I understood the inheritance was simply wonderful but it was not 'the point'. I had set myself a challenge to be free and I had diligently and with great focus kept ploughing on week, after month, after year, toward my target. This had been a second and third chakra spiritual test and I had passed it, no question. I was never outstanding at school and I was considered an oddball at work. I never had applause or prizes but I got grade A at this and I am proud of my achievement. After my inheritance I got three years grace before my next spiritual hurdle, how to heal myself from a major disease. I am still head down, focused and getting there, and get there I will. There will be another test after that, I can see another hole in one of my chakras, but let's do one at a time.

Debt can be repaid. If your debt is monumental, take professional advice, bite the bullet and do whatever it takes to clear the mess. If you are just treading water with your debt STOP SPENDING NOW. If you are partnered or married you MUST negotiate or, if necessary, hammer out a deal with your other half. If this means selling up and buying something tiny to live in, do it, because *if* there is love, the love will hold. This may well be the hardest part because you may hear some truths and find out where priorities and love really lie - it may cause considerable emotional pain. I wish you luck on this one, I really do. I would not dream of advising you about negotiating with children because I have no experience of parenthood but I do hear children and they all seem to *love* doing with their parents more than *having* from their parents.

Having done that, start the physical process. Turn your heating off and put on a big thick jumper and scarf. I am tired of listening to people whine about their financial situation when they have the heating full on and are dressed in a t-shirt in midwinter. Use the library [truly, the range of books they stock now is amazing]. Go for a long walk in a park or in the country every weekend [maybe take a book and a snack], this will bring you into contact with nature which will EARTH and STABILISE you. Buy cheap nutritious food - don't even think of convenience food, takeaways or buying sandwiches. No excuses. We can buy a large pork joint from an old fashioned butcher for £4 that will stretch to make two, sometimes three main evening meals for both of us. Get a thermos flask and by pass coffee shops. Grow your own vegetables if you can, you can grow a staggering amount in a very small space and in pots. Get real about what is important in life. What are you spending most of your money on? Is it football or haircuts? Why do you think they are so important? Is this escapism or ego driven pride? How about putting your ego in its rightful place and escaping into completely debt free living? Would you feel good about yourself? Damn right you would, and you would be the envy of all your friends. You will command respect. Once you get into the rhythm of saving you will not believe the knock on effect it will have on your life, a whole new world will open up for you and your self-esteem will soar. Things you took for granted will take on a much greater significance and treats will have you as excited as you got when you were a small child. As you get your priorities right contentment will ease into your life.

Set a goal for how you want your future life to look. From my monthly magazine treat I used to cut out pictures of agas, chickens, ponds and wooden floorboards. I put them in a file marked 'Next Home Ideas' at a time when I had not a hope in hell of getting any of them. I have them now. What you focus on expands. Make things, get creative. You don't need to spend money to impress people and if you do, you have the *wrong friends.* My pals got carefully chosen presents from charity shops. Old glass, Victorian hand towels which I washed, starched and tied with a pretty ribbon, or second hand books I knew they would love. I put effort into finding something I knew they would like and they appreciated that effort because it meant I was concentrating on them and concentrating on them meant I was loving them. Most people just want your attention, they really appreciate it.

Please try and find a level of gratitude for what you have, this is important. I think life is a gift and we don't really understand that. More and more I am wondering if life after death is vastly different from human life on Earth. Do we take for granted simple things like country walks, smelling roses, hugging and kissing loved ones? Are those sensations available to us after death? I am not sure, but I am beginning to suspect they are not because we will be energetic forms, not skin and bones. Sometimes it can be hard to find gratitude. If your life is really abysmal be grateful your lungs can breathe and your legs can move. Some people cannot even do this.

When you get to the 'W' section I will tell you about a writer who really understands about the energy of money and how to pull it towards you. Suzi Orman is another author and she has a saying, 'When you feel more you spend less'. I love this simple statement because it is so wonderfully true. Bravo Suzi! The state of 'feeling more' usually comes with age and the realization that one's years of viewing magnificent sunsets or exquisite flowers are numbered and then life takes on a sudden urgency. For those whose years are running out everything is seen and felt more profoundly and possessions matter considerably less than a smile shared, a loving touch, a good meal, or the sight of a bird in flight. Accessing and examining feelings is painful because feelings tell the truth and humans are not overly keen on that. It is easier to bypass feelings and fill the void with shopping, shopping, shopping. Emotions empty bank accounts very quickly. It was a fascination to me that the arrival of deep and profound love in my life has been the biggest shopping brake I have ever known. As my gratitude and passion for my partner has deepened so the need for retail therapy [I don't count reference books, as our groaning bookshelves can testify] has decreased. We had a rare day out in London recently and sat enjoying a roadside coffee in a smart shopping area while watching busy, busy young people hurrying past. We recalled our own busy working lives in the city. I remembered my youthful muddled thinking that if I had beautiful clothes I would somehow get a beautiful life and a nice man to share it with. How wrong I was. As I sipped my coffee I was amused by the fact that I was wearing beautiful clothes, cashmere to boot, and the entire outfit had cost me £35 in charity shops. My wonderful man had met and loved me when I was in so much pain with arthritis that I hardly cared less what I looked like. Later that day, having taken in an art gallery, we ambled through a department store and I was amazed by my detachment. I was delighted by beautiful objects but I did not want to buy them [though I was rather confused by confections that purported to be handbags, I wouldn't have known whether to hang them on a wall or eat them]. Walking through that very same shop twenty years ago I would have been a pathetic wreck anguishing over *those* shoes that were too expensive or *that* skirt that I could not afford. What a pity I wasted so much time over trivial things I thought I needed while failing to make headway towards something that would have given me lasting pleasure, like love, or learning, or a garden. I find it interesting that when you are 'feeling more' you are actually in a profound state of grace and of gratitude for life. This is probably the best form of life insurance there is. The universe will hear your minute-by-minute thank you's and give you more minutes. What a pity most of us cannot arrive at this stage of grace a lot earlier but I have a suspicion we are being offered a chance to fast track to just such a state, if we so wish. This is why we are being overloaded with continual displays of materialism. Sooner [I hope] rather than later, people are going to get bored with shopping for self-esteem. You cannot fill your third chakra with a handbag - no matter how much it cost.

Please remember too that generosity is often repaid. In the last few weeks of her life my mother questioned me over a generous offer she planned to make to someone she knew quite well who was desperately short of money. 'Absolutely, give it to them', I told her, 'you will get it back, you wait and see'. She was flabbergasted to find the exact amount she had given away was replaced from an unexpected source within a few days. 'Look at this', she said, wafting an unexpected cheque that had just arrived in the post, while staring at me open mouthed as if I was a witch. 'Quite so ..... told you', I replied, as I got on my broomstick and went home.

One last point. You MUST send out crystal clear messages about what you want. It's no good thinking, I want a new car', because you may get offered a rust bucket. Angels need specifics, they don't differentiate and don't drive [at least I hope they don't]. You need to state exactly what age of car and colour and engine capacity you want. This is not a cloud in the sky lark, it is getting straight in your head about your goals. I have asked loads of people what they want in life - but rarely do I get a clear and specific answer. Ask yourself how much money would make you feel safe. This is an important one. What would you do with a windfall, say, ten grand? Get completely clear in your mind about that sum and then ask yourself, 'What would I do with half a million pounds?'. How much would you give away .... to whom .. and why? Are you frightened of lots of money, are you a people pleaser or does money make you feel guilty? What do you want from life that money can buy? Write it down. Make a list of what you want and beside it put how much it would cost. Leave nothing out, so if you want a cottage in the country, list moving fees, solicitors fees, new curtains, the whole nine yards. Get clear about exactly how much money you need to attract. Make this an exercise to do when you have a quiet moment. It is fun to do because it gives structure to your dreams. When you have done that ask yourself, 'What do I really want from life and can money give it to me?'. Listen carefully to your answers. Be honest. I have met many women who say they want a relationship with a good man but on asking them, 'If I gave you a one-off choice of five million pounds or a really, really good man, which would you take?'. I was really surprised at how many of the women hesitated …… for quite a while. If you are a hesitating woman don't expect the man of your dreams to be just around the corner. He can't see you. There is a mountain of money blocking the view and he may not be a climber.

MASSAGE

A friend of mine, who is not in the first flush of youth, has moved into a new home that has a purpose built shower room designed for elderly disorderly joints. It got me thinking about baths and massage. It is a pity 'a massage' still has a slightly seedy connotation with us Brits. On a visit to India I was enchanted to see mothers sitting in many a doorway, massaging their babies with oil. What a shame we do not have the Turkish system of hammans, where the sexes are strictly segregated and staffed. There is no reason why we couldn't have nice warm and steamy Turkish baths here where a woman of a certain age can have a relaxing bath in mineral enriched water and know there are other women to help her get in and out if joints are creaking. Then she could be gently massaged, or thoroughly pummelled, by a female member of staff. I think these all women establishments are such a good idea and massage is so good for stimulating blood and lymphatic flow. We could have one in every village and town. It could be Women's Institute meets Topkapi. I like the idea.

MANNERS

Good manners are remembered fondly …… poor manners are remembered. 'This is not the chimpanzee's tea party, Amanda', as my parents used to say. My father insisted that no meal was started until my mother, who had prepared it, had sat down at the table. This was to show our gratitude to her for making the food. We always thanked her, cleared the table and helped wash up. She remembered her school days when she had to put down her knife and fork and place her hands in her lap between every mouthful. This makes sense for good digestion, if you think about it. I was trained at home and at school that you could not ask for the salt and pepper [and most certainly could not reach for it]. You had to wait until your next-door neighbour dining companion offered it to you. Sounds crazy doesn't it? But it taught us to pay attention to one another. I can remember the silent, open mouthed and stunned disbelief of several schoolgirls when dining at the Head's table with the new Headmistress, as her husband picked up a whole apple and ate it with his hands; took us months to recover. We were expected to cut apples up and eat each segment separately - still a step up from Mum who had to cut it up and eat it with a fruit knife and fork. All these things are history now unless you are invited to Buckingham Palace. Things needed to relax but I think we have thrown the baby out with the bath water. It seems to be eating, like everything else in life, has become a free for all, every man for himself and it is dispiriting in restaurants to see cutlery waved like a conductor's baton, open mouths mixing food like cement mixers, arms and hands all over the table and a general lunging at dishes. I don't know when just eating quietly, pleasantly and thankfully at a table became unfashionable but I do remember being absolutely appalled at an advertisement for a well-known gravy. The hardworking mother came home to find her family eating the slow cook stew she had prepared that morning. They had left not a scrap for her. I thought it sent out an insidious message, but still, as Phil McGraw so wisely says, 'You teach people how to treat you'.

If someone has taken the time to go out, choose, pay for, take home, wrap and then deliver a present to you there is absolutely no excuse for not picking up the phone, at the very least, to say thank you. I prefer hand-written, penned in ink, thank you notes on thick plain paper. It is a dying art and I think this is sad. So too, the loss of interesting, individual and beautiful handwriting. If a letter is too much effort, then send a postcard. I buy mine in bulk when I visit a museum shop because the cards are beautiful and interesting. I know it is a bit old fashioned these days but I like manners. I do not like doors shut in my face and I am always especially pleased when a man, or boy, holds a door open for me. I help people into their coats and enjoy the experience myself because it makes me feel 'cared for'. It is amazing how such a small gesture can convey so much.

It is fashionable to be boorish at the moment. This will change eventually, as all things do, but I would like to point out to those who are surly in public … what goes round comes round.

MARS

Allegedly there is no life on Mars. How would they know? If 95% of the world's population cannot see auras how would they know what a Martian looks like? Mr. Astronaut might climb out of his rocket, looking like Michelin Man with a giant mirrored visor, take a look about and announce, 'Uh, Houston, we have a dead planet', while a shimmery Martian [I like to think of a slightly camp shimmery Martian along the lines of a whispery Kenneth Williams] is standing in front of him saying, 'Hello, how can I help you today? Tea? Coffee? Martian Milkshake?', and getting no response turns to his shimmery companions and says, 'We've got *a right one 'ere!'*. His companions respond by putting up a large banner saying 'KEEP MARS CLEAN … TAKE YOUR BLOODY LITTER HOME' but Mr. Astronaut can't see it. More is the pity.

Why does life have to have cells, anyway? Isn't a breeze alive? What if we can come back as a wind? Apparently there is one planet [Saturn? I am so ignorant, it is a disgrace, I'll look it up later] that has winds going round and round at hundreds or thousands of miles an hour. Are they not alive, them there winds? Might I have a human life on planet Earth, be a heavenly ball for a while and then be a big breeze? Would I enjoy being a thousand mile an hour wind? Might be fun for a week. Jeremy Clarkson would love it, I reckon.

MAPS

I have little sense of direction. Me and maps are a not on speaking terms. I can even go in the wrong direction in London while clutching an A to Z at the right page, usually because I have turned it upside down. I was once stopped by an adorable man in Dublin. 'Are ye lost?', he enquired. 'I am', I said. I told him where I was trying to get to and he took my map and turned it clockwise several times very slowly before turning it slowly anti-clockwise several times. We spent a very happy time together being absolutely none the wiser, which appealed to my sense of humour no end.

My father would take me for long walks. The car was parked and we would be off, up puffing hill and down breathless dale. Eventually, hours later, my father would loiter near a hedge and ask me where the car was and I would confidently point over his shoulder to a distant tree line and he would point over my shoulder to the other side of the hedge behind me, while staring at me in amused disbelief. My father was a navigator in the R.A.F., but though his genes targeted my mother's ovum, the navigational ones got lost in transit. Years after he died I read in a magazine [so it must be right] that people with low haemoglobins [that's me - and haemoglobin is iron carrying red blood cells] have no sense of direction. I marched straight up to the graveyard, stood over my father's grave and could be observed gesticulating wildly and emphatically pointing to said article in said magazine. This spectacle would have amused my father greatly. I did once get directions right, though. As we sailed around Rabat in Morocco in a circular manner for the third time I insisted my partner turn the car in such and such a direction. I was loudly and triumphantly right .... but silently, secretly dumbfounded.

MAC

Mac the cartoonist of The Daily Mail. Have you got a gong yet? Sir Mac? You should have one .. because you are worth it!!! Put me out of my misery … whatever happened to Kevin Sludgebucket? And, is it true we have not gonged the designer of the Spitfire yet? No. Not possible. Inconceivable. Can't be right. Surely?

$\mathcal{N}$ Is for NICE

I have striven to be 'a nice person' all my life. 'He/she is a nice person' was one of the highest compliments my father could pay, so I suppose that is from whence my striving came. One of the most painful lessons of my adulthood has been the realisation that niceness often gets you nowhere. It made no sense. My family favoured niceness. My schooling insisted on it and my childhood religion threatened all sorts of unholy happenings should my niceness slip. I was not sure where that left me on the path of life, especially as I saw 'not nice' surging ahead, reaching heady heights of human authority and moneyed power - and beyond. Years of agonising about this have finally been resolved, mostly, by a feeling of detachment. These days I am polite, hopefully, friendly mostly but my niceness knows where the brake pedals are. This is something of a relief.

$\mathcal{N}$o

There is a saying in the self-help arena, and I like it a lot, which is, 'NO is a complete sentence'. This point is essential to grasp if you are trying to curtail your niceness. I have found that when people are pants at saying 'no' when they finally find the fifth chakra freedom to exercise this very little word they always start with their nearest and dearest. This is understandable but frustrating, if not downright infuriating. Try saying 'no' to people who are manipulating and bullying you, it is far more satisfying. If you are having problems identifying them [usually because they are right under your nose and you are in a first chakra muddle about them], let me show you how to spot the pesky critters …. they are tiring, exhausting even.

NANNY STATE

You hear much talk these days of the nanny state. Why, I pondered, do we have so many nannying programmes on the box? They are not all bad, indeed, I have watched some and learnt some, but I am mystified as to why anyone would want to appear on television to have a finger rather aggressively wagged at them inches from their nose. Extraordinary. Such a very public humiliation and this at a time when school children behave any which way and folk are so quick to claim compensation for a minor injury sustained from an uneven pavement, or something similar. It is a puzzle to me. The television is, obviously, a masterful seducer. Still, it does seem to me that while so many seek to be so publicly nannied we can hardly complain that the government is nannying us.

NAME

For rather too many years I did not like my name. I thought there were too many men in it and worse, my middle name was Caroline so there was a flaming car in there as well. I dreamt of being named Amanda Petticoat Mansell because that would have been sweet and balanced things up. My family used to call me Mandy and I did not like it. I foolishly hoped, come adulthood, that this would change. I found, however, that whenever I ventured that my name was Amanda, no matter that I was at work or a social event, within minutes I was being called Mandy. Why do people do that? Do they think it is chummy? If I pointed out my annoyance it always seemed to cause people to take offence, which I found extraordinary. Sometimes people would take offence and then use the Mandy name to wind me up. It was exhausting. I eventually circumnavigated this problem by calling myself Mansell, as I was at school. I wasn't crazy about being called by my surname but a daily battle over my first name was too tedious to contemplate.

I thought seriously about my name a year or two back and decided it wasn't too bad. I wondered if this was age or whether something more fundamental had taken place. I decided it was a bit of both. The two men in my name have taken some conquering and it has taken me far too long to utterly embrace my womanhood while simultaneously deriving my strength of character from being a woman; this I have found uncommonly hard especially in the workplace where men are expected to be assertive but women still, in some quarters, are not. While trying to be assertive I have been called hurtful names that have reduced me to tears, but I am learning and improving. Strength from softness - it is a tricky combination to learn.

Is there something more significant about names than we realise? I have a suspicion there is. I did read somewhere that each vowel has a special meaning but I can't remember what the meaning was and where I read it - so that's helpful isn't it? I think it may have come from Louise L. Hay but I can't find it in the books I have of hers. If I know someone quite well I can sometimes see a really big significance in their name and their life, or how they are living it, but other times I am completely stumped, though I must say some names make me very wary. Smith is a pretty common name and I presume comes from blacksmith, the metal worker or forge worker. Do Smiths need to find their metal, or shape their metal into something useful? If we are all here in pursuit of our authentic power we need metal [as in strength] to find it. Apologies to Winterbottoms, but I wonder if their name has deeper significance? I don't know anyone of that name, which is a pity, but if I did I would take a good look at them, listen to them, and then ponder on 'winter' and everything you do, need and are during this season more than I would ponder on 'bottom' …… but then I like pondering.

NURSING

I seemed to spend the first year of my nurse training in the sluice, but you learn a lot from poop, pee and other unpleasantries. I trained on Nightingale wards wearing a pin-striped uniform and a white starched pinny. Caps and belts of different colours were worn to distinguish which year of training you were in. On qualifying, lacy caps and cuffs were worn and silver buckles allowed. Sisters wore dark navy with white pinafores. I daresay all this sounds positively Victorian nowadays but my, we were proud of our uniforms and how smart we looked. Each hospital had its own distinctive uniform and badge and when I finally pitched up at a new hospital where a nylon pale blue check dress [nicknamed the j-cloth] was standard issue, I nearly burst into tears. It was hideous, hot and uncomfortable and I hated it. Nowadays, the most excellent girls I worked with, do not wear uniform at all. I am perplexed by this. Who is who and who is what? As I have said before, I like my pilots in a smart, dark uniform. It makes me feel safe. Of course, I understand it all boils down to the cost of laundering but still, I think the abandonment, or lack of, a smart uniform is a mistake. Uniform gives structure and confidence, not just to the wearer but to the observer. You need plenty of confidence in hospitals where raw vulnerability abounds.

I am utterly dismayed at the present method of nurse training. I met an enchanting student nurse a couple of years ago who was six months into her second year of training. I asked what allocations she had had in the last six months. She told me she was spending four days at a general practitioner's surgery and other than that had done four days on a paediatric ward. Four days! She would not even have known what was in the cupboards and don't get me started on the paediatric allocation where every parent understandably wants the comfort of a nurse with some sort of experience. All student nurses need to start somewhere but I think it is imperative the start is made on adults, not children. That poor student nurse would only have been able to stand nervously about, observe and get in the way. I suspect she will be terrified on the first day of work on a ward as a qualified staff nurse. We were terrified on our first day of staffing but we had been working on wards for three years and by then we knew what was in all the cupboards. I told that lovely student nurse that when I was in my second year of nursing I was left in charge of wards at night with one or two auxiliaries [untrained nurses] and that there was always a floating senior sister [who covered several wards] to help out, when requested, with drugs, drips, recalcitrant patients and general muddles and pickles. The student nurse's jaw dropped and she breathed, 'I would love that sort of experience'. Well she might, but she won't get it because now most of the training is classroom based. I find this completely bizarre. It is like training a plumber in a well lit classroom until he qualifies and then turfing him out to plumb in ancient buildings and towering modern skyscrapers. No matter how rigorous the training most cannot make that leap of imagination and need to absorb years of hands on experience from steady older hands. You cannot beat apprenticeships and that is what we had as student nurses when I

trained. We were guided, by the experienced, in how to *handle patients* .....
emotionally, verbally and physically because each patient is uniquely
different. It takes skill and experience to move from an aged starchy
matriarch in one bed, to a trendy architect in another. From a dying child to
a twenty stone, post surgical patient and this is just the patients, never mind
difficult doctors and distraught relatives and now there is the violence to
cope with too. You cannot learn this in a classroom, you have to be on the
wards. Better, surely, to learn these basic coping skills as a student than
when you qualify and you have to learn how to run a ward as well. I feel
passionately about this. There is something wrong at the heart of our society
when we always put money first and academic qualifications before all
other. Nurses do not need A-levels, just good basic training in anatomy and
physiology. Then they need limitless patience, physical strength,
compassion by the bucket load and top-notch skills in paying attention to the
patient. In some ways nurse training is more complicated these days because
there are far more machines and tubey equipment to deal with, but humans
do not change. You can learn how to work a machine in a classroom but you
cannot learn from a book how to work around a person on the end of a
machine because you are dealing with pain and emotions, mostly fear based.
Top grades in any science subject will not teach or prepare you to nurse the
dying. A degree will not give you the skills necessary to care for a young
man who awakes to find he is now a paraplegic. I have seen such
experiences rock older hands and devastate new nurses. I think we are in a
muddle about the role of a nurse, in some way downplaying the skill as we
have downplayed the skill of good mothering and home-making. It makes
me sad because mothers sometimes need to be nurses and nurses certainly
need to mother. A good home-maker creates a place of trust and safety and
a nurse needs to be able to do that for her patients, sometimes in impossible
circumstances. In the space of an hour a nurse may be mothering one
minute, washing a dead body in preparation for the morgue the next, then
diplomatically handling an exhausted and snappy doctor. That nurse will be
expected to handle all those situations with the same professional kindness
and understanding. How could we possibly be in a muddle about the role of
that nurse in society? It is the role of the hero, but no, we prefer coke-
sniffing celebrities whose nose repairs will be nursed by nurses who cannot
afford cocaine. It is the way of madness.

I distinctly remember my first day at the six week preparatory training we did. Arriving first at the classroom I gulped at the sight of each desk carrying a bundle of uniform encased in a navy cape and bound with tape. It looked like a parcelled up nun's habit and frightened the living daylights out of me. We immediately started learning the basics of anatomy, physiology and patient care. We learnt how to blanket-bath a patient, without them losing their dignity, by blanket-bathing each other. We lay on beds and were given bedpans to try and balance on. We had naso-gastric tubes shoved up our noses so we knew just how bloody unpleasant it was. Then we hit the wards and by week seven of my training I had laid out my first corpse. He was a love. I had prepared him for surgery and on request given his aged cheek a peck to wish him luck. I escorted him to theatre where he gave me a cheery goodbye wink and a wave. I assured him I would be on the ward to welcome him back. He came back dead. I was stunned and sad. His heart had given out on the table and they could not revive him. By the time we were in our second and third year we were old hands with dead bodies and comforted the new student arrivals when they looked ashen.

Patients don't change and they all have one thing in common, skin and emotions. Nurses need to see their patients naked, regularly, because the skin and its condition tell stories. Dry skin, thin skin, red skin, white skin, blue skin, mottled skin all tell a tale. Rashes say even more. Bottoms needed turning and rubbing every four hours or it was a pressure sore, the presence of which, when I trained, was an admission of *serious nursing failure* and thoroughly frowned upon. Blanket-bathing and spoon-feeding gave us a chance to get to know those who were seriously ill and taught us endless patience, because most patients had concerns and needed a good listening to. Aged Mr. Smith would not make a speedy recovery if he was worried that his elderly wife was not coping well at home. Fears could be allayed, the facts reported to a staff nurse or sister and she could contact the family or social services. It wasn't always worries about surgery, recovery or family, it could be pets too. Mrs. Diddlydoo might be worried sick that Twinkle the Budgie was not getting enough care from her well-meaning neighbour and might need a lot of kind reassurance - maybe a phone call or two from the nurse to check that Twinkle was perky. This is not mildly amusing frolics, it is emotional care, just as important as the latest biochemistry or wound swab results and is part of a duty of care that makes up a nurse's working day. I am not saying care is not given these days. I am saying a three-year apprenticeship at the rock face of care gave us very young student nurses a grounding in human life in all its messy and sometimes sad glory that could not be acquired sitting in a classroom. It also meant the late drop out rate was low to negligible because you would know within about three months if you were suitable for nursing. I used to hear, 'The British nurses are the best in the world', over and over again. I do not hear that now. I think it is tragic.

I was once told at a party, by a young man I should have thrown my drink at, that all nurses were failed doctors. Not so. There is an art to nursing as there is an art to being a good doctor. Don't confuse the two and never denigrate the nurse until you have been well or badly nursed and you know the huge difference between the two. Our training was to the highest standard; flat under-sheets were considered as crucial as reading cardiac monitors. If you have ever sat on a creased sheet for hours and hours with thin, sore skin and been in too much pain or too ill to move, you will know it is not pleasant and in some cases it is inviting a speedy wound. When you have seen half a buttock eaten away by a bed sore [as a result of being badly home-nursed], you will never forget it. That poor man spent months in hospital while we tried to repair the damage.

By our third training year, when working nights, we could expect a call from a nursing officer. She would ask for a ward round and we would tiptoe round whispering in the dark, giving her a full report without looking at personal or patient notes. She expected us to know everything about each patient. Name, age, diagnosis, prognosis, input, output, drugs prescribed and possible side effects or contra-indications. This was outstanding training and no matter how well or badly we did on those dark and terrifying tiptoe ward rounds we were mildly thanked or profusely congratulated; graded and awarded at ground level. One of those particularly terrifying Nursing Officers was working the night I became very ill. She took my call, saw me in Casualty, arranged a transfer to a ward and escorted me there personally. She expected the highest standards from us and when we were the patient we got the highest standards of care from her. That way we knew we were appreciated. Though I quaked with fear during those midnight ward rounds I loved that woman because she expected us to nurse well but managed, on more than one occasion, to be deaf and blind to high jinks and naughtiness. 'I can't smell curry, can I Nurse Mansell?', she once asked me. I sniffed the curry laden air, shook my head and looked all innocence. 'I didn't think I could', she replied, leaving the ward and trying not to notice kitchen windows opened in panic. Food eaten by nurses on the wards was a very serious offence in those days, but that nursing officer knew what was really important, had she seen creased sheets or food left dribbled down a patient's pyjamas she would have wiped the floor with me.

The system for training us nurses was perfect. You left home and got a small room in a nurses' home with shared bathrooms, kitchen and sitting room. Rent was taken out of your meagre salary and you paid for your food. A uniform, but not shoes [always a bugbear when you wore them out so quickly and police were issued their footwear] and first-class training was provided, which later could take you all over the world. You were worked extremely hard, got shouted at and humiliated a lot, fondled by amorous patients and doctors alike and got your own back on both. You got slightly pissed at the pub when you could afford it [rarely] and there was always a sympathetic ear from colleagues when a favourite patient died. Freddie Everest, retired policeman, wonderful man and all round good egg who made the walls shake when he sang in the loo, made nurses cry [me included] when he departed for celestial beats. I still think of him, sadly and fondly, nearly thirty years later. It was accepted that some nurses worked better during the day and some found night duty suited them and fitted round their families, so you could choose to do either, but by the time I left we were being forced to do both.

A wonderful system that worked well now torn to shreds. Nurses' homes sold off to the highest property-developing bidder when they should have been kept and enlarged. Madness. No vision. All short term gain for long term pain.

*N*ATIONAL HEALTH SERVICE

You see, if we had a National Health Service we would not be in such a pickle but we don't, we have a DCA… a Disease Control Agency and unless someone engages a common sense brain at Westminster we will not even have that in the future. We will all be paying for everything and that will be that.

Six months into my training, in 1975, my father asked me what I thought of the NHS. I told him I thought they were dishing out antibiotics like sweeties and soon they would be impotent in the face of invading organisms. Even then I was extremely dubious about free anything, because I didn't think people appreciated anything they got when they did not personally hand money over. I told my father that patients should be charged a bed fee. I thought about £5 per week would be fair and would go towards food and linen used. This would give the patients the idea of paying National Insurance Contributions to get them into hospital, no questions asked, but a bed fee would get them used to the idea that payment for usage was appropriate and necessary. My training hospital did not have a Coronary Care Unit and the Intensive Care Unit only had three beds, which were always taken with very seriously injured patients. The local population was growing and it was obvious more beds were needed, particularly for the critically ill. 'The present funding will not keep pace with technology, new forms of treatment and demand', I told my father. I was a mouthy twenty-one year old, but pretty far-sighted.

During my years of nursing, as Labour and Conservative governments came and went, I watched an increasing amount of hospital tourists abusing the system while nothing was done about it at a governmental level. I was incredulous. Cosmetic surgery was offered on the NHS while hospices for children were not state funded. It was incomprehensible. Family doctors were seen for piddling problems that any good chemist could have remedied and, worse, the public called out ambulances for outrageously, ludicrously small complaints and got away with it. This sort of abuse needed to be stamped out early. Nearly thirty years ago it cost £300 to call out an ambulance, I dread to think what it costs now. As a midwife, twenty years later, as the cut backs started to bite, I was always astounded to see dozens of suited managerial staff pouring out of the car park and into the hospital at five minutes to nine as I was [late] getting off duty. 'Who ARE all these people?', I wondered. As hospital finances became tighter I suggested to my colleagues that all pregnant women might have to take out an insurance policy against the chance of having a premature baby. My suggestion was met with howls of indignation, even though multiple births from infertility treatment was increasing and Intensive Care bed space for these tinies was not. Those same colleagues are now howling with indignation for very different and personal reasons, poor things, their jobs are unsure and some senior and highly experienced midwives have been *disgracefully* demoted.

Year after year, while working in the NHS, I watched enormous amounts of money thrown at hospitals to make them more attractive. Flashy reception desks, individual beds getting their own televisions, new chairs replacing serviceable old ones. I used to watch them being installed and think priorities were all wrong. We needed medical equipment not televisions. NHS hospitals are not hotels. State run hospitals are for sick people and are invariably noisy enough without adding entertainment noise. People don't need intravenous entertainment when they are sick, they need rest and sleep and plenty of it. Extremely sick people need the cleanest environment possible, first class medical and nursing care and then somewhere quiet to recuperate and fully heal when the danger has passed. It is damn difficult to recuperate at home, especially if you are a woman. Cottage hospitals, our national jewels and once dotted all over the country, are nearly all gone now. They were ideal for recuperation and did not require high levels of highly qualified staff, whereas county and city hospitals did. Flogging these buildings off was a staggeringly stupid thing to do and we are still in the process of getting rid of the last few. Soon there will be nowhere to put the elderly who block hospital beds and you cannot tell me it is a cheaper option to nurse them all at home, what a load of old baloney!

We are now breeding generation after generation of unhealthy children, riddled with additives, preservatives and pesticides, either fat but malnourished or thin from extreme dieting, poorly exercised, stressed with exams and not allowed to take risks. They will not heal well, full bloody stop. Nothing new in that, all through history you have had high death rates from disease and malnutrition except that nowadays there is a massive population, no-one expects to die and everyone wants compensation if something goes wrong. You will get huge increases in deaths from food poisoning, septicaemia and organ failure in the future because diets are dreadful, guts are not working properly, bowels are mucky and antibiotics have been overused. This is not hysteria, it is basic common sense deduction. My partner read out to me some staggering statistics about how fast Salmonella multiplies and spreads internally when the bowel flora is low. I can't remember the details but we were both astounded.

It does not have to be a disaster. I think the NHS is still workable, we just need a National Health Service. It's acknowledging that it is prevention, prevention, prevention and then actually DOING SOMETHING ABOUT IT. Health prevention needs to be implemented from the cradle and rammed in throughout the school years with every child having a basic working knowledge of where and how their major organs function and how to maintain their health through exercise, relaxation, bowel cleansing and nutritious food. One lesson a week right through the school years. What is the big deal? How difficult can it be? I have already made a plea for Alexander Technique teaching and mentioned iridology, neither would require huge sums or new buildings but would save billions long term. I know this will infuriate the pharmaceutical companies but what are we about ... business or healing?

Seriously straight talking from doctors, who are still taken seriously by most, needs to be directed at those who are really stupid about their diet and lifestyle. Much of the population is stuck firmly in first chakra and therefore expects to be led by professionals [including professionals in white coats]. If a doctor tells a patient, with no shilly-shallying, to bloody well lose weight, stop smoking and eat sensibly or else they will not be treated, many will pay heed - though some obviously will not, but you will never have a perfect world. You may have read what I said about the colour white in 'colour' and I think doctors need to return to their white coats because it gives them visual authority and some degree of protection. There was bound to be a problem with giving children choice at school over what they eat. Until parents see their children dying early and until the children have got their diet, health and 'you are what you eat' firmly into their heads we need an experienced nutritionist working at every doctor's surgery. You get referred by the doctor and you have to go and get a dietary check up. In fact the doctors could be seen too - that would be interesting.

Of course it is all quite positive really. The more the NHS gets into debt and the worse the standard of care the more we will be forced into self-reliance and self-responsibility towards our bodies. Third chakra here we come!

NORTHRUP

While I am in the prevention field I would recommend that every woman in the country has Dr. Christiane Northrup on her bookshelf. Her two amazing books, 'Women's Bodies, Women's Wisdom' and 'The Wisdom of Menopause' will tell you, as a woman, everything you need to know about your body and the way it works. She covers everything that can go wrong from every aspect, giving advice from conventional medicine and surgery to all the alternatives. Bravo Christiane! Thank you so much for your extraordinary work.

NOWHERE

Here is another little 'pause for a think' saying from the new agey world. If you are in one of life's jams, cannot see the wood for the trees or which way to turn and generally consider you are going nowhere, split the word nowhere into 'now here' and think again.

NOISE

I am sad at the level of noise we have to endure in modern life because silence is such a beautiful experience. They have bossily banned smoking everywhere but I could get away from smoke, I have no such luxury with music. It shrieks at me as I shop, drives me witless in restaurants and wears me out in taxis and airports. Why do we have to have it? What is it about silence that frightens people so much?

I heard on the radio that restaurants that play gentle classical music make more money than restaurants blaring out other forms of apparently popular music. I hope this catches on, because I think a silent restaurant is too terrifying for most. Pity.

O Is for OPRAH

I have much gratitude in my heart for Miss Winfrey. We are barely two months apart in age [she just pipped me, but that's an Aquarian for you] but in many ways she has been the instrument of my 'higher' education. She, and some of her extraordinary guests, have given me tools and wisdom for life that I had hoped to be given by parents and older family members. I locked into her shows sometime around 1990 taping every one so I could watch at leisure, at a time of my choosing. I tended to fast forward through the celebrity interviews, though occasionally they were illuminating, but it was through Oprah's quest for clarity in life and her special guests that I gained a sense of clarity in my own life. Thank you Oprah, and thank you, in particular, Gary Zukav, Iyanla Vanzant, John Gray, Maya Angelou, Phil McGraw, Suze Orman [they are all authors of wonderful books].

OUTSTAY

As in 'outstay ones welcome'. There is a lovely Irish saying, sadly I have forgotten the first few lines but the last three are, I think … 'when they love you so, when they want to keep you, that's the time to go'. It might be an idea to have it carved into the doorstep of No 10 Downing Street.

ORCHARDS

Gone. Hundreds, possibly thousands, up and down the country. You may not be able to plant an orchard but even if you have a small garden you can plant a miniature apple tree. You might as well, because if oil keeps going up at this rate one day soon they will not be flying apples in from anywhere. Go plant! You can even slap them against a wall and espalier them, if you have the energy. Check out apple tree growers [details at rear]. Home grown apples are delicious and there are a dizzying amount of varieties you can buy with dazzling names. How about a Peasgood's Nonsuch, Winter Quarrenden, Ross Nonpareil or Lady's Finger of Offaly in your back garden?

OPERATION

I have recently been ticked off by a young doctor for taking large doses of vitamin C. I was told it was dangerous. I took an enormously slow and deep breath. We agreed to disagree. I did not have any statistics on numbers of deaths from prescribed medication, I hear there have been *quite a few*. I have yet to hear of anyone dying from an overdose of vitamin C.

I am not advising you now. You must do what you feel is right. I am just telling you that, for myself, I would not countenance going into hospital for any pre-planned operation, large or small, without first taking large amounts of vitamins and this includes vitamin C. In these MRSA [methicillin resistant staphylococcus aureus] superbug days I would take no chances and I would want the best possible chance of a quick recovery. Had I had sufficient vitamin E before my appendix was removed, when I was eight years old, I may well not be having problems with that area of my bowel forty something years on.

My regime prior to any cold, pre-planned surgery [large or very small - and I would include plastic surgery of any description, not that I am planning any, even though my neck is heading due south] would start at least two weeks before admission. I have now found [at breathtaking cost] that I have a major problem digesting protein and this has almost certainly been around since I was a child, but has got steadily worse. I am now on a strict recovery and repair regime which means protein has to be severely restricted. If I was well I would have an extremely high protein diet prior to surgery, but as it is I would have, instead, lots of juiced fruit and masses of vegetables with the odd free range egg and small amount of fish. I am checking out a juicer that retains the fibre [expensive, I'm afraid] because juicing is great but fibre is *needed*. I would take extra Vitamin A together with [as in - at the same time] vitamin E [to prevent scar tissue - I often wonder about people with keloid scar tissue and what their assimilation or intake of vitamin E is like]. Loads of vitamin C, all the vitamin B's [as in B complex], zinc, selenium and magnesium. Plain yoghurt for breakfast with a probiotic capsule [to introduce good bowel flora] or two and that would be the best probiotic money can buy. I would eat lots and lots of iron rich food [in case I bled a lot] but would not take iron supplements as they can decrease your vitamin E, or so I am told. The night before surgery I would double my B vitamin dosage, especially B6. Post surgery would be much the same but with higher doses of vitamin C orally and later, possibly, liquid vitamin E around the scar site.

I think everyone, but most especially the elderly, should be prescribed a daily liquid mineral and vitamin rich drink for a month prior to planned surgery, in fact they could do with one daily anyway. If you are going into hospital please talk to a nutritionist beforehand. You need to be in the best possible health for surgery and don't forget that sometimes the anaesthetic takes longer to get over than the operation. Learn to breathe properly, as I have said your tummy should go up and down as your lungs go in and out.

Think of your body as being like a Ferrari - don't put two star petrol in it and expect it to go. If you are having an operation give your body what it needs to do the repair work. You prepare for work, special projects, holidays or weddings so prepare for an operation and, by the way, hospital food has not improved as far as I can see. Getting your mates to bring you take-aways into hospital is not feeding your body the *extra* minerals and vitamins it needs to do the *extra* work of *repairing*. Engage brain please.

OAK

If you plant a tree you are leaving such a positive legacy to the earth. I think I read somewhere that a thousand insects and animals can live in an oak tree and it may live for hundreds of years. What a cheap investment and glorious gift to give generations to come.

OBITUARIES

I love reading the obitituaries. There are a few writers of editorials that are not to be missed and one that makes me cackle mid-week, but most days I wonder why I still buy the newspaper now that Bill Deedes has gone to be a heavenly ball. Then I get to the obituary page and cheer up. You read about all sorts and get a glimpse into extraordinary lives that have been lived. I usually cut out an obituary that has made my jaw drop but I must have been very seriously diverted with some major personal event because I hugely regret I did not cut out the one about the RAF hero, he may or may not have been a pilot, who died around 2004 [I think]. This extraordinary individual repaired the outside of his aircraft while it was airborne over enemy territory, as I recall, during the Second World War. Such a feat of derring do I cannot believe. Imagine! I picture him hammering away in hurricane winds with a crew member hanging onto his ankles for grim death. He will doubtless be running the 'White Arrows Display Team' [see 'angels'] when I get upstairs and I shall make him tell and re-tell me his extraordinary and heroic tale.

Allowing for those who make a hundred years, I have noticed that many of the post-war generation are dying much younger than those born before The Second World War. I suspect this will accelerate and the age will drop further. I daresay the politicians who have mucked up our pensions will be relieved.

$\mathcal{P}$ Is for PATERSON

If the house was burning down and I had time to save a book I would grab James Hamilton-Paterson's 'Playing With Water'. He is a rare breed, is James. I love his words.

$\mathcal{P}$HILOSOPHY

My philosophy is 'kindness before everything with humour keeping step'. I love meeting personally honest people but I find they are few and far between. Since discovering that personal honesty is probably the most excruciatingly difficult and unpleasant task of all human endeavours I have come to the conclusion that allowing other people to do their life at their own speed is a very wise move. Minding my own business is, therefore, becoming my personal mantra. I might even go so far as to say my sacred mantra. I don't find it easy to stick to my sacred mantra because I have a rescuer archetype which is coupled with a teacher archetype and I genuinely want to pass on information that I think might help people who are in trouble, for whatever reason. Problem is, people are deaf until they want to hear and the wanting often comes with desperation. Tricky thing desperation.

I do think one's religious or spiritual beliefs are a private matter so I chewed the cud for some time on the conceit and impertinence of laying my philosophy and spiritual beliefs before you, but I decided the whole book was a giant ego trip anyway so a bit more was neither here nor there.

I was raised as a Christian; church every Sunday in best bib and tucker. My mother taught me to bob in front of the altar, sing up and remember my collection money. After the service my father would comment on the vicar's usually rather dull sermon and my mother would comment on a neighbour's new hat, or brooch or something. I was in my mother's camp. I didn't listen much to the sermon either and found hats, brooches and somethings equally fascinating. I wasn't really sure why my parents went to church and the services themselves furnished no clues. To me God seemed to be far too busy and his son was looking in a terrible state up near the altar. I thought it was thoroughly unfair having to say I was a miserable sinner at every service when I thought chance would be a fine thing. After church, on family walks, my father would crouch down, pick up a feather and ask me, 'How do you think God knew exactly when to make the feather go from brown to white?', whereupon, I would put my little hands on my little knees, stare at the feather and earnestly assure my father I hadn't a clue. My father wondered if God had run out of brown paint and we would both giggle. I thought about zebras and giraffes.'Gosh, all that paint and all that work', revised my ideas on God's busyness and decided it was getting *completely* out of hand. 'Angels, he would need lots of angels to help him paint all the animals', I decided. We would go home from our country walks to tea and marmite toast and watch black and white television. Starving children from Biafra [I think it is Nigeria now] floated across our screen and I would sit and watch in horror. 'Couldn't we send them our toast?'

At some tender age I started asking awkward questions about religion. My mother blamed my father for putting ideas into my head and my father, probably rueing the day he told me to, 'Question everything ducky', taught me as much as he knew about the other main religious beliefs followed around the globe. We talked about reincarnation and I thought it was a rollicking good idea. It might mean that I ended up starving in Biafra one day, but at least the Biafran child got a chance at tea and marmite toast. I thought this was much more reasonable and fair, so I tucked this into my God file and tried to marry multiple lives with Christian belief. I found this quite tricky, so more questions were asked of my parents about the exact nature of our religion. My father thought that the Ten Commandments were a pretty sound code of conduct. Mum thought stealing was a disgrace and you should only murder foreigners but only if you were desperate [though the definition of foreigner was hazy and there seemed to be a lot of leeway for the ones who made nice shoes or handbags]. I pondered on the Ten Commandments but I was a little small to fully appreciate the depth of not coveting thy neighbour's wife. I desperately coveted my neighbour's wife's dog but I wasn't absolutely sure if this counted as sin. I knew my father adored my neighbour's wife but I sensed he did not covet her because she had white hair and plaid slippers from Woollies. He didn't like those particular slippers but he said, 'Phwoar', and winked at me if Sophia Loren came on the box, indicating to me that phwoar and covet came with a touch of glamour and was definitely Italian.

I muddled along with this sort of dual philosophy until my teens and a change of boarding school meant I had to listen to a particularly unfortunate sermon in Northern Ireland from a politically minded vicar who did not much care for British troops. This sermon put me on high alert for opinions from servants of God that I thought were inappropriate and once I started listening out for ungodly opinions I found plenty to annoy me. Being highly opinionated myself, I came to the opinion that religion should be about forgiveness, love, kindness and understanding. It seemed to me that religion had to be fairly neutral except in a monumental crisis, though finding a definition for 'monumental crisis' kept me awake at night. I did not see much evidence of neutrality, just rules, so from then on, though I did go to church services off and on, I preferred my churches empty. I liked the silence. Still do.

It seemed to me that there was a lot of dark in the world, but I decided that there was quite a lot of light too and it struck me how so many things in life seemed to be made up of opposites. Day and night, light and dark, top and bottom, left and right, scotch and soda. I supposed you had to have opposites. You can't have all left, you have to have a bit of right. You can't have all light or all bottom, you have to have some dark and some top - a bit of balance between the two. I didn't think I could make much of an impact on the world's darkness but I thought I could work on myself and maybe find a bit of light within, so that is what I endeavoured to do. I decided to adopt a simple life strategy which was .. 'try and be kind if you can and if you can't, shut up'. I immediately regretted this rash and hasty policy decision, being unable to stick to it for even a day.

Sometime around my mid thirties someone advised me to read 'You Can Heal Your Life' by Louise L. Hay. I was impressed by her life story and how she had overcome some ghastly experiences. I thought a lot about her idea of choosing your future parents in order to learn what you needed to learn in this lifetime. I liked this idea, it made sense to me. I pictured myself as a rosy buttocked cherub staring down from my cloud and homing in on my future parents, complete with all their necessary neuroses and foibles that would perfectly assist my learning path. I could see I learnt specific lessons from my parents that I might not have learnt had I been born to the parents of friends of mine. My parents also learnt from having and responding to me - deep breathing techniques, tolerance and patience being high on the list. I imagined that all parents learnt a great deal from their offspring, sometimes learning unbearably painful lessons about life and themselves when their offspring departed early. From that point on I looked at my parents in a completely different light and I started to engage my sixth chakra awareness. Talking this over with a girlfriend, she asked what I thought my parents had taught me and before I could formulate an answer I spilled out, 'Fear, they have taught me fear'. I was astounded at what had suddenly popped out of my mouth. My parents had both served rather valiantly in the RAF during the war and had lost many friends during that time. I wondered if I was being unkind to my parents and that bothered me, but a few years later I realised virtually every parent teaches their child fear, in one way or another and that recognising and overcoming our individual fears was what life was all about. I could see that recognising a fear took personal honesty, but it took me many more years to fully appreciate the layers and depth of personal dishonesty. I did this by excavating my own fears and I am not done yet, I'm still burrowing away with my bucket and spade. For a while, as a teenager, I thought I fancied being an archaeologist. It never occurred to me I might end up excavating me.

I like the idea that we are eternal and come here many times to experience many different types of life and death. Not all human life lessons are pleasant and some are perfectly horrid, but I suppose all needs to be experienced. My childhood incomprehension over the starving children in Biafra and poverty was answered by the idea that perhaps we choose a dirt poor existence, starvation even, but then a degree of security and comfort in another life, so that both are lived and, possibly more importantly, *felt*. I have thought much about atrocities; might we choose to experience something we have inflicted upon others in a previous life? I don't know, but if that is the case it makes sense out of tragedy, though it does not lessen the pain of it one single solitary jot.

At my end, after thousands of lifetimes, I hope I eventually improve to the point that I become pure energy and unite with an energy of pure love that is God, assuming, that is, that God can bear it. I will have toned down by then …. surely? I am making a bit of a joke of this but my belief is we all carry a tiny bit of the divine spark and it is up to us to go within, find it and strengthen it. We do this by overcoming hideous life hurdles and lessons while finding love, compassion and the strength to be angry but only when it is justified which, actually, is not very often. Eventually the love and compassion over-rules the anger because we reach a point of understanding that we got ourselves into the situation where anger was the outcome. Here is the realm of self-sufficiency and loving detachment. When we are fully empowered and strengthened there is no need for another lifetime here, because all the lessons have been learnt and there is nothing left but detached compassionate love for everything.

I fully understand that there are only two emotions - love and fear. I can see that my life lessons have all been related to the chakras and I have found this tremendously helpful. Now, when I'm presented with a ghastly happening or I'm thinking uncharitable thoughts, I can stop, reverse back and look to see where my fear originated, then I can relate the fear to a specific chakra. I went through a long period of second chakra lessons, every single one was simply ghastly, but in the last few years discipline, caution, carefulness, attention to detail and self-belief have featured heavily; these are mainly third chakra lessons that have required intense concentration and stillness on my part. When I have failed to be still and concentrate, I have fallen down a mighty big and smelly old hole. I still have much work to do on both my second and third chakras. More lessons will rear up as this book is released. My fifth chakra will be challenged and I am, as usual, worrying superbly before there is anything concrete to worry about [no wonder I cannot digest protein, my poor stomach and pancreas deserve a gong … each]. I see no possible chance of getting a halo in any foreseeable lifetimes but I do draw immense comfort and hope from my beliefs and the thought that a life-path with hurdles is laid out for me. The hurdles are challenges and a pathway to my personal, authentic and internal power which is, as I see it, my link to the God force. The hurdles are not just major life events but also the daily challenges of finding kindness and courage to do and say the right thing; I can jump them, irrespective of my dislike of sport, or I can dig my heels in, it's my choice. I think the people I meet and interact with, from family, friends, colleagues, bosses, or even acquaintances and passing strangers all impart a learning experience [pleasant or not]. They are all part of my hurdle clearing. Some participants, the disempowerers, are the hurdles themselves whereas others are the trainers and support team to spur me on as I leap over the challenge. This philosophy has made me much more attentive to life.

Ever since I was a child I have been fascinated by life after death. I have read a great deal about people going to a beautiful garden and seeing loved ones and there being much joy. I have even met a few who went and came back and they all use the same expression, 'not their time', but I have also read much about people who have had near death experiences who felt unemotional. When working as a nurse I would often, mid chest depression on a patient whose heart had stopped beating, let my eyes slide up to the ceiling and silently ask the owner of the chest I was depressing if they could possibly pop back again, because many people, who have died and come back, write of floating about around ceiling level while watching the resuscitation of their body with dispassion. I have been fascinated with the 'dispassion' and have wondered if this is a state we achieve straight after death. Do we feel only joy? Do we feel [as in touch]? If we are unemotional after death, is this a state we are meant to create on earth, a state where we are not ruled by and can overcome our emotions? Does this mean I might go to heaven and share a bunk-bed with a politician and not mind? Inconceivable.

I suspect what we create on earth we recreate in some way, somewhere where dead people go, but meanwhile, in case I can't touch when I die, I plan to enjoy every minute of cuddling up to my partner, revel in every green and leafy dog walk and enjoy the sensation of shoving my nose into any scented rose that I can reach. I think I am unfathomably lucky to be alive now and though my health is still not perfect, I can still walk and enjoy, breathe and smell, touch and caress, stare and marvel, read and learn.

I see my life as a gift and every day comes a new challenge for me to hold fast to my belief that life on planet Earth can be seven shades of heaven and I am blessed to be here experiencing it. One of my dogs has just pushed her nose between my knees and I look down and see heaven in her face, whereas she is looking at me and thinking, 'Pork chops, sausages, tinned food, biscuits, anything …. *just do it'.* Perhaps a timely call or gift from the universe to remind me to stop pontificating on and give love, even if it is in the shape of a bowl of dog food.

*P*RESENTERS

I have had it watching the Chelsea Flower Show on the box. You would have thought it was about flowers, wouldn't you? No, it's about presenters. I am sick of their mugs. I want delphiniums, roses, aquilegias, sweet peas, anything flowery, I just don't want talk, talk, talking humans. And where is

Judith Chalmers? She was so professional. She understood she was presenting a destination, not herself. I want her back, because it is the same with travel programmes these days; presenters here, presenters there, presenters in jacuzzis [per ... lease]. Presenters in an hotel room pointing out the loo [good heavens! I would never have spotted it] and bouncing on the bed [an hotel with a bed - who would have thought of that?] The country? What country? Information? Don't be daft.

𝒫EACE

In the latter years of her life my mother, when she was being difficult, would growl bad temperedly at me, 'I can't get any peace', and I would look at her and think, 'Neither can bloody I'. I wondered when my peace would arrive, if ever. I am not saying I have found it but I do know that my present state of reasonable peacefulness is largely derived from not caring what others think of me. This has been hard fought for, painful and its arrival long overdue. It is not to say that I don't hit the ballistic button sometimes, I certainly do, but not as much as I used to. The saying 'what others think of me is none of my business' is perfectly true but tricky to grasp fully.

I have found a degree of peace by monitoring what I care about. I used to be keen on saying 'I don't care about ....' which meant I DID care [sometimes, very much]. If I did not care I would not bring the subject up because it would not be on registering on my radar screen. To take a step or two along a slightly more peaceful path, monitor your words carefully. If you say something along the lines of, 'We split up, she got the car and that's ok', in your eyes it is not ok that the car went and you stayed. A statement of, 'I am looking after the kids because he has gone off with his mates to watch a football match and that's ok', is not ok to you, you just think you need to be reasonable. There is nothing wrong with statements like these, I make them myself occasionally, but starting to pay attention to what you really and honestly care about is the start of a journey toward peace. In my experience there is no peace until you can make yourself heard, politely but firmly, and for me this has been hellishly difficult. Bring on the turquoise fifth chakra clearing colour. Try borrowing my mantra and 'mind your own business' because it is definitely the start of a more restful life. Occasionally we all need to interfere with loved ones who are getting themselves in dangerous situations but wherever possible let everyone get on with whatever stupid thing you think they are doing. The more you niggle at them, pointing out their foolishness, the more likely they are to carry on doing what they are doing and besides, the more you insert yourself and interfere with other peoples' lives the more you are saying, 'I am not in control of my own life'. Stand back, shut up, have a doughnut, stare at something beautiful and repeat after me, 'I mind my own business therefore I am peaceful'. Does this work? Absolutely.

*P*RAISE

I learnt something about this from a girlfriend a few years back. She was praising her young daughter's efforts at drawing. She did not just say, 'That is wonderful darling', she pinpointed several things about the picture that she particularly liked or thought were well represented. The child absolutely glowed with pleasure and I paid attention to that. A mighty lesson in a kitchen was had.

I have noticed something about the receiving of praise. If a woman, be she young or old, has had a lot of criticism from her mother she may be desperate for praise from other women or deaf to praise from other women. If I praise a woman and she does not register the praise or dismisses it, I am alerted to the possibility that she will only hear praise from a man. Likewise, if a man, be he old or young, got a lot of criticism from his father he may be desperate or deaf to praise from his fellow man. I have also noticed that if I come across a woman or man who is deaf to praise from their own sex, they are often pole-axed by gratitude if their opposite sex relays praise over-heard about them from their own sex. Are you following me? It's a bit convoluted. I will give you an example. So .... if a young footballer, with a critical father, plays well, he may be deaf to compliments from his male coach and fellow male players, but if the coach's wife, at a later date, says, 'My husband thought you played a splendid game last Saturday', he may well not be deaf but rather deafened with the applause, because he has finally heard it in the manner he needed to hear it.

Me ...... I will take praise from anyone, anything, any age, including your dog. Just gimme. When I worked at a school, I was flabbergasted at the amount of praise the boys got because I remember being genuinely praised only once at boarding school and I think the teacher was more startled than I was. It made such an impression on me that I can remember the scene vividly forty odd years later; we were visiting the Minoans and the history teacher gasped at my drawing of a Minoan floozy in elaborate costume [which made a change from the teacher gasping for breath before she launched a missile - the chalk duster was her favourite]. Such was the impact of her startled congratulation that it set me off on a lifetime trail of thinking and observation about praise and agenda free genuine praise. For too long I ignored the agendas, especially from women, because I so wanted praise, but I am wiser now. I hear well.

My father believed 'a pat on the back was worth ten kicks up the backside'. He was right. This is important in any sphere of life but most especially work. I really understood and appreciated the sentiment and during my working life, but especially during my nursing years, I always made a point of thanking staff before they went off duty. In fact I made a point of thanking everyone for work done especially the hospital porters because they are a breed apart and have always been rather special in my eyes - and a handful have been very special indeed.

I liken workers in any organisation to cogs in a wheel. If each cog is the same size and working well the wheel goes round smoothly. If some cogs are too small or lazy then other cogs are having to work harder and wear out quicker. If one or two cogs think they are superior and increase their size the wheel might not be able to move and may even stop. Each cog needs attention, care and complimenting on good work, for without this there is little sense of satisfaction and no recognition. We had an excellent senior physician at my training hospital who twinkled over his half-rim glasses, smiled and always acknowledged every single member of the hospital staff who crossed his path. He treated cleaners and fellow doctors with the same courtesy. Every ward round began with the words, 'Sorry to be a bore Sister, but could I see my patients?'. Everyone adored him, not least me. People can scrabble, *and they do*, for titles and honours but in my eyes to be genuinely loved by many for honest work, humility, kindness and courtesy, is a testament to a life well lived.

POWER

My childhood religion never comforted me in times of crisis, sadness and loss. That something awful was 'God's will' was incomprehensible to me. It seemed callous. I was to call God, 'My Father', but my earthly father would never have wanted me to be miserable, sad, or terrified so why would my heavenly Father be any different? Nothing made any sense to me until I realised it was in the reclamation of my internal power that the answers emerged and the closer to the God of my understanding I became.

I have finished writing this book and it is due to be printed but I have returned quickly to this subject because already we are seeing upheaval in the monetary markets and climate change is now on everyone's lips. Our chakra shifting is becoming more urgent. Each one of us, each little acorn, is capable of phenomenal growth, but we have to pay attention. Bear with me, please, while I take you over the authentic power lesson again. You start reclaiming your personal power in the very human and messy bits of life - families, cars, dating, work and pay. Gradually the lessons get more complicated. Families get larger or smaller, stay together or disband. Cars bring freedom, responsibility, dents or dangerous accidents. Dating brings adult relationships with all their messy bits. Work is great, sometimes, but usually a grind and money either sticks or slips through your fingers. *This is the fork in the road of life.* You can take one fork and *know* every hideous happening, large or small, is a lesson in reclaiming your internal power or you can take the other fork and *think* that every hideous happening in your life just happens to you - it's random, it's bad luck. If you take the first fork …… and keep going … then you are on a journey. You will go through and beyond second chakra external power. The lessons may come thick and fast and be very unpleasant because you are being tested. Whoever is in charge, upstairs, likes to see exactly what level of commitment you are planning to invest. Grit your teeth and plough on, becoming more and more authentically powerful and, inevitably, at some point, if you haven't already, you reconnect with the God of your understanding. You ask, 'Why?', less and less. You get more help, more often. Attachment starts to loosen its grip. You can drive a rusty banger or a Maserati and look equally commanding in either; neither will matter much and each one will have been a *conscious* choice, not an imposition or a protective statement. You become more powerful and more humble in equal measure. Detachment grows in perfect step with compassion. It is not an easy journey but it is, I believe, the one we are here to take.

I took the fork of knowing every hideous happening was teaching me and strengthening me but if you think I am now serene and spiritual, read 'zen'. While you are doing that I plan to pour myself a stiff unhealthy drink, open the newspaper and find a politician so I can practice my levels of detachment.

Look out for David R. Hawkins, M.D., and his book 'Power vs. Force', in the rear of this book.

PAINTING

I paint quite well, much to my surprise. I am much looking forward to taking it up again when this book is finished. I struggled with painting since childhood. Watercolours were far too difficult so I tried painting in oils but I could not get anything on canvas that looked remotely like the view in hand. Working outside was a nightmare, the clouds would not keep still and any passing insect would hurl themselves at the sticky paint. However, one day I was riffling through my large collection of postcards, gathered from numerous museums and galleries, when I happened upon a fairly simple still life. I thought, 'I'll try and copy that'. Lo! A revelation! I could paint! I have never looked back. So do try, do. Go get a simple picture that is quite small because I think containment is important but I have absolutely no idea why. Go for something that is very basic and easy to copy. Give Botticelli and Caravaggio a miss, you can do them next week. You may amaze yourself and if nothing else you will be delighted with your new found attention to detail, form and colour in every day life.

PRISONS

I do not believe in the death penalty. You cannot take the dreadful risk. We have hanged innocent people - no appeal court for them. If a loved one of mine was murdered I would want that murderer locked up for life but not in a cell with nothing to do. Inmates should work and for those unskilled inmates who are going to be released soonish, they have to be trained at something, they just do. Of course this will cost and of course you will need more staff and probably many more expensive prisons. So? We send billions to the EU each year, why don't we decide to do something to improve our country?

I daresay some of the prisoners will pick up something heavy or sharp and do something nasty, but locking up inmates for twenty three hours a day is not working and it is ludicrous to send them out into the community without a skill. You are going to need more prisons anyway because more and more people are feeding a drug habit and many more will go wonky in the head because of poor nutrition, damaged leaky guts, viewing violence daily on a screen of some description and insufficient loading of first and second chakra from difficult or abusive childhoods. You might as well prepare pro-actively for this by building more prisons now so you are equipped and ready to start the emotional and physical repair work and retraining. It is just accepting what is and doing something constructive about it. We can afford it because we can't afford not to.

PUNCTUALITY

I think it is the height of a big ego trip to be known for being late. There is nothing ditsy or disorganized about it, it is just rude, arrogant, attention seeking and based in fear of not being noticed. Fine at 12 years of age, but really, in adult life - get professional help and a wristwatch.

PETS

I want to make a plea about cages. Let's all lock ourselves in a room the size of a public lavatory, live there for a month and see how we like it. Pets give so much pleasure and deserve a life that gives as much freedom as possible. Imagine being kept in a tank or cage all your life. A life sentence but no crime committed. Never to feel natural sunlight or a gentle rain falling on your skin. Never to smell your native land's smells or hear other animals go about their busy lives. Never to be able to see plants and trees, blue sky or clouds. Never to be able to rub your skin against the bark of a tree, scuttle about, slither through leaf litter, feel a breeze on your skin. Sometimes never to have a companion to talk animal talk to, or just to make you feel a little bit safer. We have Amnesty International for humans, yet we imprison animals, without thought, all across the country.

It just makes me feel so sad. We humans love, want and sometimes demand our freedom. We love sensations. Think of all the huge number of different sensations we enjoy in the space of a year. Running, jumping, climbing, touching, mucking about in the garden or on a beach, seeing different sights from all angles, dodging rain showers, enjoying the sun, yet all, all denied to many of our pets. Let us just look at the animals we bring into our lives and wonder if they are getting a life we would want. *Please.*

Q Is for QUARTZ

I adore crystals. I have bought many and I still have a yen for a socking great clear/white crystal to tower on a window sill where I can stare at its awesome majesty and marvel how it came to be. Years ago I bought a crystal to wear as a pendant and I followed instructions on 'clearing' it by running it under clean water and sending it positive thoughts or affirmations. I am not now pooh-poohing these actions because my choice of crystal was interesting [it was scimitar shaped and I was just beginning to start cutting up swathes of my life that I did not like the look of] but I think it is best to appreciate that crystals are just crystals and stones are just stones. Though their purchase and certainly their colour will be making a personal statement they are unlikely to uplift you to a place of your dreams without you putting in a great deal of intent. You have to do the work to make them work, if you get my drift.

QUEUES

They used to drive me to distraction. I would steam and foot tap, huff and puff and generally exhaust myself. These days I transport my mind from the queue to something or somewhere pleasant and peaceful and resolutely refuse to become irritated and to my satisfaction I find, should I be concentrating strongly on pleasantness, the queue disappears.

QUEEN

Queen Elizabeth II has been my monarch all my life. I have said, 'Good morning', to her though I suspect she may not remember me. I am not offended because I like her. I think she has done the most extraordinary 'job' in the most extraordinary way. I admire her sense of duty, her discipline and her ability to just 'be'. I fear greatly that when she dies this country is going to be deeply distressed, I might even go so far as to say the country will be plunged into a deep mourning and possible depression because I do not think we realise how lucky we have been nor do we understand what her presence has meant to the nation. We shall not see her like again. It bothers me, especially as so many other aspects of our lives are pitching toward crisis point in the future.

$\mathcal{R}$ Is for Right

Have you heard the one ….. 'do you want peace or do you want to be right?' I want both - no question.

$\mathcal{R}$ELATIONSHIPS

I have talked about relationships in 'love' but I have a few more observations that I want to mention. The belief that love relationships should be, 'I need you because I want you', not, 'I want you because I need you', never settled completely into my gut where all my 'Truths' eventually bed down. I now think that need is the main element that brings people together. The need is the glue to hold the participating people together while they learn the lessons they have signed up for. The relationship is where you get the chance to learn how not to need. You take the chance if you are ready.

For many years I was baffled at social events by couples who made continuous disparaging remarks about each other; remarks that appeared lightweight, or in jest, though sometimes they were downright hostile. I did not understand why two people stayed together when they so obviously disliked one another, but now I understand many people have an almost primeval fear of being alone and it is often a case of 'any relationship is better than no relationship'. Though this is changing rapidly now, there is still a great deal of status attached to being partnered. During my formative years, a woman was a bit of a hopeless case without a boyfriend, which made me an ongoing disaster zone. Today, the status attached to being partnered or married often encompasses a social circle, a house and, probably more importantly, an income, for which some will hold on tenaciously, putting up with any degree of ghastliness within a relationship in order to do so. I have always struggled to understand this because I would rather live in a shack than inhabit a house, of any description, with a disagreeable partner.

While watching couples interact, I have noted that quite often a person selects a partner to 'fill in' a missing character trait. Usually the missing trait is emotional but sometimes it is physical too - such as when a short man chooses a very tall woman or an incredibly feminine woman [extra yin] chooses a hulking great cave man [extra yang]. Ideally [when there is spiritual growth within a relationship], the short man can become tall in his evaluation of himself and the ultra-feminine lady can find wielding a spanner is a breeze under the instruction of her cave man. Then there is the extrovert married to the introvert, each person filling in the missing part in the other and therefore perhaps trying to strike some sort of balance. The extrovert needs to begin introverting and the introvert to open up and find their expression, yet often I see men who cannot do small talk but choose a wife that can and then complain that she never shuts up. No lesson learned there, folks. No balancing out. When I met my partner I was a raging pessimist and he was way too optimistic but we have learnt from each other and now I am much more perky and he is much more wary. We have tried, in this at least, to strike a more healthy balance, but there is plenty more to work on in our partnership.

As a midwife I was enormously privileged to be on close and intimate terms for several hours with couples. During the pain and rawness of labour, the relationship between a man and wife was exposed down to its bare bones. In the early hours of long labours, while contractions were not too painful and all consuming, couples would sometimes talk to me about how they met each other. I would listen carefully but often would silently wonder why people had chosen to come together and share a roof, because some couples seemed to lack compatibility, cohesion or, sometimes, even closeness. It was not until I had left midwifery that I began the process of working out the point of relationships but then, slowly, I began to realise we choose people to learn specific lessons. I believe this is part of the realm of the sacred contract [more later]. One of the most fundamental lessons is to learn to manage and survive alone, so the sudden break-up of a relationship, for whatever reason, will bring this lesson in to sharp focus. Within relationships people often choose a partner with similar characteristics to one of their parents in order to work through unfinished emotional business. To give you one very simplistic example, a timid woman might chose a bullying husband [echoing her bullying father who may or may not be around - or even alive] to learn to stand up to him. The woman will choose to either submit to her bullying husband, find some degree of resolution [this often comes with age or a husband's infirmity] or she may decide she has had enough and take the necessary action which may involve packing her bags - or even packing his bags. Self-empowerment is something that timid people have to learn and it is a lesson that will come back and back [in differing formats], each return offering a chance to take appropriate action and undertake some level of spiritual growth. Action comes when there is a recognition of one's own victim role playing as well as external bullying [both second chakra], a desire to build some self-esteem [third chakra] and an acknowledgement that enough is enough, using your voice [fifth chakra] to express that feeling.

Another element to relationships is an identical character trait, even between couples who superficially appear as different as chalk and cheese. To take an example would be ... say, a thrusting businessman with a vicious temper married to a quiet 'stay at home' wife. Docile wifey appears to be sweetness and light, but actually harbours thoughts of lacerating unpleasantness but never, or rarely, expresses them. The link between the two would be acid thoughts, his expressed, hers unexpressed. Other links can be idleness, weakness, competitiveness, selfishness, resentment, manipulation and so on. They don't all have to be negative traits but mostly they are, because we are human. The 'acid thoughts' relationship will hold while the two are both chucking acid about, but a split may come when one of them starts thinking about the milk of human kindness [changing his/her vibration] and the other [who is not ready for the change] can't keep up. Making a deliberate step toward shifting, stopping or healing an underlying trait can be the trigger for a relationship break down, but this shifting can be done unconsciously so that, when the breakdown comes, all looks like incomprehensible turmoil but at a deeper level one person has recognised a change in vibration within the relationship and has found it too hard to live with. Let me tell you a story.... I once met a lovely man on holiday, who told me a tale of his happy marriage of nearly twenty years, with its many shared interests. His wife suddenly asked for a divorce. He was completely shattered, almost unable to breathe, because he had not see a fault line developing within his marriage. As I paid attention to him and listened very carefully to all the little details of his story, particularly relating to his wife, I could feel where the problem lay. I suspected his vibrational rate had changed quietly and undramatically over the years of his marriage to the point that his wife could not keep up. Their two vibrations were out of kilter, so she left. She left to be with someone who matched [exactly, judging by what he told me] her vibrational rate. This did not mean that he was in some way superior, it is just that people move at different speeds. Some have much repair work to do on a specific issue related to a specific chakra and it may be that this man had a large challenge in a different chakra ahead [purple featured a great deal in his belongings and clothing; I suspected his next major challenge would be intensely spiritual, whereas his ex-wife still had work to do on her first and second chakra divide]. I told him about vibrational rates and reassured him that I was absolutely certain that there would be someone in the future who would match his vibration, someone to love and journey with him on the next leg of his life experience. He did a tiny double nod and then went very quiet on me, though his body language was peaceful. Later in life he will be able to look back on his divorce and fully understand it. As the years pass I am able to look back on my life and view, from sixth chakra, what were, at the time, absolutely inexplicable events. I can now see that all those happenings, even the most ghastly ones, were necessary for my spiritual development; my reclamation of my internal power base. With each insight is the opportunity to soften my heart, to bridge my diaphragmatic divide between third and fourth chakra. It is my call.

For many years I thought the high divorce rate in this country was dreadful but know I understand it is revolution before evolution - revolution is rarely pretty or comfortable. The up-side of all this turmoil is an opportunity for phenomenal fast-forward personal spiritual growth. Our youngsters, many from shattered families locked into welfare and drug addiction will have, by far, the greatest chance for growth; the choice to perpetuate the misery or walk, with dedication, away from it. A positive decision, for them, will be incredibly difficult but we all face a fork in the road at some point in our life. We can stay on the 'they/he/she did that to me' road, or take the other route toward our individual third chakras. If you look at relationships in this light you can see that all is an illusion. Relationships are our greatest teachers and the more uncomfortable the relationship the greater the chance to grow …. or stagnate. It is our call.

ℛELIGION

I once went to an interview [of sorts], which was not going well, when a woman asked me if I was a regular churchgoer. I thought about my answer only to find her staring at me and impatiently tapping her pen. I shifted into a lower gear and answered, 'At times', because I felt my honest answer would have unnerved her. 'At times - so not all the time?', she repeated, stating the obvious. She peered at me in an irritated manner and dangerously carried on with an edgy, 'Well, do you *like* singing hymns and carols - that sort of thing?'. Eyeing her, I dropped my head in a gesture that, to most who know me well, means I may be about to charge because religion is sticky territory as far as I am concerned. I thought quickly about giving her my views on religion versus spirituality, belting out hymns versus silent contemplation, but decided discretion was the better part of valour. I raised my head. 'Yup, absolutely', I reassured her. She calmed down, but I knew she thought I was trouble.

I went through a phase as a child that frightened the living daylights out of my mother. I became absolutely fascinated with a local Carmelite convent. I bought an enormous set of black rosary beads and hid them under my bed. My mother's hair nearly turned white when she found them and they were confiscated. She needn't have worried. Should I ever have sidled, nun like, through the door of a convent I would never have got past the first 'obedience' hurdle. I think my fascination with that convent was visual, more than anything else. Nuns have always held me spellbound. The older and more extravagant their habits and headgear the more stunned, stilled and silent I am. Was I a nun in a previous life? Definitely. Had to be. It is all so familiar. It is not just convents that fascinate me, I love all old churches and cathedrals, the emptier the better. I have to visit them, it is imperative, like a calling. I love their serenity and silence, their thick and often damp walls with their testaments to love and loss. I love churchyards with a passion because they remind me of my mortality and how each second is precious, whether I am well or unwell, happy or sad, amused or irritated. However, I have ceased going into a church in order to seek, or ask for, guidance because, I believe, we are being guided [and taught] every single minute of our waking day.

We found ourselves in Lincoln cathedral not so long ago, staring reverentially upward at this awe-inspiring building. Over the infuriating and intrusive loudspeaker I was instructed to thank God for the beautiful building. It is never a good idea to loudly instruct me to do anything, so I did nothing of the sort. I thanked the medieval stone masons instead [who must have been mighty plucky judging by the height of the roof].

On our extensive travels we inevitably find ourselves in places of worship of differing religions because they are a draw and a fascination to both me and my partner. Our experiences have confirmed to us that we are all so very much the same. We have been struck how each religion teaches, in different ways, how to bring the sacred into our most basic and daily lives. These small acts of reverence, respect and even healing are not widely known. I think this is really sad. Despite my deep fascination of the subject, I am often appalled by the application of religion. I remember meeting a cold Christian missionary in a hot, poor country. He had steel blue eyes and would truck absolutely no opposition of spiritual thought from either me or my partner. What is this demand? This rigid fear of difference? How can such fear possibly stem from the teachings of Jesus? That missionary frightened the living daylights out of both of us. I was confused by his moral superiority and concerned that he was living and preaching to people who lived such poor but honest lives. Not much in the way of mod-cons for them, they lived biodegradeably and many worked the soil by hand, so had a great understanding and reverential respect for the land that fed them. The missionary was offering them salvation, but I felt that they were already living with integrity and respect in their own garden of Eden. I have given up on religion for now, but strangely I feel an urge to study theology coming on. I should have known this might be a possibility because, twenty-five years ago, I met a very young American who planned to quit his job in the forces and study theology. I remember being completely, but quietly, stunned and not a little admiring.

In the future, I fear we will lose countless small churches all over the land unless some really dramatic decisions can be quickly made. I am relieved to hear some are already being used as places for meeting or for children's playgroups. Would it be possible to use rural churches for silent retreat, guided by retired or part-time clergy? We so badly need a point of focus for silence in our incessant noisy world. We have musical concerts, including jazz, in our church. I think it is wonderful. What about plays? We could have regular plays on a biblical theme - what fun. Shakespeare classes! Gosh, that would be fabulous!

REINCARNATION

I picked up and read Jenny Cockell's 'Past Lives, Future Lives' several years ago. This is a quiet and sincere little book. When I got to the future lives bit, I clearly remember sighing and thinking, 'Yup, that feels about right to me'. I just don't see us getting to grips with our passion for consuming until all the oceans are as Jenny describes.

Her book throws up extraordinary questions of time and space and how we perceive them. Perhaps her vision of the future gives humanity hope but I fear it offers little comfort to most of our animal species. It is beyond tragic.

If you have children or grandchildren I would recommend you read it. Forewarned is forearmed, as they say.

REMEMBER

For years I have had a major block with remembering names, even with people I know well. I have learnt a trick that works really well, but only WHEN I remember to use it. The trick is, on being introduced to someone, that I repeat their name to myself several times and say, 'I will remember that'.

If your memory is starting to fail, you can improve things. By looking at the condition of the top portion of your iris an iridologist can tell you if changing your diet would help. If you sleep with a lot of pillows and/or you don't do much brisk walking [helps the muscles pump the blood back up your body] you may need to look at improving the circulation to your head. Exercise is crucial, but herbs can help [see a fully trained herbalist] and it might be wise to see an osteopath. Low levels of one of the B Vitamins, niacin, can affect the memory and make you agitated. Get hold of an Adelle Davis book, if you can, and read what she says about memory loss. If you can't get hold of wonderful Adelle, then see an experienced nutritionist. I wonder about low levels of zinc and memory loss. Please also think bowels. Your intestines get a little bit more tired every year. Chew your food, eat lots of vegetables, avoid micro-waved ready meals and get some gentle exercise, but, above all, remember to have some fun.

RATS

My partner was born under the Chinese sign of the rat and I am the horse. Apparently this is a disastrous combination. We like to buck trends and anyway, my partner is good with horses and I am rather fond of rats, I think they get a bad press. I got to thinking about rats once. Imagine if you were a round ball in heaven and wondered what it must be like to try a short life form where you are hated and persecuted. Might you opt for a lifetime as a rat?

S Is for S.M.I.L.E

Stands for ………. stillness, manners, intention, listening and elegance. This is what I try to aim for as a modus operandi [method of living] as I tiptoe through my life. Stillness is mighty attractive in a man. Few men have it and short men need it because stillness makes them appear taller. I think men and women with stillness make others feel comfortable and safe.

Manners, intention and listening I have already covered. Elegance is not just confined to dress because if it was I would never make the grade. I can manage elegant dress when necessary but I always end up galloping home, with sore feet, itching to ditch the heels and tightness. I would like to walk elegantly but I never learned to cruise like a goddess, though I once walked behind a young French girl [a receptionist in an Egyptian resort hotel] who walked to perfection. I tried to copy her, walking behind whilst endeavouring to emulate her exquisite gait. My partner assured me I was not successful. We often talk about that young lady and still look for someone to match her peerless elegance but as yet, models included, we have not seen anyone to touch her. I am, however, endeavouring to be elegant of thought and speech. I'm finding it damned hard work and impossible when politicians come on the telly. I instantly turn into Eliza Doolittle using language that would make a sailor blush. However, with age and boredom from hearing the same old rubbish, I am improving. Sometimes I can keep quiet and just roll my eyes, but mostly I maintain my elegance by not turning the telly on in the first place. Such a blessed relief.

SMILE

A smile is always nice to get. An inner smile is ravishing to achieve. I am working on it. No luck yet.

I have two little sayings, which are: 'the smile is too bright' and 'the loudest laugh covers the most pain'. I have noticed that an overused dazzling smile can be a cover for great insecurity, unhappiness and fear and those that laugh loudest are often holding deep emotional pain.

About twenty-five years ago I was travelling on the London Underground when a stranger smiled at me. She was an attractive young woman, from the States [I reckoned] accompanied by her husband. They were dressed in tennis clothes, clutching rackets, he was reading a newspaper. I don't know what it was about her smile that threw me completely. I was, quite literally, stunned and then profoundly grateful. Maybe I was at a low ebb and that is why it had such an effect on me. That stranger will never know how much I appreciated and marvelled at her smile. Sometimes it is the very simplest things that carry great weight and momentum - so go smile at a stranger. They may need it desperately and even recall it thirty years hence.

SELF-SABOTAGE

I have been a major saboteur of my life at times. I have watched breathtaking displays of sabotage in others and wondered, stupefied, why a course of self-destructive action would be taken by a seemingly intelligent person. Now I believe I understand completely. We vibrate, as does every thing on the planet, and we hold ourselves in vibrational holding patterns of self-belief. Should something sunny, wonderful and perhaps wished for thing come into our lives …… but deep in the darkest depths of ourselves we do not believe we deserve it [or are afraid of it], we will sabotage. No matter how pleased we say we are or how much we dance and clap with delight, if we don't think we are worthy of it we will push it away, or lose it. It might be in hours, or months, or years but we will self-sabotage. We will jam our finger on our self-destruct button, press hard and when our life goes 'boom!', we will blame everyone but ourselves.

In this way, large sums of money evaporate, dream jobs are lost and partnerships go awry. This is why people are late for the job interview they *say* they desperately wanted. Why people slap you in the face [metaphorically or literally] when you have been kind to them. Why people take completely unnecessary risks in their private lives and work knowing there is a good chance they will be found out. Think about your moments of self-sabotage. Think about your friends and colleagues, then raise your eyes and look at the big risk takers. Think big and global, for self-saboteurs are not confined to the poor and ordinary folk.

SUN SIGNS

You may think astrology is a load of old rubbish, I couldn't possibly comment. However, if I am short on laughs I get out and reread Linda Goodman's book 'Sun Signs'. She has me, Aries woman, down to such a 't' I think she must know me personally. Hilarious!

Also, each sign has a major lesson in life to learn. It might be worth looking up your sign and your lesson, it will help you to pay attention.

SKILLS

Oh hallelujah! Our great leaders have finally cottoned on to the fact that millennia of apprenticeships can't have been all wrong. What a relief. I did a three year apprenticeship when I trained as a nurse and I learned more on the wards from the oldies [anyone over thirty] than I did in the classroom. These days I have to fill my lungs very deeply and calmly every time I am greeted by a certain type of 'hello'. It is the 'hello' of the twenty-something who is not an apprentice [but should be] and who thinks and acts like they are in charge. These days, they seem to be everywhere, running everything. I cannot seem to gain access to a voice from anyone with grey hairs and lumpy bits. Where are they? Lurking behind closed doors, behind appointments I can't get, presumably. Not that these twenty year olds are not adorable, mostly they are, but when you are conducting business or trying to get something fixed, that certain 'hello' usually indicates you are not speaking to someone with years of experience [experience of anything, but work would be nice]. It means you are going to get the statutory answer, one given from on high, the high you cannot get access to. Sometimes I think it must be easier to talk to God than to talk to someone who is really, really in charge.

Thank heavens the Queen is now eighty, making white hair and sensible quite 'the thing'. She timed that well, didn't she? Perhaps now we can have a bit of balance and a general realisation that wrinkles do not go hand-in-hand with senility. Of course, not everyone with white hair is intelligent and wise, but mostly they are pretty sensible, except when it comes to their diets.

I am not quite white haired and I am not yet a fountain of wisdom but I have paid attention and I have clocked up a mighty amount of experience. This attention and experience tells me things are going to get much, much tougher for most and for a considerably long time ahead [like lifetimes]. This means everyone, but most especially the young, will need a multitude of skills to survive in the future. If I might make so bold as to offer some advice to those leaving school, please try and learn as many skills as possible. Any skills. Apprentice yourself to anyone who can teach you anything, whether they want you around or not. Find a talented wrinkly, glue yourself to them and learn. Please wise up and pay attention. Don't just sit in front of your computer or television as there may come a time when you, or your parents, cannot afford the electricity to turn them on. A mobile phone may become a luxury you will have to do without and, anyway, you learn more talking to someone when you can read their face and body language. The job market, especially in the UK, is shrinking and the global population is growing [for the time being, anyway]. Communication skills are vital all through life but especially in interviews and the workplace because they put you ahead of the rest of the competition. These skills are, at present, woefully ignored in most schools and even, sadly, in most homes. If you are teenager with a tendency to mistake grunting for talking you are at a *profound disadvantage.* If you lack communication skills, go and find someone who is good at communicating and watch their every move. Then copy. In the workplace you are at a profound *advantage* if you can approach someone with a smile, maintain eye contact and then greet them politely. We have noticed on our travels in India and South East Asia that the children stop grunting at two years of age and are either shyly charming or skilled and inquisitive communicators by their early teens, often using a self-taught foreign language. In our new found global marketplace these teenagers may get the work you so badly need. Pay attention.

Go to the granny and grandpa generation and ask them to teach you their skills. Hurry up - do it before that generation are dead and gone taking their knowledge with them. How is your handwriting? Not important? Think again. You can tell a great deal about people from their handwriting and some people write so beautifully they make a living from it. Can you write a business letter or a decent job application letter? I have stared in open mouthed incredulity at some business letters. I once saw a handwritten letter on a piece of torn off lined scrapbook notepaper from a woman applying for a job. What could she possibly have been thinking? Did she think that letter would be taken seriously or that it showed her in a good light? Did she engage brain at all? Unlikely, it seems. Whatever you are doing now, at school or working, if you don't know how to write, type or spell a job application or business letter, find someone who does and ask them to teach you. This is a life skill, as important as learning to drive a car….. and by the way, pretty flowery notepaper is NOT APPROPRIATE when applying for a job or answering an advertisement. Neither is notepaper with teddy bears on it - you are sending out a clear signal that you are immature. Grow up. Get serious, or someone else will get the job you want.

Learn to do woodwork, metalwork [particularly welding], fix simple engines, crochet, knit, prune apple trees, cook, ice cakes, make jam and preserves, keep ferrets, gain hunting skills or a language, embroider, sew, repair shoes, restring beads or pearls, milk a cow, stitch leather. If nothing else you will be a richer and more interesting person because most of these are creative skills and creating is what makes people come alive and become uniquely individual. Most people can do computer games but could you catch a mole without resorting to a large explosive device? You may think this is hilarious and so out of the ark it would bore Noah, but the fact is anything you can do with a mobile phone, or a computer, some teenager somewhere else in the world can do too - possibly better, probably cheaper and very likely in more than one language. They may also be able to catch a rat, so a mole might not be too much of a problem. Survival is not just about cooking out of an empty tin and snaring rabbits on wet and windy Brecon Beacons with the SAS. Survival is about learning to live life whatever life brings you. Right now you may live in a housing estate with hot and cold running everything, your food comes from a parent and electricity comes with the flick of a switch, but please know this: all through history most governments have had common-sense by-passes and ours is no different. Our economic situation could change catastrophically and very suddenly. It is a distinct possibility that this could happen in this country and it may be on the horizon, so please go out and learn those skills. DO IT. What you have learnt from someone older may put food on your plate in years to come. Ignore anyone who laughs at you, because they are the fool, not you.

By the way, moles move lightning fast if you think catching one is a breeze. They are also, some wise country man told me recently, very, very high in vitamin E. I wonder why that should be? Could we slap a mole on a burn?

SPEAK SOFTLY

I was talking to a charming American gentleman, whom I met on a dog walk recently. We discussed Theodore Roosevelt's saying .. 'There is a homely adage which runs - speak softly and carry a big stick, you will go far'. I believe this saying originates from Africa. The American gentleman expressed the view that this meant having the courage of your convictions, which fascinated me because I never interpreted it that way. In my way of thinking it meant 'speak softly but make absolutely sure they know you have a Chieftan tank, primed and ready to fire, parked quietly in the woods behind you'. To interpret it in chakra language it would be 'speak softly from your fifth chakra, but carry a big stick in your second'. Now, however, I am looking again at 'having the courage of your convictions' and thinking maybe that American gentleman was right all along.

SIRENS

I can't be doing with those whoop-whoop-wheeee sirens. I can't tell which direction they are coming from or judge their speed. I want to go back to nuh-nuh, nuh-nuh. Why do we have to copy the Americans with everything?

SPELL IT OUT

We are bombarded with words now, but most of us have limited attention spans. You sometimes need a degree in engineering to open or lock a suitcase and instruction books, if read, could take days to finish. I wish messages could be spelt out more, in a simple way. In 1983 I learnt a huge but simple lesson, because it was spelt out to me. I was working on an Intensive Care Unit and on a day off I purloined my father's car [because I only had a moped at the time] and took the family dog I semi-shared with my parents to the vet for his annual MOT. Whilst the vet examined the dog, my eye wandered around the room alighting upon all sorts of drugs, many of which I recognised because they sounded similar to the ones I gave in alarming numbers to my patients during a nursing shift. I mentioned this to the vet and he asked me what I thought his drug bill was per month. I pondered on the size of his practice and the lack of large farm animals in the surrounding area and tentatively suggested several hundred pounds. '£18,000 a month, £24,000 on a bad month', he informed me [you can now, in 2007, more than double the last sum]. I was speechless. You could have knocked me over with a feather because I had recently bought a tiny house for a little over the former figure and was really struggling to pay the mortgage and feed myself. Now, I was already of the opinion that the NHS was in deep trouble with it's pill bill, but this vet's bombshell of a reality-check really brought it home to me. It spelt out the problem in no uncertain terms. I tried to imagine what the hospital drug bill would be per month. I thought of the cost of all the drugs I gave to a patient in one shift. On my return to work I told my colleagues the story. Their jaws dropped too. I suggested to my senior colleagues that price tags should be attached to everything we use in the hospital. This was met with about as much enthusiasm as most of my ideas, but I believe it is pretty much standard practice now. I decided the government needed to 'spell out' how much money went where and to whom, but thought this was an unlikely scenario. Once we, the people, the breadwinners, knew exactly how much government cost, we might get more than a tad restless.

I think it was Machiavelli who said, 'Man's greatest weakness is his lack of foresight'. I will, if I may be so bold, Niccolo, add a Manselli to a Machiavelli and say that, 'Man's greatest weakness is his lack of foresight and lack of imagination'. I meet very few people who can imagine, or even try to imagine, what it must be like to be in someone else's shoes, life, bank balance, country or predicament. Often, therefore, there is a need to spell things out in simple language that a young child could understand. My partner does huge mileage in his working day and sometimes used to get let down by clients cancelling appointments at the very last minute, wasting his time, petrol and money. He bemoaned the fact to me. 'Spell out your working day to them, in a pleasant manner', I instructed him, 'because they cannot imagine what your day consists of'. He did this. Client's eyes widened, pennies dropped and now he very rarely gets let down.

Office workers think farmers just drive tractors all day and farmers think office workers just push paper around, but an office worker might have to drive miles to work [might even get stuck behind a tractor while doing so], and farmers have to push ludicrous amounts of paper around because governments everywhere have completely lost the plot and cannot stop interfering. I really think we all need to spell out what we do and how we work. I don't think television helps much; all those hospital soaps astound me, where do they get the time for so much dialogue between colleagues? I remember someone bemoaning to me their stressful high-powered office work and my countering back to them how stressful I found laying out young bodies and how I hated de-lousing some adults who had crabs and lice attached to every hair on their body from head to foot, including eyebrow and nostril hair. There was a pause for a jaw drop and I realised that person had no concept of what my nursing work entailed, but then I probably did not understand their life. My mother, bless her, also lacked imagination. At the end of my eleven hour night shift I walked around the corridor to the orthopaedic ward and asked the staff if I could visit my Mum, who had had her hip replaced. Still in uniform and with that post-shift facial pallor that affects most night-workers I asked my mother how her night had been. '*You won't believe what has been going on here!*', she steamed. 'The nurses have not stopped all night - they have worked their socks off. Up and down, up and down. Patients yelling, buzzers going, doctors visiting. I hardly got a wink of sleep you know.' This went on for several minutes as I sat in tired and confused amazement that my mother was seemingly unable to grasp that I had been doing much the same, all night long, a couple of wards away from her bed. I could not even spell it out to her, she needed to actually see me doing it to believe it.

How about a new television programme? A full day in the life of a farmer, a lawyer, a nurse, a refuse collector, a hairdresser, a tailor, a tree surgeon, a soldier and so on. We could all be amazed, educated and have reality spelt out to us.

SHOPPING

I am exhausted by the choice. So many shops, so little to choose. Now our local supermarket has expanded and I am greeted with a huge expanse of olive oil or mayonnaise. I want reasonable olive oil and mayo made with eggs from happy chickens, but I am worn out reading all the labels. I have decided I want time - not choice. Occasionally I work up some excitement and ponder a shopping expedition to one of East Anglia's larger towns. Then I think about the drive, the parking [if you are lucky], the trailing from the car parking, the browsing of the same choice in multiple shops and then the drive back. I think I will stay at home. I prefer the excitement of local charity shops. I am an aficionado. A con-oi-sur, as my Kiwi friend says. I was in tight over the chest silk and too long in the arm cashmere when people thought charity shops were about as much fun as bungee jumping with a frayed rope. In fact, I was rummaging before bungee jumping was even thought of. In those heady, glorious, distant days I had the shops to myself. They were stuffed to the gunnels and full of 1940's treasures and more. There were always drawers full of belts and gloves and scarves and shelves of handbags. Heart a flutter with possibility, I would pounce on a treasure; an old but glorious suede or leather handbag with its very own suede backed mirror inside and a special compartment for lipstick! Raptures!

'Nowadays', says I, with thinning lips, 'every bloody Tom, Dick and Harry is in the charity shop'. And that is exactly right - men. What is more, they simply do not seem to understand that they get in my way. I am not the same woman that smiles with grace and humour outside the premises. For me that doorway is a threshold of Jekyll and Hyde proportions. Once in, I become a woman of murderous intent. A woman of whom Sherlock Holmes would be proud. I miss nothing. My radar alerts me to good cloth and vintage anything from fifty paces. As I make my completely focused advance upon my quarry, arm outstretched, what happens? A man walks in front of me and then hovers. What the bloody hell is he looking at frocks for, at his age? Don't answer! Women I understand. I always check the women as I come through the door because I can spot serious competition a mile off and sometimes it can resort to speeded up comedy if the competition spots me and we both hurtle through the rails, at lightning speed, trying to find a gem first.

My mother never got the hang of it and never recovered from me finding a serious gold chain and paying 20p for it. I refused to take her, ever again, after she haggled over a silk scarf at rock bottom price in a Sue Ryder Shop.

I told her it was 'a disgraceful carry on' and she responded by glowering at me and doing the one thing that riled me more than most of the things she did - she lit up a cigarette in the car. We drove home in stony silence. Actually, I secretly envied her cohones [Spanish for balls] because I am useless at haggling. My mother was fleeced on more than one occasion by a smooth talking antique salesman ....

Me ... 'How *could* you have fallen for *that* line?'

Mother ...'He was so nicely spoken; he nearly went to Eton, you know'.

Me, incredulously ... *'Nearly?!?'.*

However, mother would take no such line from a grocer. Velvet tones were wasted on her if they came from a man in a pinafore [unless he was caressing a cabriole leg], she would get that cheddar at trade price if it was the last thing she did. Mortified, I would silently slide out of the shop, red-faced and heated enough to warm a small town. We would drive home in stony silence. Again.

I have such happy memories of my golden years in charity shops when there was proper rummaging to be had. Pretty china and Victorian glass, linen sheets, velvet draught excluders and everything you could possibly need for the kitchen. In those days you could buy electric goods too [very heaven!], and all were carried home triumphantly to my little nest. My mother called a truce to stony silences for a month when I presented her with a bullseye - a pair of unworn Ferragamo shoes that fitted like a glove on her poor, sore, aged feet. She wore them until she died. Suddenly my CSR's [charity shop raids] were full of promise. She would furnish me with a shopping list, ignoring my response that, 'You don't tend to find Aspreys and Hermes goods round these parts, Ma'. Nowadays the charity shops are thinned out and far too tidy for my liking. Too much nylon, too many men and worse ..... new goods .... whatever next? It is tragic, but still, I had the best of the days.

SMALL

Never underestimate the small things in life. I know the saying goes 'the best presents come in small packages' and it is true that expensive personal adornments usually come in small boxes, but I am talking about small acts of kindness and generosity, or a few kind words, that fill a great big gaping hole.

I am not shy about handing out compliments, so don't be shy giving them to me. A few days ago a woman in a divine hat and an equally divine pale blue old [that is about as technical as I can get] open-top sports car drove past me in a car park. The sight was a feast for the eyes and I told her how much I had enjoyed it. She thanked me. I think genuine compliments are lovely and I prefer them to be succinct. My most favourite ones have been when nothing was said but an appreciative look spoke volumes. I have always thoroughly disliked lengthy, oily compliments from men of a certain age. I know what they are trying to say and the answer is, 'No. Bog off, or talk to me sensibly'.

I have been immensely moved over the years by small acts of kindness. A bunch of daffodils from a colleague when I was having a rough time. A hug from another colleague when my heart was breaking. Sweet words of support from a friend when life just seemed all too much. A girl friend who turned up and silently weeded for me when I was so desperately ill and the garden was turning into a jungle [and would have silently left had I not heard the clink of trowel on stone]. A pretty image on a postcard and a few thoughtful words can make someone's day. You may or may not be aware of this, but birthday cards mean much more to the middle-aged and elderly [especially if they live alone] than they do to youngsters. Youngsters tend to rip open the envelope, check the content and abandon the card but a card to someone of less than tender years is so often rather reverentially displayed and admired. A birthday card and a posy of garden flowers in a jam jar left outside a front door can mean so much.

I have found cupping someone's elbow and saying how sorry you are eases distress faster than anything, and if you don't know what to say to someone's woe or death loss, say just that .. 'I don't know what to say'. I remember talking to a lovely man who had just lost his most beloved wife of many years. He was devastated to be told he would soon meet someone else. He didn't want to meet anyone else, he just wanted to talk, uninterrupted about his wife's devastating illness and death. He deserved to be allowed to do just that. All he asked and needed was a small listening kindness.

The elderly want your time and they can be time consuming but don't forget that you will be elderly and quite possibly lonely one day too. Try and stop for a quick chat, it is the small acts of kindness that empower you personally because lots of little acts of kindness make one big kind person who has more authentic power than they realise.

SACRED CONTRACTS

All about me, these days, I see the possibility of sacred contracts. I am humbled and fascinated. I think every relationship we have is a sacred contract and the contract is made before our arrival. I have an irrational fear of two countries, Germany and China. I have not visited the former but while working in Hong Kong I trekked into the New Territories, viewing the sight of distant China with an anxiety that was much deeper than economic concern. My mother said the first thing she noticed about me, at birth, was that I had two small marks in different places, one brown and one white. Truly, the white one looks and feels like a scar. My feelings say it was a bullet hole. I have no proof of course but I don't think I need proof. The mark, as far as I am aware, has little to do with my life right now, but still, I fear Germany and my feelings say that is where the mark was made.

I had a complicated relationship with my mother. Ever since I was a very small child I always had these strange and persistent feelings of guilt about her. After she died, a kinesiologist [muscle tester] did a past life question and answer on me [I am sure you think this is completely off the wall, but I can assure you muscles can answer yes and no - this is simple to test by holding a bottle of water and a bottle of bleach - the latter will make your muscles weaker, if only fractionally]. When the kinesiologist had finished her 'yes and no' questioning, she told me of a past life in China where, as some sort of monk or priest, I fathered a child. I let that child down very badly and was mightily punished for my actions. That child was my mother in this lifetime. Perhaps that explains my inexplicable feelings of guilt with my mother and perhaps, when I die, I will find out if this story is true. It feels true to me. I still fear [and yet am fascinated by] China.

I have had more lives, I believe. Mundane ones, so I obviously failed to make the grade as an Egyptian princess - darn it. I have had, on several occasions, a vivid daytime image of lying mortally wounded in the lower abdomen; a Union soldier in the American Civil War, the grass around me sticky with the blood of other fallen soldiers. My name was John, my wife was Mary [hardly original, but there we have it]. Is this true? I don't know. I don't fear America but I watched that outstanding documentary 'The American Civil War' [by Eric or Pete Burns?] with such very still silence.

I met my partner when I was forty-five. I cannot remember thinking, 'I am in love with him', I just remember feeling I had to be with him. I had to and it was hideous because he was married to someone else at the time. He had the same feeling. Now, as I look back over my life I see events that pointed, several times, to him. At the age of thirteen my boarding school closed down. Our theatrical cupboard was stuffed with lovely things that we were told were going to charity. I suppose we were being naughty, just for once, but us girls were taking a few bits and bobs. There were velvet robes and feather boas that I loved but did not take. Instead I picked up two small objects that were meaningless and pretty much worthless. I had to have them. I stared at them for years wondering what on earth had made me take them, yet now they are such a strong link to my partner, relating specifically to him and his ancestry, I can hardly believe it. In one of my early jobs a colleague told me of the town of her birth which had an unusual name. I kept badgering her. 'How do you spell it? Where is it? What is it like?'. She got rather irritated with me. There are dozens of places with unusual names but this one struck *such* a cord with me that for years I jumped if I heard anyone mention it. My partner was, at the time, living in that town. In London, as a nurse, I stood behind a policeman one night as he questioned a drug addict. The world went quiet for a moment - stilled - I stared at the policeman's back while listening intently to his East End of London accent. 'He's in the East End', my feelings said, 'your man is a Cockney'. My partner was born and pretty much raised in the East End of London. In my late thirties I took a photograph of a painting of a Spanish nobleman in a national art gallery. I can't remember if I was allowed to take the photograph but I would have done it anyway, though I am not a law breaker as a rule. I had to have a photo of that painting. When it was developed I used it as a bookmark. When my man finally turned up in my life he looked just like the Spanish nobleman in my postcard and he had Spanish ancestry too.

Do our sacred contracts talk to us over the years? I think they do and I think we tend to ignore them or fail to realise their importance. I do believe my contract was to wait for my partner, it explains unexplained feelings I have had since my teens. I also believe that when I have tried in some way to break, shift or remake my contract doors have slammed in my face and relationships have gone awry. I should have waited. I should have been patient. I came here to learn patience, after all. We think we are here to have a nice time and wail when we are not. I believe we are here to participate in our contracts in order for us to learn and then to take our power back. I also believe that when we fully understand this, we can then start having a nice time.

SHOPKEEPERS

My biggest worry about big business is that, within them, too many people become salaried workers with little understanding of the nature of business. The nation of shopkeepers that Napolean described, dismissively perhaps, was a nation that was soundly rooted in the hard reality, savagery even, of selling, for without the sale there was no bread on the table. For hundreds of years our small shops were family run and mealtime conversation would have educated the next generation on the finer points of buying in and selling on. A shopkeeper's son or daughter had [hopefully] first chakra tribal support, a very early introduction into some major second chakra lessons, a chance to take over the business and explore third chakra while verbally [fifth chakra] standing their ground with tricky customers.

I have always felt that at some point in one's life there comes a time when you consider how you may serve. There are a thousand ways of giving back, but to serve well as a shopkeeper is to enhance the nation while personally enhancing your character. Having tackled a shop once myself I have huge admiration for small shopkeepers, whatever their wares. The fact that they are so bullied and hounded by national and local government just makes them more heroic in my eyes.

SUCCESS

I don't know what your definition of success is but mine is contentment. Quiet contentment. I have met more quietly content folk in rural villages than I see striding through city streets. We have the following framed on our wall ....

To laugh often and much;
to win the respect of intelligent
people and the affection of
children; to earn the appreciation
of honest critics and endure the
betrayal of false friends;
to appreciate beauty;
to find the best in others;
to leave the world a bit better;
whether by a happy child,
a garden patch or a
redeemed social condition;
to know even one life has
breathed easier
because you have lived.
This is to have succeeded.

RALPH WALDO EMERSON
AMERICAN ESSAYIST, PHILOSOPHER AND POET
[1803 - 1882]

I remind myself to read this on a regular basis. I think it is beautiful, succinct and true. However, underneath this we have another framed saying ……….

We are here on earth
to do good for others.
What the others are here for,
I don't know.

WYSTAN HUGH AUDEN
ENGLISH POET
[1907 - 1973]

T Is for TRADITION

I am for maintaining our traditions as well as creating new ones. Our somewhat eccentric customs and colourful traditions give us, in many ways, our identity and act as boundary keepers and restraining bonds. These customs and traditions usually require a coming together [usually a joyful reconnection] of the tribe in some form or another and act as a reminder that, 'No man is an Iland, intire of it selfe', as John Donne taught all those years ago.

*T*EACHERS

I know I have already said it but I am going to say it again because it is hugely important and it needs spelling out in plain language. Who is currently really pissing you off? They are your teachers. They are here to highlight your problems. Find a friend, have a coffee and a rant or a moan. Get that off your chest. When you are done, clear off home, or somewhere quiet, and ask yourself some deep and meaningful questions. First, what is it about this infuriating teacher that annoys you and exactly where might you have expertly hidden that very same trait? Be honest. I know - it's a nightmare. I hate doing this exercise myself but we all have to grow up. It's time. Second, have you been playing doormat? If so, re-read what I said about boundaries, second and third chakra and get yourself into navy blue. Third, if you have honestly written both those possibilities off, is this pain in the rear-end teacher the road sign that says leave this place/person and seek pastures new? If so, be brave, re-read 'commitment' and use colour to help you. If you are getting a nasty life lesson and you are foaming at the mouth - whether it is a snipey carpy letter from the bank or a higgledy piggledy dispute with a loved one - wear some mid to dark blue colour [NO stripes or checks]. It will help you calm down and see the bigger picture.

Now, swerving slightly off the subject, I once gave a friend [who I am fond of] a stern ticking off because she had suicidal eating habits. This woman was not in the first flush of youth and not given to raising her voice in protest, let alone anger. As I ticked her off, this relatively mild-mannered woman gave me a look much like a distressed puppy but, luckily, I was watching her jaw muscles which were clenching in irritation. I pointed out what was happening. Outright denial on her part because she did not know she was doing it but I was, in her eyes, the teacher [and a bossy one to boot] but I was also reminding her of someone. I was replaying a ticking off scene, almost undoubtedly from her childhood. Her anger, so well hidden for too many years did not show in most of her demeanour, but her clenching jaw said it all. We need to pay attention to the small signs. People who really annoy you affect your digestion and therefore your biochemistry - let that go on for long enough and then comes the ill health. It is best to find out what they are teaching you, quick smart, and then move on with your life. It is a way to stay healthy. Not 'the' way but 'a' way.

One last thing. I have been taught by teachers absolutely everywhere. On trains, planes and in shops. I have had major life lessons in supermarkets from a casual remark made by a fellow shopper who was a stranger. In fact, I have learnt more in the every day ordinary process of living than I ever learnt in any classroom or lecture theatre. I have done this by paying attention to tiny details and small comments. Your teachers are all around you. Your world, wherever you live, is your classroom. Are you paying attention?

TRAINS

I visited Japan and went to a railway station. *It was immaculate.* I got on a bullet train. No-one said, 'Mind the gap', because there wasn't one. The train was spotless, you could have eaten off the floor. The loos were a symphony of sweet smelling cleanliness. Japan does not heave with foreigners who clean for low wages, the Japanese clean themselves and most thoroughly and exquisitely they do it too. The train was so smooth you could write a letter while travelling at .... er, improbable speeds. No-one in Japan chucked rubbish out of their gardens on to the railway banks. What, pray, is the matter with us?

Could it be about attitude? Perhaps we need to start young. Why don't we get schoolchildren to clean their own schools? Do I hear howls of indignation? I remember a story from my childhood of a young man longing to join the army but devastated when he failed the practical test for [I think it was] Sandhurst [but don't quote me]. The story I was told was that though he did splendidly in written and oral testing he was given the practical task of washing the floor of a room. He started, with his mop and bucket, by the entrance door. He failed the test.

I remember being stunned by a new young recruit to the hospital who flatly refused to take a bedpan from me. She said there was no way she was cleaning it out - yet bedpan cleaning was most specifically within her job remit. She did not stay long. I thought about my early nursing days when unpleasant jobs were absolutely accepted as par for the course. As I emptied the bedpan in the sluice I wondered incredulously where this high-handed attitude had first been birthed. From whence did this attitude of superiority come? Why was changing a nappy acceptable to most women but emptying a bedpan not? Why is cleaning a floor demeaning instead of being a practical skill that will come in handy all through life? I think collectively 'the tribe' has failed the younger generation. It has not instilled a disciplined acceptance of what is perceived as 'demeaning work'. Instead, the younger amongst us have been quickly introduced into second chakra lessons. However, without the tribal insistence that the young perform menial and sometimes smelly work, there can be no understanding, or reference point, when it comes to them to perform, later in life, the altogether different but equally unpleasant tasks of third chakra. Grit is learnt from the crib.

TALK

My partner has suddenly become of the opinion that men do not talk nearly enough. Hurrah! I have come to the conclusion that the world is split between talkers and non-talkers. Talkers, I have noticed, are split into revealers and concealers. The revealing talkers teach you a lot in their revealing, while the concealing talkers bombard you with endless detail while failing to actually reveal anything about themselves and their inner workings. I think the non-talkers have an easier time in life. My parents talked too much and I was privy to things I did not need to know at such an early age. It sometimes made me frightened and often confused. Then there was the dilemma of what to do with the information I had been given. I found various filing cabinets in my brain and stored it there, failing that I pretended I was thick. People rarely questioned this, which is interesting. I really admire people who can sort out their problems without chewing them over with friends or loved ones. I have met a few who are able to do this but only a handful; I admire these people. However, I have met many who will not talk about their problems at all until things get completely out of hand. In these cases it is up to us to pay attention to people who are pressure cookers about to explode and offer a chance to release their steam before they do some irreparable damage. Talking things over with one you trust is invaluable because you can get so bogged down with problems that encircle your brain like the M25 in rush hour, but a fresh view can clear the traffic log-jam and get you motoring in the right direction again.

*T*ONGUE

If you want to know what yours should look like find a rosy cheeked and healthy small child [assuming you can find one these days] and ask them to stick their tongue out at you. Probably best to ask their parents' permission first, in these hysterical times. I am NOT an expert on tongues. I have had no formal training but I have read a bit here and there. My tongue tells me how my health is and I take its messages very seriously. I am wondering [just wondering mind you] if tongue observation could be another preventative health measure against bowel cancer.

Stick yours out and have a gawp in the mirror. Is it a nice and slightly rounded shape, pink and healthy? Your tongue is a *vital* visual link to the state of your gut and digestion. Bad tongue - bad health. Do you have wind? Prod your tummy all over. Anything going ouch? Get help from someone trained and experienced and do it now please. I am really sorry to say this but a doctor would not be my first port of call if I had a tongue that looked like it had died a week ago. As a child, if taken to the surgery, our family doctor always looked at my tongue, eyes, hands [both sides], nails, felt my neck glands and pulse and more often than not palpated my tummy and took my temperature. While this went on my mother was asked about my waterworks, bowels, appetite and sleep patterns. Sadly, this does not seem to be deemed necessary now.

A healthy tongue does NOT have large or small cracks, in singles or multiples. It does not look like a map of the British Isles [geographic tongues point to prolonged B vitamin deficiency], nor is it white coated [this is showing an overgrowth of unhelpful gut bacteria] or very smooth with large taste buds at the rear. These all point to one or more B vitamin deficiencies. Stay seated please. I don't want you rushing out to the pharmacy or health food shop just yet. Keep absolutely calm and carry on reading …………...

Smelly breath can be a lack of vitamin B6, but check your teeth [have you flossed between them recently, or do you have rotten and smelly food particles wedged in your pearlies?]. Gums [healthy gums need Vitamin C], tonsils, bowels and *anger,* expressed or unexpressed, can all point to smelly breath. Sometimes vitamin B6 is low if your tongue is burning. Large, beefy or slightly swollen tongues and/or scalloped edges [where your tongue has rested on your teeth] can mean you are low on the B vitamin pantothenic acid, but don't take B's in isolation, taking one in excess can deplete another, get professional help. It is your diet and how you eat it; your bowels and how you clear them; your emotions and how you deal with them. A magenta coloured tongue can mean low B2, but get your neck [and therefore blood supply] checked by someone who understands muscles and bones, in that order. Alexander Technique is good, but look at how you stand first. Are you always looking downwards? Are you disappointed with life? Afraid to look up at the horizon?

Smooth shiny tongues can be a sign of Low B12 and/or folic acid. A bright red tongue can point to low niacin amide [also called nicotinic acid or B3, and steady as you go, too much can cause a hot prickly red rash, but it passes fairly quickly]. A sore mouth generally can point to B6, or folic acid or niacin amide [B3]. Don't look at your tongue and panic. You may have a gluten intolerance and/or leaky gut in which case you need expert advice from an expert nutritionist. What do you eat for breakfast, or have you nervily skipped it because your tummy is in secret knots? Do you chew your food? Skip lunch or eat on the hoof? Sweeties? Choccy? Sugar? Cheese every single day? Lots of coffee, little water? What are your bowels up to? What is your intake of all the B vitamins? My very best little book, The Vitamin and Mineral Counter [Murdoch Books, Consultant Editor - Dell Stanford] is, tragically, out of print but you may find it in the library. Your digestion is affected by your emotions, so clear them. Dump the emotional garbage any way you fancy. Use colour, Bach Flower Remedies, see a homeopath, a hypnotist, use Thought Field Therapy, have a holiday, have a drink, bawl your eyes out, stop being heroic, or stoic, or coping. Sing, shout, lose your temper, dump your boyfriend, whatever. Just swerve off your present path, plead silently for help and then pay very silent and very serious attention to little tiny messages from the universe. If you keep very, very quiet don't be surprised if someone talks to you, someone you can't see. Invisible talkers should always be helpful and friendly. If they are not - see your doctor and look at the colours you wear.

My tongue used to frighten the living daylights out of me but it has improved greatly, though there is still work to do. My taste buds are starting to reappear along a tongue that was smoother than an ice rink, with fissures to fox any potential skaters and fluted edges to finish off the design. Now my tongue is looking prettier my sense of taste and smell is also vastly improved. No wonder I used to put so much salt on my food, I couldn't taste the flavours in anything. I hardly use salt at all these days, except on my boiled eggs. If you are a woman and planning a family take a look at your tongue and check Daddy's too. If it is not pink and perky start working on it and please, please, talk ... just talk to a nutritionist about your diet before you get pregnant. That tiny growing baby in your uterus deserves the best start in life and its little body is depending on every mouthful of food you put in your mouth. What food are you giving it and how often? What don't you like eating that the baby might need?

*T*RANSPORT

I drive a Dovo. This is a cross between a dog and a Volvo. My partner, who was either a bloodhound or a Parisian parfumier's nose in a previous life, says my car stinks. I tell him I have met men who smell worse. One of my dogs has made a hole in my seat and I wonder if I should have bought leather instead of fabric seating, but I was in my vegetarian phase when I bought the car. Still, my dogs are capable of making holes in anything, be-bulbed flowerbeds and carpets are a speciality and leather is not a hint of a problem. What to do? I am in a transportation dilemma. Should I buy a new car? But there is nothing wrong with the one I have ... in my nose. It is slightly battered and scratched but I call that character and, anyway, about these parts hedgerows move, especially when they see me coming. Should I get a new seat and drive my Dovo into the sunset? Go green and convert the engine so it propels itself on alcohol? What sort of alcohol? Sounds like a damned waste to me. I ponder on the shape of my future transport [horse and cart?] while soaking in the bath, as my dog makes holes in the bathmat. My neighbour once told me an Arabian [sounds so romantic] gentleman once told him, 'My grandfather had a donkey, I have a Cadillac, my son will have a jet plane and my grandson will have a donkey'.

Maybe I should buy an electric car, but I do so hate plugs, they make me nervous. Still, you wouldn't have to check the oil would you? I remember being asked to check the oil on a strange car so I lifted the bonnet and started looking for a shepherd's crook type thing. I don't do instruction books, not if I can possibly avoid them. Half an hour later I was fuming and making highly explosive racist remarks about a specific foreign car manufacturer. I gave in and started slapping the pages of the instruction book but was still none the wiser. Eventually I found what I was looking for and I pulled out something that looked as if it had been designed by John Paul Gaultier. I was incredulous and then thoroughly depressed. The design world had left me behind. I was trapped in a shepherd's crook of time.

Cars are not what they used to be. I rather miss the days of the banger. I had one where the windscreen wiper had to be operated manually and a friend had one whose horn only worked if you opened the bonnet and pushed things together. A policeman stood watching, incredulously, as my mate demonstrated to him the horn-honking procedure. In those days people were not as angry as they are today and everyone had a sense of humour. I sold a banger when I moved to a city and months later I got a phone call from the police describing the car. 'Are you no longer the owner of said veer-hickle?', the policeman asked me.'I am not', I replied, wondering how on earth he had tracked me down to my present employment. 'Your car has been used as a getaway car following a robbery', he informed me as I struggled to suppress a serious attack of the giggles. 'But that car can only do forty miles an hour downhill with the wind behind it, officer', I informed him, thinking it best not to mention that it also suffered from a fuel injection problem which brought the car to a regular standstill and required me, the driver, to leap out and give an almighty kick in a specific spot near the petrol tank. This was tricky in busy three lane traffic but caused no end of amusement to a car overloaded with raucous student nurses. I never found out who robbed what and made off in my old car, more is the pity.

I always fancied a Jensen Interceptor. I like their bottoms. I don't think I will have one now, but never say never, I say. My partner prefers small sporty affairs with massive mileage to the gallon because he does massive mileage. I am past sporty now. He likes the wind on his face. I like my hair in place. I have got an original wrap around cotton scarf that buttons at the back of my neck which I wear with dark glasses but I fear I cannot pull off the Audrey Hepburn look. There is too much of me and the much is getting on.

*T*ECHNOLOGY

Computers are amazing, aren't they? All our new technology is spellbinding and awesome but it has a bit of a drawback because chakra lessons are limited when dealing with a machine. Chakra development requires human to human contact and interaction. This is a worry to me, in this, our technological age.

$\mathcal{U}$ Is for UNDERWEAR

I have turned into my mother. I suppose it was inevitable. I spent years teasing her about her knickers and though I have not yet reached her baggy standards I fear I have alighted upon her height of elastic. I am not going to spell it out, my partner is beyond begging for a drop in height but I am resolute. I did lacy wispy for years *and a fat lot of good it did me*. Upon acquiring a pair of knickers that could be used to polish a large car a gorgeous man appeared in my life, so I am not tempting fate.

My mother, and I am sure she won't mind me telling you this story [?!] had a very high pain threshold. Just as well. I have some of her knicks from WWII days and very silken they are too, but like most women of her era she embraced nylon with gusto. My father eventually put his foot down with the nylon sheets after sparks were seen when he turned smartly over in bed. Still, nylon was the order of the day for undies. No matter what I said, or offered, Mum's knickers were vast, man-made and once, having had a tinkle, she swept them on and the upward gust included a drowsy wasp having a nap under the loo seat. You know wasps can sting more than once. Too ghastly .... *and she was heroic.*

Some years ago, I went to an old-fashioned corner of an old-fashioned department store. I perused rows of large white catapults and alighted upon a whisper of silken salmon pink and café au lait lace. I seized an appropriate approximation with gurgles of delight just as a matronly figure in navy appeared at my shoulder. 'Would madam like to try it on?' Madam would. 'Would madam like to be measured for a well-fitting brassiere?' Madam most bloody well would not, but madam was far too well brought up and suffered from a split personality when it came to saying what madam thought, so madam smiled through gritted teeth and said, 'Thank you'. A tape measure appeared - it looked like a guillotine. Madam was measured and it was not good news. The navy blue presence assured madam she had the perfect bra for such a bilateral edifice, whereupon she disappeared off to fetch it. She reappeared and held it aloft. Kangaroo hammocks. Hideously practical but not even a sliver of salmon or lace. 'I WON'T', I thought, but the presence was formidable and knowing. I hated her, but I knew when I had met my match.

Some weeks later, because I had to, I closed my eyes, put on my kangaroo hammocks and miserably got dressed. I looked in the mirror and lo........ two perfect hemispherical lobes twinkled back at me. I had SHAPE!!

Sometimes navy blue presences *know things.*

*U*RINE

Please try and notice what your pee looks like, smells like and how much you do. If you get sick your doctor may ask you just these questions. Backache can be kicked off by a kidney infection - do you know where your kidneys are yet? Urine should be very pale straw yellow coloured and it should not smell. Fishy smelling urine means trouble - get thee to a doctor, quick smart. Don't take your urine specimen with you in an orange juice jar, like my mother did, having failed to wash it out properly and resulting in my father's urine sample being so full of orange juice sugar that there was total panic at the hospital. Dark coloured urine [but be sure it is not blood] often means dehydration - drink water. If you suffer repeatedly from cystitis get help from a nutritionist, but check out who is pissing you off. Pinky coloured or urine with tiny shreds or clots of blood also points to infection, or something - get thee to a doctor. I find if I over alkalanise my body by reducing meat, increasing vegetables and cutting out tea and booze my urine quickly starts developing a whiff. A stiff scotch soon remedies *that*............. and that is my excuse and I am sticking to it.

You should be widdling about two litres out daily and putting two litres of fluid back in - some of which will be in your food. Measuring could be a messy nightmare so I would not worry about it too much, just keep an eye on the colour and roughly how much you do and how often you go. You need to know these things, you really do ... and Mums, you need to know these things about your young children, you really do. It's important.

While in am in the piddling department may I make a bold suggestion and suggest you buy yourself a really useful present? A slipper bedpan. You won't use it for a decade, maybe two, but when you need one you can't find one and when you need one it is urgent. We had a happening when a friend badly injured her knee. She could not move or be moved, poor thing, without screaming with pain. Her bladder was filling mightily so a china potty was fetched but was too big and tall for her to use so a slim flat plastic slipper pan was sought high and low, with no luck. As her bladder swelled, frantic phone calls were made to various medical type establishments and on-call nurses without actually resorting to a hospital. Computers they had, but bedpans they had not. I suppose you could pee into a computer in an emergency, as long as it was a very small pee. Eventually it was a bin-liner and multiple towels to the rescue. It seemed to be just another indicator of how far we have come from the basics. You can get the innermost hinterlands of your body exposed on a screen but a bedpan is harder to come by.

V Is for VALIDATION

A bit like a woman moaning that she cannot grumble in front of her man because he hears the grumble and offers a solution whereas she just wants an ear to grumble into, it is difficult to heal an emotional wound without validation. I have found that it only takes one genuine, empathic and kind person who is able in some way, maybe not even verbally, to validate a hurt and in that moment of validation a whole suitcase of pain can be dropped and a lighter life begin.

I used to measure my hurts against the survivors of Auschwitz or starving children in Africa and think, 'Shut up Amanda, just shut up'. I cannot even attempt to empathise with those children or those survivors and trying to usually makes me tearful. I think it is healthy to measure your good fortune against human tragedies of greater magnitude. Our hurts may seem pathetic against such a backdrop but hurts unhealed ulcerate away at our fabric and sharing a hurt to a kind and sympathetic other releases one and teaches another.

*V*ITAMINS

There is a saying, by Hippocrates I think, 'Let food be your medicine, let medicine be your food'. I was unsure when I heard it. Food equals medicine? I am not unsure now, he was damn right was Hippo all those thousands of years ago.

I don't know much about minerals and vitamins but I will give you what I do know because the first step in getting a better life is to take control of your body. To do this you need to know where things are, how they work and what they need. Most of us know where our lumpy bits are, or should be, on the outside, but not many know where they are, or should be, on the inside. It helps if you know where your liver is and to be able to point to kidneys, spleen, bladder etc., so do get an anatomy book and look.

There is endless discussion about the necessity, or not, of taking supplements. There is absolutely NO QUESTION that you are best off getting your requirements from a well chewed plate of nutritious food, but food is not what is used to be and pollutants, additives and stressful emotions take their toll on your biochemistry. I am not a banner waving anti-drug therapy person, I take the odd pain killer and anti-spasmodic myself. If I got cancer I would probably mix conventional Western treatment with alternative therapies, though my main cause of concern would be that I had not paid attention to my feelings. That my Rheumatoid Arthritis was a message from me to me [and it was not talking to anyone else] is a definite. I had failed miserably to listen to my feelings after my mother died, when my feelings were telling me to sit by an ocean, stare and do nothing for a year while my overworked and exhausted body repaired and my mind cruised and silenced. Then, and only then, should I have returned to work, but I knew better than my feelings and I am now paying the price for that outrageous arrogance. What I know now is your health is in your hands and in your mind but that the keeping of it or reclaiming of it is your decision and yours alone. I have come to understand that this is a spiritual decision.

I have said this before, but you are getting it again [sorry], it is fundamentally important to EAT THREE BALANCED MEALS A DAY. You can get away with being silly about your food for many years but sooner or later [and these days it is getting a lot sooner] your body will start to complain, or worse. If you have not fed your immune system expect double trouble. A bowl of breakfast cereal and a cup of tea every morning is NOT a balanced meal, especially if you are doing work that involves physical work. Your body will need some protein and carbohydrates at breakfast despite what you, stonking great ego, think it needs. Eat sensibly, lots of fruit and vegetables. If you are pregnant eat doubly sensibly because you too are doing physical work, you are building a baby and every single part of that baby will need different minerals and vitamins to grow. It is often the case, I have noticed, that the person who thinks they do not need to see a nutritionist is the person who needs to do exactly that. I look back on my years as a midwife and despair that I knew nothing about nutrition then. How could I have been so stupid?

Get enough protein, most people [probably you] don't. Most of us watch telly while eating sometimes, we certainly do, but it is a really bad habit. Television flashes lights at you and throws up all sorts of emotions. You just do not need that while your stomach and the rest of your digestive organisation is trying to get down to peaceful work. Try and imagine someone doing something that really annoys you while you are eating and then imagine your stomach thinking the same thing as you turn the telly on and start chewing. Sit down at a table while you eat. Try and be peaceful, don't have a row, fume or just generally get over-emotional over a plate of grub because it does not help digestion, nor does walking and eating at the same time. Don't eat if you are upset [I adore shellfish of all types yet I am allergic to one type of food only, oysters. I think it is because the very first time I had them my stomach was in emotional knots and my body put oysters and knots together and now, still, says, 'No thanks', spectacularly]. Tea and coffee are not particularly good for you, but most of us like one or the other and most of us drink too much of one or the other. If you drink a litre of plain water a day it reduces your craving for hot drinks. Chew your food and give yourself as much time as you can spare to relax after a meal. Remove as much stress from your life as you possibly can, this takes discipline, so acquire some and also some fifth chakra vocalisation. Get some proper nutritional advice - either read nutritional books or see a professional.

I am just going to do a basic vitamin and mineral run through. I am not trained in this, I am just trying to raise your awareness. If you need more information get hold of an Adelle Davis book on nutrition if you can. The Optimum Nutrition Bible by Patrick Holford, is excellent and widely available. Take a serious illness seriously. I was talking to a teacher of nutrition recently who told me that my glandular fever [at age thirty-three] followed by chicken-pox and multiple post-viral infections over two years was my first *major* warning sign that my immune system was in serious trouble. I knew at the time I was very unwell but I had to go to work because I had to pay my mortgage. I should have gone to the best nutritionist in the country there and then, though quite how I would have paid for it I don't know. On my credit card I suppose. If you are poorly and not improving get professional help, seek the best and pay for it, for you are nothing without your health.

VITAMIN C. Low levels can mean lots of head colds, dry hair and skin, poor healing and infections, cramps, bruising [if you are having excessive bruising, bleeding gums or nosebleeds see your doctor immediately]. Your whole body needs vitamin C and you need more if you are poorly or healing from anything. It is not stored so you need a daily or regular intake, especially during the winter coldy/fluey months. I take 1000mgs every two to three days, more often and higher dosage if I think a cold is impending or I start sneezing [watch out for repetitive sneezing attacks it can be your distressed liver talking to you]. If I was back in full health I probably would not need to take a Vitamin C supplement regularly as I eat a lot of fruit. Personally I would keep a pot of vitamin C handy and with me at all times if I was working away from home and especially if I was commuting. A sneezey fellow passenger can pass on their bugs in a nano-second and you may be an hour or more away from your home supply of supplements. I give all my animals [dogs, cats, chickens, but not the fish in the pond] oral Vitamin C, in preference to antibiotics when they are poorly, injured or have an infected anything. We have one cat who is always fighting and getting disgusting pus-filled wounds which I have to clean and drain. Luckily this cat will swallow enormous horse pills of vitamin C. The wounds are clean and clear in a matter of a few days. Our other cat is a beast with pills and you need a paramedic standing by with a blood transfusion [for me - not the cat], but fortunately he has a strong immune system and heals quickly anyway.

If you overdo the vitamin C you get a rumbly tummy, possibly an achey rumbly tummy and diarrhoea that may smell of orange juice. That goes for humans or animals. I once gave a dog at death's door such a huge dose of vitamin C that when I told my new vet [years later] he went white. The dog recovered briskly with no side effects at all. A month later the dog had a bit of a health wobble and I gave him 3000mgs of vitamin C orally. Within an hour he went into the garden and squirted out a fountain of orange juice diarrhoea. I immediately stopped the supplements [but I did wonder about offering his rear end to the Ministry of Defence; liquid poop warfare, fast, biodegradeable and a preferable option to our nuclear capabilities. What do you think, is it a goer? We could get instant world peace]. ALWAYS, always see a vet if you have a sick dog [or any animal], but ask them about vitamin C and see what they say - frankly, if your dog is barely a cocked leg from heaven's gate you don't have much to lose. Be careful if you are taking large doses, I seem to remember too much can knock out a mineral [copper, possibly].

If you smoke, you use up loads of vitamin C and, obviously, the more people you are around, or work with, the higher your contact with bugs will be. Stress, booze and pollution all remove this vitamin. Try and get your daily allowance through food, particularly fruit. Kiwi fruit is good and we heard recently that eating the skin [wash first] is a good aid to digestion. I don't know how much of the vitamin is lost when fruit and vegetables are held in cold storage for a long period of time. I have read conflicting accounts, but I have also heard the period of storage these days is very long indeed. Cooking in general, but especially prolonged boiling or washing, will reduce the vitamin's content. I read that rose hips and hot chilli peppers are very high in vitamin C; your kisses would be interesting to say the least. You need vitamin C to maintain healthy collagen [a protein that is the principal constituent of connective tissue which holds cells together, you don't want your cells running away now, do you? They might head for the pub without you]. Connective tissue is in skin, tendons, ligaments, bone, walls of blood vessels and cartilage. It is therefore essential for everyone and probably even more so if you do a lot of running and jumping about. Footballers take note. I take Vitamin C for any type of injury, even a slight muscle strain. Strong connective tissue gives some protection against recreational drugs, pollution and that sort of thing. I would take it daily if I lived in a large city. Little children need it for healthy teeth formation and both children and adults need it to maintain healthy gums and to stop teeth falling out.

VITAMIN A. Repeated head colds and recurrent infections [sometimes thrush and cystitis]. Styes on your eyelids, excessive mucous in the corner of the eye [often seen in the elderly], itchy eyelids, pain in the eyes, problems with vision, ulceration of the mouth and cornea, infertility problems, dry hair, poor nails, rough and/or lumpy skin on the backs of the upper arms, dry and rough skin [especially elbows and knees], dandruff, pimply spots or big boils CAN point to a shortage of Vitamin A [but you may have other deficiencies too]. It is stored in the body and you can take too much and make yourself very ill indeed. Don't be silly about it, especially if you are pregnant when it can be *dangerous* for the *baby*.

I was deficient in this vitamin for years probably from childhood when I had continuous colds. It is formed in the body from carotene found in a variety of fruit and vegetables [carrots and apricots particularly]. Mild deficiencies can present with impaired vision, especially night vision [so if you are blinded by oncoming car lights you have a problem], if you get tired eyes after watching telly, or a need to wear sunglasses all through the year. Don't get muddled with red, or gritty eyes which can be low B vitamins, talk to a nutritionist. If you are exposed to a lot of light, full on or reflected, you will use up a lot of Vitamin A [think open-top sports cars, skiing, sailing, photography studios, printing/exposure to light reflected off white paper and anyone doing fine concentrated work with their eyes, such as sewing]. If you blow your nose when you do not have a cold and there is rather too much in your handkerchief think Vitamin A shortage. You need it for healthy mucous membrane [which is up your snoz for starters, plus middle ear, throat, lungs and bladder - so repeat infections in these areas may be a pointer] and it will, therefore, be a first line of defence against airborne bugs like head colds. I take my supplements in the form of cod liver oil but be aware of the latest research into the alleged alarming amounts of mercury in fish. Eating liver is good, I am not keen but I force myself. Don't eat a polar bear's liver, it will kill you because it is so high in Vitamin A, but I did read somewhere the highest level ever recorded was in an aged python. I have no idea if this is correct and absolutely no intention of trying to find out.

B VITAMINS. Water soluble, not really stored, needed daily. The soothers for agitated people. I think low Bs [like low magnesium] are becoming an epidemic in this country. I would not be at all surprised if low Bs are not a major contributing factor to obesity - people get twitchy and upset and reach for a soothing fatty meal to, quite literally, 'pour oil on troubled water'. Either that or they reach for drugs or booze which removes even more of their Bs. I am a big fan of old fashioned remedies, like Epsom salts for magnesium, poultices on boils, dandelion tea as a diuretic, that sort of thing. I am a huge fan of Brewer's Yeast because a *good quality* Brewer's is stuffed with B vits and lots of other minerals [please read the labels for *maximum* contents]. However, I would not recommend it to everyone because it is yeast. Having said that there are a lot of confused elderly folk who would probably do well on a daily dose of Brewer's if they do not have a yeast intolerance [you could pop a spoonful of Brewer's into a cup of soup each day]. There is too much confusion in the elderly, these days. I blame food production, diet and damaged leaky guts.

B1 Thiamine - needed for protein utilisation - low levels indicated by poor concentration, *irritability, depression,* heart problems, poor muscle tone, tingling hands and feet.

B2 Riboflavin - sore watery eyes, cracks in the corner of your mouth, *confusion,* poor healing.

B3 Niacin - muscle weakness, depression, *confusion,* some skin problems.

B5 Pantothenic Acid - scalloped edging to tongue often a sign - you need it for your brains, *nerves,* skin, hair, gut, energy and it's a component in production of the *body's own stress hormones.*

B6 Pyridoxine - *confusion, depression,* skin problems, low immunity, skin tingling in extremities.

B12 Cobalamin - tricky one - don't know much other than responsible for pernicious anaemia and can affect *nerves.*

Think ANTI-STRESS THERAPY when it comes to B vits. Stress comes in all shapes and sizes and is a normal part of daily life, it is your reaction to it that counts. Read 'tongue' if you haven't already. I have covered this in 'iridology' but I use up lots of B's because I am twitchy and I have multiple contraction furrows in each iris. If you are twitchy too you might need to look at increasing your intake, remembering that bullies and boundary issues deplete supply and panic attacks can be an early warning sign of low stocks, then look at the immense stress of a sudden event like bereavement, a serious accident, an operation, a divorce … whatever. This is when you need to shove extra B's in. No husband of mine, serving in the armed forces, would go to fight without a huge supply of B's. Bugger the grenades, he would have bottles and bottles of B's dangling from his waistband. I'd be Miss Popularity herself with the top brass at H.Q. ………. you can imagine. Early greying hair and baldness may be signs of low B's. I don't understand why so many men are going bald these days, unless it is God's only way of accessing their seventh chakra [this is a joke]. Don't just accept changes in and around your body, research! There is no excuse these days when everyone has access to mountains of information. If you are depressed, you may need extra B's. I should have given my Mum biotin ….. probably, don't know, but it might have helped her [read what Adelle Davis had to say about the B Vitamins]. You need the B's for your skin too [as well as vitamin E]. I am bothered that we are developing so much skin cancer and I am wondering if there is not more to it than just a hole in the ozone layer. If I had surfing sons I would probably be on the beach too, rattling a bottle at them. Aren't you glad you are not a child of mine? If I develop high cholesterol or high blood pressure I will first check my feelings, chuck my emotions out and then hurl B vitamins at my body.

FOLATE OR FOLIC ACID. *Depression,* painful mouth and tongue, slow growth and development especially nerves, vital for growing foetus. It is not found in an awful lot of foods and if you don't like vegetables you are in trouble. You can get it in pulses, nuts, liver and yeast extracts.

BIOTIN. Still being researched. Tiredness, hair loss, *depression* and some skin complaints. You find it in eggs, cheese and yoghurt, also in Brewer's yeast, liver, nuts brown rice and whole wheat.

VITAMIN D. Poor bone density in children [rickets] and the old, also poor muscle tone. There is a theory that we are not getting the same degree of vitamin D as our ancestors because we scrub ourselves free of our natural skin oils when we bathe or shower every day. We would probably do better if we were all a bit whiffy - not keen on the idea myself - because the D is absorbed more efficiently when these oils are present on the skin. You need some sunshine, so if you are in an office all day make sure you get outside at the weekends and allow some sun on your skin but don't spend eight hours butt-naked and kipper-flat getting a tan, because that is silly. You need vitamin D to stash your calcium, get a decent night's kip and settle your ragged nerves. There is some Vitamin D in milk, butter and free range eggs [at the merest hint of a blue sky my chickens hurtle out of their run, clutching their towels and suntan lotion, grab the sunniest spot, flatten themselves out, wings askew and sunbathe for hours at a time. 'Anyone for D?', I joke to them; no response, but they complain if I cast a shadow]. Fish is good, so get it while you can because your children probably will not if Jenny Cockell is right [see 'reincarnation']. Kippers, mackerel, sardines that sort of thing. Cod liver oil is, of course, a good supply of D, but ONLY take the recommended dose and be careful with children [though Adelle swore by it, refrigerated, given after every main meal, with vitamin E, for really healthy children]. I would certainly look at my Vitamin D intake in any bony injury but especially a fractured bone that was slow to repair, as well as ensuring I was getting enough protein, calcium, B Vitamins and Vitamin C [especially if there was a skin wound too].

VITAMIN E. Fat soluble, so stored, so be careful. Poor wound healing, inside and out. Wheat germ is high in this vitamin which is required for the formation of every cell, but especially skin and muscle [the heart is a muscle, so I am wondering about that]. My partner treats many people [including me] whose muscles feel as if they split under his fingers, so it makes me wonder about hernias and vitamin E. I am only wondering, I don't know. I seem to need a large quantity of this vitamin, otherwise I find I am struggling to lift or dig in the garden. Women need *a lot* of Vitamin E during the menopause - that's me folks, as if I don't have enough on my plate. You will need it to heal wounds without excessive scarring. I have been told that brown marks on the backs of hands are a sign of low Vitamin E, I don't know if this is correct but I have some liver spots and it seems to me they have shrunk a bit since I have been taking Vitamin E supplements, but then I take lecithin and inositol periodically too [it is never ending, isn't it? I can't pronounce them either]. It is very popular to have vitamin E in beautifying face creams these days but I have been chucking it at my face and in my mouth for many a year and I have yet to feature on the front cover of Vogue magazine.

VITAMIN K. I really don't know anything about it except it is essential to prevent haemorrhaging [newborn babies are given it routinely because they are low in Vitamin K at birth]. Eat your leafy greens and don't boil them, steam them.

INOSITOL AND CHOLINE. Err, don't know anything really. Maybe a link with high cholesterol and low inositol and there is a link with the liver and choline but I am not sure what.

MINERALS ....

MAGNESIUM. Anxiety, maybe *depression*, cramping, hand tremors, heart irregularities. My feeling is we have a major problem with the lack of it but I don't know why. Maybe the dinosaurs ate it all, maybe it is due to modern farming methods, maybe God ran out of Epsom salts when he made Britain, maybe it is tied in with low B vitamins, who knows? It is a soother, it is essential. I wish I had given it to my Mum. Eat your nuts, pasta, seafood, dried fruit, seeds and wholemeal bread and make sure you get plenty of B vitamins. Both magnesium and B's are in Brewer's yeast. If you have a bit of a shaking hand, try upping your magnesium [and B vits] *significantly* in your diet and if you suffer from restless legs at night do the same. If your hand tremor and/or restless legs are really bad you may need significant amounts of the *right type* of magnesium [I take high daily doses of magnesium citrate malate in powdered form, from a pulled apart capsule, in water with added liquid vitamin B6]. Seek professional help.

CALCIUM. Bony problems, cramps, heart and blood pressure problems, achy joints, poor sleep. I have been told low calcium is really rare, but low magnesium is everywhere. I believe it. Look at bottled water and check the ratio of calcium to magnesium, I think it should be two Ca to one Mg. Obviously it is in dairy products, fish, leafy greens, some nuts and other things.

POTASSIUM. It is not that common but we were alert for it in hospital in the seriously ill with excessive sweating, vomiting and diarrhoea. Keep it in mind if you are very ill at home. Watch out for excessive thirst, cramps and confusion. It is in loads of things, fruit and veg, meat and fish and dairy.

SODIUM. Again you are more likely to see it in someone who is really ill or in someone who is drinking way too much water. It is hard to avoid in food.

PHOSPHORUS. Weak muscles, weak bones. It is in loads of food.

CHLORIDE. Don't know, don't think it is much of a problem, sorry to be unhelpful.

IRON. Anaemia. It is a component part of your oxygen carrying red cells and assists in energy production. Found in parsley, some nuts, pork, pumpkin seeds, prunes, cooked dried beans, dried apricots and raisins.

SULPHUR. Probably not much of a problem unless you have a serious food toleration problem. It is in a lot of food.

SELENIUM. Muscle weakness. I think you need vitamin E and some iodine to absorb and keep it [talk to a professional who knows]. I believe it is important in keeping your immune system ship-shape and Bristol fashion. Found in liver, nuts, wheat germ, whole grains, sea creepy-crawlies, meat and eggs.

CHROMIUM. High blood sugars and cholesterol. If you have a family history of diabetes definitely get your chromium levels checked and do a bit of research. Positive Health Magazine is great for information. I know I am probably low in chromium when I start thinking about chocolate and I know it is seriously low if I find myself loitering with intent outside doughnut shops. An iridologist can see potential blood sugar problems in the iris.

IODINE. Needed, like vitamin E [and other things], tyrosine [amino acid] and maybe selenium, for the production of thyroxin [thyroid gland]. Don't muck about with your thyroid, ALWAYS get it checked by your doctor but also talk to a nutritionist because you may be low on other things if your thyroid is wonky [remember fifth chakra too - turquoise, turquoise and learn to say 'No!', *nicely*]. Iodine is found in lots of different foods but particularly kelp and other sea vegetables.

MANGANESE. Healthy bones, cartilage, nerves and tissue, assists red blood cells, stabilises blood sugar/insulin production and your brain needs it. Found in wheat germ, wheat bran, sea vegetables, some nuts, peanut butter and a host of other food.

MOLYBDENUM. I can't pronounce it either. You need it to chuck out uric acid and various other nasties and it makes your teeth look perky. Found in tomatoes, wheat germ, some meats and some beans.

I think that is it. I am not trained in this so please, please research yourself. Always consult a doctor immediately if you are poorly and if you think you are low on something but I would always recommend a visit to an experienced nutritionist as well.

VIOLENCE

I am enormously saddened at the amount of violence being produced and categorised these days as entertainment. I have had several experiences, over the years, of meeting people who are completely impassive to violence on the screen but who shrink, puke, or faint at the sight of real blood. I am still confused by this.

Twenty-five years ago, or more, I was working in London and was given a free press ticket to see the film 'Raging Bull' at ten o'clock, or thereabouts, in the morning. Nurses used to get quite a few free tickets to theatre, ballet and cinema but it was a rarity by then, so I thought I would grab the offer. I knew the film was about boxing. I tootled off to the cinema and during the film I averted my eyes to a lot of the close-up shots of the boxing and watched the press men instead. I walked out about two-thirds of the way through the film. I could not bear the violence - not the boxing, it was the other violence in it. From the cinema I walked to the Casualty Department where I would later start my shift and I hoped there would not be too much blood about. While walking, I thought about how impassive the press men appeared to be to the violence they saw on the screen and compared it to the reaction in Casualty of many horrified and white faced on-lookers, male and female, who saw the actual results of the real life night time violence. I thought then, what I think now ……. we are in a muddle.

Nowadays, violence is everywhere. They have studies [who pays for them?] to see if watching violence induces violence. Now there's a thing. Studies! I ask you? I know the violence on television and in films will not stop but what I would like is a bit of understanding and balance. Boxers are trained to take non-stop raining blows on their bodies. Their bodies are honed and their musculature is like armour. Most bodies do not have this and if you kick someone repeatedly in the abdomen and ribs you could quite possibly kill them. This needs to be understood I think, just as it needs to be understood that the kicker is coming from a place of absolute *fear and self-loathing..*

Still, I was cheered by a new boxing film. My partner, who once boxed himself [but not as well as his father], got the dvd of the film 'Million Dollar Baby'. 'It's a boxing film, darling, but I think you might enjoy it', he said with an over-optimistic tone. We settled on the sofa and I popped a cushion on my lap, should the need arise to cover my face. A fascinating film [such a *vast* amount of *green* too]. I was relieved, here at last was the reality of violence. Bravo Clint Eastwood! And I never thought I would say that.

W Is for WILDE

Stuart Wilde. Something of a character who can arouse strong opinions. Here is my opinion. All his books have been absolutely invaluable to me and out of our hundreds of books they form part of my 'precious collection', the ones I refer back to when I am heading off track and getting confused. When I first came upon his work I could not stand his 'Hey man, cool dude' approach, but he has toned down and I have lightened up and who knows, he might read this book and think it is a load of old rubbish …. and that's fine .. he's just not getting a glass of *my* Shiraz.

He is pretty wacky, there's no doubt, and his books are not for most but he writes so well about attracting and making money that I recommend these specific books to everyone who is either struggling to financially make ends meet or starting a new business. I will list them at the back.

WEATHER

I am certain we do have global warming. Who am I to argue with scientists about the ozone layer? I am sure they are right but I have just taken my dogs for a walk, in June, in East Anglia, wearing winter clothes and wellies. I blame Glastonbury myself - always a mud bath. The weather is changing but it has always changed. They skated on the Thames .. erm, sometime in the 17th century? Maybe later. I have sunny memories of a warm childhood summers. I daresay this is entirely inaccurate and I was freezing my blue knees off in cotton frocks. Are we responsible for climate change? I don't know but we cannot go on as we are living, that's for sure, so changes must be made. I see outside loos making a comeback. I'm planning one. Not keen on large spiders though - could make my bladder freeze up. Problem.

There is something bothering me that no-one seems to mention and that is rivers. Until we decided to breed in ridiculous numbers and poo in a flushing loo, virtually all the rain went into the land which drained into rivers which went into the sea. There must be much, much less water getting into the sea these days because we are busy washing our lettuce [ludicrously flown in from somewhere] and keeping golf courses green. We are also flushing bleach down our drains which will reach the sea eventually and will need diluting. I read that the Colorado river is not a shred of its once mighty self. What sort of an impact does this excessive water usage have on the oceans? It must lower them, surely, mustn't it? Would that make glaciers melt? I don't know. Is Mother Earth thinking, 'Hell's teeth - too much bleach - let's melt an ice cube to stop the fishes burning their skin off?' [I feel guilty every time I have my bleached blonde highlights now]. And another thing I don't understand - they take oil out of the earth and pump water in and they remove peat bogs. What does that do? Heat us up or cool us down? Sensible answers on a postcard please. Better still, hilarious ones, because I am depressed enough about it as it is.

WATCHES

If you are stuffed for cash and have a much loved old wind-up watch that belonged to Grandpappy but it is not longer ticking - have a holiday. Go to Asia or beyond and take your watch with you. Fixed in a jiff for a piddling amount. In Vietnam they even repaired the plastic wheel on my suitcase in a few hours for a few quid. We always take our watches and jewellery for repair when we are off on our adventures. Huge apologies to our local jeweller whom we genuinely love and adore.

WOLF

I have always had a thing for the four -legged variety but now I have fallen in love with a two legged wolf. My partner knows, so that's ok. The object of my passion is Leonard of many names. He is in his eighties. We have not met, but I feel I know him and already he inhabits my life and makes me laugh. His clothes are a source of amazement and his brain a source of wonder. His twelve life lessons filled me with happiness and hope. Happiness that I had done quite well, so far, and hope that I could definitely do better. Leonard is a teacher. Leonard is an artist. Leonard approves of passion, in fact he insists on it. I just love Leonard. The book 'The Treehouse' is a gem. Thank you Naomi Wolf, you have been gracious enough to share your father with the world and what a gift you have given us.

I remember discussing love with a friend. 'Affection', she said, 'it is all about affection'. My eyes swept up and right [neuro-linguistic programming - visually constructing], my thoughts contained and framed in a window exposing a smudged and grey rain filled day. 'Ahh', I replied, but deep in my body I felt something was missing. It took me quite a while to locate and fully embrace the missing element. It is, for me, passion. I have always had passion but it is so much a part of me that I failed to see how much it affected me by its absence. I have endless passion about endless things. From dogs to daisies, cobwebs to chakras, tea to thunder, rivers to roses. And my man. My man who understands and does not deride my passions. My man who, even when he is driving me absolutely n u t s …… I still love with a passion.

WAKE UP

There are plenty of books about now that would give you sleepless nights. I would recommend that you read this one ….. 'Wake Up! Survive and Prosper in the Coming Economic Turmoil' by Jim Mellon and Al Chalabi. It might make you feel a little nauseous but it is simply written and gives sensible advice.

WELFARE

If you are on welfare payments I strongly suggest you read the above book. The economy is slowing, people are feeling the pinch, tax payers are getting tired and fed up. I feel a pendulum swing coming on and the problem with pendulum swings is they can throw the baby out with the bathwater. Everyone needs a safety net but the safety net is way too big, holding far too many people and we are going to pay the economic price now. It is not going to be nice. Get yourself some skills as fast as you can.

$\mathcal{X}$ Is for X Rays

I once read that having an x-ray uses up a lot of the B vitamins. I have no idea if this is correct but the last time I had an x-ray I took a B complex just to be on the safe side.

I am a little short of things under X, so moving swiftly on ....

Y Is for YOBS

Always have been. The Brits have been yobs for centuries. We love a good scrap and we have been drinking ourselves senseless since mead was drunk and probably even before that. To introduce twenty-four hour drinking was, therefore, insanity.

YOGHURT

Keep it plain, the creamy ones are simply gorgeous and I adore them but they are not the very best for maintaining health. Read the labels and aim for one with as many helpful bacteria as possible. Eat daily.

YORKSHIRE

Ok. *What is their problem?* Why do they always have to tell you, 'I'm a Yorkshireman'. Yeah? And? Then they tell you that their county is the best in England. It is not. It's nice, lovely in parts, but it is not THE BEST. Get a grip.

YIN AND YANG

In the Orient, yin is female and yang is male. Now, most men like yin women and most women like yang men, but it is tricky in this day and age when woman have had to yang up to cope with a working life and men are expected to yin down [as it were] in order to cook, change nappies and understand why the state of a woman's hair is more important than national security. Too much yang attracts yin and vice versa, irrespective of what sex you are. We all need to get a bit of balance. If you are too yangy try wearing pale pink and if you are too yinny try pillar-box red .... add white to red and you get pink - interesting.

Z Is for *ZZZZZZZ*

Sleep. I know that people know about chronic sleep deprivation, but knowing about it and going to bed at a reasonable time is quite a different matter. Time and again my partner treats people who put their horses cosily to bed at six but they are still watching television and snacking on rubbish at midnight. Bodies need sleep to repair. There is a very old saying that goes something like ….. 'every hour of sleep before midnight is worth three after'. Children, especially, need long hours of sleep while their bodies do double the work, repair and grow. How can people say they love their children but fail to ensure their child gets a healthy body to carry them through life?

Tomorrow morning, when you wake up, just remind yourself of this: while you slumbered, your heart kept pumping, lungs kept breathing, blood was made, cells died, pee stored, poop amassed, liver slogged, nails and hair grew and that is just for starters. Have a healthy enriching but light supper and go to bed early at least once or twice a week. Nine o'clock. Ten o'clock is just ok as long as you are asleep by five past ten. Get your ego under control and have some respect for your body. If you are a night owl you can still go to bed early allowing your body to rest while stretched out and fully supported. Read a dull book [obviously not this one], it sends me to sleep in no time.

Snorers are invariably exhausted, so exhausted that they don't even recognise it. Take a holiday for a week and sleep all day and all night. If you do this and can do this, you know you are seriously knackered. If you go back to the same routine after the holiday it will not be long before your body starts having problems. I am bored with being told how much sleep is sufficient for the average adult. What the hell is average? Are we not unique individuals with unique bodies? Outside of siblings [and even here there are differences] while we were being formed did we have the same mother, same pregnant mother's diet, same pregnant mother's anxieties? No, we did not. It was only just over a hundred years ago that most people [except the wealthy and their poor servants] went to bed when it got dark in the winter.

Our bodies have had to adapt to far less sleep and in doing so have been pushed to the limit in just a century. There are many factors to poor sleep but low B vitamins [especially B6] is one, poor digestion [heavy late meals means the gut is working overtime at night], alcohol and coffee are some of the offenders. Calcium will help you sleep but low magnesium can keep you awake.

Emotions aside, I know I pushed my body to breaking point working years of night-duty and coping with high levels of stress. Though I made sure I got extra sleep during my nights off and always prepared nutritious meals to take to work and to come home to, I did not appreciate how much I needed my B vitamins and how little my diet and supplements were supplying. Though not a coffee drinker [which removes B vits at speed], I drank strong tea at work which probably removed what little B's I put in and probably some iron too. That whole period of my life exhausted my adrenal glands and I am now paying the price.

Apparently there are sleep clinics in Britain but I don't know where. I should have got my mother to one; in painful retrospect, I think it may have helped her enormously. I do think medically supervised induced sleep can be very healing. I nursed for many years and often the newly admitted elderly patients would get little rest in hospital because of the noise and commotion and, before long, they were wandering around in a confused state. I do wish we could get round to giving the elderly [in hospital and out] a fortified mineral and vitamin drink every day and ensuring they get a decent night's kip. I would also apply this principle to elderly pets, particularly dogs. I have seen really poorly and extremely confused old dogs improve hugely after just one night of proper sleep. I read a lovely story once about a young vet who was working many years ago. He went to a house to see a sick dog. He told the owner it was a very poorly woolly-woofer and needed 'putting to sleep' - only he didn't give it enough of whatever vets give. A few days later he called in to visit the dead dog's owner, to see if she was fairly chipper, but was astounded to see the dog cheerily greet him at the door. His owner told him that the dog had had a lovely sleep.

Occasionally I go through a phase of not sleeping well. I take, just before bed, B6, B complex, magnesium and a big glass of milk for the calcium.

This usually works, but valerian is another option. Lettuce is good, apparently. If you can't take milk, try a calcium tablet [they make fizzy ones these days if you find pills difficult to swallow] but do watch your magnesium [cocoa is good] levels. If none of these work and you are desperate to sleep, try meditating. Lotus positions do not feature in this household. I meditate flat on my back with my head on a comfortable pillow and my body snuggly under a duvet. You can do the same. Just switch off your busy brain and concentrate really hard on staring at the back of your eyelids. When you have practised this for a while you will often start to see faces or portions of faces. It is quite fascinating. Who are these people? I have absolutely no idea. They will either deeply relax you, which is the next best thing to actual kip, send you to sleep, or they will push off so you can see yet more fascinating things.

ZEN

I love the idea but how to put it in practice? I'm a bit of a hoarder myself. I once heard of a man who was clearing out the house of his dear departed parents. They had been magpies and the son had found a full box labelled 'string too small to use'. I hooted with laughter at this because I come from a family of magpies and I am trying to dissuade myself of a tendency to think, 'It could come in handy', to a broken clothes hanger. It does not come in handy, it just goes in the green house awaiting a call from a small and exhausted sweet pea that needs something to cling to. The call never arrives but the hanger stays, providing a climbing frame for spiders. My mother hoarded everything and, 'So useful for travelling!', was her standard response to my incredulous expression on opening a bulging cupboard or drawer full of unusable, untouched and fairly ridiculous items. If I got tough with her, she would pounce, as much as she was able, to retrieve jettisoned articles with the words, 'I'll need that come the revolution'. I could not argue with that one. These days I do manage to put small bits of string on the compost heap, but I fear I have not progressed much further than that. My mother is sniggering at me from her cloud, when, that is, she is not trying to locate its hallmark.

I have a yen for zen. I have a longing for a very plain simple house but I have a confession to make: the zen house that is in my mind has multiple, large but discreet, cupboards. Big enough to house armies of magpies. Perhaps we should stay put and have a clear out. I keep saying I am going to give everything the heave-ho. I can't do it. I come over all hot at the thought. I must do it, I must. Courage! Detachment!

ZOOS

We have to have them because it is the only way we can save species while we destroy their habitat. One day, when we have come to our bloody senses and there are a lot less of us human savages, those saved species will, hopefully, be re-introduced back to their rightful homes. Meanwhile, please, please can we give them some space. Not cages but enclosures big enough for them not to go out of their minds.

ZUKAV

I am relinquishing this book. I am surprised I have so much to say. My partner says he is not surprised at all, in a tone I don't much care for. I shall take that comment as a compliment and resolutely ignore the eye rolling. I started writing two years ago and wondered how it would end. How could I have been so forgetful? Gary Zukav will close me down exquisitely.

For a man who fought in the Vietnam War, Gary seems to have found a level of peace that is still eluding me. I will list his books shortly, do read them because he is a gentle teacher. Oprah Winfrey visited him in his home and retreat. He hadn't a clue who she was; he did not have a television. What he did have was an extraordinary spiritual partner, Linda. Oprah asked him to appear on her show. He agreed. Sometime later he courageously admitted to Linda that he had developed 'feelings' for another woman. Linda, with eye-popping wisdom and equal courage asked him, 'What are you afraid of?'. Gary thought carefully about this and then admitted, 'I am afraid of appearing on Oprah'. Having discovered the *cause* of his *fear*, his *feelings* for this other woman *evaporated.*

Gary gave an extraordinary performance [with Linda in the audience] and, within it, he told the tale I have just told you. By being so honest and open he taught us to tell the truth and face our fears. I knew I was watching a major spiritual teacher for our time. I think Gary's feelings were his fear and that he developed emotions for another in order to throw up some sort of distraction. By confronting his fear the emotion left.

Truly, there are only two emotions, love and fear. We all have our own uniquely individual fears and need much courage to face and reveal them, but the extraordinary thing about revealing fear is that often invokes a kindly response and it certainly repairs huge third chakra holes. I do not have Gary's skills but what I have learnt and observed from my life I offer you. I really hope I have made you chortle once or twice because laughter is a healer and, sadly, it is thin on the ground these days. This book has been hugely important healing exercise for me and if anything within it has been helpful to someone, somewhere .... well, job done and much fun I have had in the writing of it.

A per centage of the profits of this book will go
to The Hand of Friendship. The "Villa Emilia" Project,
which is helping to educate children [and their mothers] in Bolivia.
This is a registered charity [No. 1108120]. Registered address,
12 Shortlands, Ipswich, IP8 3RA, UK.

THANK YOU

To my late parents.
Hugely missed.
Through their triumphs
and their tragedies
they taught me so very much.

To my spiritual partner Larry.
I could not have written this book
until I understood what love really is.
You have shown me.

To every single member of my family.
You have been my greatest teachers
whether you knew it or not.

To all my friends.
Past, present and future.
Ditto.

To my godmother Esther.
For a lifelong
master-class in listening with kindness
and for setting
impossibly high standards
that I struggle
to emulate each day.

To Alison Englefield
[and Clare Calder-Marshall].
For tackling my wild punctuation
and editing
with such humour, enthusiasm
and wisdom.

To all the animals
that have shared my life.
Each and every one bringing
its own unique
gift and lesson in
how to live in the moment.

To planet Earth.
For allowing me to stand
upon you
and
gaze in wonder
at your extraordinary beauty
and diversity.

AUTHORS AND BOOKS THAT HAVE MADE THE BIGGEST IMPACT ON MY LIFE

New [and second hand] books available by mail order from Inner Bookshop, Oxford [01865 245301 - mail@innerbookshop.com]. Or ...Tao of Books, [tao is pronounced dow, I think] which is based in Pulham Market, Norfolk. [0845-3456-222 - www.taobook.com].

Dr. CAROLINE MYSS
Anatomy of the Spirit [The Seven Stages of Power and Healing] ISBN 0-553-50527 Bantam Books
Why People Don't Heal And How They Can ISBN 0-553-50712-5 Bantam Books
Sacred Contracts [Awakening Your Divine Potential] ISBN 0-553-81494-X Bantam Books
Invisible Acts of Power ISBN 0-7432-6371-5 Simon & Schuster
Tapes of her lectures are also available

Dr. CAROLINE MYSS AND NORM SHEALY MD
The Creation of Health ISBN 0-609-80323-9 Three Rivers Press [I would recommend this book to every person who treats sick people, in whatever capacity.]

NORM SHEALY MD
Miracles Do Happen ISBN 1-85230-688-2 Element Books

ADELLE DAVIS [out of print - you will have to check second-hand bookshops]
Let's Get Well   ISBN0-7225-2701-2 Thorsons
Let's Eat Right To Keep Fit   ISBN 0-04-641034-1 Unwin Paperbacks
Let's Have Healthy Children   ISBN 0-451-14319-1 Signet Books

PATRICK HOLFORD
The Optimum Nutrition Bible ISBN 0-7499-1855-1 Piatkus

GARY ZUKAV and LINDA FRANCIS
All his books but particularly
The Heart of the Soul   ISBN 0-7432-2068-4
[However 'The Dancing Wu Li Masters' is heavy duty physics -
I understood not a word]

JAMES HAMILTON-PATERSON
PLAYING WITH WATER ISBN 0-333-44716-6 Macmillan
GRIEFWORK ISBN 0-09-980960-5 Vintage
GERONTIUS ISBN0-09-979120-X Vintage
He is not a therapist, as such, unless you are healed by his extraordinary
flow of words.

THOMAS HANNA
Somatics ISBN 0-7382-0957-0 Lifelong Books
Highly recommended to all body working therapists - really easy to
understand pictures.

Dr. CHRISTIANE NORTHRUP
Women's Bodies, Women's Wisdom ISBN 0-7499-1925-6 Piatkus
The Wisdom of Menopause ISBN 0-7499-2214-1 Piatkus

STUART WILDE
The Trick to Money is Having Some! ISBN 1-56170-168-8 Hay House
The Little Money Bible ISBN 1-56170-393-1 Hay House
and if you are ready for super-wacky stuff ....
The Whispering Winds of Change ISBN 1-56170-160-2 Hay House

LOUISE L. HAY
You Can Heal Your Life ISBN 1-870845-01-3 Eden Grove

DAVID R. HAWKINS MD
Power vs. Force ISBN 0-9643261-1-6 Veritas Publishing
The Eye of the I ISNB 0-9643261-9-1 Veritas Publishing

Dr. CHRISTINE PAGE
She is an English doctor. I highly recommend all her books but particularly
Frontiers of Health ISBN 0-85207-256-2
Published by The C. W. Daniel Co. Ltd.

PETER JACKSON-MAIN
Practical Iridology ISBN 1-903258-74-X Carroll & Brown

ECKHART TOLLE
Anything he has written but particularly
A New Earth   ISBN 0-141-10782-1 Penguin Books

MARTHA BECK [hilarious!!]
Finding Your Own North Star ISBN 0-7499-2401-2 Piatkus

JOHN C. PEIRRAKOS MD
Core Energetics ISBN 0940795-08-6 Life Rhythm Publication

JENNY COCKELL
Past Lives, Future Lives ISBN 0-684-83216-X Fireside

GARY CHAPMAN
The Five Languages of Love ISBN 1-881273-15-6 Northfield Publishing

NAOMI WOLF
The Treehouse ISBN 1-84408-244-X Virago

JEAN SHINODA BOLEN MD
Goddesses in Everywoman ISBN 0-06-091291-X HarperPerenial
Gods in Everyman ISBN 0-06-250098-8 Harper & Row

SUZE ORMAN
The Courage to Be Rich ISBN0-09-182682-9 Vermilion Books

VALERIE V. HUNT
Infinite Mind ISBN 0-9643988-1-8 Malibu Publishing

JOHN E. UPLEDGER
SomatoEmotional Release ISBN 9 781556 434129 North Atlantic Books
Highly recommended to all body working therapists

PIERRE PALLARDY
Gut Instinct [what your stomach is trying to tell you] ISBN 1-59486-542-6
Rodale

RACHEL CARSON
Silent Spring ISBN 0-14-022404-1[published 1962] Pelican Books

THEO COLBORN, DIANNE DUMANOSKI & JOHN PETERSON MYERS
Our Stolen Future ISBN 0-349-10878-1 Abacus

JIM MELLON AND ALI CHALABI
Wake Up! Survive and Prosper in the Coming Economic Turmoil
ISBN 1-84112-691-8   Capstone

DR. F. BATMANGHELIDJ
Your Body's Many Cries For Water ISBN0-9530921-6-X Tagman

Dr. PAUL CLAYTON
Health Defence ISBN 0-905553-66-7 Accelerated Learning Systems Ltd

DEBBIE SHAPIRO
Your Body Speaks Your Mind ISBN 07499-1595-1 Piatkus

THE VITAMIN AND MINERAL COUNTER
Consultant Editor: Dell Stanford ISBN 1-903992-03-6 Murdoch Books
Sadly out of print, maybe someone can persuade them to do a re-run

THOMAS GRINER
What's Really Wrong With You ISBN 0-89529-658-6 Avery Publishing

LINDA GOODMAN
Sun Signs ISBN 0 330 23390 4 Pan

JULIET DE BARAICLI LEVY
The Complete Herbal Handbook for the Dog and Cat
ISBN 0-571-16115-4 Faber and Faber

DUCHESS OF DEVONSHIRE
Counting My Chickens ISBN 1902421051 Long Barn Books

OTHER WRITERS TO LOOK OUT FOR
WAYNE DYER [any of his books and tapes- he is very funny]
ELISABETH KUBLER-ROSS
THE DALAI LAMA
IYANLA VANZANT [wonderful woman - hilarious to listen to]
DR. PHIL MCGRAW
JACK KORNFIELD
THOMAS MORE [both of them, but mainly the author of Care of the Soul]

OSTEOPATH [Connective Tissue Release]
RICHARD KEMP, D.O., M.C.S.P., M.R.O.F.,
The Langham Osteopathic Clinic, Suffolk [he also works in London].
Tel: 01206 272720 [www.myosteopath.net]

ANCIENT HERBAL REMEDIES
[www.resourcesforlife.net - 0800 0744279 [free phone]

APPLES - [mail order] Deacon's Nursery [01983 840750
deacons.nursery@btopenworld.com